ATLAS OF CHINA

McGraw-Hill Book Company

New York
St. Louis
San Francisco
Düsseldorf
London
Sydney
Toronto
Mexico
Panama
Montreal
New Delhi
Rio de Janeiro
Singapore
Kuala Lumpur

ATLAS *of* CHINA

Chiao-min Hsieh

Professor of Geography
University of Pittsburgh

Edited by

Christopher L. Salter

Associate Professor of Geography
University of California, Los Angeles

The editor for this book was Nancy E. Tressel, the editing supervisor was Janine Parson, and the designer was Merrill Haber. Its production was supervised by Joseph Campanella. The text was set in Century by University Graphics, Inc., and place names on the maps were set in Futura.

The ATLAS OF CHINA was printed by Halliday Lithograph Corporation and bound by The Book Press, Inc.

Library of Congress Cataloging in Publication Data

Hsieh, Chiao-min, 1921–
  Atlas of China.

  Bibliography: p.
  1. China—Maps. 2. China—Economic conditions—Maps. 3. China—Historical geography
—Maps.
  I. Title.
  G2305.H83 1973   912'.51   72-8717
  ISBN 0-07-030628-1

McGraw-Hill Atlases

Consulting Editor Norman J. W. Thrower, University of California, Los Angeles

General Drafting Corporation and Norman J. W. Thrower: *Man's Domain: A Thematic Atlas of the World*
Chiao-min Hsieh and Christopher L. Salter: *Atlas of China*
Judith Tyner: *The World of Maps and Mapping*

CONTENTS

List of Maps   ix
Preface   xiii
Editor's Foreword   xv

Part I PHYSICAL   1

STRUCTURE   3

The Development of the Science of Geology in China   3
Tectonic Structure of China   8
Three Ancient Land Masses   8
Earthquakes   10

LANDFORMS   13

Landform Characteristics   13
The Plains   15
The Basins   15
The Hilly Regions   15
The Plateaus   15
The Mountains   16
Special Kinds of Landforms   16
    Loess   16
    Karst   16
    Glaciation   18
The Coastline   19

CLIMATE   22

Three Control Features   22
Temperature and Rainfall   25
Climatic Boundaries and Classificaton   32
China's Fog   32

HYDROLOGY   40

Drainage Systems   40
China's River Network   42

The Rate of Flow, or Run-off, of China's Rivers   *44*
The Silt Content of China's Rivers and the Problem
   of Flooding   *45*

SOILS, FLORA, AND FAUNA   **49**

Soils   *49*
   Areal Distribution of Lowland Soils   *49*
   Vertical Distribution of Mountain Soils   *51*
Vegetation   *51*
Distribution of Animals   *54*

Part II CULTURAL   **59**

PEOPLE   **61**

Population Size and Distribution   *61*
The Overseas Chinese   *63*
Minority Groups of China   *65*

TRANSPORTATION   **69**

Railroads   *69*
Highways   *74*
Air Transport   *74*
Marine Commerce   *74*
Inland Water Transportation   *78*

AGRICULTURE   **81**

Food Crops   *81*
Animal Husbandry   *86*
Economic Crops   *88*
Forestry   *90*
Marine Resources   *90*

MINING AND MANUFACTURING   **95**

Mineral Resources   *95*
   Coal   *95*
   Oil   *95*
   Iron and Steel   *97*
   Other Metals   *97*
   Nonmetallic Minerals   *100*

Manufacturing   *100*
   Manufacturing Prior to 1952   *100*
   The First Five-Year Plan   *100*
   Manufacturing Since 1957   *104*

Part III REGIONAL   **111**

NORTH CHINA   **113**

The Lower Yellow River Region   *113*
The Upper Yellow River Region   *118*

CENTRAL CHINA   **128**

    The Lower Yangtze Region   *128*
    The Middle Yangtze Region   *133*
    The Upper Yangtze Region (Szechwan Basin)   *137*

SOUTH CHINA   **145**

    The Southeast Coast Region   *145*
    Taiwan   *148*
    The Kwangtung and Kwangsi Region (including
      Hainan Island)   *162*
    The Yunnan-Kweichow Region   *168*

THE NORTHEAST (MANCHURIA)   **178**

INNER MONGOLIA   **183**

SINKIANG   **189**

TIBET   **196**

CITIES   **199**

Part IV   HISTORICAL   **219**

    Very Early History   *221*
    The Ch'un-Ch'iu Period (722-481 B.C.)   *223*
    The Contending States (480-221 B.C.)   *223*
    The Ch'in Dynasty (221-206 B.C.), The First
      Empire   *223*
    Earlier and Later Han Dynasties (206 B.C.-220 A.D.) *227*
    The Three Kingdoms (220-265)   *229*
    The Western and Eastern Tsin Dynasties (265-420) *231*
    Northern (439-581) and Southern (420-589)
      Dynasties   *233*
    The Sui Dynasty (581-618)   *233*
    The T'ang Dynasty (618-906)   *236*
    The Five Dynasties (907-960)   *239*
    The Sung Dynasties (960-1279)   *239*
    The Yüan (Mongol) Dynasty (1280-1368)   *243*
    The Ming Dynasty (1368-1644)   *243*
    The Ch'ing (Manchu) Dynasty (1644-1911)   *248*
    Modern China (1911-   )   *250*

    Bibliography and Map Sources   **263**
    Glossary   **268**
    **Appendix: Detailed Agricultural Regions of
      China**   **269**

    Indexes
      **Index to the Physical, Cultural, and Regional
        Maps Parts I, II, and III**   **272**
      Index to the Historical Maps (Part IV) **277**

LIST OF MAPS

PART I
PHYSICAL

Map No.	Map Title
I-1	China
I-2	Physical Features

Structure

Map No.	Map Title
I-3	Geology
I-4	Geologic Cross Sections
I-5	Geotectonic Regions
I-6	Rifts and Faults
I-7	Regional Seismic Activity
I-8	Maximum Earthquake Intensity

Landforms

Map No.	Map Title
I-9	Block Relief Diagram
I-10	Serial Profiles
I-11	Loess Landforms of the Middle Yellow River
I-12	Thickness of Loess Soils
I-13	Distribution of Karst and Limestone
I-14	Vertical Cross Sections of Karst Landforms in Kwangsi
I-15	Glaciation
I-16	Coastal Landforms

Climate

Map No.	Map Title
I-17	Climatic Data for Selected Stations
I-18	Winter Air Masses
I-19	Summer Air Masses
I-20	Surface Winds: January
I-21	Surface Winds: July
I-22	Average Annual Temperature
I-23	Average Annual Precipitation
I-24	Average Number of Days with Precipitation
I-25	Average Number of Days with Frost
I-26	Average Number of Freezing Days
I-27	Climatic Regions According to the Köppen Classification
I-28	Maximum Snow Accumulation
I-29	Season of Maximum Hail
I-30	Average Annual Humidity
I-31	Annual Potential Evapotranspiration
I-32	Distribution of Mean Annual Fog Days

Hydrology

Map No.	Map Title
I-33	Major Drainage Systems
I-34	River Patterns
I-35	Length of Major Rivers
I-36	River Run-off Zones
I-37	Volume of River Run-off
I-38	Run-off Isopleths
I-39	Classification of Underground Water
I-40	Degree of Water Hardness
I-41	Chemical Properties of Surface Waters

Soils, Flora, and Fauna

Map No.	Map Title
I-42	Soil Types
I-43	Soil Temperature Categories in Eastern China

Map No.	Map Title	Map No.	Map Title
I-44	Selected Soil Profiles	II-39	Machine-Building Industries
I-45	Vegetation Types	II-40	Degree of Industrialization
I-46	Zoogeographical Regions	II-41	Economic Regions
I-47	Number of Species of Mammals		
I-48	Distribution of Some Large Mammals		
I-49	Distribution of Some Small Mammals		

PART II
CULTURAL

PART III
REGIONAL

| | | III-1 | Regions of China |

North China

People

| | | III-2 | Regions of North China |

II-1	Population Distribution
II-2	Population Density
II-3	Distribution of Overseas Chinese
II-4	Ethnic Minority Groups
II-5	Languages

Lower Yellow River

| III-3 | Political |
| III-4 | Changes in the Course of the Yellow River and Extension of its Delta |

Transportation

| III-5 | Landforms |

II-6	Railroads
II-7	Railroads Built by Foreign Powers
II-8	Pao-chi to Ch'eng-tu Railway via Tsinling Shan
II-9	Railroad Construction by Years
II-10	Railroad Administrative Systems
II-11	Railroad Equipment Manufacturing and Repair Centers
II-12	Highways
II-13	Air Routes
II-14	Inland Waterways

III-6	Cross Section from the Inner Mongolian Plateau to the Central North China Plain
III-7	Percent of Land Cultivated
III-8	Percent of Cultivated Land in Wheat
III-9	Percent of Cultivated Land in Cotton
III-10	Percent of Cultivated Land Irrigated
III-11	Industries

Upper Yellow River

III-12	Political
III-13	Relief
III-14	Block Diagrams of the Han-chung Basin
III-15	The Physiographic Development of the Yellow River
	a. Initial Stage
	b. Later Stage
	c. Final Stage

Agriculture

II-15	Land Use
II-16	Major Crop Assemblages
II-17	Rice
II-18	Wheat and Soybeans
II-19	Maize, Barley, Millet, and Sweet Potatoes
II-20	Peanuts and Tea
II-21	Additional Agricultural Products
II-22	Cattle
II-23	Swine
II-24	Sheep
II-25	Horses
II-26	Cotton
II-27	Silk, Rubber and Vegetable Oils
II-28	Major Fishing Grounds
II-29	Fish of the Coastal Region
II-30	Detailed Agricultural Regions
II-31	Generalized Agricultural Regions

III-16	Wind Erosion
III-17	Water Erosion
III-18	Oasis Distribution in Kansu
III-19	Water Conservancy Projects on the Yellow River
III-20	Tsaidam Basin
III-21	Geologic Development of the Tsaidam Basin
III-22	Land Use
III-23	Industries

Central China

| III-24 | Regions of Central China |
| III-25 | Block Diagrams of the Yangtze |

Mining and Manufacturing

Lower Yangtze

II-32	Coal, Oil, and Natural Gas
II-33	Selected Metals
II-34	Nonferrous Metals
II-35	Nonmetallic Minerals
II-36	Development and Location of Industries
II-37	Stages of Industrial Growth
II-38	Electric Power

III-26	Political
III-27	Stream Network of the Yangtze Delta
III-28	Land Use in the Yangtze Delta
III-29	Settlement of the Yangtze Delta
III-30	Textile Industries of the Yangtze Delta
III-31	Land Use in the Lower Yangtze
III-32	Industries of the Lower Yangtze

Map No.	Map Title

Middle Yangtze

Map No.	Map Title
III-33	Political
III-34	Relief
III-35	Industries
III-36	Land Use
III-37	Percent of Land Cultivated
III-38	Percent of Cultivated Land in Rice
III-39	Percent of Cultivated Land in Wheat

Upper Yangtze (Szechwan Basin)

III-40	Political
III-41	Physiography
III-42	Relief
III-43	Temperature
III-44	Precipitation
III-45	Industries
III-46	Agricultural Regions
III-47	Percent of Land Cultivated
III-48	Percent of Cultivated Land in Wheat
III-49	Percent of Cultivated Land in Maize
III-50	Market Towns and Their Fair Days

South China

III-51	Regions of South China
III-52	Profile of the Hsi Chiang

Southeast Coast

III-53	Political
III-54	Relief
III-55	Land Use
III-56	Industries

Taiwan

III-57	Taiwan
III-58	Administrative Districts
III-59	Vertical Profiles
III-60	Landforms
III-61	Köppen Climatic Regions
III-62	Soils
III-63	Geology
III-64	Natural Vegetation
III-65	Agricultural Regions
III-66	Sequence of Settlement
III-67	Population
III-68	Minerals
III-69	Industries
III-70	Highways and Railways
III-71	Taipei
III-72	T'ai-chung
III-73	T'ai-nan
III-74	Hsin-chu
III-75	Chia-i
III-76	Hua-lien
III-77	T'ai-tung

Kwangtung and Kwangsi

III-78	Political
III-79	Relief
III-80	Industries
III-81	Land Use
III-82	Percent of Land Cultivated
III-83	Percent of Cultivated Land in Rice

III-84	Percent of Cultivated Land in Sugar Cane in Kwangtung
III-85	Amount of Cultivated Land per Draft Animal

Yunnan and Kweichow

III-86	Political
III-87	Relief
III-88	Percent of Land Cultivated in Kweichow
III-89	Percent of Cultivated Land in Small Grains in Yunnan
III-90	Percent of Cultivated Land in Rice
III-91	Percent of Cultivated Land in Wheat
III-92	Percent of Cultivated Land in Maize
III-93	Industries
III-94	Physiographic Diagram of the City of Tsun-i and Its Surroundings, Northern Kweichow
III-95	Block Diagram of Tien Ch'ih
III-96	The Development of Tien Ch'ih
III-97	Landforms of the Tien Ch'ih Area
III-98	Land Use in the Tien Ch'ih Area
III-99	Irrigation of the Tien Ch'ih Area

Manchuria

III-100	Manchuria
III-101	Political
III-102	Relief and Profile
III-103	Precipitation and Temperature
III-104	Annual Number of Days with Snow
III-105	Annual Number of Frost-free Days
III-106	Agricultural Regions
III-107	Land Use
III-108	Industries

Inner Mongolia

III-109	Inner Mongolia
III-110	Political
III-111	Landforms
III-112	Land Use
III-113	a. Precipitation and Temperature
	b. Ethnic Groups
	c. Land Use
	d. Grasslands
	e. Animal Ownership per Capita
	f. Crops
III-114	Industries

Sinkiang

III-115	Sinkiang
III-116	Political
III-117	Ethnic Groups
III-118	Relief
III-119	Interior Drainage Patterns
III-120	Development of the Tien Shan Geosyncline
III-121	Turfan Depression and Profiles
III-122	Land Use
III-123	Industries

Tibet

III-124	Tibet
III-125	Political

Map No.	Map Title
III-126	Relief
III-127	Relief Profile
III-128	Land Use and Industries

Cities

Map No.	Map Title
III-129	Peking
III-130	Tientsin
III-131	Tsinan, Shantung
III-132	Cheng-chou, Honan
III-133	T'ai-yüan, Shansi
III-134	Sian, Shensi
III-135	Lan-chou, Kansu
III-136	Hsi-ning, Tsinghai
III-137	Nanking, Kiangsu
III-138	Soochow, Kiangsu
III-139	Nan-ch'ang, Kiangsi
III-140	Ch'ang-sha, Hunan
III-141	Wu-han, Hupeh
III-142	Ch'eng-tu, Szechwan
III-143	Chungking, Szechwan
III-144	Hangchow, Chekiang
III-145	Foochow, Fukien
III-146	Canton, Kwangtung
III-147	Nan-ning, Kwangsi Chuang Autonomous Region
III-148	Kuei-lin, Kwangsi Chuang Autonomous Region
III-149	Kuei-yang, Kweichow
III-150	K'un-ming, Yunnan
III-151	Harbin, Heilungkiang
III-152	Shen-yang, Liaoning
III-153	Ch'ang-ch'un, Kirin
III-154	Dairen, Liaoning
III-155	Urumchi, Sinkiang Uighur Autonomous Region
III-156	Lhasa, Tibetan Autonomous Region

Map No.	Map Title
PART IV	
HISTORICAL	
IV-1	Comparative Boundaries of Selected Dynasties
IV-2	Ch'un-ch'iu Period, 722–481 B.C
IV-3	Contending States, c. 350 B.C.
IV-4	Ch'in Dynasty, 221–206 B.C.
IV-5	Earlier and Later Han Dynasties, 206 B.C.–220 A.D.
IV-6	Three Kingdoms, 220–265
IV-7	Western and Eastern Tsin Dynasties, 265–420
IV-7a	Eastern Tsin Dynasty, 317–420
IV-8	Northern and Southern Dynasties, c. 450
IV-9	Sui Dynasty, 581–618
IV-10	T'ang Dynasty, 618–906
IV-11	T'ang Dynasty, c. 700
IV-12	Five Dynasties, 907–960
IV-13	Sung and Chin Dynasties, 960–1279
IV-14	Yüan Dynasty in Inner Asia and China, 1280–1368
IV-15	Yüan Dynasty in China, 1280–1368
IV-16	The Grand Canal in the Yüan Dynasty
IV-17	Ming Dynasty, 1368–1644
IV-18	Ch'ing (Manchu) Dynasty, 1644–1911
IV-19	The T'ai Ping Rebellion, 1850–1864
IV-20	Spheres of Foreign Influences in the 19th Century
IV-21	Route of the Long March, 1934–1935
IV-22	Control of China, 1941
IV-23	Communes, c. 1961
IV-24	Nuclear Research and Resources, c. 1960
IV-25	Military Administrative Zones, c. 1960
IV-26	Centers of Higher Education, c. 1964
IV-27	Contemporary Political Map of China

PREFACE

China grows larger and larger in the world's eyes. The visit of President Nixon to Peking, the ever-increasing volume of press and radio releases emanating from mainland China, the continuing deficiencies in its statistical reporting, and the complexity of its administrative structure all emphasize the need for more information about this phenomenal land.

Ever since the change of government in mainland China in 1949, the Communist government has been engaged in a program of rapid transformation in industry and economic life. As a result, the surface of contemporary China has undergone tremendous change, perhaps unequaled in the history of the nation. Many new railroads and highways have been built, many new irrigation and water control projects have been launched, agriculture has been expanded, new industrial regions have appeared, and new urban centers have developed. But while many books on the China of today have been published in the Western world, few scientific maps have appeared, either in public or in academic circles, to make graphic the changing situation on the mainland.

Parallel to the economic developments, an inventory of the country's resources has been made by survey parties, and many new data on geological structure, surface configuration, soil, climate, hydrology, and flora and fauna have been published. Yet few attempts have been made to put these new data systematically into maps, and few atlases of China showing these features have been published.

And mainland China's changing surface is poorly understood in the West.

This atlas incorporates information on recent industrial and economic development and many of the new resource data as a means of increasing understanding of the landscape of China. In order that the reader may visualize countrywide distributional patterns and the relationships between environmental phenomena and human activities, the maps in this volume make a scientific presentation of the principal characteristics of the country, including its physical environment, cultural configuration, regional characteristics, and historical evolution. The texts accompanying the maps explain key features and discuss their causes and effects. Taiwan, as well as mainland China, is covered.

The first part of the atlas presents the physical environment of mainland China, making use of the post-1949 data on geological structure, landforms, hydrology, climate, soils, and vegetation. The second part is devoted to cultural and especially economic geography. Particular attention is given to new railways and highways, water control, irrigation projects, agricultural expansion, new industrial regions, and new urban centers. The third part, utilizing a regional approach, shows the characteristics of Northeast China, North China, Central China, and South China, as well as inner Mongolia, Sinkiang, Tibet, and Taiwan.

The fourth part is historical. Especially in a rapidly changing country like China the importance of time sequence cannot be overstated. This atlas therefore devotes a series of maps to the historical geography of different dynasties in order to trace adequately the changing interrelationships between land and people from earliest times. Depiction of the geographic setting in successive periods presents a picture of processes rather than of static conditions.

The preparatory work on the atlas has shown clearly how unsatisfactory and incomplete are the available basic data and how far we still are from a complete inventory. A tremendous amount of exploratory work has yet to be done. Still, the formidable task of evaluating the basic information on China already available has been faced, and an attempt has been made to incorporate it all in the atlas. Much energy has been spent in collecting, assembling, analyzing, and classifying the data and in producing maps that represent the data accurately. The present volume may be incomplete, but it at least lays the foundation for further work.

The Social Science Research Council generously awarded me for the preparation of this volume two large grants, without which the atlas could not have been completed. I also wish to thank the Center for International Studies of the University of Pittsburgh and especially its director, Dr. Carl Beck, for financial help in hiring cartographers to finish the plates for the last part of the atlas.

As is frequently the case with work of this type, the number of individuals who have assisted directly and indirectly is so large that it is not feasible to name them all; special thanks, however, are due to key persons.

In deep gratitude for his warm support during the planning stages, this atlas is dedicated to the memory of my former teacher Dr. George B. Cressey, Maxwell Professor of Geography at Syracuse University.

The original impetus for the atlas was provided by the late Dr. John M. H. Lindbeck, Director of East Asian Studies, Columbia University, whose initiative and continued interest have contributed substantially to its final realization.

The late Dr. Arch C. Gerlach, Chief Geographer for the United States Geological Survey, gave me much support and encouragement during his tenure as Chief of the Map Division of the Library of Congress.

On a fall 1972 trip to Russia, Eastern Europe, and Taiwan, I secured a new political map of China reflecting many boundary changes and a world atlas containing 1970 area and population figures for China, both published by the China Cartographic Institute in Peking, December 1971. Since my book was already in production it was too late to change the boundaries of existing maps. However, I have incorporated this new data in the last map of the atlas, *Contemporary Political Map of China,* with an accompanying chart showing up-to-date area and population figures for the 30 political units of China (22 provinces, 5 autonomous regions, and 3 autonomous municipalities).

I also wish to thank Dr. Norton S. Ginsburg, Professor of Geography at the University of Chicago, for his significant help during the early work on the atlas.

I am indebted to my colleagues at the University of Pittsburgh Dr. Hibberd V. B. Kline, Jr., for his encouragement and consistent support, and Dr. Louis Peltier, for his assistance in deciding upon many special terms to be used.

Many scholars and specialists have helped with the preparation of maps. In particular, I want to thank Dr. K. Y. Lee, Geologist for the United States Geological Survey, for his help with the *Geology* map, and Dr. Shin-ying Hu of the Arnold Arboretum of Harvard University, for the *Vegetation Types* map.

The wisdom and talent of many skilled professionals have been necessary for the cartography. Thanks go first to my wife, Jean Kan Hsieh, former Lecturer in Geography at Trinity College in Washington, D.C., who has been a constant critic and adviser and who has designed many of the maps. Mrs. Tashiko Mechlenburg has also contributed her excellent talent in the creation of a large number of maps. Mrs. Jeanne Tsou Liu, former graduate student at the University of Wisconsin, did many valuable maps. Mr. Louis F. Campbell, Jr., former graduate student at the Catholic University of America, drew many preliminary maps. Mr. Howard Ziegler, Cartographer in the Department of Geography, University of Pittsburgh, has also contributed much, especially in the historical section. I also want to thank Mr. Chao-tsai Lee for his beautiful Chinese calligraphy which appears on the cover of the atlas.

Finally, I want to thank Professor Christopher L. Salter of the University of California, Los Angeles, for his tremendous work in editing my atlas. Without his help it could not have been satisfactorily completed.

Chiao-min Hsieh

EDITOR'S FOREWORD

Certain procedural explanations here will make the *Atlas of China* more usable. Orthography is primary among these items. Anyone who has worked with Chinese in English translation knows the agonies of the numerous variations in the romanization and transliteration of Chinese place names. After reflection on the various means of achieving uniformity of place names in the maps and the text, I decided to establish a simple and reasonable touchstone and shape the atlas by it. In the Physical, Cultural, and Regional sections, place names have been brought into conformity with the spellings of the United States Board on Geographic Names (the Board's second edition on Mainland China, 1968) as manifest in the 1971 edition of the CIA's *People's Republic of China Atlas,* the only deviation being that I have used occasional spelling options for places fixed firmly in Western literature in a linguistically impure form—for example, Chungking and Nanking instead of Ch'ung-Ch'ing and Nan-ching. In addition to the imperfect city transliterations, adherence to convention has introduced somewhat awkward redundancies in the spellings of some physical features, particularly in the case of mountains and mountain systems. Hence you find Tsinling Shan and Yin-shan Shan-mo (North China) which, if translated literally, would mean the Tsin (Ch'in) Mountain Range Mountains and the Yin Mountain Mountain Range. Such indelicacies are bothersome, but I decided early in the editing of this atlas to adhere to some recognized standard rather than to compound further the place name confusion already existing in the English view of China. In the Historical section all place names through the Ch'ing Dynasty have been brought into conformity with the 1966 Albert Herrmann *Historical Atlas of China.* Follwing, 1911, the spelling is the same as that of the other three sections of the atlas.

In the initial production of the maps Taiwan was included at the same scale as the mainland. I felt that serious oversimplification was caused by this small-scale representation, so Taiwan has been omitted from the small-scale graphics in almost all cases and has been treated separately in the Regional section.

The indexes for the *Atlas of China* have been structured to locate all places mentioned in the text. The March 1969 CIA *Administrative Atlas of Communist China* is suggested for a more inclusive gazetteer.

In conclusion I wish to give very special thanks to several people, all of the University of California, Los Angeles. Miss Magdalen Woo has been involved from the outset with responsibilities ranging from translation to preparation of the index. She has done a magnificent job. Miss Patricia Caldwell has been reworking, redrafting, and redoing maps for more than a year in an attempt to attain uniformity and clarity in this atlas. Four other people have been involved in special ways: Professor Norman J. W. Thrower had the wisdom to encourage McGraw-Hill to publish the Hsieh map collection; Mrs. Louise Wilhelm made many improvements in the flow of the text; Mr. Noel Diaz executed the evocative map of China which opens the atlas; and Miss Susan Woodward redrafted some of the Taiwan maps.

Here, then, is Professor Chiao-min Hsieh's *Atlas of China,* and may it serve you well.

Christopher L. Salter

I. PHYSICAL

Structure

The Chinese landscape is a bold and broken one, plunging from the highest plateau on earth in the west to the rolling hills and coastal plains of the eastern seaboard. The extent and boundaries of today's China, and the variety of its landforms, are shown in Maps I-1 and I-2. By referring to these, and to the more detailed thematic maps, the reader will be able to follow the discussion of structure, landforms, climate, hydrology, soils, flora, and fauna in the Physical section of the atlas.

It should be noted that, wherever terms such as Central China, the Northeast, South China, etc., are capitalized, reference is specifically to the geographic regions discussed in Section III of the atlas.

THE DEVELOPMENT OF THE SCIENCE OF GEOLOGY IN CHINA

At the turn of the twentieth century the development of geology in China was stimulated by foreign geologists, such as F. von Richthofen (German), B. Willis (American), and A. W. Grabau (American). In 1916 the National Geological Survey was established, and from then on Chinese geologists carried on geological surveys of their own. Many geological data were collected, scientific monographs were published, and knowledge of the Chinese geological environment was broadened. For example, a 14-sheet geological map of eastern China with a scale of 1:1,000,000 and a geological map of the entire country with a scale of 1:3,000,000 were published.

In 1939 Li Su-Kuang (J. S. Lee) published his well-known book *Geology of China,* which was based on his analysis of China's geological structure from a geomechanical point of view. Later on, in 1945, Huang Chi-Ch'ing (T. K. Huang) published his book *The Main Tectonic Features of China,* which was based on stratigraphic analysis of ancient deposits and which made an attempt at a tectonic and orogenic differentiation of China.

From 1950 to 1960 Chinese geologists, together with some Russian geologists, such as V. M. Sinitsyn, proceeded actively with the study of stratigraphy, paleontology, mineralogy, and mineral resource location in China. The focus was on tectonics, and as a result the book *Principles of Geotectonics of China* (in Chinese), together with a tectonic map, with a scale of 1:4,000,000, was published. The book was edited by Chang Wen-yu and others on the staff of the Institute of Geology, Academia Sinica, in China. Map I-3 draws from a variety of these sources to show the complexity of the geology of China; Map I-4 shows a series of geologic cross sections.

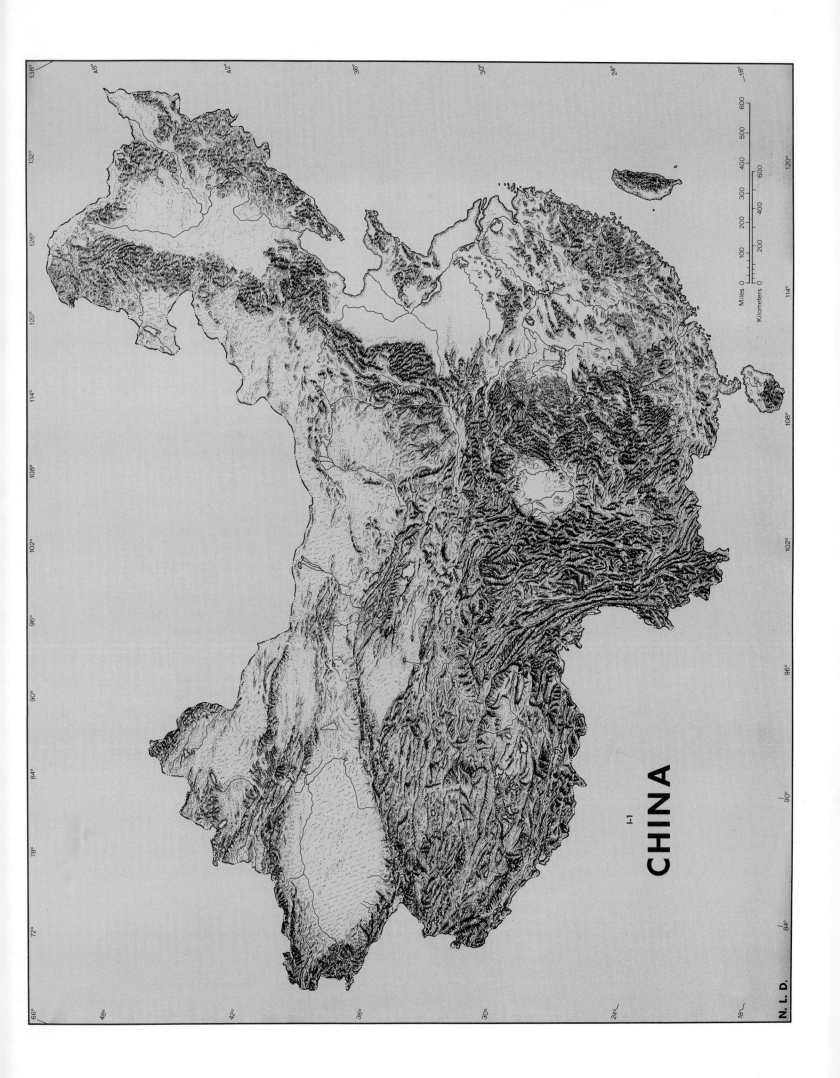

I-1

CHINA

N. L. D.

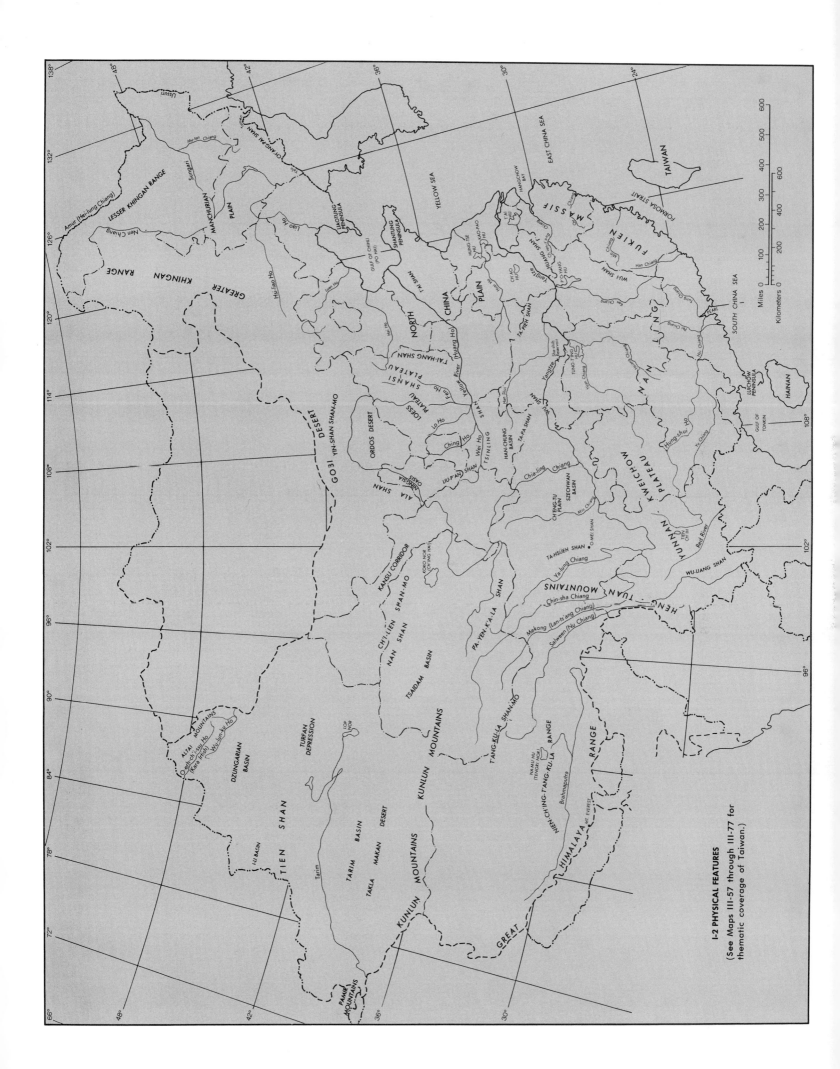

I-2 PHYSICAL FEATURES

(See Maps III-57 through III-77 for thematic coverage of Taiwan.)

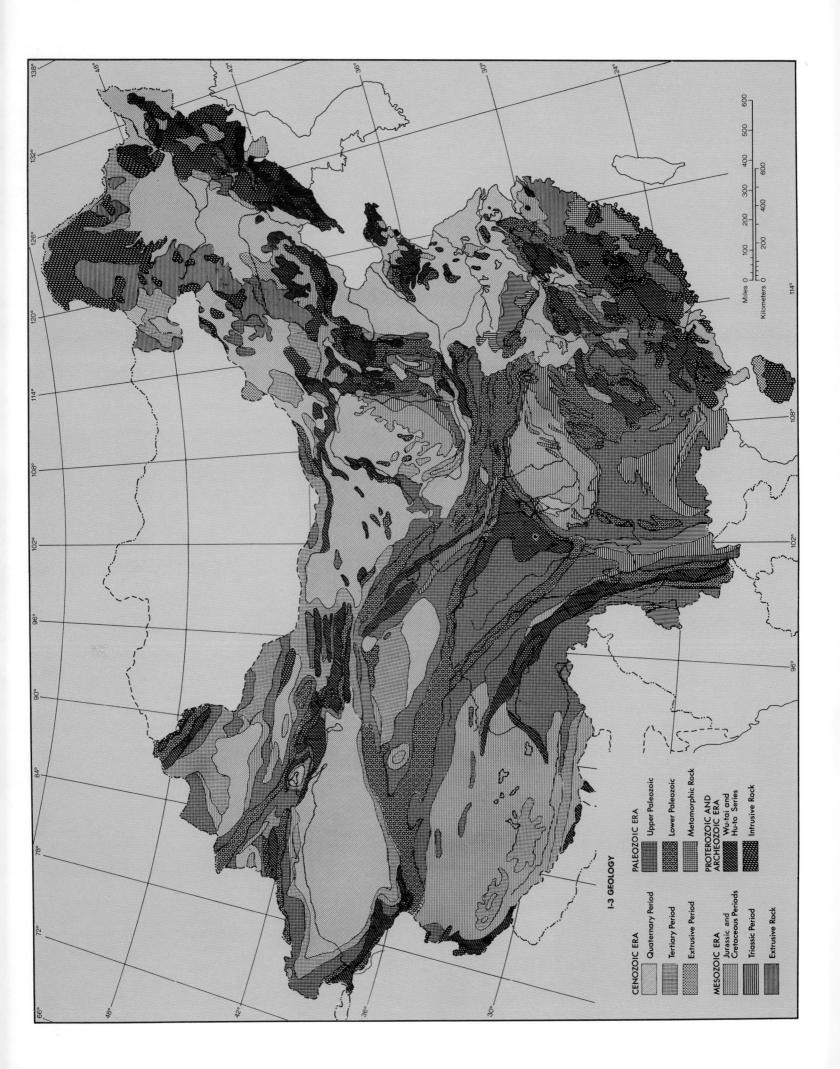

I-3 GEOLOGY

CENOZOIC ERA
Quaternary Period
Tertiary Period
Extrusive Period

MESOZOIC ERA
Jurassic and Cretaceous Periods
Triassic Period
Extrusive Rock

PALEOZOIC ERA
Upper Paleozoic
Lower Paleozoic
Metamorphic Rock

PROTEROZOIC AND ARCHEOZOIC ERA
Wu-tai and Hu-to Series
Intrusive Rock

Miles 0   100 200 300 400 500 600
Kilometers 0   200   400   600

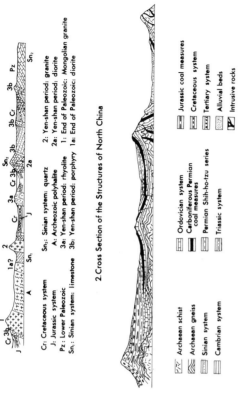

1. Cross Section from Inner Mongolia to East Liaoning Hills (near the head of Yalu)

Cr: Cretaceous system
J: Jurassic system
Pz: Lower Paleozoic
Sn₁: Sinian system: limestone

Sn₂: Sinian system: quartz
A: Archeozoic polyhalite
3a: Yen-shan period: rhyolite
3b: Yen-shan period: porphyry

2: Yen-shan period: granite
2a: Yen-shan period: diorite
1: End of Paleozoic: Mongolian granite
1a: End of Paleozoic: diorite

2. Cross Section of the Structures of North China

Archaean schist	Ordovician system	Jurassic coal measures
Archaean gneiss	Carboniferous Permian coal measures	Cretaceous system
Sinian system	Permian Shih-ho-tzu series	Tertiary system
Cambrian system	Triassic system	Alluvial beds
		Intrusive rocks

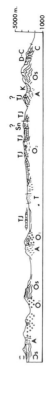

3. East-west Structural Cross Section of the Yunnan-Kweichow Plateau

T: Miocene (mainly Triassic) strata
Pz₂: Upper Paleozoic
Pz₁: Lower Paleozoic
Psn₁: Pre-Sinian: lightly metamorphosed rocks
Psn₂: Pre-Sinian: deeply metamorphosed rocks

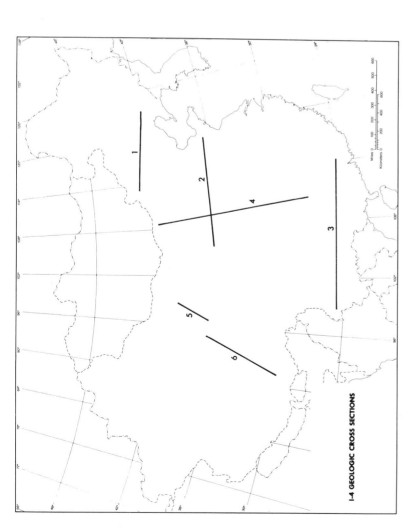

1-4 GEOLOGIC CROSS SECTIONS

4. Cross Section of the Structural Frame of China

Base of continental core: metamorphic-sedimentary rocks	Folded Paleozoic strata
Pre-Hu-to system: intrusive rocks	Paleozoic intrusive rocks
Hu-to system: mulde aggradation	Undisturbed Paleozoic and Mesozoic strata
Hu-to system: intrusive rocks	Fractures in folded rocks

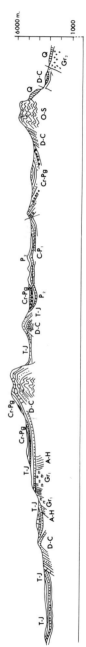

5. Cross Section from Tsinghai to Kansu Corridor

A: Pre-Sinian
Sn: Sinian
Os: Lower Paleozoic metamorphic rocks
D: Devonian
C: Carboniferous System (with volcanic rocks)

T: Triassic metamorphic rocks
TJ: Triassic-Jurassic
K: Cretaceous
O₁: Paleozoic (?) granite
O₂: Mesozoic granite

6. Cross Section from Ko-erh-mu (in Tsinghai) to Lhasa (in Tibet)

Q: Quaternary loess
Cr-Pg: Cretaceous Tertiary sandstone and pebbles
J: Jurassic coal measures
T-J: Triassic-Jurassic purple and green sand and limestone Series
P₂: Upper Permian coal measures
C-P₁: Carboniferous to Lower Permian: sand and limestone

D-C: Devonian to Carboniferous: sandstone and volcanic rocks
O-S: Ordovician-Silurian: green Schistose rocks, Phyllite, marble and volcanic rocks
A-H: Pre-Sinian gneiss and crystalline Schistose rocks
Gr₁: Caledonian (or older) Gneissic granite
Gr₂: Hercynian Porphyry granite

TECTONIC STRUCTURE OF CHINA

As a result of recent extensive geological exploration in mainland China, voluminous material on regional geology has been gathered by various Chinese geological organizations—the Institute of Geology, Academia Sinica, the Ministry of Geology, the Peking and Ch'ang-ch'un geological institutes, and the South-central Mining and Metallurgical Institute. Several variants of the tectonic map of China have appeared, along with a number of articles and monographs.

There are two principal schools of tectonic analysis. The one championed by J. S. Lee is called geomechanistic and is the study of geological structure from a mechanical point of view, using mathematics, physics, and engineering sciences. The historical-geological school, with its traditional and orthodox study method, enjoys the greater popularity.

In general terms, there are two distinctive geotectonic units, or two different structural systems, in China. One is a series of elongated enclosed unstable zones, or geosynclines. They are highly plastic and intensely deformed. These broad folded belts are interspersed with troughs of various dimensions. It is this series of geosynclines that has produced the great ranges of the Himalayas, the Kunlun, and the Tien Shan in the western part of China, as well as the island of Taiwan.

The second unit, the China platform, is bordered by the folded belts of the Altai, Tien Shan, Kunlun, and Himalayas. This platform can be divided into two parts, the east and the west, with the north-south division line following approximately the trace of the Liu-p'an Shan, on the west edge of the loess plateau, and passing through the Tsinling Shan, on to the western edge of the Szechwan Basin and continuing along farther to the eastern edge of the Tibetan Plateau.

Stable partial massifs, or blocks, are Dzungaria, Tarim, Tsaidam, Ala Shan, and Tibet. These blocks, with their near-oval shapes extended in the latitudinal direction, were formed after intensive tectonic movements during the Cretaceous period. They are enclosed by folded mountain ranges, but they have retained their stable platform appearance. These stable blocks have served in their depressed sections as the bases for long-time accumulation of sediments, including carbonates, gypsums, and easily soluble salts.

The uplifting and growth of the Khingan, Himalaya, Tien Shan, and Kunlun ranges all began in the Tertiary period, and they continue today. These processes in the more elevated western segment of the China platform predetermined the intensive erosion and the accumulation of conglomerates, loam, sands, and thick layers of deltaic alluvium in the east China lowlands.

These various regions are shown in Map I-5.

THREE ANCIENT LAND MASSES

Beneath all young deposits in China—below the sands of great plains, the loess slopes and valley bottoms, and other consolidated conglomerates, sandstones, shales, and limestones—lies an ancient complex of hard crystalline rocks which forms the foundation of China's continent. During past geological periods this ancient land mass was never wholly submerged beneath the sea. However, while these ancient crystallines underlie most of China, they are evident at the surface in relatively few localities.

On the surface of China stand three old masses which are structurally so rigid that they are called massifs and shields. In southeast China appears the remnant of the old rocks of *Cathaysia*, which contain the granites and porphyries in the provinces of Fukien and Chekiang, as well as those in Shantung and Liaoning further to the north. The second remnant is found in Inner Mongolia and is called *Gobia*. This Paleozoic massif is partly buried by Tertiary sand, clays, and basalt flows. The third and most preserved of these permanent massifs is *Tibetia*, located in the high western part of China.

Between these three crystalline rock masses are thick sedimentary deposits. From the beginning of the Paleozoic period up to the Jurassic, shallow seas occasionally invaded the land, leaving in their wake limestones, sandstones, and shales. During the Carboniferous and Jurassic periods came the widespread deposition of coal beds.

As a result of the configuration of ancient land masses, the structural patterns in China have three distinctive strike sets: northeast-southwest, west-east, and north-south (Map I-6).

The first strike set, from northeast to southwest, is the Cathaysia trend, which is shown in the mountain ranges of the Liaotung and Shantung peninsulas, the hills of Fukien Province, the Greater Khingan Range between Mongolia and Manchuria, the T'ai-hang Shan between the loess plateau and the North China Plain, and the eastern edge of the Yunnan-Kweichow Plateau.

The second set of structural alignments extends from west to east. It is represented by the Himalayas and by the Yin-shan Shan-mo; this range is the divide between North China and Mongolia, and is developed in the land mass of Gobia. Another important east-west mountain range is the Tsinling Shan, a continuation of the Kunlun, which lies be-

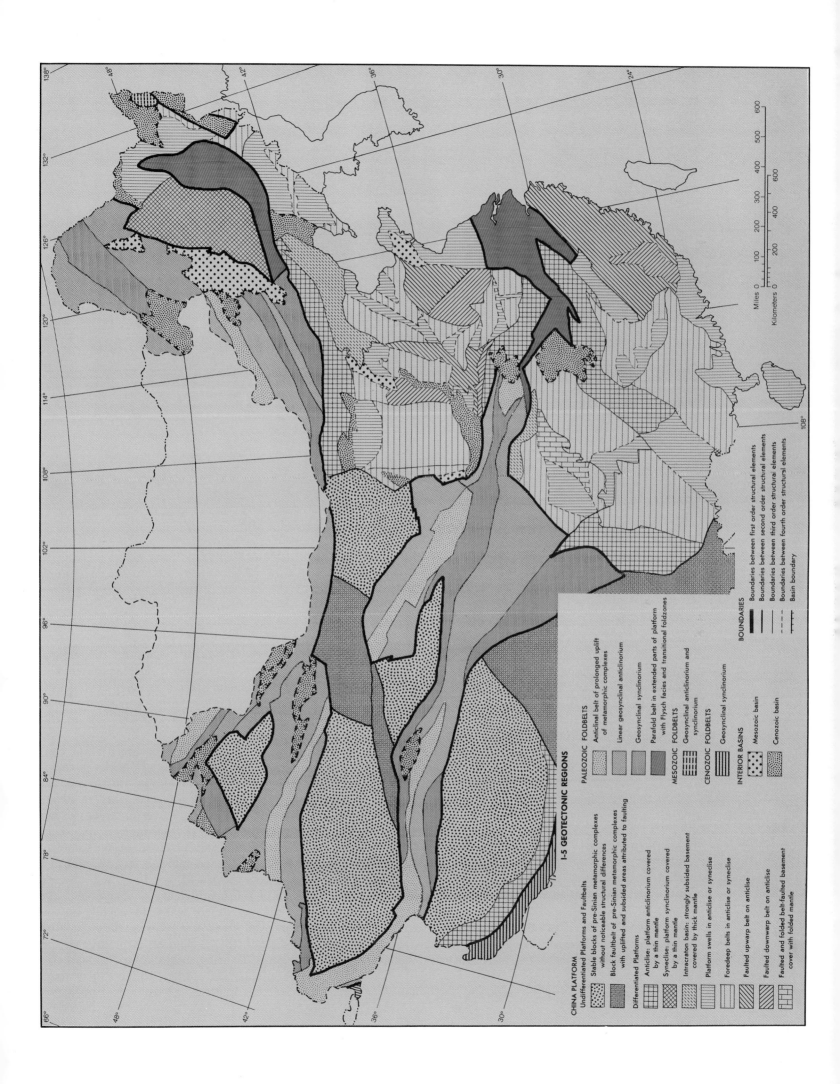

I-5 GEOTECTONIC REGIONS

CHINA PLATFORM

Undifferentiated Platforms and Faultbelts

Stable blocks of pre-Sinian metamorphic complexes without noticeable structural differences

Block faultbelt of pre-Sinian metamorphic complexes with uplifted and subsided areas attributed to faulting

Differentiated Platforms

Anticlise: platform anticlinorium covered by a thin mantle

Syneclise: platform synclinorium covered by a thin mantle

Intracraton basin: strongly subsided basement covered by thick mantle

Platform swells in anticlise or syneclise

Foredeep belts in anticlise or syneclise

Faulted upwarp belt on anticlise

Faulted downwarp belt on anticlise

Faulted and folded belt-faulted basement cover with folded mantle

PALEOZOIC FOLDBELTS

Anticlinal belt of prolonged uplift of metamorphic complexes

Linear geosynclinal anticlinorium

Geosynclinal synclinorium

Parafold belt in extended parts of platform with Flysch facies and transitional foldzones

MESOZOIC FOLDBELTS

Geosynclinal anticlinorium and synclinorium

CENOZOIC FOLDBELTS

Geosynclinal synclinorium

INTERIOR BASINS

Mesozoic basin

Cenozoic basin

BOUNDARIES

Boundaries between first order structural elements

Boundaries between second order structural elements

Boundaries between third order structural elements

Boundaries between fourth order structural elements

Basin boundary

Miles 0 100 200 300 400 500 600

Kilometers 0 200 400 600

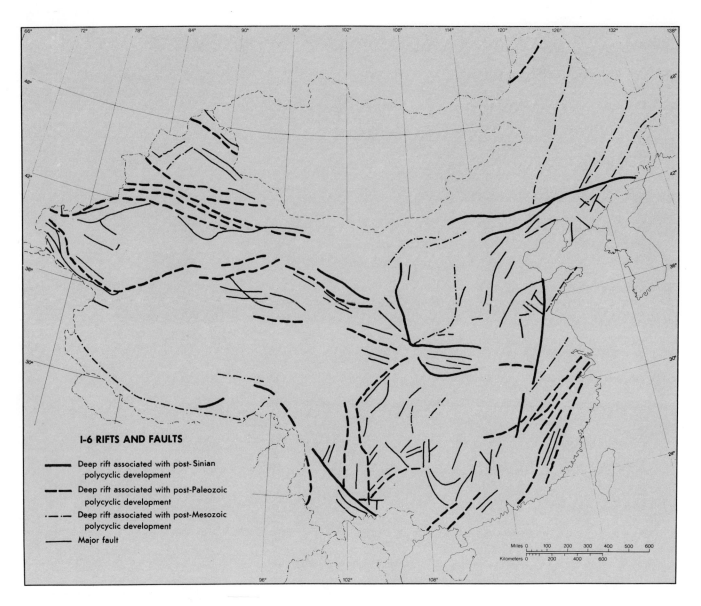

I-6 RIFTS AND FAULTS

———— Deep rift associated with post-Sinian
      polycyclic development

– – – – Deep rift associated with post-Paleozoic
      polycyclic development

–·–·– Deep rift associated with post-Mesozoic
      polycyclic development

———— Major fault

Miles 0   100   200   300   400   500   600
Kilometers 0   200   400   600

tween the Yangtze and the Yellow River and forms
the backbone of China. In South China there is the
Nan Ling range, which also has an east-west strike
and is the divide between the Yangtze and Hsi
Chiang.

The third structural trend, from north to south,
is well developed in the land mass of Tibetia. It is
reflected in the mountain ranges of the Ala Shan
and Liu-p'an Shan and the Heng-tuan mountains
on the eastern edge of the Tibetan Plateau.

EARTHQUAKES

China is a seismically active country, and a thorough
scientific examination of historical records of the
past thousand years, together with comparisons of
geological data, has enabled Chinese scientists to
provide an overall picture of seismicity in China
(Map I-7).

China's long history of recording earthquakes
dates back three thousand years to the Shang
Dynasty (1766 B.C. to 1122 B.C.). Explanation of the
earthquake phenomena started as early as 780 B.C.,
and an instrument for measuring earthquakes was
developed by Chang Heng in 200 A.D., during the
Later Han Dynasty.

In spite of this historical documentation con-
cerning earthquakes, China was late in the development of the study of seismology. With modern
industrial development, it was necessary to incorporate anti-earthquake measures in construction
of multistory buildings in the seismic regions. This
required a correct assessment of the seismic danger
in various areas, and maps showing seismic intensity
became necessary (Map I-8).

Because of the insufficiency of instrument observations, the assessment was made mainly on the
basis of historical statistical records, supplemented
by knowledge of the geological structure of the
seismic regions. To bring these data to a systematic
and properly classified order, China's historians
(members of the Institute of History, the Third

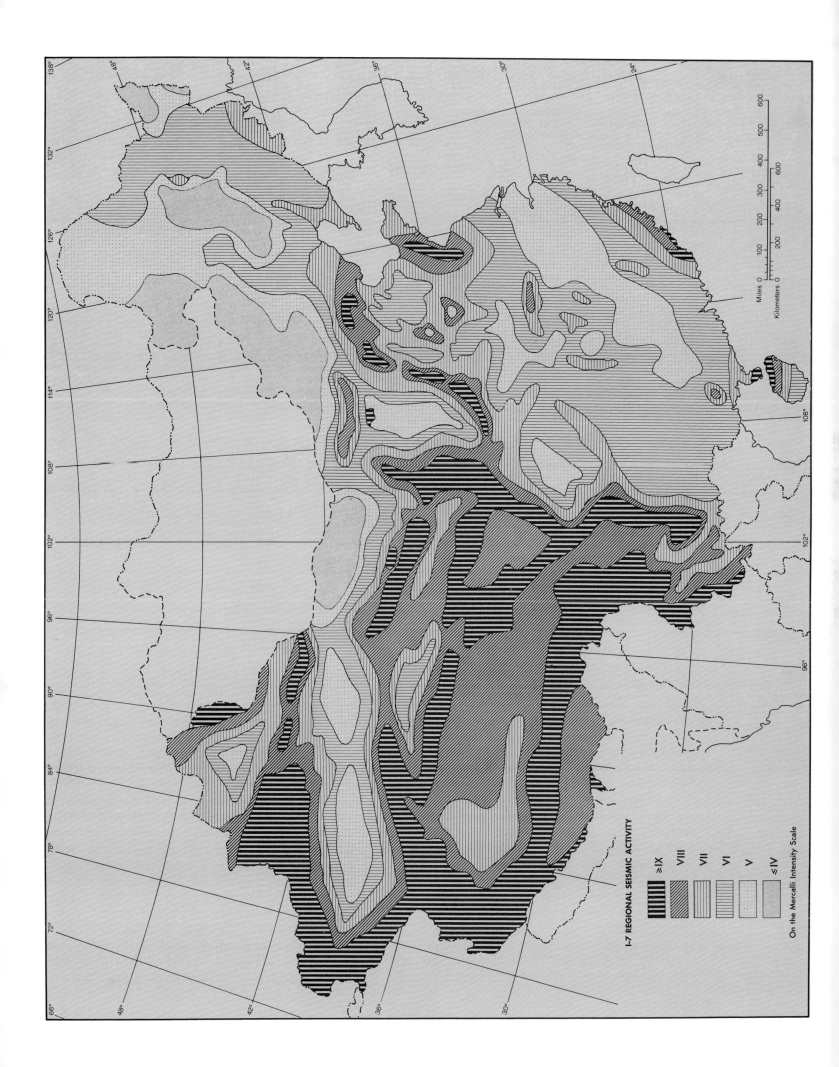

I-7 REGIONAL SEISMIC ACTIVITY

≥IX
VIII
VII
VI
V
≤IV

On the Mercalli Intensity Scale

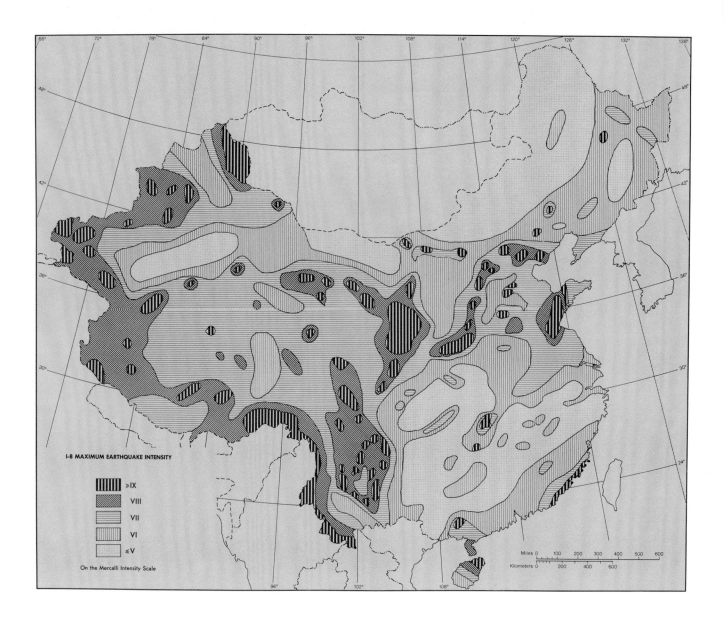

I-8 MAXIMUM EARTHQUAKE INTENSITY

▉	≥IX
▧	VIII
▦	VII
▤	VI
░	≤V

On the Mercalli Intensity Scale

Branch, Academia Sinica) spent two years examining over 8,000 diverse literary sources containing information about earthquakes—official chronicles, local gazetteers, notes, sketches, poems, articles, newspapers, archives of the Imperial Court, and oral reports by the aged. This effort resulted in the recent publication of the *Chronological Tables of Seismic Data on China,* in which over 15,000 descriptions of past earthquakes are collected.

From these data it is evident that there have been recorded in China 883 earthquakes, from 1000 B.C. until 1955, with an intensity greater than VI on the Mercalli Intensity Scale.

The seismologists of the Institute of Geophysics, Academia Sinica, have analyzed and systematized these historical data and, supplementing them with the records of modern instrument observations, have compiled the *Catalogue of Chinese Earthquakes.* The first volume of the catalogue reports 1,180 earthquakes of VI or greater on the

Mercalli Scale in the period from 1189 B.C. to 1955. The catalogue also provides information on the beginning of the tremors, the loci of the epicenters, the estimated intensity, and the principal features of the devastation. The second volume has been compiled in district-by-district form; it is designed as a reference manual for building construction.

Historical records show that 1,600 of China's 2,060 *hsiens* (counties) have suffered earthquakes. If each *hsien* is considered as a unit and marked with the highest degree of earthquake violence occurring there, isopleth lines showing five different earthquake intensities can be constructed. This is what has been done in Map I-7, Regional Seismic Activity. Such isopleths show that in southeastern China earthquakes are weak. However, in the western areas of Tien Shan, Sinkiang, the Himalayas, the Kansu Corridor, the Wei Ho Valley, the loess regions, Yunnan Province, and in western Szechwan Province earthquakes are more intense.

Landforms

The landforms of China are diverse and complex, with elevations ranging from the 8,880-meter peak of Mt. Chomolungma (Everest) to the Turfan Depression, which is 154 meters below sea level. Between these extremes are extensive plateaus, desert sand dunes, alpine glaciers, alluvial plains, precipitous canyons, and irregular coasts. Unusual landscapes are formed by loess hills, limestone karst formations, and glaciated mountains.

China's varied topography derives in part from the interaction of three characteristics: (1) The land decreases in elevation from west to east, (2) most of the major mountain ranges run from west to east, and (3) the land mass is broken up by great variety in landforms (Map I-9).

LANDFORM CHARACTERISTICS

1 The Land Mass in China Is High in the West and Low in the East.

Starting in the extreme west with the Tibetan Plateau ("the roof of the world"), the west-to-east inclination might be compared to a three-section staircase divided by two notable steps (Map I-10).

The higher step consists of the Kunlun and the Ch'i-lien Shan-mo, which constitute the northern boundary of the Tibetan Plateau, and the Ta-hsüeh Shan, which form the eastern edge. The altitude of this step approximates the 3,000-meter (10,000-foot) contour line. The second step, which is 2,000 meters lower, follows the Greater Khingan Range, the T'ai-hang Shan, the Wu Shan (which enclose the Yangtze gorges), and the eastern border of the Yunnan-Kweichow Plateau.

In the elevations between these two steps are plateaus and basins such as Inner Mongolia, the loess plateaus in the northwest and in North China, the limestone plateaus in South China, and the Szechwan Basin.

East of the second step is a belt of depressions with elevations below 500 meters. This includes the Manchurian Plain, the North China Plain, and the mid-Yangtze lake region.

Still further east are the elevated land masses of the eastern Manchuria upland, the mountains and peninsula of Shantung, and the Fukien Massif, which is known as the southeastern coastal hills. Farther to the east are the shallow depressions of the Yellow Sea, the East China Sea, and the South China Sea.

2 Most of the Major Mountain Ranges in China Have a West-East Orientation.

At intervals across the above-mentioned elevated and depressed stretches, the major mountains, or watersheds, run in general from west to east. In

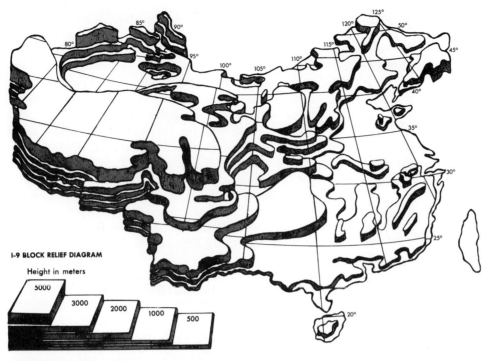

I-9 BLOCK RELIEF DIAGRAM

Height in meters

5000
3000
2000
1000
500

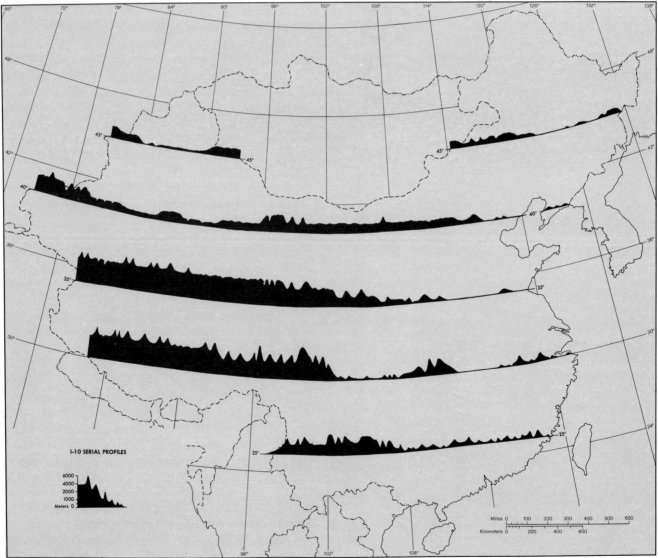

I-10 SERIAL PROFILES

6000
4000
2000
1000
Meters 0

Miles 0   100   200   300   400   500   600

Kilometers 0   200   400   600

the west are the Altai, which are the northern edge of the Dzungarian Basin; the Tien Shan, which divide the two basins of Sinkiang; the Kunlun, which separate Sinkiang from Tibet; and the Great Himalaya Range, which forms the mighty boundary between China and India.

Eastern regions are also cut by three mountain ranges. Farther north, the Yin-shan Shan-mo separate Inner Mongolia from the North China Plain. To the south, the Tsinling Shan lie between the North China Plain and Central China; and still farther south, the Nan Ling divide Cental China from South China.

This combination of longitudinally descending steps and latitudinally folded belts of mountains superimposed upon each other gives China's land surface an approximate checkerboard pattern.

3 The Landforms of China Are Varied.

With respect to slope and relief, the land surface of China may be generalized as plain, basin, hill, plateau, and mountain. About 11 percent of China's area is in plains; 16 percent, basins; 34 percent, plateaus; 9 percent, hills; and 30 percent, mountains. Elevation is distributed as follows:

Elevation	Percent of total area
Over 5,000 meters (over 16,404 feet)	16
2,000–5,000 meters (6,561–16,404 feet)	17
1,000–2,000 meters (3,280–6,561 feet)	35
500–1,000 meters (1,640–3,280 feet)	18
Under 500 meters (1,640 feet)	14
	100

These five general kinds of landforms are described below.

THE PLAINS

China's coastal plains cover more than 1 million square kilometers, or 11 percent of its territory, and provide its principal farmlands. The notable coastal plains, each with an area of approximately 300,000 square kilometers, are the North China Plain in the lower reaches of the Yellow River, the Manchurian Plain, and the middle and lower Yangtze. The Canton lowland is also a smaller plain. Rich soils, extensive irrigation, and centuries of intensive farming have made these areas not only the granary of China but also one of the world's greatest centers of agricultural production. Most important of the smaller interior plains are the Ch'eng-tu Plain, with an area of 6,000 square kilometers, the plains of the Wei Ho, and the Ningsia Oasis region, all of which

have been widely irrigated and cultivated to form agricultural centers and support large populations. These interior plains comprise approximately 1 percent of the total land area.

THE BASINS

About one-sixth of the total land area of China is basins, of which the four largest are the Szechwan, Tarim, Dzungarian, and Tsaidam Basins. Fringed by lofty mountains, these basins are part of the primary structure of the land rather than the result of deposition. Aside from Szechwan, where special climatic conditions provide ample rainfall, the inland location of these basins causes a dry climate which has made them steppe and desert regions. Local agriculturalists make use of melting snow from the surrounding mountains to irrigate their fields in fertile and picturesque oases. The more temperate Szechwan Basin is called "heavenly country" by the Chinese, because of the rich soils and humid climate which enable it to produce a wide variety of crops.

THE HILLY REGIONS

The hilly regions constitute about 9 percent of China's total area. Their slopes, interspersed with fluvial plains and small basins, make them ideal for terracing and the cultivation of a wide variety of field crops and tree crops. A few hills of over 1,000 meters, such as T'ai Shan in Shantung, and others in Anhwei, in Kiangsi, and in Chekiang, have become nationally known tourist and pilgrimage centers owing to their traditional religious significance and the concentration of temples on their flanks.

THE PLATEAUS

Located in western and central China, the plateaus occupy a third of the country's total area and include Tibet, Inner Mongolia, the loess plateau of Shansi and Shensi provinces, and the limestone Yunnan-Kweichow Plateau. Each has its own appearance and special features. Tibet, with an elevation of over 4,000 meters, is the world's most extensive tableland. Here are found seemingly endless snow-covered peaks, salt lakes, steppe tundras, and relatively flat valleys. The plateau of Inner Mongolia, bounded on the south by the Great Wall, on the east by the Greater Khingan Range, and on the west by Ch'i-lien Shan-mo, is broad, flat, and rather uniform in its surface.

Averaging 1,000 meters in elevation, the loess, or *huang-tu*, plateau to the west of the Tai-hang Shan is capped with a thick layer of fine, fertile silt, largely wind-transported loess. The sparseness of vegetation leaves the fine loess open to erosion by wind and water. The limestone of the Yunnan-Kweichow Plateau stands at an elevation between 1,000 and 2,000 meters. Water erosion has led to well-developed karst topography, including isolated peaks, pinnacles, gaping sinkholes and caverns, and lapiés, as well as small, fertile intermontane plains, known locally as *pa-tze*.

THE MOUNTAINS

The mountains of China reflect the geological structure of the land and provide the skeleton around which it is formed. The mountains produced by the Yen-shan revolution of the Cretaceous period run from northeast to southwest, while those formed during the earlier Caledonian and Hercynian revolutions of the Paleozoic era strike east-west, and others created during the Jurassic period have a north-south orientation.

The ranges running northeast-southwest include the Ch'ang-pai in eastern Manchuria and the Wu-i in Fukien. The east-west mountains, which resemble the fingers of a giant hand stretching across China, include the Altai, Tien Shan, Kunlun, Nan Ling, and the Himalayas. At approximately longitude 96°E, the east-west direction of the Himalayas suddenly veers to the south, forming the Heng-tuan mountains, which are the north-south ranges. The erosive action of the Salween, Mekong, and upper Yangtze (Chin-sha Chiang) has carved these mountains into spectacular gorge regions.

SPECIAL KINDS OF LANDFORMS

Loess

Loess, or *huang-tu*, covers an area of over 200,000 square kilometers and is an important natural feature of the landscape in China. It is a loosely compacted fine yellow silt composed largely of quartz, aluminum oxide, and organic particles, whose size varies from a diameter of $\frac{1}{16}$ to $\frac{1}{32}$ centimeters. It is not stratified but is well developed in vertical

joints, forming gorge-like gullies standing several decameters above the ground, traditionally making transportation difficult (Map I-11).

The accumulation of loess began when North China was mostly grassland. Apparently, strong outblowing winds from the Gobi Desert deposited silt on the grasslands, which eventually were buried under these aeolian deposits. In places the loess is more than 70 meters deep, burying the original bedrock landforms and forming an undulating tableland (Map I-12). Today the "sandy winds," or dust storms, in spring in North China indicate that loess accumulation is still in progress.

This aeolian silt, which is deposited in a thick layer of loose mantle, is easily dissolved by underground water, causing depressions, and landslides and making the region particularly susceptible to earthquake damage. Devastation of plant cover on unterraced loess slopes has made soil erosion a serious problem. The silt content of the rivers and the amount of erosion in the region are proportional to the extent of the loess area drained by the particular stream.

In addition to cultivation, the most notable human use of loess is for the cave dwellings which are excavated from loess banks. These caves are cool in summer and warm in winter, providing a very comfortable home, but the farmer must climb to his "roof" to cultivate his fields, and also must live with the danger of collapse because of earthquakes.

Karst

The areas of Kwangsi, Kweichow, and Yunnan are classic examples of karst topography (Map I-13). For centuries high temperatures and heavy rainfall have caused erosion and solution of the massive limestone strata which dominate this region, and the dissolving of the limestone has resulted in the spectacular landscapes for which the area is known. Isolated hills rise almost vertically from the ground in some places as the only remnants of the original mass of limestone, while in other places deep sinkholes and canyons dissect the original surface. Still other areas have been eroded into a profusion of steep hills, leaving only traces of the old surface. Caves and underground drainage ways penetrate the subterranean regions, and creeks which begin on the surface suddenly disappear to become underground streams. The environs of Kuei-lin, the capital of Kwangsi, is particularly enchanting and has the reputation of having the most beautiful scenery in China. This karst scenery is often the dominant landscape feature of Chinese landscape paintings.

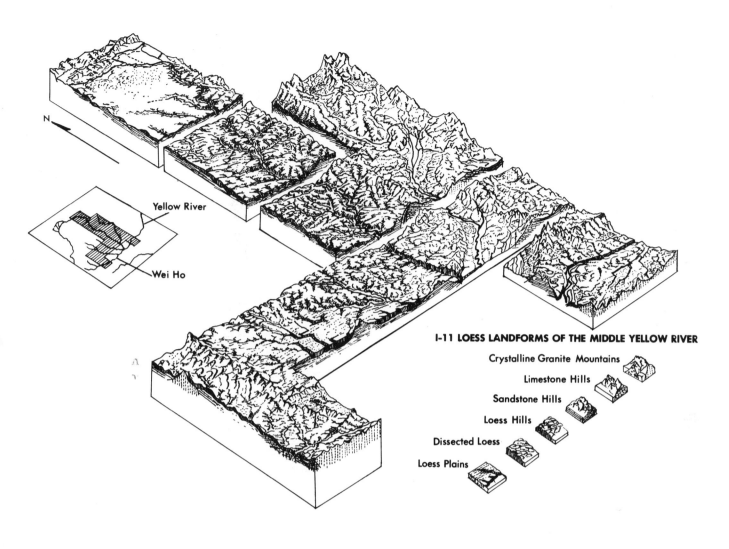

I-11 LOESS LANDFORMS OF THE MIDDLE YELLOW RIVER

Yellow River

Wei Ho

Crystalline Granite Mountains

Limestone Hills

Sandstone Hills

Loess Hills

Dissected Loess

Loess Plains

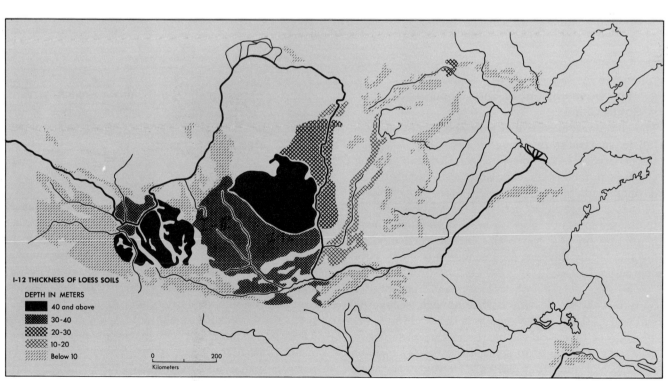

I-12 THICKNESS OF LOESS SOILS

DEPTH IN METERS

- 40 and above
- 30-40
- 20-30
- 10-20
- Below 10

0   200
Kilometers

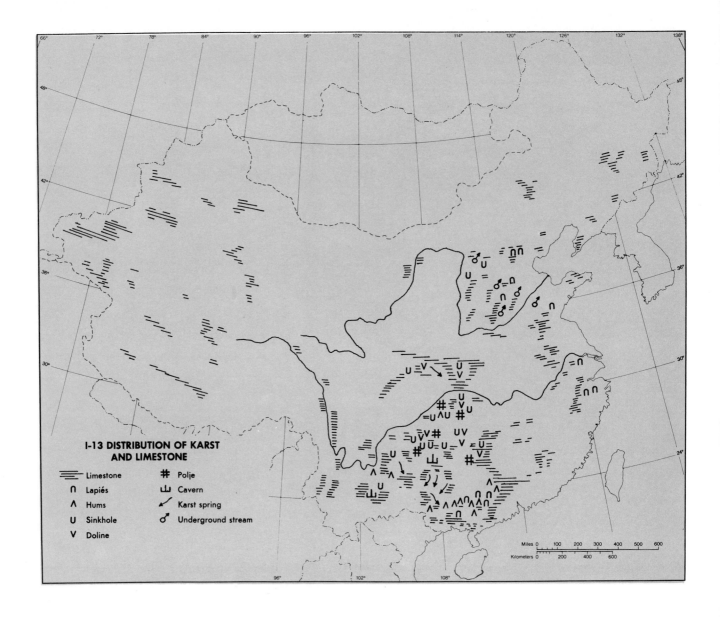

**I-13 DISTRIBUTION OF KARST
AND LIMESTONE**

≡ Limestone # Polje
∩ Lapiés ⊔ Cavern
∧ Hums ⤢ Karst spring
U Sinkhole ♂ Underground stream
V Doline

The Development of Karst Topography
in South China

The combination of sultry heat and abundant rainfall in southwestern China is extremely favorable to the processes of limestone solution and erosion. Geological factors in this area also facilitate the development of well-pinnacled karst topography. This is a region of an active mesa where numerous faults are present, and collapse occurs with even slight movement in the earth's crust. Vertical joints are also highly developed. Because of the structural characteristics and the great thickness of the limestone (often over 500 meters), erosion and solution by running water develop landforms such as caverns, sinkholes, steep valley canyons, and cliffs. The strong rock layer and the nearly horizontal structure cause the rock body to separate at joints, forming stone peaks and stone pillars. However, the solubility of limestone and the water permeability of the

joint system also make it difficult for random stream erosion to occur along the rock sides, so that sharp topographic forms of varying sizes and shapes abound (Map I-14).

Glaciation

Modern research has shown evidence of Pleistocene glaciation in many parts of China, including the mountains of northwestern Hupeh, parts of Ta-pieh Shan, the Yangtze Valley, and the mountains on the western border of the Red Basin of Szechwan. Other areas with traces of glacial action include the Greater Khingan, Ch'i-lien Shan-mo, and Tien Shan, as well as the provinces of Kweichow, Yunnan, and northern Kwangsi. Apparently polyglaciation predominated in both northern and southern China, with periods of warm (genial and subtropical) climate alternating with the glacial periods.

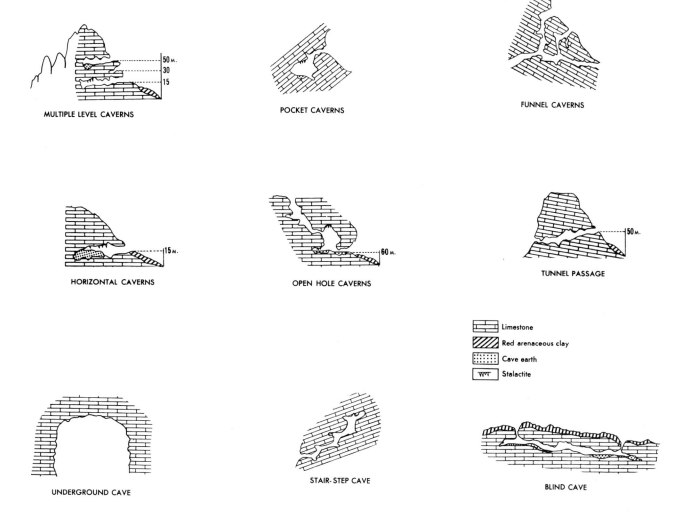

MULTIPLE LEVEL CAVERNS

POCKET CAVERNS

FUNNEL CAVERNS

HORIZONTAL CAVERNS

OPEN HOLE CAVERNS

TUNNEL PASSAGE

Limestone
Red arenaceous clay
Cave earth
Stalactite

UNDERGROUND CAVE

STAIR-STEP CAVE

BLIND CAVE

I-14 VERTICAL CROSS SECTIONS OF KARST LANDFORMS IN KWANGSI

The Quaternary Glacial Deposit Distribution in China

J. S. Lee in 1922 discovered glacial deposits along the T'ai-hang Shan and for the first time suggested that the modern glaciation of the Quaternary was not limited to the western part of China, but also occurred in eastern China. From 1933 to 1937 Lee published essays on the Quaternary glacial deposits of China. These essays were the pioneering work on glaciation in China and are partly responsible for Map I-15.

In western China, recent glacial deposits are found in the Tibetan Plateau, the Ch'i-lien Shan-mo, the Tien Shan, and the Altai Mountains.

In southern China, including east Szechwan, Kweichow, Kwangsi, Hunan, Hupeh, south Anhwei, Chekiang, Kiangsi, Fukien, and Taiwan, there also exist glacial landforms and glacial deposits. However, the glacial landforms have been subjected to extensive river erosion and as a result have been generally destroyed.

THE COASTLINE

China's 20,000-kilometer coastline, extending from the mouth of the Yalu River on the Chinese–North Korean border to the Chinese–North Vietnamese border in the south, is one half the length of the equator.

Hangchow Bay divides China's coast into two parts. North of the bay the coast is sandy, with the exception of the rocky shores of the Shantung and Liaotung peninsulas; south of the bay it is mostly rocky.

The northern part of Kiangsu Province and the land along the coast of the Gulf of Chihli (Po Hai) are

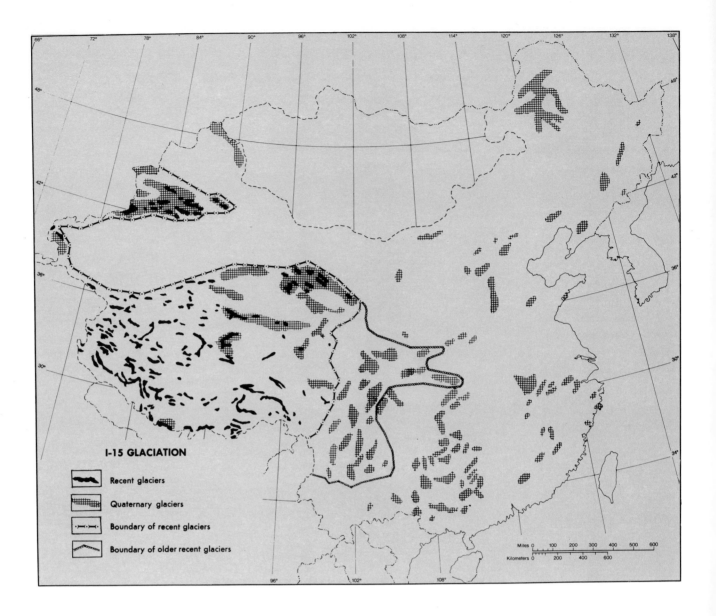

I-15 GLACIATION

—━━━ Recent glaciers

▥▥▥▥ Quaternary glaciers

·—╳—· Boundary of recent glaciers

▵▵▵▵ Boundary of older recent glaciers

famous salt-producing areas; they are also rich in marine products. The Shantung and Liaotung peninsulas, with their rocky coasts and their many harbors and islands, provide favorable shipping facilities.

The rocky coast south of Hangchow Bay is interrupted occasionally by patches of sandy shoreline at the mouths of some rivers. The rocky coasts have many indentations that are suitable for construction of ports and development of a fishing industry.

The coast of China includes both submergent and emergent types. Emergence characterizes the formation of the coast north of Hangchow Bay, and submergence the coast south of that bay. A traveler voyaging south from Shanghai to Canton will see an irregular rocky coast with numerous islands and bays and many good harbors; but on a trip north from Shanghai to Tientsin he will see a flat, straight shoreline with no islands other than sand deposits and with few good harbors.

China's coast has not been stable, especially in the southeastern section, where the irregular, rocky coastline, the drowned character of many rivers, the many islands and bays, the lack of large deltas, and the spits and bars all definitely suggest submergence. However, in the same region the wave-cut terraces, marine shell deposits, and shallow water offshore are evidences of emergence. As a whole, the coast of southeastern China is of the compound type, having been first submergent in the early Tertiary period and then raised in the Quaternary (Map I-16).

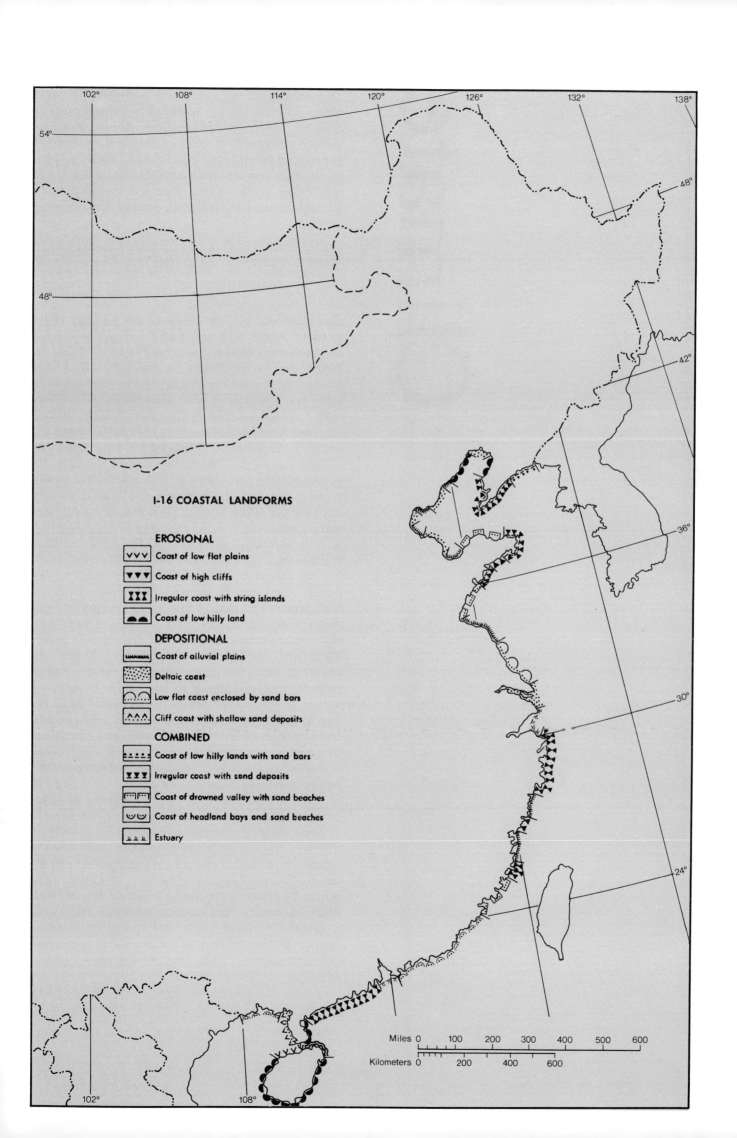

I-16 COASTAL LANDFORMS

EROSIONAL

ⱽⱽⱽ	Coast of low flat plains
▼▼▼	Coast of high cliffs
ⅠⅠⅠ	Irregular coast with string islands
▬▬	Coast of low hilly land

DEPOSITIONAL

ⱽⱽⱽ	Coast of alluvial plains
⣿	Deltaic coast
◠◠	Low flat coast enclosed by sand bars
ᴧᴧᴧ	Cliff coast with shallow sand deposits

COMBINED

⁚⁚⁚⁚	Coast of low hilly lands with sand bars
▼▼▼	Irregular coast with sand deposits
▭▭	Coast of drowned valley with sand beaches
◡◡	Coast of headland bays and sand beaches
ⱳⱳⱳ	Estuary

Miles 0 100 200 300 400 500 600

Kilometers 0 200 400 600

Climate

In a country as large in extent and varied in land-forms as China, there is bound to be a broad range of climates. Temperature zones represented in China include equatorial, tropical, subtropical, warm-temperate, temperate, and frigid, while humidity types can be classified into humid, subhumid, subarid, and arid (Map I-17). Three features control China's climate: monsoons, mountain ranges, and cyclones.

THREE CONTROL FEATURES

The monsoons are the result of the peculiar alignment of Asian land and water. China is located on the eastern edge of the great Eurasian continent, facing the Pacific Ocean on the east. In winter the heat of the earth is quickly lost by outward radiation and the interior land mass becomes intensely cold, causing the build-up of extremely high-pressure air masses. At the same time the Pacific Ocean develops a relatively low-pressure air mass above its surface due to the longer retention of the heat absorbed during the summer and fall. This strong polarity between the high-pressure land mass and low-pressure ocean surface gives rise to steady seaward winds.

In summer, alternatively, the land becomes warmer than the ocean, and thus low pressure develops on the land, while high pressure shifts to the ocean. As the winds always blow from the region of high pressure to that of low, this changing of pressure centers causes the wind to swing around from the winter pattern, changing its direction in accordance with the seasonal temperature changes. In winter it blows from the land to the ocean, and in summer from the ocean to the land. During the winter monsoon, the winds in northern China are usually from the north and northwest, while in central China they are from the north and northeast. The summer monsoon is dominated by south, east, and southeast winds in the north, and by predominantly southeast winds in the south.

The winter monsoon consists chiefly of polar continental air masses (cP) and land-transformed or sea-transformed polar continental air (LNcP or SNcP). Originating in the Mongolian anticyclone in winter, these air masses are cold and stable and influence the weather of a great part of China. The summer monsoon consists of three air masses with different origins: the tropical maritime (mT), the equatorial maritime (mE), and the polar maritime (mP). Of these, the last is not tropical in origin and is least important. The first two are warm and unstable air masses (Maps I-18 and I-19).

Since the winds that blow from the continent are dry and cold and those that blow from the ocean

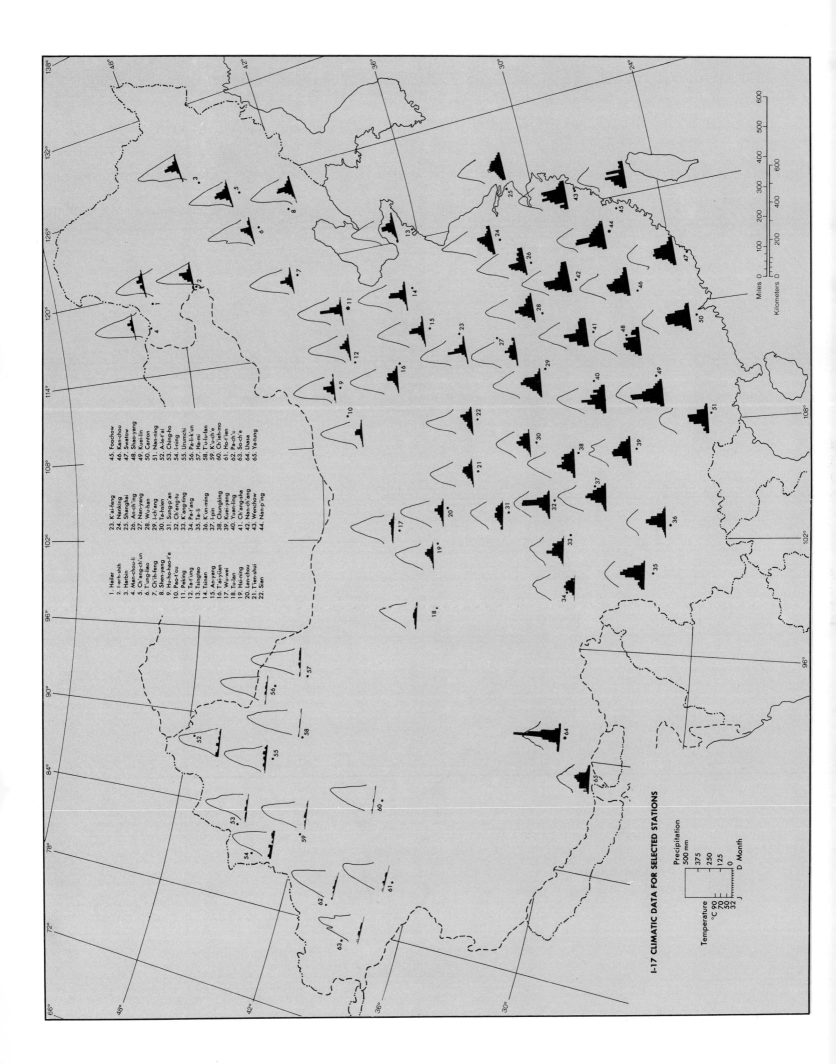

I-17 CLIMATIC DATA FOR SELECTED STATIONS

1. Hailar	23. K'ai-feng
2. I-erh-shih	24. Nanking
3. Harbin	25. Shanghai
4. Man-chou-li	26. An-ch'ing
5. Ch'ang-ch'un	27. Nan-yang
6. T'ung-liao	28. Wu-han
7. Ch'ih-feng	29. I-ch'ang
8. Shen-yang	30. Ta-hsien
9. Hu-ho-hao-t'e	31. Sung-p'an
10. Pao-t'ou	32. Ch'eng-tu
11. Peking	33. K'ang-ting
12. Tai'ung	34. Pa-t'ang
13. Tsingtao	35. Ta-li
14. Tsinan	36. Kun-ming
15. An-yang	37. I-pin
16. T'ai-yüan	38. Chungking
17. Wu-wei	39. Kuei-yang
18. Tulan	40. Yüan-ling
19. Hsi-ning	41. Ch'ang-sha
20. Lan-chou	42. Nan-ch'ang
21. T'ien-shui	43. Wenchow
22. Sian	44. Nan-p'ing

45. Foochow	
46. Kan-chou	
47. Swatow	
48. Shao-yang	
49. Kuei-lin	
50. Canton	
51. Nan-ning	
52. A-k'o-t'ai	
53. Ching-ho	
54. -ning	
55. Urumchi	
56. Pa-li-k'un	
57. Hami	
58. T'u-lu-fan	
59. K'u-ch'e	
60. Ch'ieh-mo	
61. Ho-t'ien	
62. P'o-ch'u	
63. So-ch'e	
64. Lhasa	
65. Ya-tung	

Precipitation

500 mm
375
250
125
0

Temperature

°C 90
70
50
32

D Month

Miles 0 100 200 300 400 500 600

Kilometers 0 200 400 600

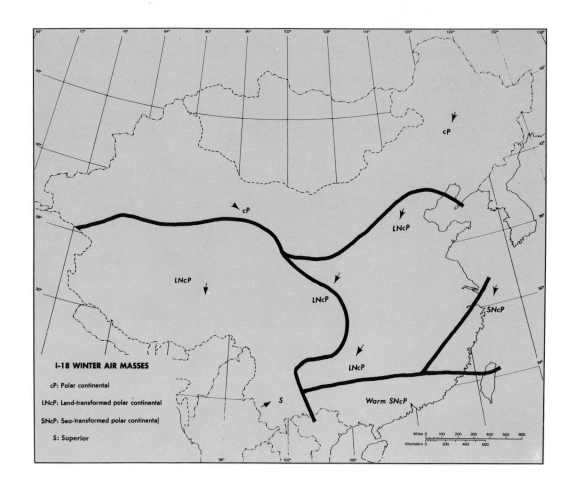

I-18 WINTER AIR MASSES

cP: Polar continental

LNcP: Land-transformed polar continental

SNcP: Sea-transformed polar continental

S: Superior

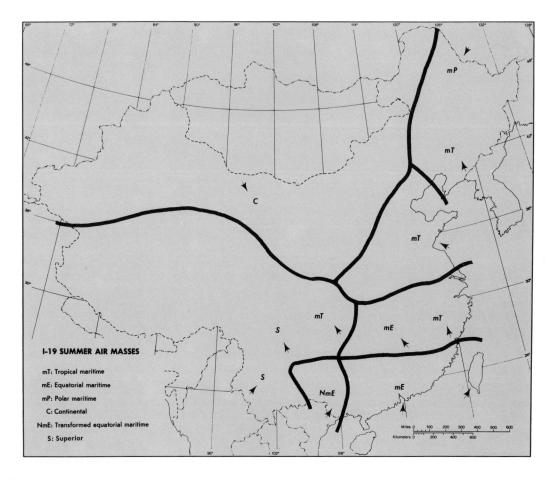

I-19 SUMMER AIR MASSES

mT: Tropical maritime

mE: Equatorial maritime

mP: Polar maritime

C: Continental

NmE: Transformed equatorial maritime

S: Superior

are moist and warm, rainfall reaches its maximum in summer and its minimum in winter (Maps I-20 and I-21).

The east-west arrangement of the mountain ranges presents barriers to the rain-bearing winds from the south in summer and the cold winds from the north in winter. Three pairs of cities—Sian and Wan-hsien, Cheng-chou and Hankow, and Süchow and Nanking—present examples of the influence of the mountain barriers on precipitation. Both cities of each pair are located at approximately the same longitude, but each pair is separated by the Tsinling Shan. Wan-hsien, Hankow, and Nanking, all south of this range, have an annual rainfall of more than 750 millimeters; Sian, Cheng-chou, and Süchow, all north of the range, have only half as much annual rainfall, or approximately 375 millimeters.

At China's location, extratropical cyclones are the usual cause of abrupt weather changes, especially in the spring. About 70 percent of such cyclones originate in China, 27 percent in Siberia, and 2 percent in India. The largest incidence of cyclones is in April and the smallest in August, with the spring season accounting for an average of 35 percent of a year's storms. Winter accounts for 26 percent, autumn for 20 percent, and summer for 19 percent. Along the coastline, however, an additional factor is the occurrence of the tropical cyclones (typhoons) of the western Pacific. These fierce marine storms pound the coasts, especially during August and September.

TEMPERATURE AND RAINFALL

Temperature and amount of rainfall are the main indicators of the climate of a region. The temperatures in North China and South China are not widely different in summer, but they differ markedly in winter. During winter the isotherms are close together, extending from west to east, parallel with latitude; in summer they are far apart, having an almost longitudinal orientation and in general lying parallel to the coast (Map I-22).

The rainfall in different parts of China shows even more variation than the temperature (Map I-23). Atmospheric moisture in China comes mostly from the Pacific, so that the rainfall decreases from southeast to northwest; it is 2,000 millimeters annually along the southeastern coast, 750 millimeters on the southern slopes of the Tsinling Shan, and less than 375 millimeters along the Yellow River. The northwest is so dry that it depends for its water supply on the melting of snow on top of the flanks of the Tien Shan and Altai.

In terms of annual rainfall, China can be divided roughly into four zones: humid, arid, subhumid, and subarid (or semi-arid). The humid zone includes areas south of the Tsinling Shan and the Huai Ho, where the annual rainfall averages 750 millimeters and sometimes reaches 2,000 millimeters in the south-east coastal hilly regions. These places are well known for rice, tea, and subtropical fruits and plants. The arid zone includes the areas north of the Yin-shan Shan-mo and Kunlun mountains, such as Sinkiang, Inner Mongolia, and other parts of the northwest, where the annual rainfall is less than 250 millimeters. Here the air is dry, and except where there are irrigated oases, most of the land is steppe and desert. Shortage of rain here is due, first, to the long distance from the sea and, second, to mountains and plateaus which prevent the moist wind from blowing in from the southeast. The land lying between the two zones ranges from semi-arid to subhumid, with an average annual rainfall of between 250 and 750 millimeters.

China's rainfall not only is distributed unevenly throughout the country but also varies widely from season to season and year to year. Disparity is greatest in the lower Yellow River regions and the northwest. For example, Peking's average annual rainfall over sixty-nine years was 630 millimeters, but the extremes in that period were 1,084 millimeters and 168 millimeters. The Hsi Chiang area in South China has the most reliable rainfall (Map I-24).

Over 80 percent of the annual rainfall occurs between May and October, the period of the summer monsoon. In the semi-arid and arid regions, the heaviest rainfall is concentrated in July and August. The coincidence of greatest rain with highest temperature is beneficial to agriculture, especially to rice cultivation.

The length of seasons also varies. Some places have a long winter and practically no summer, while others are warm year round and have no real winter. Using monthly average temperature as a guide for dividing the four seasons, summer is defined as the period when temperatures are above 22°C and winter as that when temperatures are below 10°C; spring and autumn are the periods when temperatures are between these extremes. According to this definition, in the areas south of the Nan Ling there is no winter, and summer lasts from five to eight months. Most of the area of the Tibetan Plateau, as well as northern Heilungkiang Province, has long winters and virtually no summer. The rest of the country enjoys four seasons, although winter is longer than summer in the North and summer is longer than winter in the South.

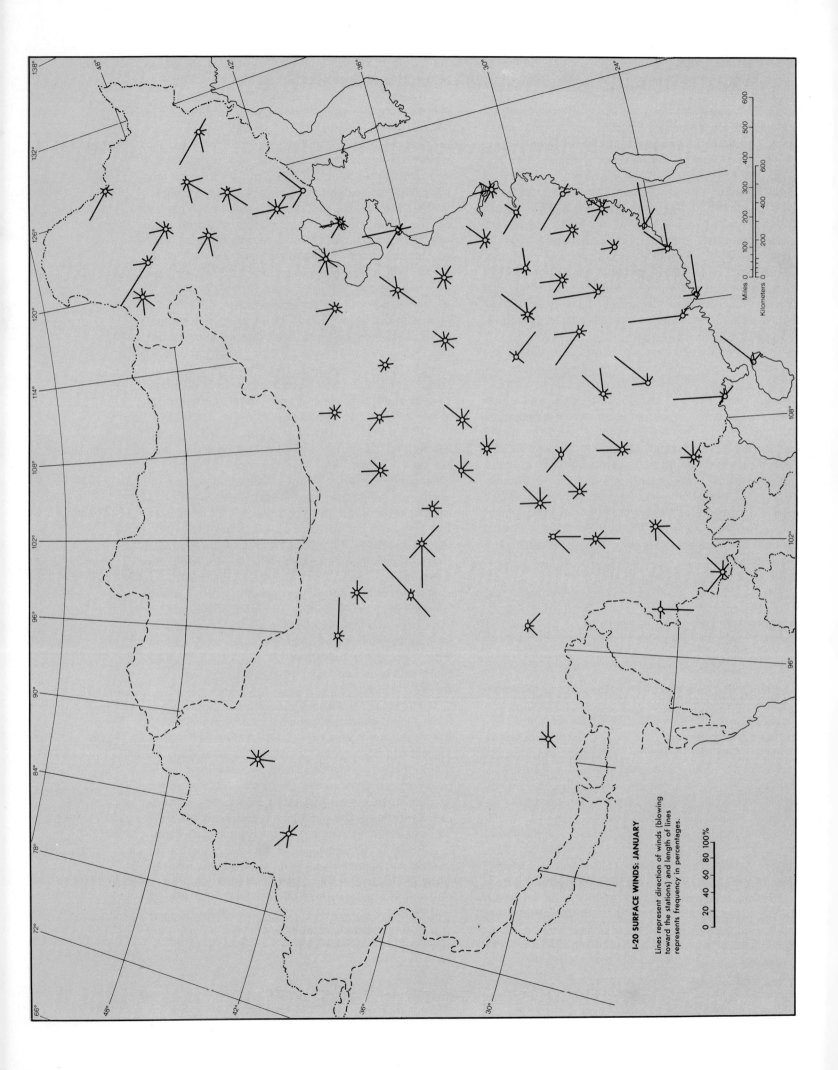

I-20 SURFACE WINDS: JANUARY

Lines represent direction of winds (blowing toward the stations) and length of lines represents frequency in percentages.

0 20 40 60 80 100%

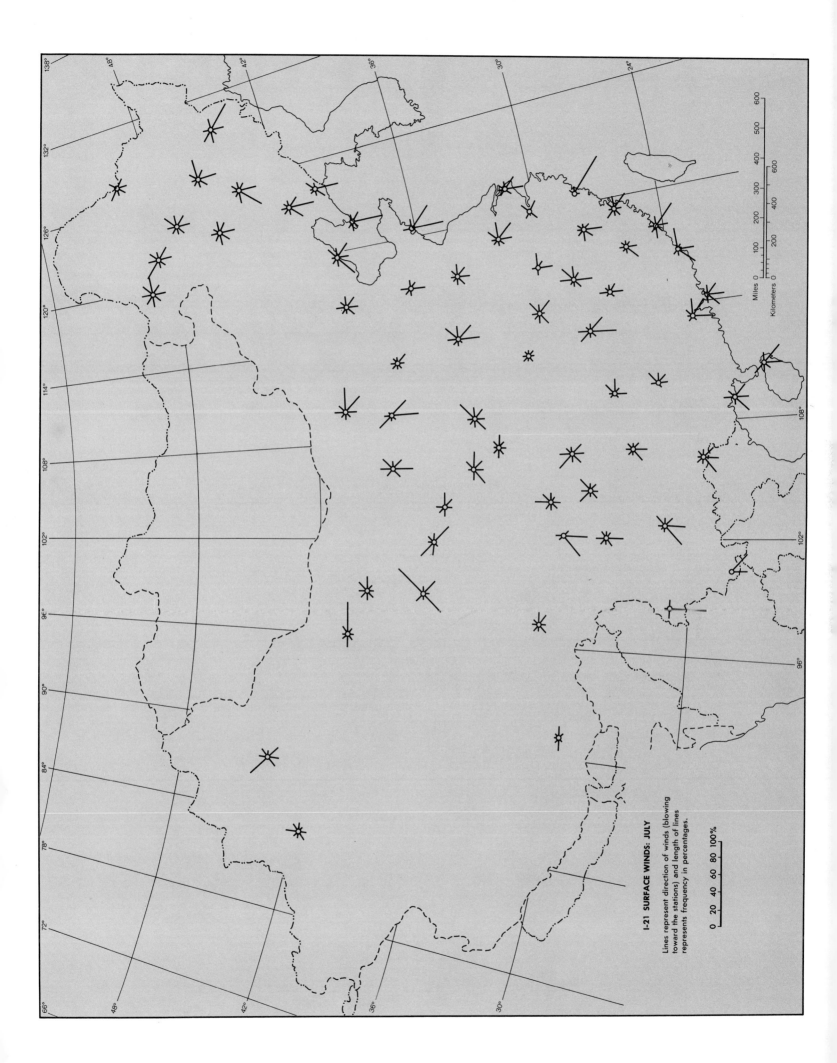

I-21 SURFACE WINDS: JULY

Lines represent direction of winds (blowing toward the stations) and length of lines represents frequency in percentages.

0 20 40 60 80 100%

Miles 0   100   200   300   400   500   600
Kilometers 0   200   400   600

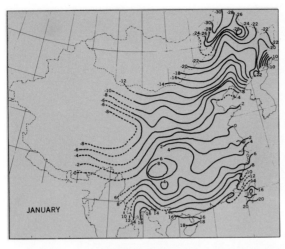

JANUARY

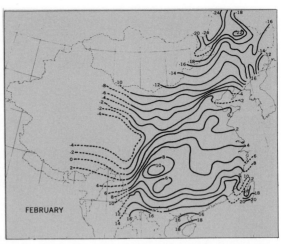

FEBRUARY

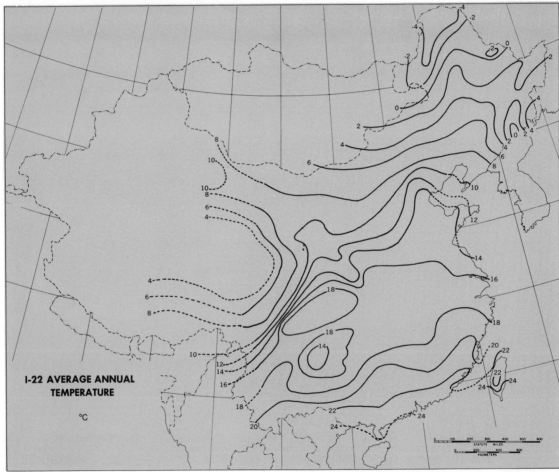

I-22 AVERAGE ANNUAL TEMPERATURE

°C

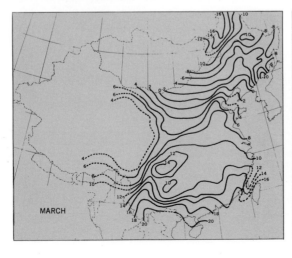

MARCH

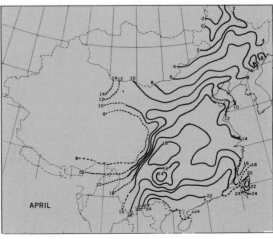

APRIL

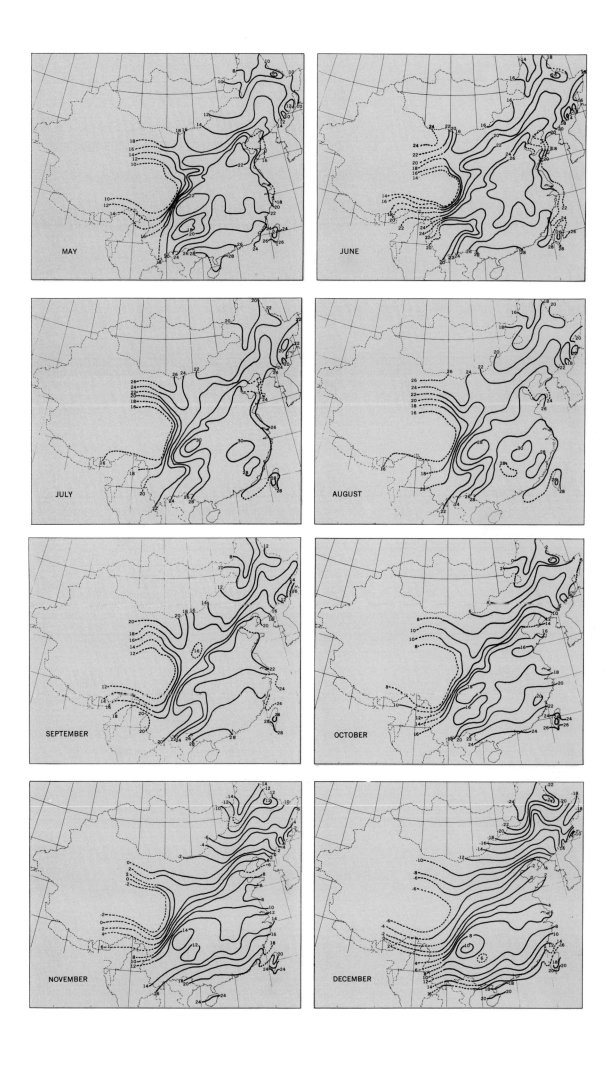

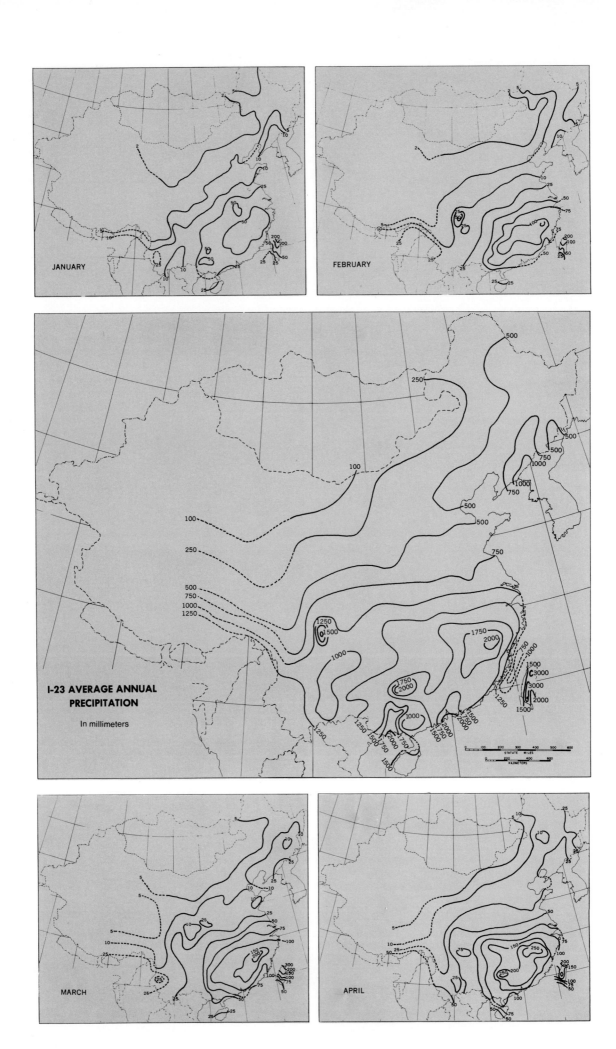

JANUARY

FEBRUARY

I-23 AVERAGE ANNUAL
PRECIPITATION

In millimeters

MARCH

APRIL

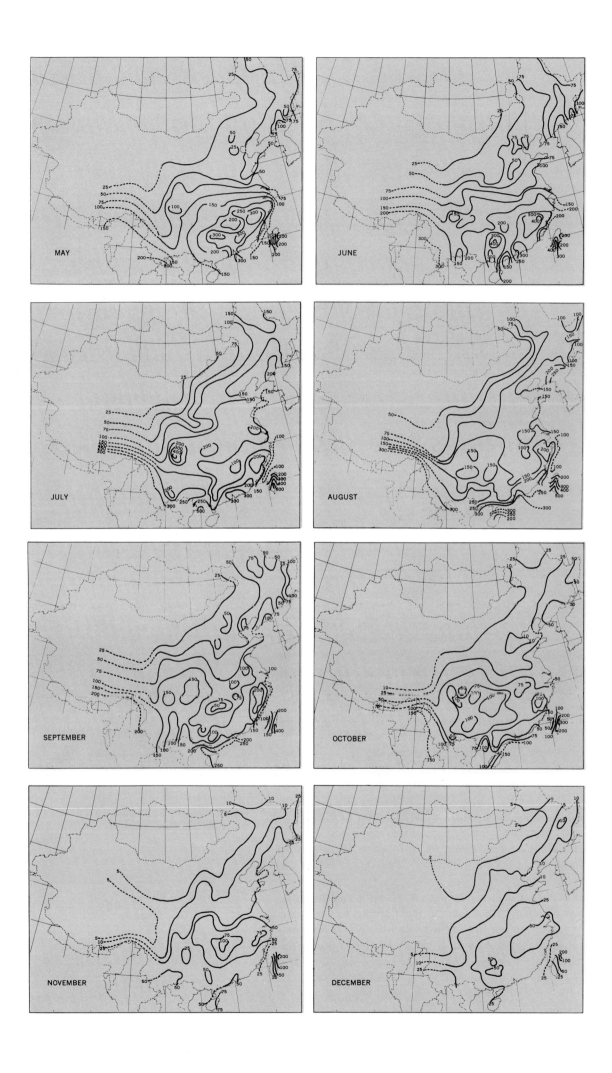

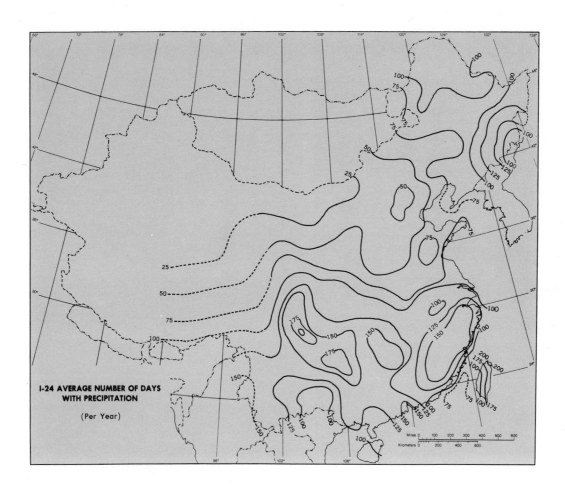

I-24 AVERAGE NUMBER OF DAYS
WITH PRECIPITATION

(Per Year)

CLIMATE BOUNDARIES AND CLASSIFICATION

China has three important climatic boundaries that are closely related to cultivation. The first is the −6°C January isotherm, which roughly coincides with the Great Wall and is the boundary between the areas of spring wheat (to the north) and winter wheat (to the south). The second is the isohyet of 750 millimeters, which parallels the Tsinling Shan and the Huai Ho and also coincides with the 6°C January isotherm. This line is the northern limit of rice cultivation. The third boundary is the 10°C January isotherm, which separates the area growing two crops of rice per year from that growing only one; that boundary coincides with the freezing isotherm south of the Nan Ling (Maps I-25 and I-26).

Climatically, China can be divided into approximately east-west belts, which are closely related to their patterns of agriculture. They are listed in the table below.

According to Köppen's classification, China has climatic types varying from tropical A to polar or mountainous E climates. Generally, three broad zones can be discerned, with the southeast part dominated by Monsoon Climate including the A, C, and D types, the northwest by Dry Climate (B) and the southwest and Tibet by Highland Climate (E) (Maps I-27, I-28, I-29, I-30 and I-31).

Name of belt	Location	Crops	Growing season
Sai-pei	North of Great Wall	Spring Wheat	140 days
Ho-pei	North of Yellow River	Wheat and Millet	222 days
Huai-pei	North of Huai Ho	Wheat and Cotton	250 days
Huai-nan	South of Huai Ho	Rice and Bamboo	285 days
Chiang-nan	South of Yangtze	Silk and Tea	300 days
Ling-nan	South of Nan Ling	Two Crops of Rice, Olives, Lichee Nuts, Sugarcane, Oranges, and Other Fruits	All year
Hai-nan	Hainan Island	Palm Trees and Tropical Fruits	All year

CHINA'S FOG

The distribution of fog along China's coast varies with the distance from the sea. Islands located near the coast have more days of fog than places

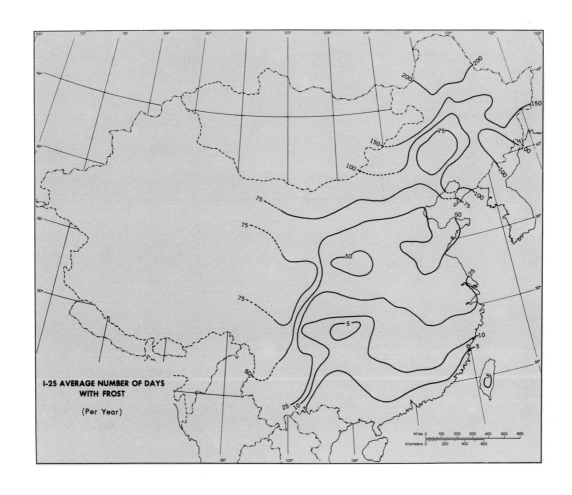

I-25 AVERAGE NUMBER OF DAYS WITH FROST

(Per Year)

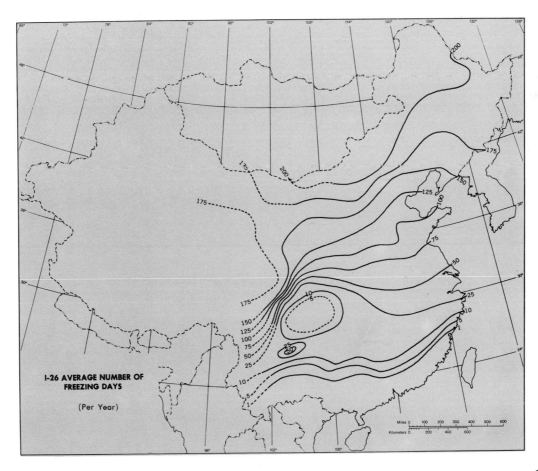

I-26 AVERAGE NUMBER OF FREEZING DAYS

(Per Year)

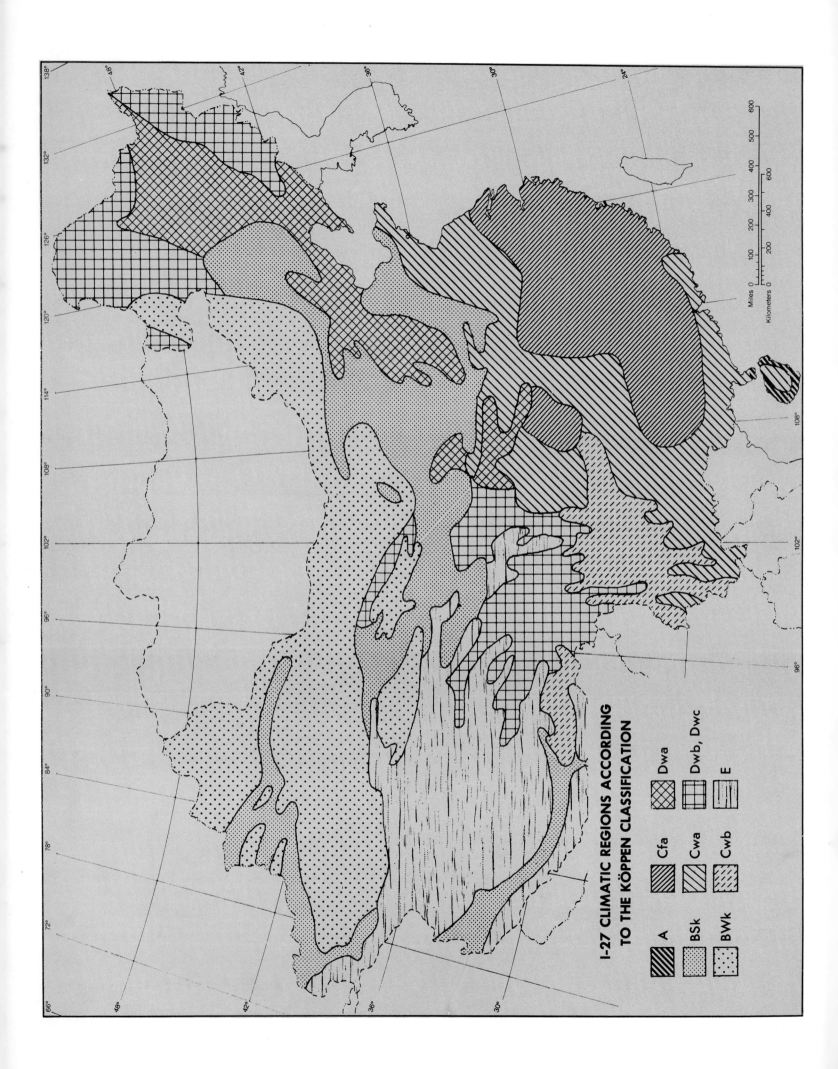

I-27 CLIMATIC REGIONS ACCORDING
TO THE KÖPPEN CLASSIFICATION

A   Cfa   Dwa

BSk   Cwa   Dwb, Dwc

BWk   Cwb   E

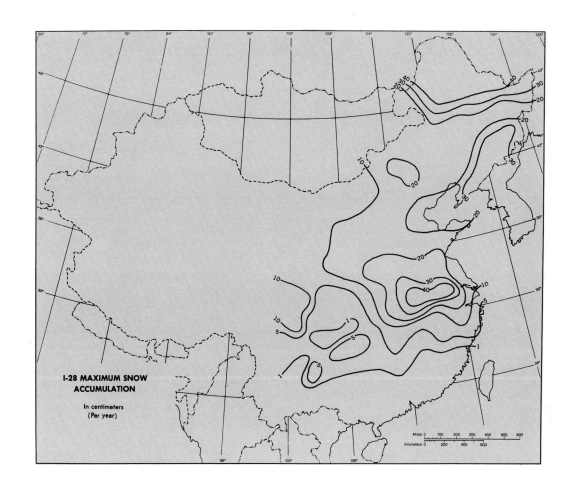

I-28 MAXIMUM SNOW ACCUMULATION

In centimeters
(Per year)

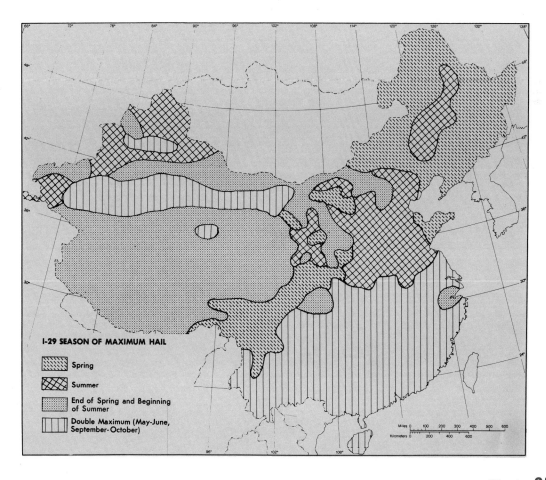

I-29 SEASON OF MAXIMUM HAIL

Spring

Summer

End of Spring and Beginning of Summer

Double Maximum (May-June, September-October)

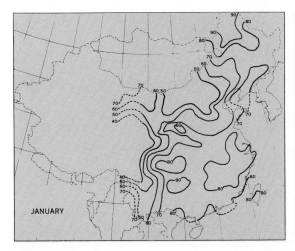

JANUARY

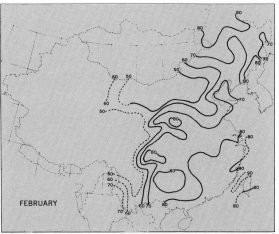

FEBRUARY

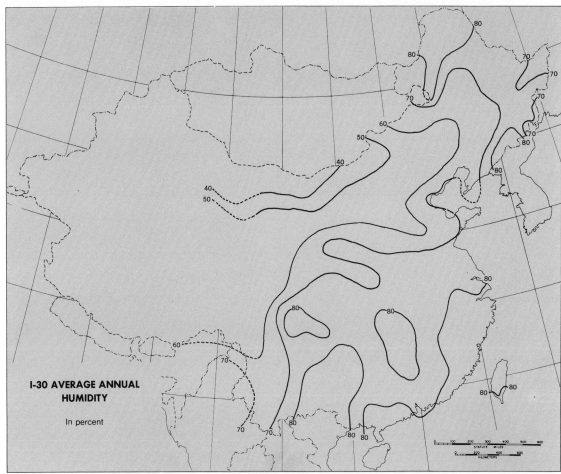

**I-30 AVERAGE ANNUAL
HUMIDITY**

In percent

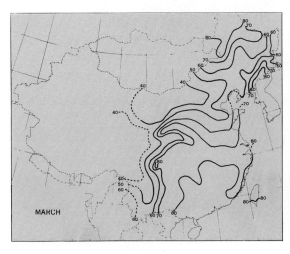

MARCH

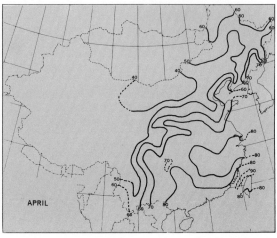

APRIL

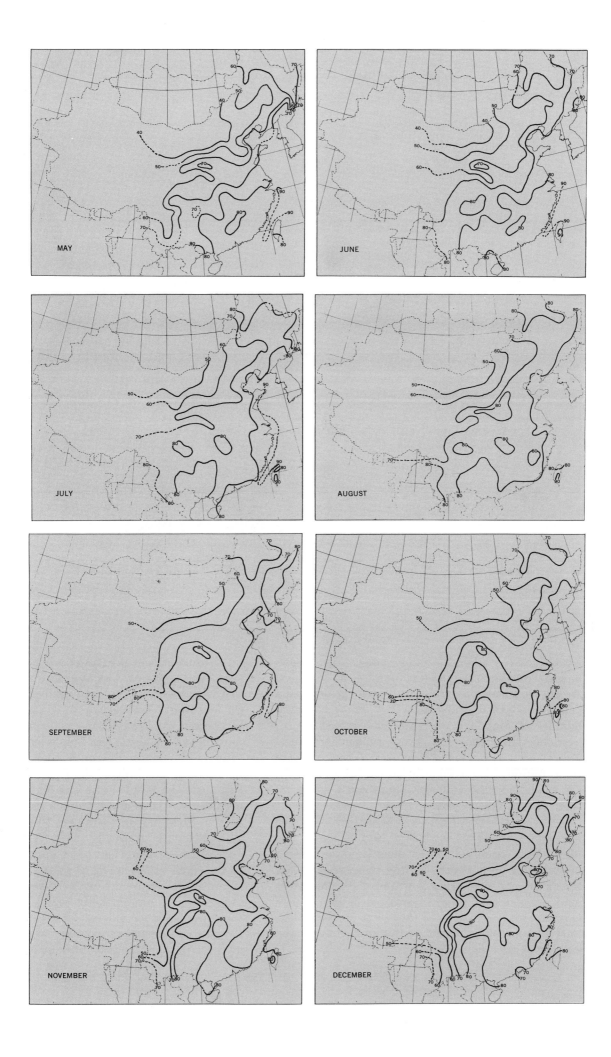

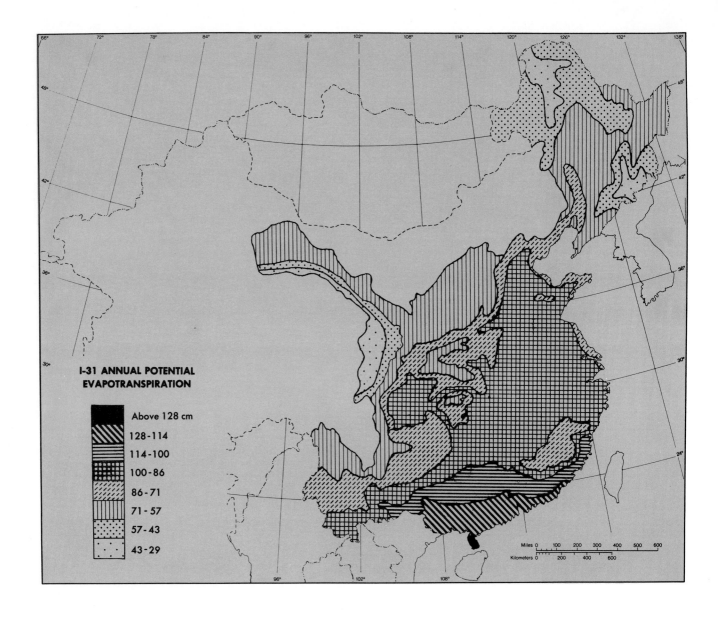

I-31 ANNUAL POTENTIAL
EVAPOTRANSPIRATION

■	Above 128 cm
	128-114
	114-100
	100-86
	86-71
	71-57
	57-43
	43-29

located in the adjacent inland areas. The coastal areas having the greatest number of fog days are the southeast part of the Shantung Peninsula and the mouth of Hangchow Bay, where the total number of fog days per year may exceed 80, or over one-fifth of the year. From the northern tip of Taiwan and the Chekiang coast to the coast of Shantung, fog days per annum total more than 50. On the whole, any point along China's coast has more than 20 fog days a year.

There are several general characteristics of the fog along China's coast which should be recalled as Map I-32 is consulted. First, most fog occurs either in spring or in summer. During these seasons the southeast monsoon winds blow from the ocean to the land, are warmed as they first pass over warm ocean currents, and are cooled as they next pass over the East China (cold) Current; it is this cooling of the air that gives rise to the fogs.

Second, as one proceeds northward up the coast, the peak fog period falls later in the year. On Hainan Island or in the Gulf of Tonkin the month having the most fog is February or March; along the Kwangtung coast the fog peak moves to April; in the Formosa Strait or along the Fukien coast it moves to May; in Hangchow Bay or on the Chekiang coast it falls in June; and along the coast of the Shantung Peninsula the month with the highest incidence of fog is July. Thus as we move from the south coast area to Shantung in the north, the month with the most fog days gradually shifts from February to July. This phenomenon corresponds with the shift in the route of the warm current. From spring to summer the warm current increases in energy, and as it takes a more northerly course, its influence on the superjacent air masses grows stronger.

Also, the lowest frequency of fog days occurs in the late summer and autumn, especially in the

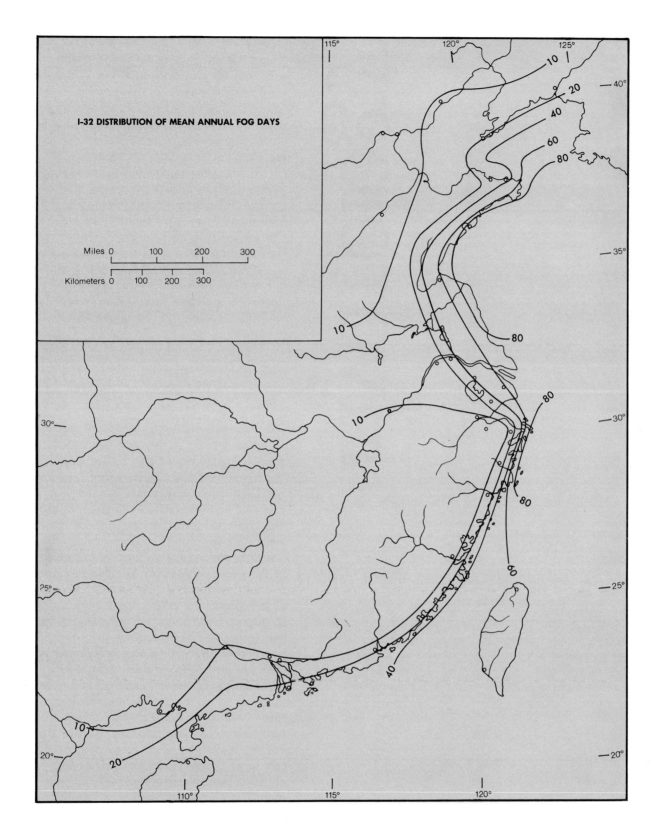

I-32 DISTRIBUTION OF MEAN ANNUAL FOG DAYS

months of September and October. The reason may be that during this time the southeast monsoon retreats and is replaced by the dry winter monsoon. The moisture in the air has decreased, and the temperature of the continental air mass increases as it approaches the sea. Therefore fogs cannot be formed.

Lastly, the concentration of fog days in the spring and summer is characteristic only of the coastal region; as one proceeds inland, the total number of fog days per year becomes far fewer than that of the off-shore islands, and the distribution of fog days inland shows no sharp peaks of concentration.

Hydrology

Hydrologic works in China began very early. The Grand Canal was constructed between the seventh and thirteenth centuries A.D., and rain gauges were widely used by the early fifteenth century (Ming Dynasty), before they were used in any European country. At present, there are approximately 2,000 rain-measuring stations and 6,800 river-gauging stations in mainland China.

Using the slogan "Coordinating scientific research with production practices," the mainland government has set the specific objectives of the nation's hydrological work as follows: to collect river discharge data at thousands of stream-gauging stations, to improve the soil moisture supply, to reduce silt in the Yellow River, to construct dams and drainage works, to extend irrigation facilities, to control floods, to maintain banks and levees, and to build additional canals for transportation.

DRAINAGE SYSTEMS

China's river systems carry 2,784 cubic kilometers of water a year, an amount surpassed in quantity only by the rivers of the Soviet Union and Brazil. The river systems are essential to industrial and agricultural development, and are one of China's most valuable natural resources. Programs are being undertaken to harness the rivers: to provide wide-scale irrigation, hydroelectricity, flood control, and transportation facilities, as well as to bring new lands under cultivation by utilization of river silt, making previously barren areas fertile. More than 95,000 kilometers of the streams are considered navigable, and the water energy has the potential for generating 540 million watts of power. Of China's rivers, there are 5,000 having a drainage area of more than 100 square kilometers (Map I-33).

China's general surface configuration—with high elevations in the west and low elevations in the east—results in most rivers flowing from west to east and emptying into the Pacific Ocean. This Pacific drainage characterizes about 57 percent of the total Chinese territory. However, the central and western plateau regions are surrounded by mountains which provide a watershed for interior drainage. Nearly 36 percent of China's rivers flow into the basins of these areas, with the water being mostly absorbed in downward percolation. The majority of these streams have their sources on the slopes of the mountains bordering the plateaus. The flow into the Indian Ocean (7 percent) accounts for virtually all other drainage.

The continental divide runs from the Greater Khingan Range in Inner Mongolia to northwestern Ningsia, then along the Kansu Corridor, across the

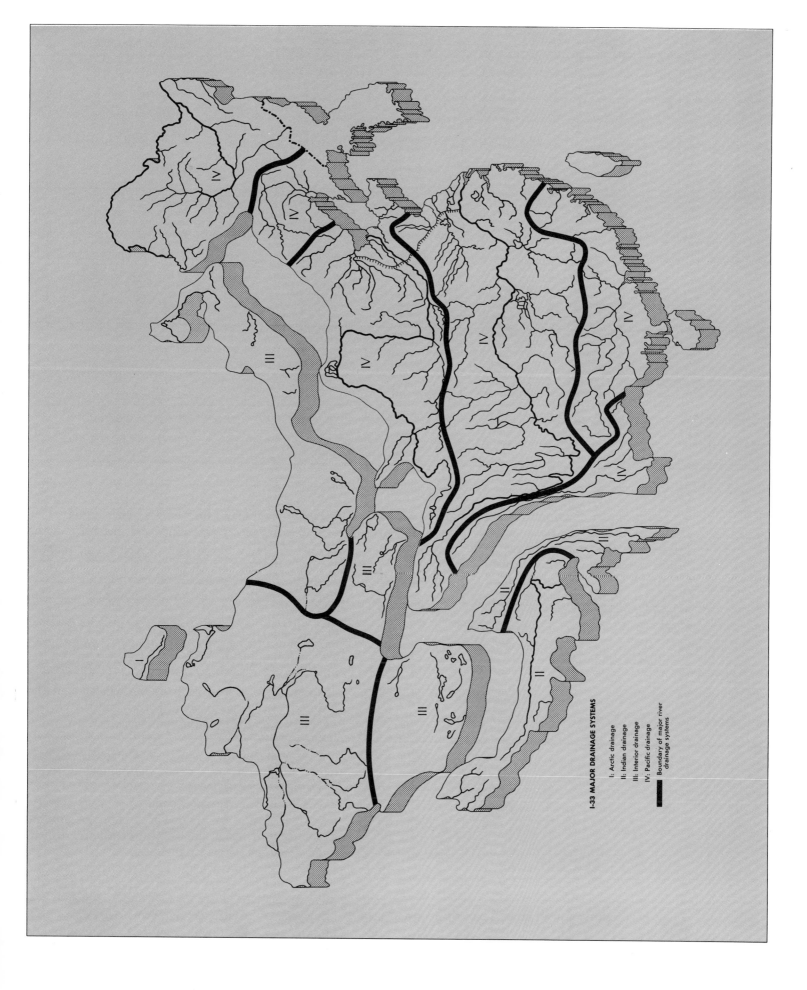

I-33 MAJOR DRAINAGE SYSTEMS

I: Arctic drainage
II: Indian drainage
III: Interior drainage
IV: Pacific drainage

▬▬ Boundary of major river
drainage systems

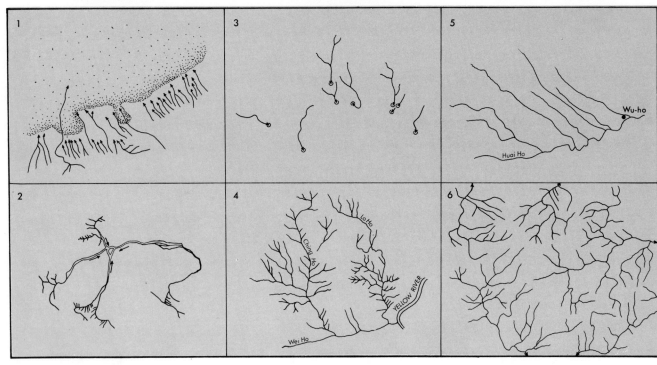

Blind rivers in southern Tarim Basin of Sinkiang

Blind rivers of southern Kweichow in limestone caverns

Trellis pattern in Honan and Anhwei

Concentric pattern in Tarim Basin of Sinkiang

Dendritic pattern in Shensi

Radial pattern in Heilungkiang

I-34 RIVER PATTERNS

western border of Tsinghai, and through the western third of Tibet to the Indian border. East of this line the rivers flow out to the sea, while west of it they flow inward to the interior plains and basins. The Tarim River is the only exception to the rule that the streams of interior basins are short, shallow, intermittent, and poorly defined, often carrying water only in the rainy season (Map I-34).

The following table shows the statistical distribution of China's river systems and drainage outlets:

Drainage outlets	Area (square kilometers)	Percent of total
Pacific Ocean	5,440,540	56.7
Indian Ocean	663,750	6.9
Arctic Ocean	40,340	0.4
Total Exterior Drainage	6,144,630	64.0
Interior Drainage	3,452,370	36.0
TOTAL	9,597,000	100.0

CHINA'S RIVER NETWORK

The headwaters of most large Asian rivers are located in three areas of China. The Tibetan Plateau is the origin of such long rivers as the Yangtze, Yellow, Mekong, Brahmaputra, Ganges, and Indus. The second important river source lies generally in the center of the country and includes the Greater Khingan Range, the T'ai-hang Shan, the Shansi Plateau, and the Yunnan-Kweichow Plateau. Major rivers originating here are the Sungari, Hsi-liao, Hai, Luan, Pearl, Red, and Hsi rivers. The third area extends over the eastern coast of China and includes the Ch'ang-pai Mountains in Manchuria, the Shantung Hills, and the southeastern coastal hills. These mountains and hills are the headwaters of many short rivers, such as the Tumen and the Yalu on the Chinese-Korean border and the Ch'ien-t'ang, Min, and Han in the southeastern coastal area (Map I-35).

Annual rainfall is higher in the southeast than in the northwest; as a result the number of rivers in the northwest is fewer.

To gain a better understanding of China's rivers, the country may be divided into eight geographic areas, each of which has certain distinctive hydrological characteristics (Map I-36).

In Manchuria, where the major rivers are the Amur, Sungari, Nen, Tumen, Yalu, and Liao, the highest water level occurs in August, which is the rainy season. Melting ice and snow also cause a high flow in spring, but floods result from clogging by ice flocs rather than from the large volume of water.

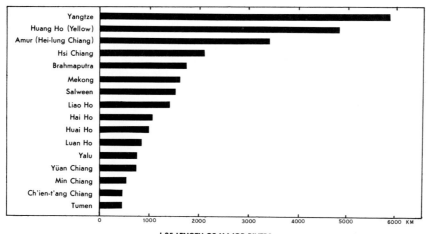

I-35 LENGTH OF MAJOR RIVERS

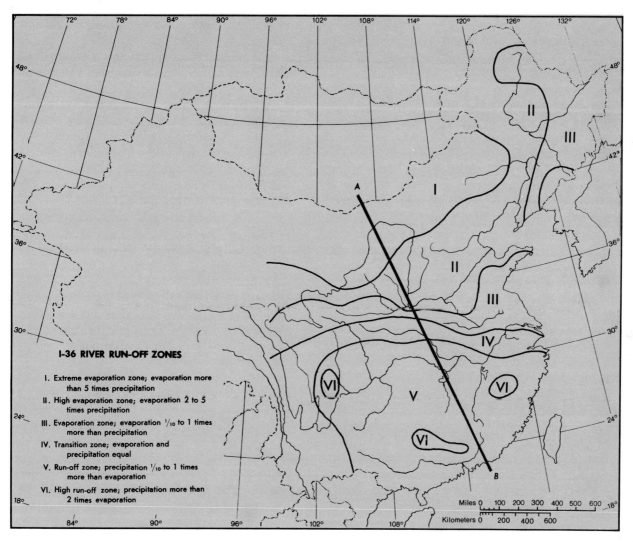

I-36 RIVER RUN-OFF ZONES

I. Extreme evaporation zone; evaporation more than 5 times precipitation

II. High evaporation zone; evaporation 2 to 5 times precipitation

III. Evaporation zone; evaporation 1/10 to 1 times more than precipitation

IV. Transition zone; evaporation and precipitation equal

V. Run-off zone; precipitation 1/10 to 1 times more than evaporation

VI. High run-off zone; precipitation more than 2 times evaporation

PROFILES OF PRECIPITATION, RUN-OFF, AND EVAPORATION

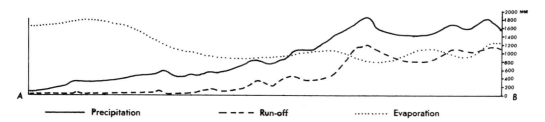

—— Precipitation   - - - Run-off   .... Evaporation

The rivers of this area are frozen from late October or early November until March. The lowest water levels occur in January and February.

North China includes the Huai, Hai, and Yellow rivers, all of which have their highest water levels in August. Melting snow brings high water in the spring, but since the volume of snow on adjacent mountains is limited, floods are more frequently caused by sudden summer showers. The lowest water level occurs in May and June, when high temperatures and low humidity result in a high evaporation rate. The exception to this is the Yellow River, which derives much of its water supply from the melting snows of Tsinghai. The Yellow River reaches its lowest water level in December and January.

In South China, the plentiful rainfall of the tropics and subtropics gives rise to large rivers such as the Yangtze, Hsi, Ch'ien-t'ang, Kan, Min, Wei, and Pearl rivers and the various rivers in Taiwan. The highest levels and floods occur during the typhoon season, July to September.

The main rivers of southwestern China are the upper Yangtze, the upper and middle Yu, and the upper Hsi, Red, Mekong, and Salween. Since this region is seldom affected by ice melt, high water levels occur during the rainy season in July and August, and the lowest levels coincide with the dry weather of February. Owing to their deep beds, the rivers in the mountainous areas seldom flood.

The Tsinghai-Tibet area is the source of many rivers, such as the Indus, Salween, and Mekong, as well as the more northerly Yangtze and Yellow rivers. Melting snow and ice result in a high spring water level, but gradual melting makes the high-water season poorly defined. The maximum water levels occur during the rainy season (July through September), and the headwaters of the river are frozen from October to March.

The streams of Inner Mongolia are dispersed over wide plains where sand, high winds, gully diversion, sparse rainfall, and a high evaporation rate result in intermittent streams. Since the principal source of water is rainfall, many of the streams carry water only after a storm. Underground springs supply a very few tiny streams, which are the most dependable sources of water in this arid region.

In the northwest, melting snow and glaciers from the Tien Shan, Kunlun Mountains, and Ch'i-lien Shan-mo provide the chief sources of water for the desert and semidesert areas. Although the snow begins to melt in March, ground absorption and a high evaporation rate keep the water level very low, except for the period from June to August when there is rain. Flow in the upper reaches is perennial, but dispersal in steppe and desert land leaves little water in the lower reaches of these streams, which are dry from October to late May.

The Altai area includes the O-erh-ch'i-ssu and Wun-lun-ku rivers, which are fed by abundant snow and rainfall. Spring floods are caused by the coincidence of spring rains and melting snow, and the midseason high water level occurs in July. Freezing from November to March results in low water levels from November to April.

THE RATE OF FLOW, OR RUN-OFF, OF CHINA'S RIVERS

Before discussing the run-off of China's rivers, it is necessary to define the term "rate of run-off." Rate of run-off is the amount of water flowing past a given point (cross section) of a river within a given period of time. It is usually expressed in cubic meters per second.

In China 32 rivers average a run-off of more than 200 cubic meters per second, and 11 exceed an average of 1,000 cubic meters per second (Maps I-37 and I-38). The Yangtze ranks fourth in volume of run-off among the world's rivers, being surpassed only by the Amazon, Congo, and Indus. The Yangtze at its mouth has the highest run-off of any river in China, 32,620 cubic meters per second. The Hsi and Amur rivers have a high run-off, averaging 11,000 cubic meters per second.

The Yellow River has only one-twentieth of the run-off of the Yangtze. The run-off of the Yellow River is roughly equal to that of the Ch'ien-t'ang Chiang, though the latter's drainage area is only one-fifteenth that of the Yellow River. The rate of run-off of the Min Chiang is three times greater than that of the Yellow River, although the Min Chiang's drainage area is only one-twelfth that of the Yellow. These differences in water flow are primarily a result of climatic variations and differences in stream density.

If all tributaries are included, only three rivers, the Yangtze, Amur, and Hsi, have an average annual run-off of more than 10,000 cubic meters per second.

China's total run-off of 2,784 cubic kilometers annually, or 9.21 cubic meters per second per square kilometer, accounts for 8.5 percent of the world's total. This is 40 percent of Asia's total run-off and exceeds the total annual run-off of Europe.

In China the mountainous areas have a greater run-off than the plains, and the east coastal region has a greater run-off than the western interior. This distribution corresponds with the rainfall pattern of China.

In general, southern China has an average run-off rate of 20 liters per second per square kilometer, and the rivers along the southeastern coast have a rate of 35 liters per second per square kilometer. However, this rate decreases northward. For example, the Yangtze River has an average rate of run-

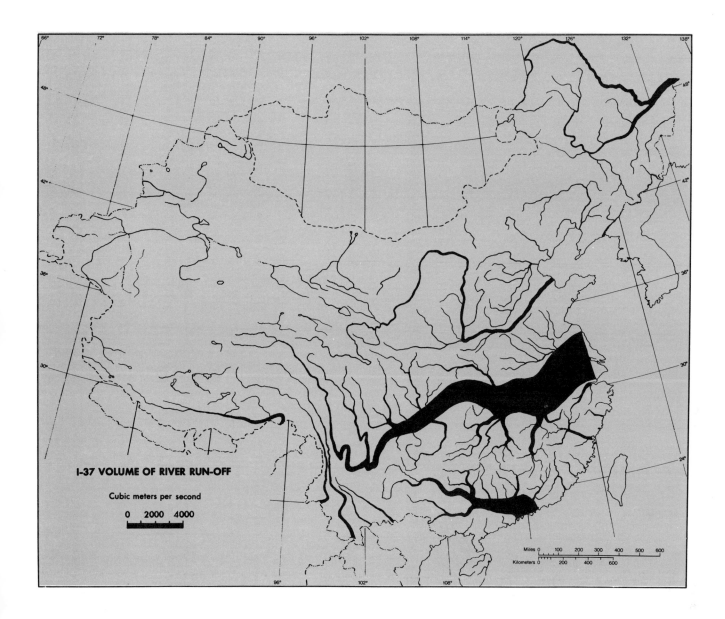

I-37 VOLUME OF RIVER RUN-OFF

Cubic meters per second

0   2000   4000

Miles 0 100 200 300 400 500 600
Kilometers 0 200 400 600

off of 18 liters per second per square kilometer, the Huai has a rate of 5.52 liters per second per square kilometer, and the Yellow, Hai, and Liao rivers have a rate of only about 2 liters per second per square kilometer. In Manchuria the rate of run-off again increases, the Amur having a rate of 5.31 liters per second per square kilometer and the Yalu a rate of 15.01 liters per second per square kilometer. The area of interior drainage has the lowest rate of run-off, less than 1 liter per second per square kilometer.

THE SILT CONTENT OF CHINA'S RIVERS AND THE PROBLEM OF FLOODING

The silt content of China's rivers varies among regions. For example, such Manchurian rivers as the Amur and the Yalu have a low silt content, since the region has sufficient vegetation to retard soil erosion. By contrast, the Yellow River flows through the loess region and has a very high silt content, since erosion in this area is severe. These regional differences are summed up in the table below:

THE COMPARATIVE EROSIONAL FORCE OF SELECTED RIVERS IN CHINA

River	Drainage basin area (square kilometers)	Silt per year (millions of metric tons)	Average silt (grams per cubic meter)	Erosion (millions of metric tons per square kilometer)	Years to erode a 1-meter depth
Amur	1,620,170	29.8	110	18	83,300
Sungari	436,000	25.6	315	59	25,430
Liao	116,760	29.0	7,305	249	6,000
Yellow	684,470	1,360.0	32,200	9,987	760
Huai	121,330	14.3	560	118	12,700
Yangtze	1,010,000	490.5	1,090	485	3,090
Ch'ien-t'ang	31,300	5.0	121	160	9,400
Min	54,700	8.0	114	145	10,300
Hsi	330,000	86.0	406	266	5,640

Additional information on China's hydrology is given in Maps I-39, I-40, and I-41.

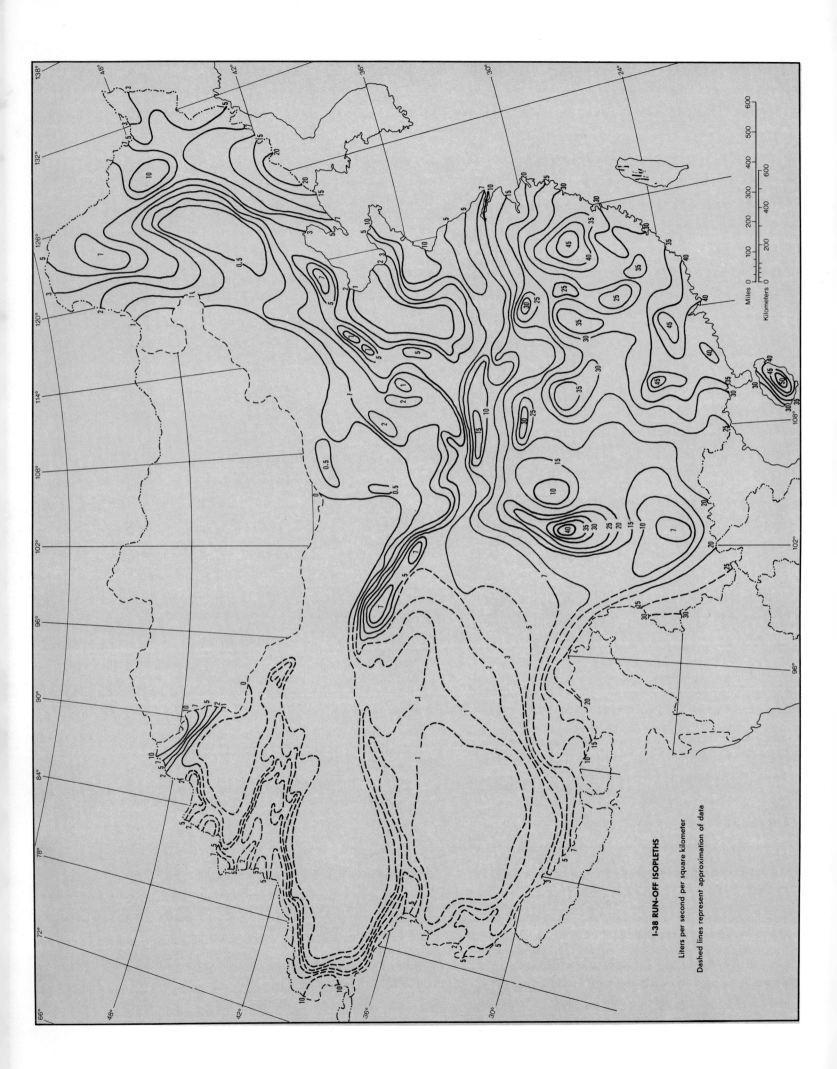

I-38 RUN-OFF ISOPLETHS

Liters per second per square kilometer

Dashed lines represent approximation of data

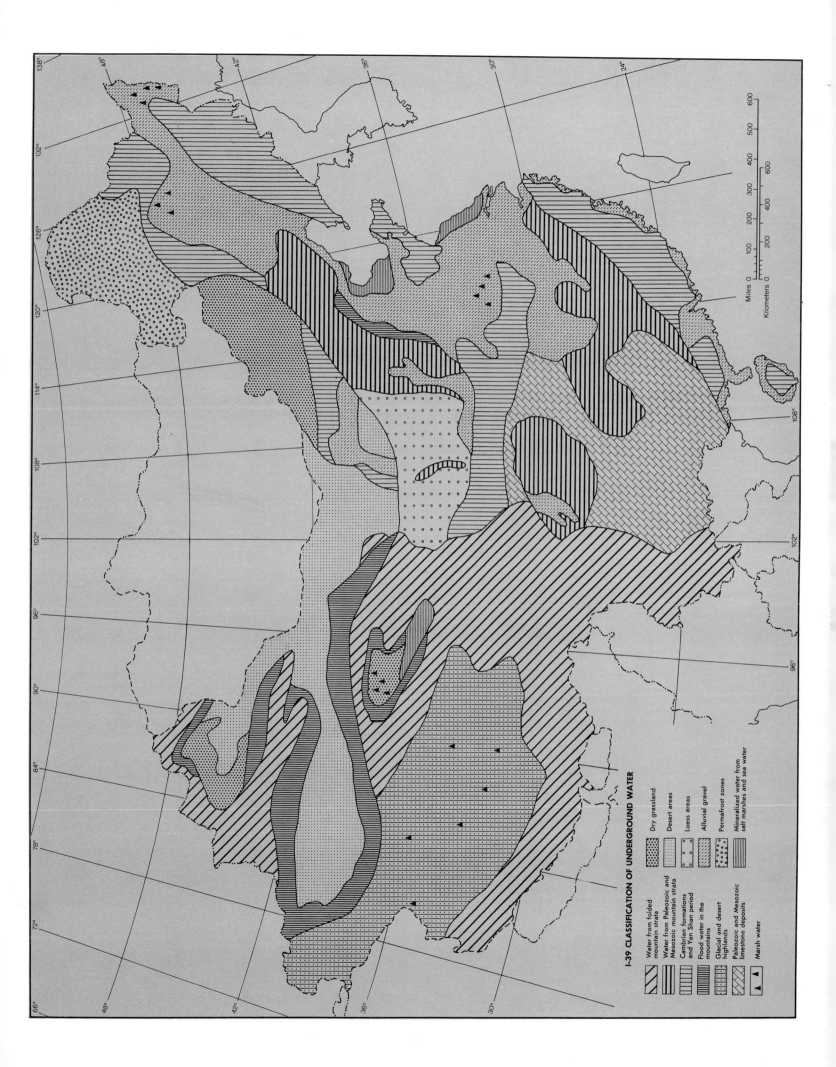

I-39 CLASSIFICATION OF UNDERGROUND WATER

- Water from folded mountain strata
- Water from Paleozoic and Mesozoic mountain strata
- Cambrian formations and Yen Shan period
- Flood water in the mountains
- Glacial and desert highlands
- Paleozoic and Mesozoic limestone deposits
- Marsh water
- Dry grassland
- Desert areas
- Loess areas
- Alluvial gravel
- Permafrost zones
- Mineralized water from salt marshes and sea water

Miles 0 200 400 600

Kilometers 0 100 200 300 400 500 600

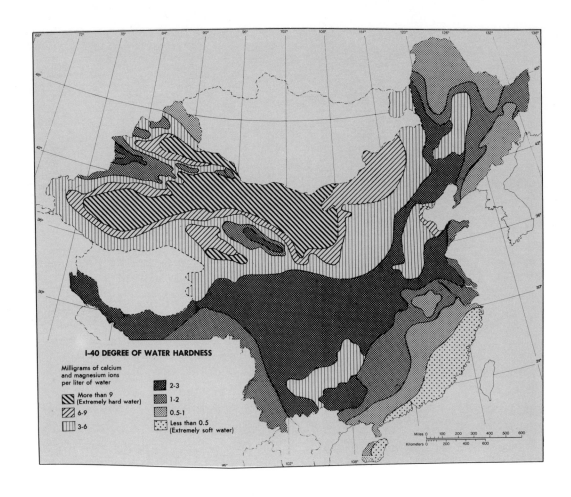

I-40 DEGREE OF WATER HARDNESS

Milligrams of calcium
and magnesium ions
per liter of water

- More than 9 (Extremely hard water)
- 6-9
- 3-6
- 2-3
- 1-2
- 0.5-1
- Less than 0.5 (Extremely soft water)

Miles 0 100 200 300 400 500 600
Kilometers 0 200 400 600

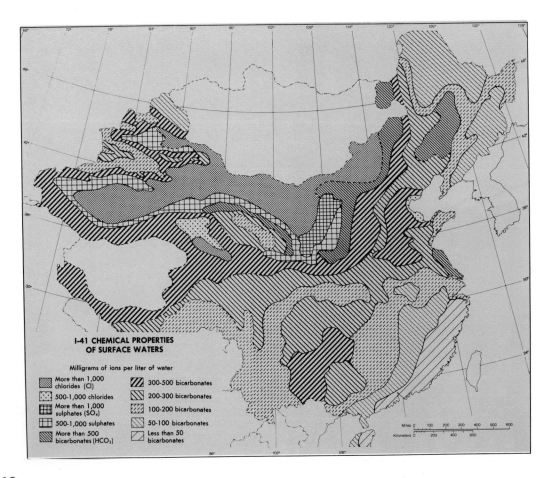

**I-41 CHEMICAL PROPERTIES
OF SURFACE WATERS**

Milligrams of ions per liter of water

- More than 1,000 chlorides (Cl)
- 500-1,000 chlorides
- More than 1,000 sulphates (SO₄)
- 500-1,000 sulphates
- More than 500 bicarbonates (HCO₃)
- 300-500 bicarbonates
- 200-300 bicarbonates
- 100-200 bicarbonates
- 50-100 bicarbonates
- Less than 50 bicarbonates

Miles 0 100 200 300 400 500 600
Kilometers 0 200 400 600

Soils, Flora, and Fauna

Map I-42 shows the distribution of soil types in China.

Areal Distribution of Lowland Soils

The distribution of lowland soils is the result of a number of environmental factors: latitude, distance from the sea, the effect of high mountains, and changes in climate and vegetation (Map I-43). Consequent zonality may be generalized into two realms: the oceanic type and the continental type. Along the seacoasts, soil is developed under relatively humid forest vegetation. The sequence of areal occurrence from north to south along the coast is podzolic soils, brown earths, korichnevyi soils, yellow korichnevyi soils, red-and-yellow earth, and red earth. The continental types are developed under the semi-arid and arid climate conditions in the inland regions. The progression from north to south for the continental type of soil distribution is desert soils, sierozems, brown soils, and chestnut soils.

There are also phase changes from east to west. In the eastern cool-temperate belt of Manchuria and Inner Mongolia, there is an approximate east-west sequence of podzolic soils, gray-forest soils, leached chernozems, chernozems, dark chestnut soils, light chestnut soils, brown soils, sierozems, and desert soils. In the warm-temperate belt of North China and northwestern China, the east-west sequence is brown earths, korichnevyi soils (sometimes spelled korichnevie), siero-korichnevyi soils, sierozems, and desert soils. In Central China there are yellow korichnevyi soils in the north, yellow earths in the south, and yellow earths and mountain soils to the west. In the subtropical belt of South China, the longitudinal phase change shows no sharp difference.

The name "korichnevyi soils" was introduced by I. P. Gerasimov. Such soils are developed under temperate forests and shrubs. In China they were formerly called "forest brown pedocals" and "noncalcic brown" or "Shantung brown soils." The name "siero-korichnevyi soils" was also introduced in China by Gerasimov. These soils were formerly called "imperfectly developed chestnut earths of the loessial region" by James Thorp. Also, yellow korichnevyi soils were formerly called "claypan soils" in the region of the lower Yangtze River by Thorp and "concretional yellow earth" in Szechwan by C. K. Lee and H. Yu.

The majority of the soils of China have been affected by human activity. Sod-forest soils and skeletal soils are usually found in mountainous regions which have undergone deforestation.

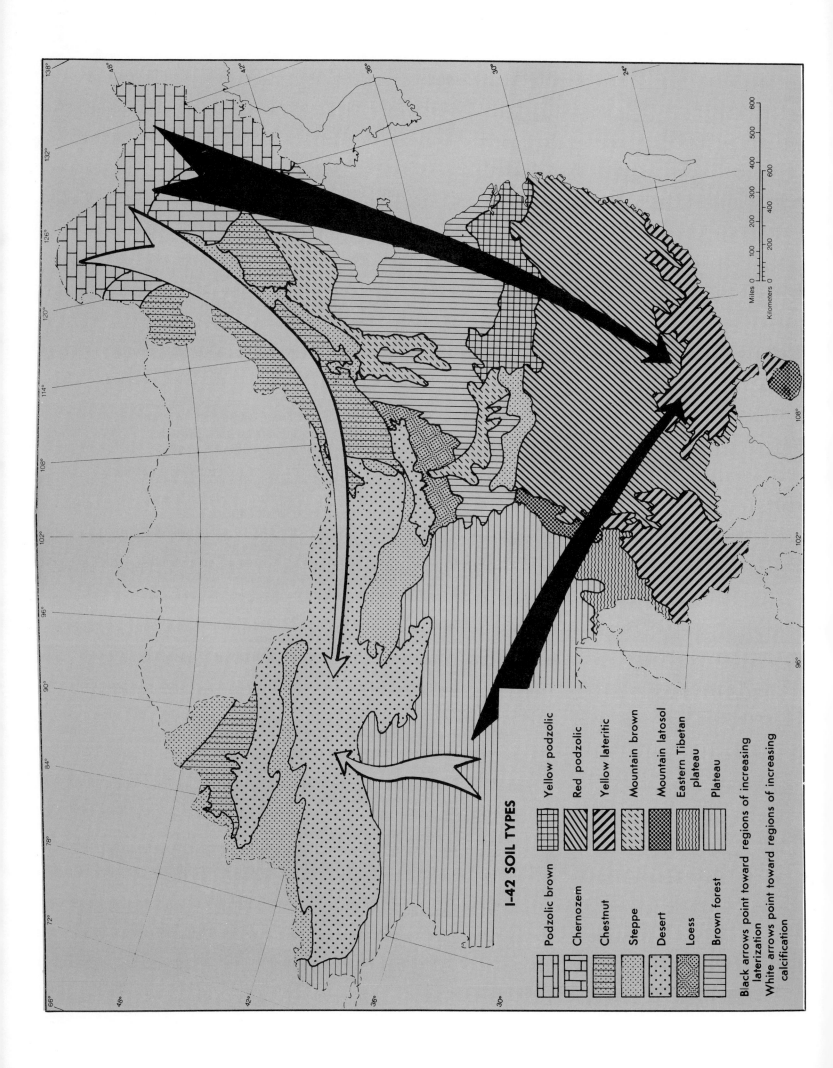

I-42 SOIL TYPES

Podzolic brown		Yellow podzolic	
Chernozem		Red podzolic	
Chestnut		Yellow lateritic	
Steppe		Mountain brown	
Desert		Mountain latosol	
Loess		Eastern Tibetan plateau	
Brown forest		Plateau	

Black arrows point toward regions of increasing lateralization

White arrows point toward regions of increasing calcification

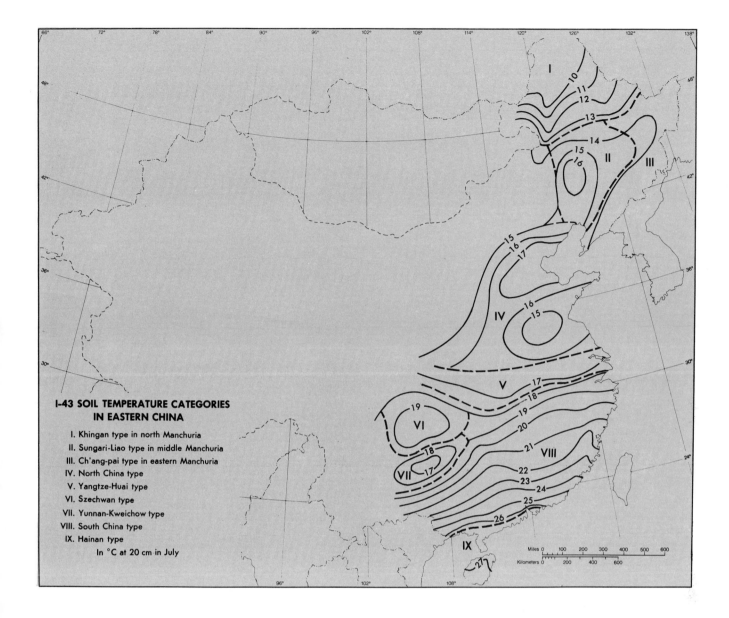

Erosional soils develop when rolling hills are cultivated but unterraced. Plowed surface soils occur in the flat cultivated lands of the flood plains and terraces of China. Highly modified paddy soils occupy virtually the entire central and southern lowlands of China.

Vertical Distribution of Mountain Soils

Soils in mountainous regions vary greatly as a result of differences in elevation, steepness of slope, and the character of the parent rock, climate, and vegetation in a given zone. In China there are five generalized vertical soil zones (Map I-44). They are:

1 Mountain podzolic soils—as exemplified at Hsi-kuei-t'u-ch'i (Ya-k'o-shih), Inner Mongolia

2 Mountain steppe soils and mountain dark korich-nevyi soils—Po-ko-to Shan, Sinkiang; and Yin-shan Shan-mo, Inner Mongolia

3 Mountain brown earths and mountain korich-nevyi soils—Ta-pa Shan, Shensi; and Wu-liang Shan, Hopeh

4 Mountain yellow earth and mountain gray-brown earth—Huang Shan, Anhwei; and Chiung-lai Shan (just north of O-mei Shan), Szechwan

5 Mountain yellow earths and mountain podzolic soils—Tien-tsang Shan, Yunnan

VEGETATION

There are six major forest types which form broad bands on the land surface in a more or less latitudinal sequence. From north to south these bands are the boreal coniferous forest, the mixed northern hardwood forest, the temperate deciduous broadleaved forest, the mixed forest, the evergreen broadleaved forest, and the rainforest (Map I-45).

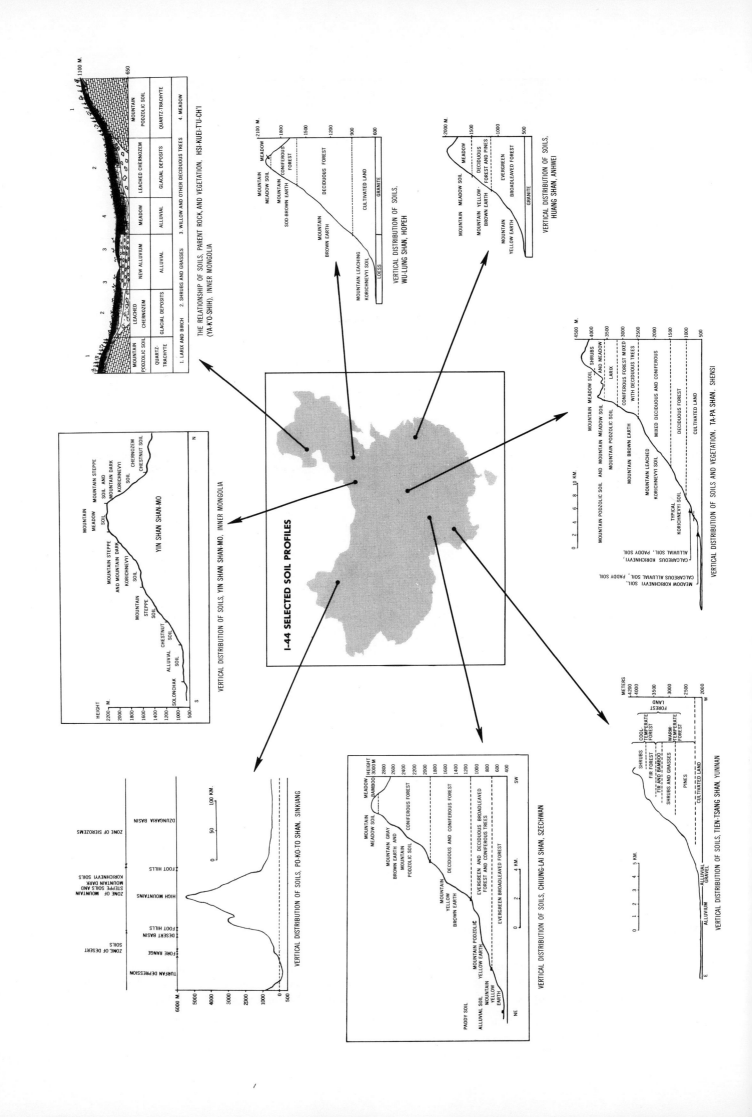

I-44 SELECTED SOIL PROFILES

THE RELATIONSHIP OF SOILS, PARENT ROCK, AND VEGETATION, HSI-KUEI-T'U-CH'I (YA-K'O-SHIH), INNER MONGOLIA

MOUNTAIN PODZOLIC SOIL	MOUNTAIN MEADOW	LEACHED CHERNOZEM	MEADOW	NEW ALLUVIUM	LEACHED CHERNOZEM	MOUNTAIN PODZOLIC SOIL
QUARTZ-TRACHYTE	GLACIAL DEPOSITS	GLACIAL DEPOSITS	ALLUVIAL	ALLUVIUM	GLACIAL DEPOSITS	QUARTZ-TRACHYTE

1. LARIX AND BIRCH   2. SHRUBS AND GRASSES   3. WILLOW AND OTHER DECIDUOUS TREES   4. MEADOW

1100 M.
650

VERTICAL DISTRIBUTION OF SOILS, WU-LUNG SHAN, HOPEH

2100 M.
1800
1500
1200
900
600

MOUNTAIN MEADOW SOIL
MOUNTAIN MEADOW
CONIFEROUS FOREST
MOUNTAIN SOD-BROWN EARTH
DECIDUOUS FOREST
MOUNTAIN BROWN EARTH
CULTIVATED LAND
MOUNTAIN LEACHING KORICHNEVYI SOIL
GRANITE
LOESS

VERTICAL DISTRIBUTION OF SOILS, HUANG SHAN, ANHWEI

2000 M.
1500
1000
500

MOUNTAIN MEADOW SOIL
MOUNTAIN MEADOW
MOUNTAIN YELLOW-BROWN EARTH
DECIDUOUS FOREST AND PINES
MOUNTAIN YELLOW EARTH
EVERGREEN BROADLEAVED FOREST
GRANITE

VERTICAL DISTRIBUTION OF SOILS, YIN SHAN SHAN-MO, INNER MONGOLIA

HEIGHT
2200 M.
2000
1800
1600
1400
1200
1000
800
500

MOUNTAIN MEADOW SOIL
MOUNTAIN MEADOW SOIL AND MOUNTAIN DARK KORICHNEVYI SOIL
MOUNTAIN STEPPE SOIL AND MOUNTAIN DARK KORICHNEVYI SOIL
CHERNOZEM
CHESTNUT SOIL
MOUNTAIN STEPPE SOIL
CHESTNUT SOIL
ALLUVIAL SOIL
SOLONCHAK

YIN SHAN SHAN-MO

S   N

VERTICAL DISTRIBUTION OF SOILS AND VEGETATION, TA-PA SHAN, SHENSI

4500 M.
4000
3500
3000
2500
2000
1500
1000
500

MOUNTAIN MEADOW SOIL
SHRUBS AND MEADOW
MOUNTAIN MEADOW SOIL
CONIFEROUS FOREST MIXED WITH DECIDUOUS TREES
LARIX
MOUNTAIN PODZOLIC SOIL AND MOUNTAIN MEADOW SOIL
MOUNTAIN PODZOLIC SOIL
MIXED DECIDUOUS AND CONIFEROUS
MOUNTAIN BROWN EARTH
DECIDUOUS FOREST
MOUNTAIN LEACHED KORICHNEVYI SOIL
CULTIVATED LAND
TYPICAL KORICHNEVYI SOIL
CALCAREOUS KORICHNEVYI, ALLUVIAL SOIL, PADDY SOIL
MEADOW KORICHNEVYI SOIL, CALCAREOUS ALLUVIAL SOIL, PADDY SOIL

0 2 4 6 8 10 KM.

VERTICAL DISTRIBUTION OF SOILS, PO-KO-TO SHAN, SINKIANG

6000 M.
5000
4000
3000
2000
1000
500

DZUNGARIA BASIN
ZONE OF SIEROZEMS
FOOT HILLS
ZONE OF MOUNTAIN STEPPE SOILS AND MOUNTAIN DARK KORICHNEVYI SOILS
HIGH MOUNTAINS
FOOT HILLS
DESERT BASIN
FORE RANGE
ZONE OF DESERT SOILS
TURFAN DEPRESSION

NE

0   50   100 KM.

VERTICAL DISTRIBUTION OF SOILS, CHIUNG-LAI SHAN, SZECHWAN

HEIGHT 3000 M
2800
2600
2400
2200
2000
1800
1600
1400
1200
1000
800
600
400

MEADOW
BAMBOO
MOUNTAIN MEADOW SOIL
MOUNTAIN GRAY BROWN EARTH AND MOUNTAIN PODZOLIC SOIL
CONIFEROUS FOREST
DECIDUOUS AND DECIDUOUS BROADLEAVED FOREST
MOUNTAIN YELLOW BROWN EARTH
EVERGREEN AND DECIDUOUS BROADLEAVED FOREST AND CONIFEROUS TREES
MOUNTAIN PODZOLIC YELLOW EARTH
EVERGREEN BROADLEAVED FOREST
ALLUVIAL SOIL MOUNTAIN YELLOW EARTH
PADDY SOIL

SW   NE

0 1 2 3 4   KM.
0   2   4 KM.

VERTICAL DISTRIBUTION OF SOILS, TIEN-TSANG SHAN, YUNNAN

METERS
4200
4000
3500
3000
2500
2000

COOL-TEMPERATE FOREST
WARM-TEMPERATE FOREST
FOREST LAND
SHRUBS
FIR AND BAMBOO
FIR AND BAMBOO
SHRUBS AND GRASSES
PINES
CULTIVATED LAND
ALLUVIAL GRAVEL
ALLUVIUM

W   E

0 1 2 3 4 5 KM.

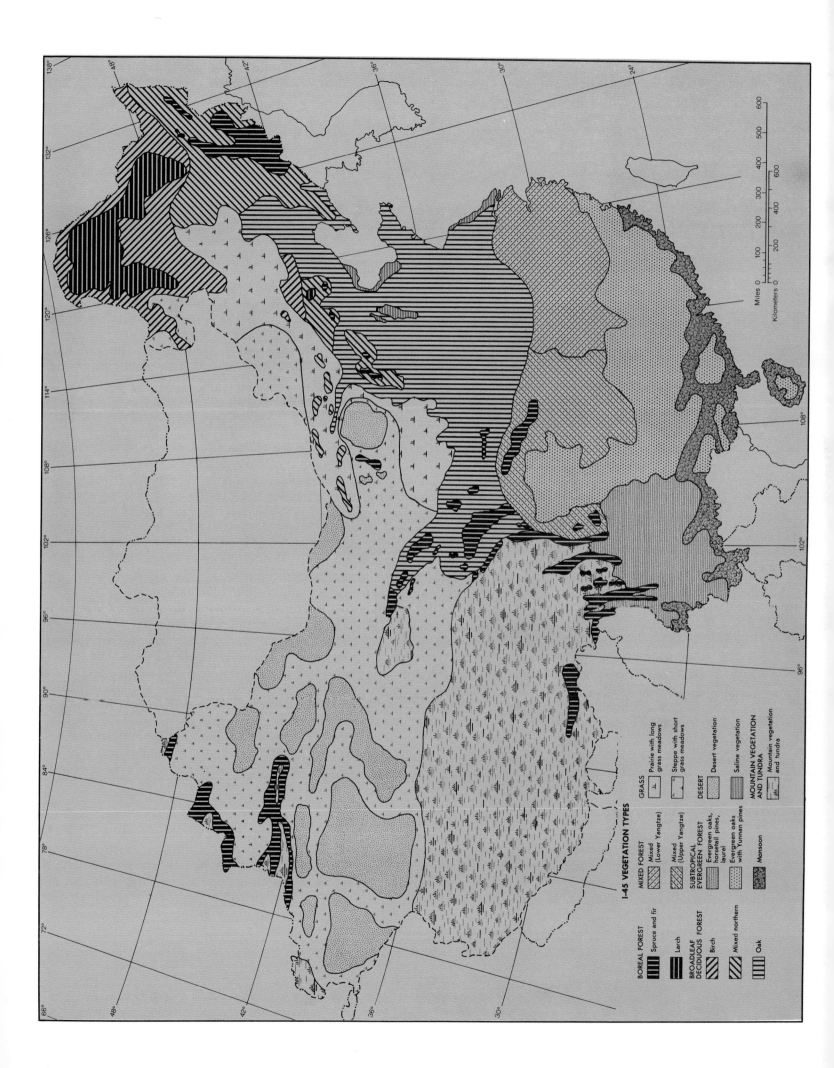

I-45 VEGETATION TYPES

BOREAL FOREST
Spruce and fir
Larch

BROADLEAF
DECIDUOUS FOREST
Birch
Mixed northern
Oak

MIXED FOREST
Mixed (Lower Yangtze)
Mixed (Upper Yangtze)

SUBTROPICAL
EVERGREEN FOREST
Evergreen oaks,
horsetail pines,
laurel
Evergreen oaks
with Yunnan pines
Monsoon

GRASS
Prairie with long
grass meadows
Steppe with short
grass meadows

DESERT
Desert vegetation
Saline vegetation

MOUNTAIN VEGETATION
AND TUNDRA
Mountain vegetation
and tundra

Miles   0   100 200 300 400 500 600
Kilometers 0 200 400 600

	Grassland		Woodland		
	Desert Turfan (Sinkiang)	Steppe Pao-t'ou (Inner Mongolia)	Mixed Northern Hardwood Forest Ch'ang-ch'un (Kirin)	Evergreen Broadleaf Forest K'un-ming (Yunnan)	Rainforest Canton (Kwangtung)
Soils	Desert Soils	Chestnut and Brown Soils	Podzolic Soils	Red-and- Yellow Earth	Red Earth
Rainfall (Inches)	0.8	11	25.7	51	88
Days of Rain	6	56	103	132	155
Growing Season (Days)	—	151	143	258	356

The steppe-desert in China's northwest is essentially in the region of internal drainage in the heartland of the Eurasian land mass. The vegetation types occur as concentric rings surrounding a salt lake (nor), a dried-up lake basin, or an immense desert such as the Takla Makan at the center of the Tarim Basin. The innermost ring is desert scrub; then come bands characterized by alkaline-saline plant communities, steppe, and finally vast expanses of short and tall grasses. Along the periphery of the concentric zones is a transitional belt of mixed grass and woodland.

Superimposed upon the general pattern of latitudinal bands of forest types and concentric rings of steppe-desert is the altitudinal differentiation of vegetation types. In the mountains of the southwest the vegetation ranges from the rainforest on the lower slopes through the evergreen broadleaf forest, the deciduous broadleaf forest, and the boreal coniferous forest of spruce and fir to the alpine scrub and meadow and, lastly, perpetual snow.

No genuine understanding of the vegetation in China is possible without realization of the fact that the nation is founded on two great natural plant formations—the woodland in the east and the grassland-desert complex in the west. The division line occurs approximately on an arc drawn from K'unming in Yunnan to Harbin in the Northeast.

DISTRIBUTION OF ANIMALS

Of the world's six major zoogeographical regions, China includes two, the Palearctic and the Oriental. The Tibetan Plateau, Sinkiang, Inner Mongolia, the Northeast, and all areas north of the Yellow River lie in the Palearctic region, while central and southern China and the southwest lie in the Oriental region (Map I-46). Although the parts of China in the Oriental region constitute a much smaller land area than those in the Palearctic, more animal species are found in the former than in the latter. Throughout the world, the number of species found in a region decreases as one moves north. The seeming exception is the southern Tibetan Plateau, which shelters fewer species than lands farther north; this is explained by the elevation, rigorous climatic conditions, and desert character of the plateau. Elevation alone gives it the features of a much more northerly region.

From the Himalayas to the Tsinling Shan, the line dividing the Palearctic and Oriental regions is clearcut, but to the east the division is much less distinct. The large transitional area in northern and central China has led many scholars to disagree on just where the line should be drawn. The north-south orientation of the Heng-tuan mountains on the eastern flank of the Tibetan Plateau also makes Yunnan a transitional area. The Oriental region embraces Central and South China.

The distinctive environmental conditions of the two major zones provide habitats for characteristic animal species (Map I-47). Important mammals native to the Palearctic zone are the river fox, jerboa, horse, camel, tapir, mouse hare, hamster, and forest jerboa. The distribution of some of these mammals extends into the Oriental region as the result of natural dispersal and migration. Within the Oriental region, South China produces several species not found in the Palearctic zone, including the tree shrew and the gibbon. Other monkeys and apes are found throughout the Oriental region, as are civet cats, Chinese pangolins, bamboo rats, and "chrysanthemum-headed bats."

In all the diverse climatic and geological environments there are deer or antelope, bears (including the giant panda, which, however, is found only in a narrow region along the Yangtze), wolves, pigs, and rodents. Species within these classes are adapted to the specific area in which they flourish (Maps I-48 and I-49).

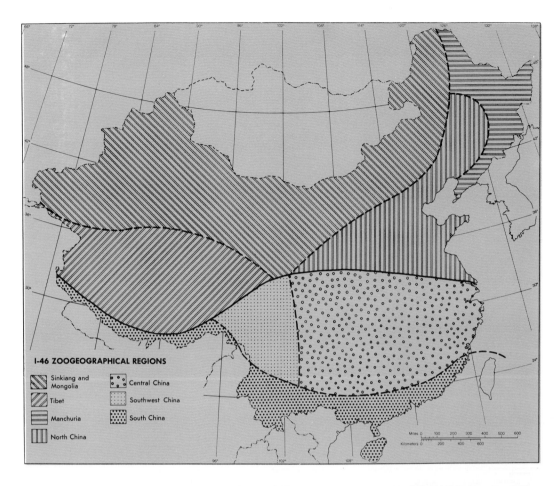

I-46 ZOOGEOGRAPHICAL REGIONS

Sinkiang and Mongolia

Tibet

Manchuria

North China

Central China

Southwest China

South China

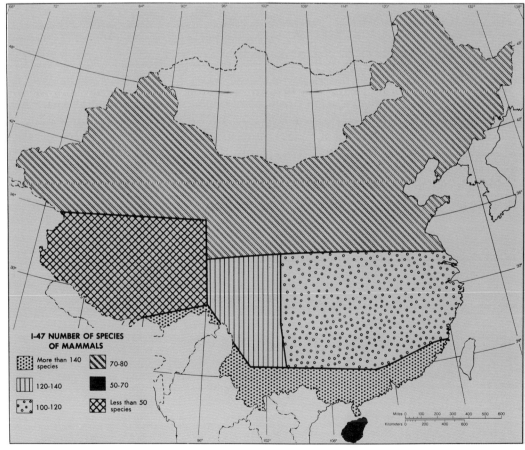

I-47 NUMBER OF SPECIES OF MAMMALS

More than 140 species

120-140

100-120

70-80

50-70

Less than 50 species

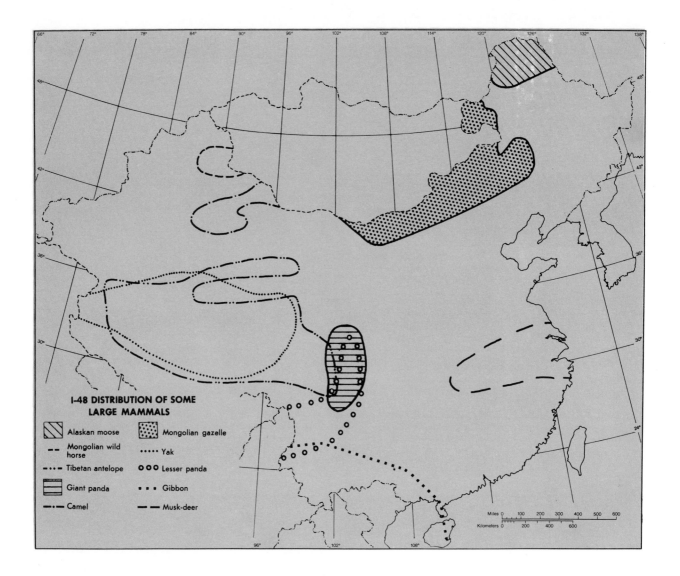

I-48 DISTRIBUTION OF SOME LARGE MAMMALS

Alaskan moose		Mongolian gazelle	
Mongolian wild horse		Yak	
Tibetan antelope		Lesser panda	
Giant panda		Gibbon	
Camel		Musk-deer	

Finally, in discussing animal distribution, we cannot overlook the influence of human activity. In China Proper (the eastern third of China), intensive cultivation and clearing of forests have sharply reduced the number of surviving forest animals and increased the number of plains animals, especially the small rodents which thrive in cleared fields. In the Northeast, fur trappers have also diminished the population of fur-bearing animals. Current programs of wildlife conservation are aimed at stopping this trend, and at the same time programs are being developed to control animals injurious to humans, ranging from fieldmice to tigers and wild pigs.

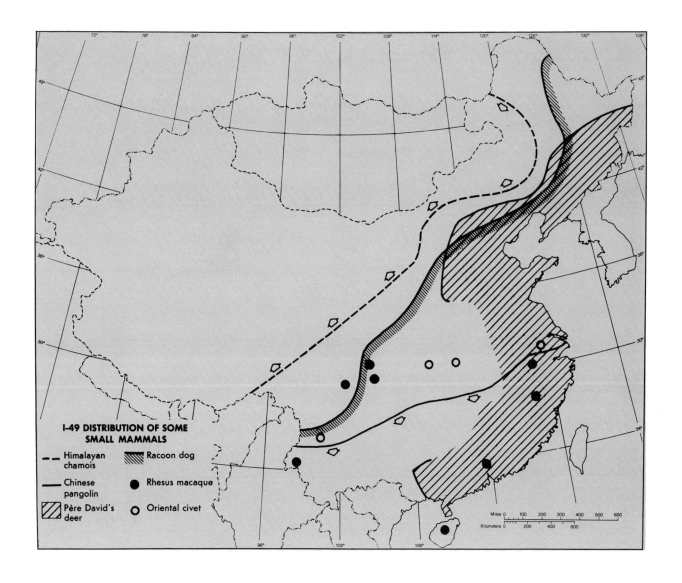

I-49 DISTRIBUTION OF SOME SMALL MAMMALS

- - - Himalayan chamois

▨▨▨ Racoon dog

—— Chinese pangolin

● Rhesus macaque

▨ Père David's deer

○ Oriental civet

II. CULTURAL

People

The exact size of China's population is a subject of controversy, though it is well known that it is the most populous country in the world: Its people constitute between one-fifth and one-quarter of the world's population, or between 680 million and 825 million people. While China has a long, unbroken record of population statistics, the early estimates included only portions of the total population, and the accuracy of these, as well as later counts, is difficult to ascertain. Chinese emperors were primarily interested only in the number of farmers, taxpayers, and men for military service. In estimating the total population, indirect methods were used, such as calculating the number of people on the basis of the amount of cultivated land, levels of salt consumption, or post office traffic. With those methods the count was little more than guesswork.

During recent decades no fewer than 50 estimates of China's population have been made, with the figure of 475 million generally accepted as accurate for the late Nationalist period; this figure was also used by the Communist regime when it came to power in 1949.

POPULATION SIZE AND DISTRIBUTION

In November 1954 the Peking government announced that as of June 30, 1953, a census showed China had 582.6 million people on the mainland, 7.5 million on Taiwan, and 11.7 million overseas. It is difficult to be certain about the accuracy of the 1953 census, or the increments to the population since then. However, on the basis of that year's count, and judging by what is known of population growth in China, it seems probable that the Chinese population is almost twice as great as that of the United States and the Soviet Union combined (Map II-1). China's population in 1970 was 697,600,000 according to a pocket atlas published by the China Cartographic Institute of Peking.

Communist China's 1953 census report included demographic characteristics such as the rate of population growth, age distribution, and sex composition. These figures were obtained from a sample survey of 30,180,000 persons in 29 provincial cities.

The age-group figure reported in the sample showed that China was a young country. About 45 percent of the people were younger than 20 years of age, 35 percent were between 20 and 44, 13 percent between 45 and 59, and 7 percent over 60.

Another distinctive feature of the Chinese population is uneven spatial distribution. The deserts of western China are among the emptiest regions of the globe, yet few places can match the crowded conditions in the delta region of the Yangtze. For

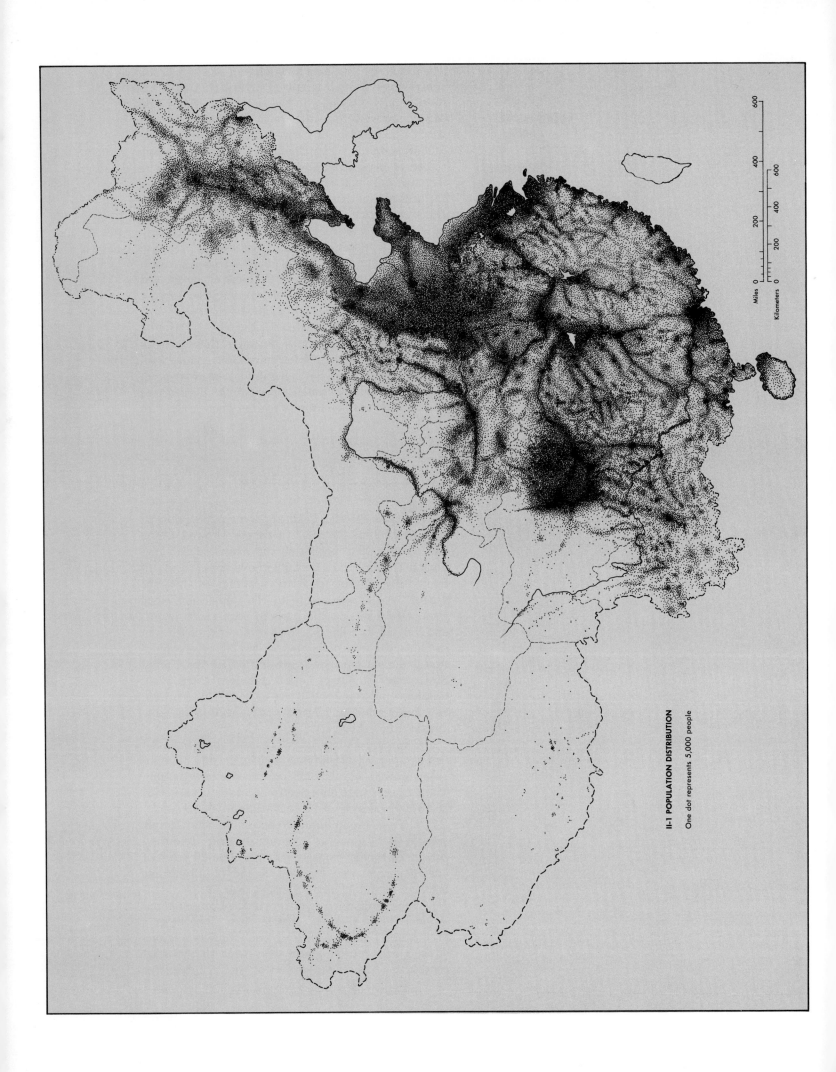

II-1 POPULATION DISTRIBUTION

One dot represents 5,000 people

Miles 0   200   400   600

Kilometers 0   200   400   600

example, the six coastal provinces of Hopeh, Shantung, Kiangsu, Chekiang, Fukien, and Kwangtung had in 1953 a total population of more than 255 million, about 33 percent of the country's total, but these provinces constitute only 7 percent of China's land area (Map II-2).

In order to visualize the picture of the uneven distribution pattern of the Chinese population, a geographer has pointed out that if a line is drawn from the city of Ai-hui, in the extreme of the Northeast, to the city of T'eng-ch'ung in Yunnan Province, the area southeast of the line contains only 36 percent of the total area of the country but is home to approximately 96 percent of China's population. Northwest of the line the area contains 64 percent of China's area, yet the population is only about 4 percent of the total.

Even today, about 75 percent of China's people live in 15 percent of the country's territory. The areas which stand out as centers of population are located on the eastern coastal plains and the hilly lands situated east of an imaginary line formed by the Greater Khingan and T'ai-hang mountain ranges and the eastern border of the Yunnan-Kweichow Plateau. (This is roughly congruent with the line from Ai-Hui to T'eng-ch'ung.) The only population center west of this line is Szechwan, the most agriculturally productive province in China. The Yangtze delta and the lower reaches of the Hsi Chiang have an average population density of over 770 persons per square kilometer (2,000 per square mile). The North China Plain and the southeastern coastal region of China each have more than 230 persons per square kilometer (600 per square mile). In contrast, the population of Sinkiang averages about 5 persons per square kilometer (12 per square mile). Inner Mongolia and Tibet also have sparse populations. China's largest cities are concentrated east of the line mentioned above: Shanghai, Peking, Tientsin, Shenyang (Mukden), Wu-han, Canton, Chungking, Nanking, Harbin, Ch'ang-ch'un, Fu-shun, T'ai-yüan, Ch'eng-tu, Sian, Tsingtao and Dairen (Lü-ta) all have populations of more than 1 million. The largest cities west of the line are Lan-chou and Pao-t'ou, which have populations approaching 1 million.

THE OVERSEAS CHINESE

Some 18 million Chinese are now living outside mainland China. They are found in almost every country. It was not until relatively modern times that population pressure and internal problems in China caused people to seek refuge and opportunity overseas. The first significant outmigration occurred before the first contact with Europeans, during the early fifteenth century, when there was substantial emigration from China to Southeast Asia.

In the middle of the seventeenth century the changeover from the Ming to the Manchu Dynasty encouraged additional emigration. When the Manchu troops overthrew the Ming Dynasty, thousands of coastal residents in the southeastern provinces sought refuge on Taiwan. Some Chinese even fled to Kyushu, Japan, and formed a small community in the city of Nagasaki. Contacts with Europeans also opened new horizons, resulting in a further exodus. In 1810 tea cultivation was introduced into Brazil, and before the opening of the treaty ports in China in the early 1840s, organized Chinese emigration to Brazil to aid in the growth of this industry was taking place. Also in the first half of the nineteenth century, Chinese settlement began in the Indian Ocean area.

The 1840–1850 decade marked the beginning of China's contact with the West on an unprecedented scale. The establishment of Hong Kong as a free port in the early 1840s, and of Canton and Amoy as treaty ports in 1842, provided further foreign economic opportunities and, hence, the impetus for Chinese emigration in the modern period. Eight hundred laborers from Amoy arrived in Cuba in 1847—the beginning of large-scale Chinese emigration to the New World. Two years later Peru received contract Chinese laborers to work on cotton plantations. In 1849 the news of the discovery of gold in California reached China, and in that year the first group of Chinese arrived in California to join the gold rush. In 1849 also, Chinese laborers appeared in New South Wales in Australia; and in 1851 the discovery of gold in that area, and later in Victoria, stimulated Chinese emigration to Australia during the latter half of the nineteenth century. By 1850 Chinese workers had to be brought in to Hawaii to work on the sugar plantations because disease and frequent warfare among the feudal chiefs there had resulted in the rapid decline of the supply of native labor in the islands. In the same year the construction of a railroad across the Isthmus of Panama was started, and Chinese were imported for construction work.

Throughout most of the nineteenth century Chinese emigrants moved mainly southward across the South China Sea to Southeast Asia and Australia or eastward across the Pacific to the New World. The opening of the Suez Canal in 1869 stimulated trade between Europe and Asia, and during the 1870s Chinese began to wander westward to and through Europe.

The Chinese emigrants have come almost entirely from coastal provinces, particularly Kwangtung and Fukien, but in the past several decades there has been a small but constant flow of Muslims from

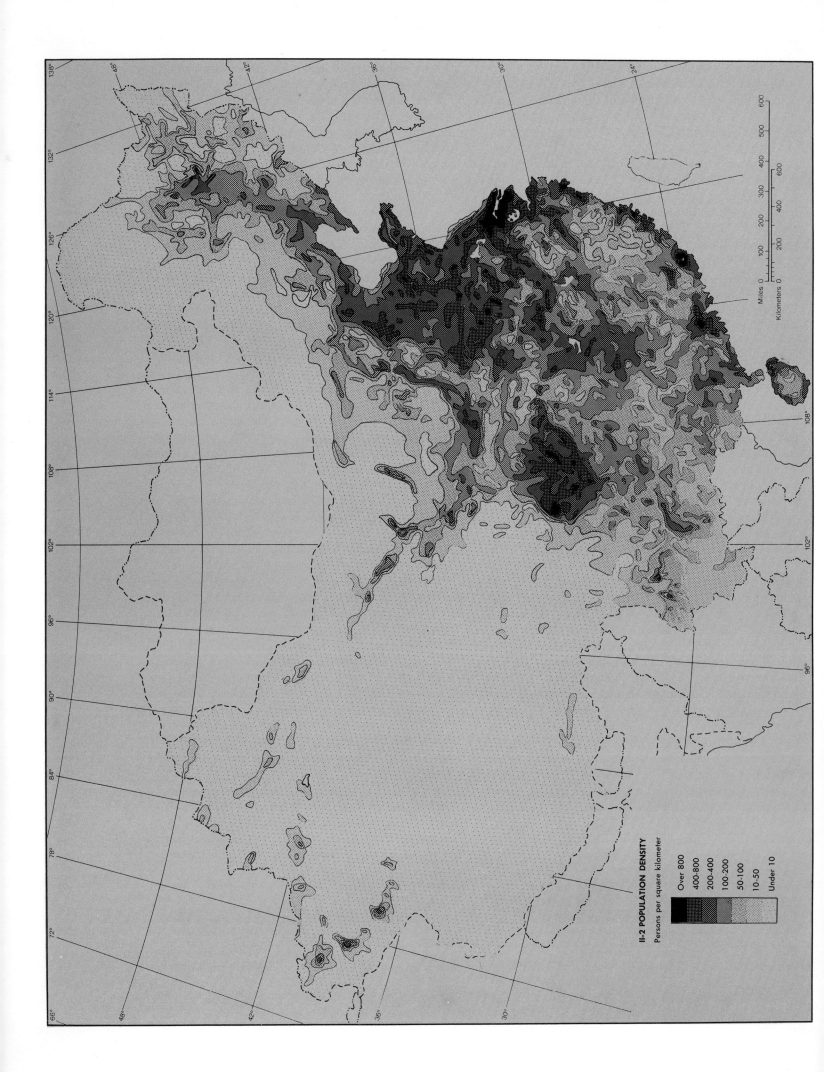

II-2 POPULATION DENSITY
Persons per square kilometer

Over 800
400-800
200-400
100-200
50-100
10-50
Under 10

Miles 0 100 200 300 400 500 600

Kilometers 0 200 400 600

the northwestern provinces to Saudi Arabia to take up permanent residence. After the formation of the People's Republic of China in 1949, the outmigration of Chinese Muslims to Southwest Asia increased.

In 1963 there were 3,197,091 Chinese in Hong Kong, 160,764 in Macao, and 16,420,910 living outside mainland China and Taiwan—the largest emigrant Asian ethnic group. If we assume that the total Chinese population in that year was about 650 million, it would follow that approximately twenty-one out of every thousand Chinese reside outside their own country (Map II-3). Of the Chinese abroad, 96.6 percent are in Asian countries, and in general the distribution pattern of the Chinese abroad can be characterized as tropical, coastal, and urban. More than 90 percent of the overseas Chinese make their living within the tropics. The majority of them are found south of 18°N, the parallel of latitude which passes a few miles south of the island of Hainan.

In the higher latitudes their numbers decrease rapidly. The United States is the only mid-latitude country that has a Chinese population of more than 100,000. The overseas Chinese populations in Canada, Japan, Korea, and Great Britain are the next largest agglomerations.

Overseas Chinese tend to gather more on islands or along coasts than in the interiors of continents. In Southeast Asia the largest concentrations of Chinese are along the north shore of the Gulf of Siam, the west coast of the Malay Peninsula, and the western section of the north coast of Java. In the Caribbean they are found mostly in Cuba, Jamaica, and Trinidad. In Africa they are far more numerous on the islands of Mauritius and Madagascar than on the continent itself. In North America the Chinese tend to be most numerous in California and in the Northeast.

Many "Chinatowns" all over the world are associated with metropolises of considerable size. Thus 90 percent of the Brazilian Chinese live in São Paulo, 57 percent of the Bolivian Chinese in La Paz, and 50 percent of the Peruvian Chinese in Lima.

Chinese emigration has been induced by conditions both in China and abroad. The factors within China itself which stimulated emigration included poverty, rural unemployment, civil war, and famine. The attractive foreign factors included employment opportunities created by the exploitation and development of the tropical world by European countries and by the shortage of laborers in industrializing countries. In recent decades, however, the primary occupations of the overseas Chinese have been restaurant work, retail trade, agricultural labor, handicrafts, light industry, and mining.

Although more than 70 percent of the people of China make their living by farming and related activities, few Chinese abroad have chosen to be independent farmers.

MINORITY GROUPS OF CHINA

Like the United States, China is a country composed of many ethnic groups. While an overwhelming majority of China's people are Han, or ethnic Chinese, there are some 35.5 million who retain non-Chinese customs, religions, and languages. These people live mainly in the fringe areas of China: to the north, northwest, and southwest of China Proper.

The lands inhabited by these peoples are as varied as the inhabitants themselves. The Inner Mongolian Autonomous Region is a steppe lying north of the Great Wall and south of the Gobi Desert. It is a semi-arid area, barely able to support the people who live there. The Mongols in this area and scattered throughout the rest of China number about 1.6 million.

In the deserts and the mountains of Sinkiang we find the Uighurs, the Kazakhs, and the Kirghiz. These Turkic peoples number about 4.5 million and have as many differences among them as they have similarities.

On the high plateaus south of the Kunlun Mountains and north of the Himalayas we find some 3 million Tibetans. These people are also found south of the Himalayas, as well as in parts of Szechwan, Tsinghai, and Yunnan provinces. They live on the mountain slopes or on high intermontane plateaus, where the climate is very cold and dry.

The plateaus and mountains of southwestern China are the home of a great variety of peoples of predominantly Tibeto-Burman stock as well as some of Austro-Asiatic stock. Among these groups are the Chuang, the Yi, the Miao, the Li, the Lisu, and the Yao. There are also some Thai and Burmese in this area.

Ningsia Hui Autonomous Region, on the western edge of the loesslands, is the home of a majority of the Huis, a group of Han Chinese set apart because of their Islamic religious background. There are also numerous small pockets of Huis scattered throughout other parts of China.

In addition to these groups, there are the Manchus and a number of Koreans in the Northeast. The full variety of ethnic minorities is shown on Map II-4, with its associated table. The languages of these diverse groups are shown on Map II-5.

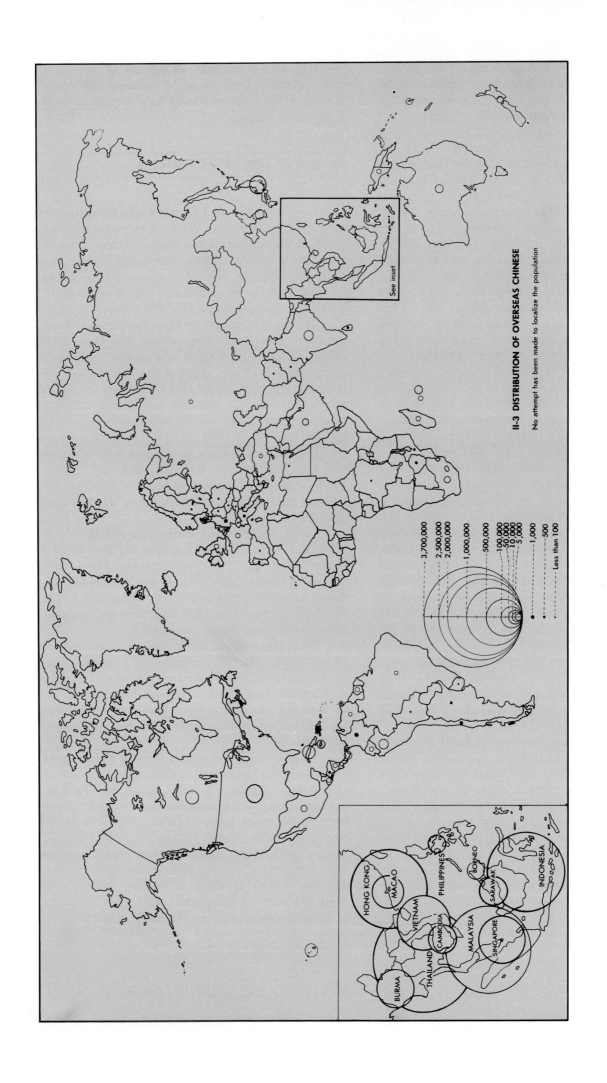

II-3 DISTRIBUTION OF OVERSEAS CHINESE

No attempt has been made to localize the population

3,700,000
2,500,000
2,000,000
1,000,000
500,000
100,000
50,000
10,000
5,000

1,000
500
Less than 100

See inset

HONG KONG
MACAO
VIETNAM
CAMBODIA
THAILAND
BURMA
PHILIPPINES
BORNEO
SARAWAK
MALAYSIA
SINGAPORE
INDONESIA

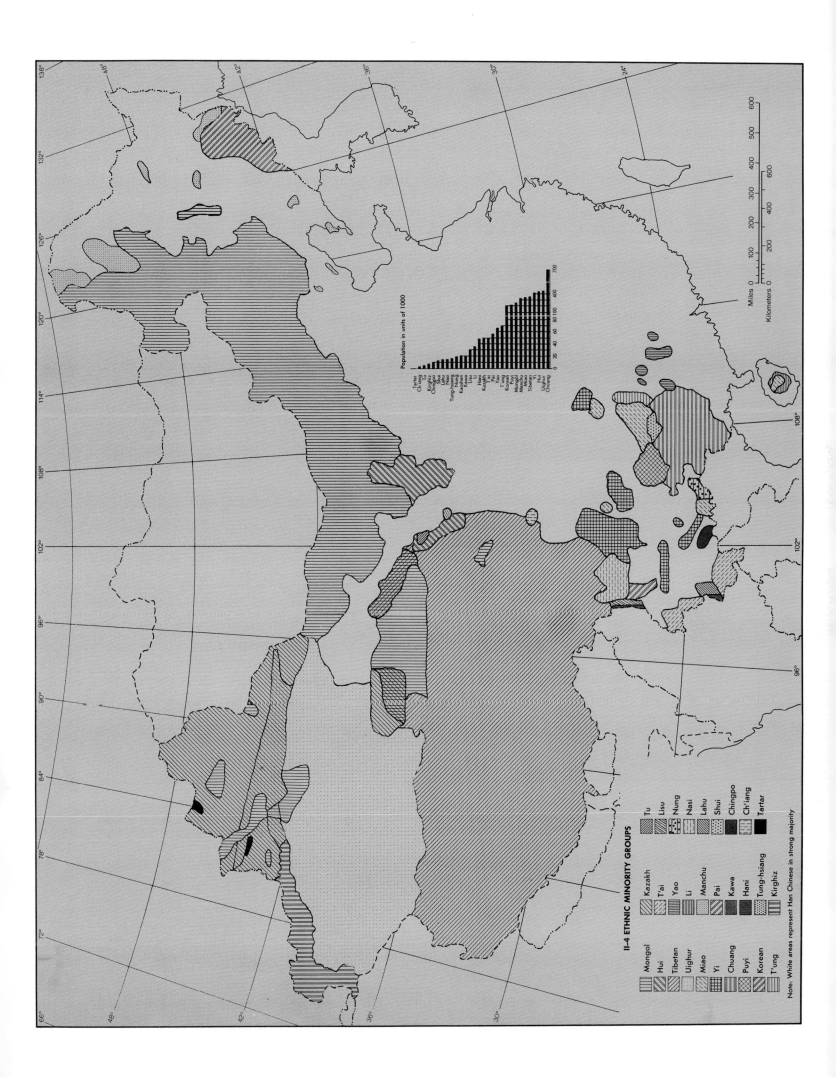

II-4 ETHNIC MINORITY GROUPS

Population in units of 1000

Tartar
Ch'iang
Tu
Kirghiz
Chingpo
Kawa
Lahu
Nasi
Tung-hsiang
Nung
Korean
Lisu
Li
Han
Kazakh
Tai
Pai
Yao
T'ung
Puyi
Mongol
Manchu
Miao
Tibetan
Hui
Uighur
Chuang

0 20 40 60 80 100 200 300 400 700

Mongol	Kazakh	Tu
Hui	T'ai	Lisu
Tibetan	Yao	Nung
Uighur	Li	Nasi
Miao	Manchu	Lahu
Yi	Pai	Shui
Chuang	Kawa	Chingpo
Puyi	Hani	Ch'iang
Korean	Tung-hsiang	Tartar
T'ung	Kirghiz	

Note: White areas represent Han Chinese in strong majority

Miles 0 100 200 300 400 500 600

Kilometers 0 200 400 600

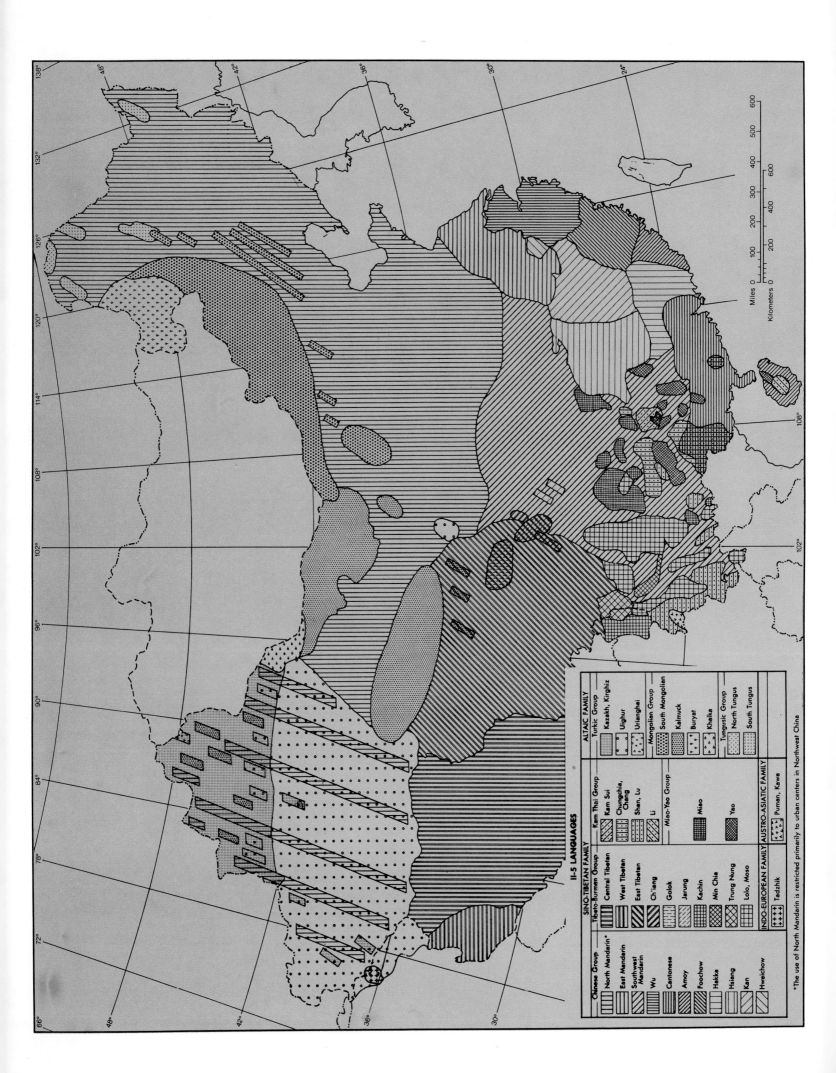

II–5 LANGUAGES

SINO-TIBETAN FAMILY

Chinese Group		Tibeto-Burman Group		Kam Thai Group	
	North Mandarin*		Central Tibetan		Kam Sui
	East Mandarin		West Tibetan		Chungchia, Chang
	Southwest Mandarin		East Tibetan		Shan, Lu
	Wu		Ch'iang		Li
	Cantonese		Golok		**Miao-Yao Group**
	Amoy		Jarung		Miao
	Foochow		Kachin		Yao
	Hakka		Min Chia		
	Hsiang		Trung Nung		
	Kan		Lolo, Moso		
	Hweichow				

ALTAIC FAMILY

Turkic Group		Mongolian Group		Tungusic Group	
	Kazakh, Kirghiz		South Mongolian		North Tungus
	Uighur		Kalmuck		South Tungus
	Urianghai		Buryat		
			Khalka		

INDO-EUROPEAN FAMILY
Tadzhik

AUSTRO-ASIATIC FAMILY
Puman, Kawa

*The use of North Mandarin is restricted primarily to urban centers in Northwest China

Transportation

The key to economic growth in China is the creation of an effective transportation system. Throughout China's history, fundamental economic problems have been closely allied with those of distribution: Famines would have been averted if surplus foods from other areas could have been moved into the stricken region; rich timberlands of the southwest have not been opened to development because of their poor surface linkage with population and industrial centers. The Communist government recognizes this transportation deficiency and has accordingly made the development of modern transport facilities a major part of successive Five-Year Plans.

Railroads are the primary means of transportation, in terms of volume of cargo and passengers moved, as well as of distance covered; in the economic plans, railroads are described as the "main line" carriers, with water and road transport occupying subordinate positions (Map II-6). Although water transportation is the cheapest means of moving bulk cargo, this form of transportation is always subject to limitations of natural conditions, and two-thirds of China is beyond the reach of navigable, cargo-carrying waterways. The Yangtze, Hsi Chiang, and Sungari river systems will always be important thoroughfares, but for the nation as a whole, the railroads form the backbone of the transportation system. Motor vehicle and air transport are too expensive for massive bulk and long-distance carrying and therefore have been relegated to subsidiary roles in major commodity movement. In China, highways function to provide short-distance hauling and as railway terminal connecting links, while airlines are reserved for urgent transportation between distant points. Only in Tibet does a highway serve as the main link with the rest of China.

RAILROADS

Before the Sino-Japanese War most of the capital for China's railroads was supplied by foreigners, and the routing of main lines was designed to benefit the investors. Construction was often of low quality, with both narrow and standard gauge tracks, antiquated station and siding equipment, and a limited supply of rolling stock, all of which was imported. The greatest density of railroad track was in Manchuria and along the eastern seaboard in North China; these areas accounted for more than three-quarters of the total rail system. South of the Yangtze River there were only a few routes, and west of an imaginary line from Lan-chou to K'un-ming practically no railroads existed. Such uneven distribution resulted from the interplay of a number of factors.

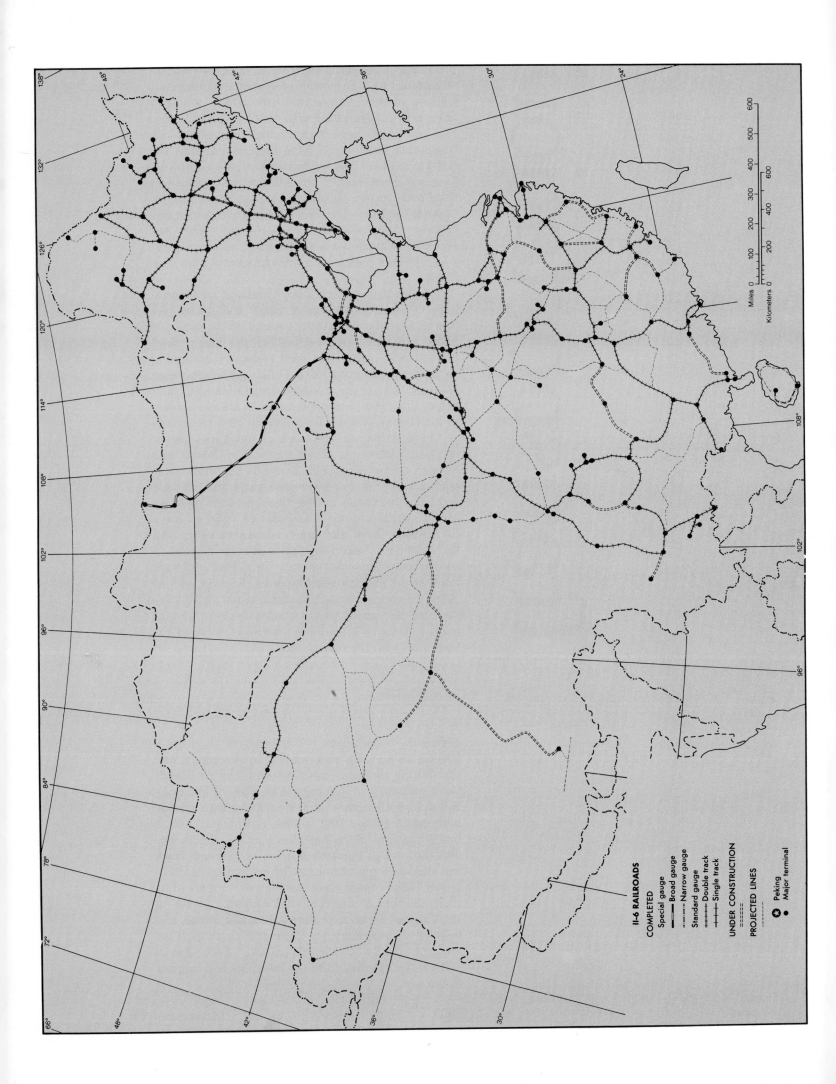

II-6 RAILROADS

COMPLETED

Special gauge
——— Broad gauge
– – – Narrow gauge
——— Standard gauge
═══ Double track
—+—+— Single track

UNDER CONSTRUCTION
═══════

PROJECTED LINES
– – – – –

✪ Peking
● Major terminal

Miles 0   100   200   300   400   500   600

Kilometers 0 200   400   600

By far the most influential of these factors was the scramble for concessions by the great powers at the end of the nineteenth century. Manchuria fell within the Russian sphere as soon as the Chinese Eastern Railway and its southern branch were completed. Germany obtained the concession to build the Tsingtao-Tsinan Railway and a section of the Tientsin-P'u-k'ou Line, enabling that country to exploit the minerals in Shantung Province. The British attempted to open up a corridor across China from Burma to Shanghai. The French built the K'un-ming–Haiphong Railway in an attempt to connect the Luichow Peninsula with southwestern China. Japan inaugurated an active railway development program in Taiwan. Belgium took over the project of the Peking-Hankow Railway, while American capital was called upon to build the southern section of this railroad, the Canton-Hankow line (Map II-7). A combination of foreign and Chinese capital funded the so-called Lung-hai Line from Kiangsu west in the direction of the Kansu Corridor.

Damage during the anti-Japanese and civil wars was heavy. When the Communist regime came to power in 1949, the task of rebuilding and developing the railway system was enormous, and during the "People's Reconstruction" period from 1950 to 1952 intensive effort was put into improving all existing rail lines. By 1952, 24,000 kilometers of railroad track were usable, an increase of 118 percent over the 11,000 kilometers functional in 1949.

The Five-Year Plans included programs designed to link the whole country in a single network of transportation. Special emphasis was placed on connecting the potentially productive southern and southwestern regions with each other and with the rest of the country. Northwestern railway construction has also been dramatic, with the dual aims of (1) making Sinkiang's mineral resources accessible to the industrial centers of eastern China, while at the same time developing local industrial complexes, and (2) bringing the minority peoples of northwestern China into closer political and cultural contact with Peking.

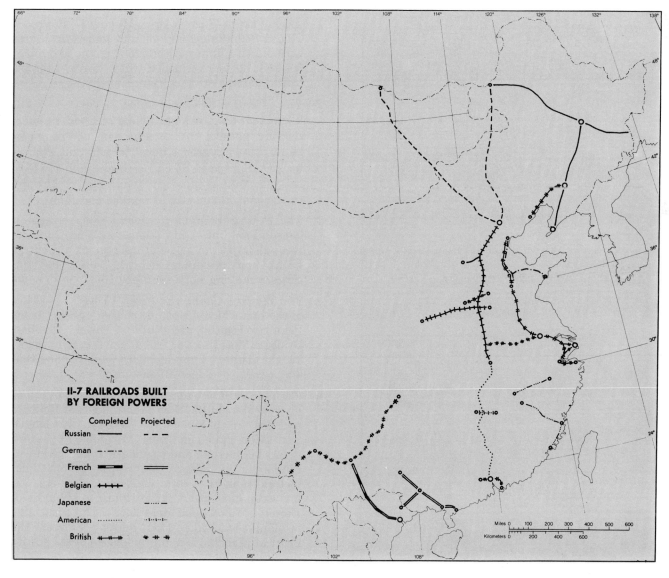

II-7 RAILROADS BUILT BY FOREIGN POWERS

	Completed	Projected
Russian		
German		
French		
Belgian		
Japanese		
American		
British		

The first railroad to be added by the Communists was the 549-kilometer line between Chungking and Ch'eng-tu. The railroad was completed in 1952, giving Szechwan an easy outlet for its varied agricultural products, such as cotton, rice, tung oil, fruit, and sugar. Another major line was then constructed, connecting Ch'eng-tu with Pao-chi on the Lung-hai Railroad (Map II-8). Thus the formerly isolated province of Szechwan was joined with the rest of the country via Chungking or the Lung-hai Railroad.

II-8 PAO-CHI TO CH'ENG-TU RAILWAY VIA TSINLING

The previously constructed Lung-hai road from the port Lien-yün-kang on the Yellow Sea to T'ien-shui in Kansu Province was extended to Lan-chou, the capital of Kansu. A further extension, begun in 1952, reaches from Lan-chou westward through Sinkiang toward the Russian border and is named the Druzhba ("friendship") line after the name of the Soviet border station. The completed line is to have a length of 2,331 kilometers between Lan-chou and Druzhba. By 1960 the line had reached Urumchi, the capital of Sinkiang. It has presumably been continued no further than this point.

Another international line, connecting China with the Soviet Union through Mongolia, was completed in 1956, shortening the distance between Moscow and Peking via Ulan Bator by 1,091 kilometers.

The total length of railroads today in China is approximately 40,000 kilometers (25,000 miles), an increase of more than 12,000 kilometers (7,500 miles) since pre-World War II days. There has also been a marked growth in the area served by railways. The following are presently the major trunk lines:

1 *The Peking–Shen-yang (Mukden) Railroad.* This is 840 kilometers long and joins Manchuria with North China. Although this line is double-tracked, it is overloaded with heavy railroad traffic moving to and from Manchuria.

2 *The Tientsin-Shanghai Line.* This is 1,310 kilometers long, a longitudinal railroad running roughly parallel to the seacoast. It connects two great industrial cities, Tientsin and Shanghai, via Nanking. It carries coal, lumber, steel, and pig iron southward, while the northward traffic consists mostly of textiles and flour.

3 *The Peking–Wu-han Railroad.* This is also a longitudinal line, 1,211 kilometers long, running through important agricultural regions of Central China and providing another outlet for the cargoes moving north and south.

4 *The Wu-han–Canton Railroad.* This is a section of the line which forms one continuous link from Peking to Canton, and it utilizes the new Wu-han Bridge. This line is 1,088 kilometers long, making the distance from Peking to Canton along this line a total of 2,299 kilometers.

5 *The Harbin Railroad.* This comprises two former lines in Manchuria, the Chinese Eastern Railway and the South Manchuria Railway. Its length from Man-chou-li in Inner Mongolia to Harbin is 928 kilometers, and its length from Harbin to Sui-fen-ho in eastern Manchuria is 552 kilometers, making a total of 1,480 kilometers. A line extending from Harbin south to the port of Dairen is 1,368 kilometers long. The entire line is double-tracked. This railroad crosses the heart of Manchuria and provides an outlet for its diverse products.

6 *The Lung-hai Railroad.* This is the longest east-west rail line. It runs from Lien-yün-kang in Kiangsu, the old name of which was Hai-chou, to Lan-chou, the old name of which was Lung-chou; thus its name is a combination of words in the two earlier place names. The total length of the line to Lan-chou is 1,782 kilometers. Westward from Lan-chou, as described above, this line has been completed to Urumchi and is projected eventually to the Soviet border for a total length of 4,113 kilometers.

7 *The Shanghai–Chu-chou Railroad.* This is 1,128 kilometers long, running from Shanghai in a generally southwest direction, via Hang-chow, until it joins the Wu-han–Canton Railroad at Chu-chou in Hunan. This east-west line plays a prominent economic role by integrating the eastern, central, and southern regions of China.

Map II-9 shows the historical sequence of Chinese railroad construction.

Extension of railways has been matched by large-scale bridge and tunnel building; in particular, three crucial railway bridges have been constructed since 1949. They are:

1 *The Wu-han Bridge.* The largest bridge in Asia, the Wu-han Bridge has 1,700 meters (5,600 feet) of double-deck construction with double track and six highway lanes. It crosses the Yangtze at the triple cities of Hankow, Han-yang, and Wu-ch'ang. This bridge—the first to span the Yangtze—not only is a triumph of engineering skill but also represents a major link in the nationwide transportation system: The Yangtze is no longer a barrier to north-south rail movement.

2 *The Chungking Bridge.* This was completed in 1959 to provide rail linkage for all of Szechwan Province.

3 *The Nanking Bridge.* This provides an uninterrupted rail connection between Tientsin and Shanghai.

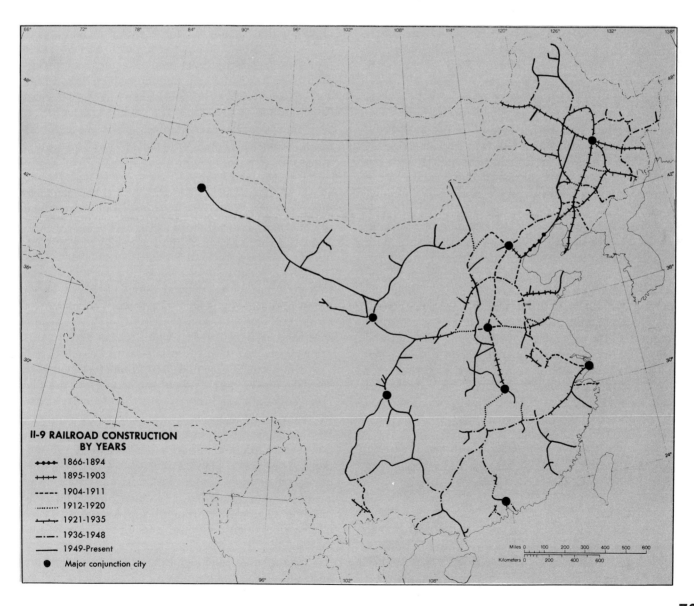

II-9 RAILROAD CONSTRUCTION
BY YEARS
++++ 1866-1894
+++ 1895-1903
----- 1904-1911
.... 1912-1920
+--- 1921-1935
-.-.- 1936-1948
——— 1949-Present
● Major conjunction city

Map II-10 shows the administrative systems for Chinese railroads, and Map II-11 locates the support centers for the rail network.

HIGHWAYS

China's highway network, like its railroad system, is concentrated in the coastal provinces: Eastern China accounts for three-fourths of the total highway mileage and one-third of the total land area of the country. However, although the highway density of northwestern China is low, highways continue to play a critical role in transport within this region since rail lines service only a small part of the area (Map II-12).

Lan-chou is the focal point of the highway network of northwestern China. Southeastward from Lan-chou a highway extends to Sian and eastern China, functioning as a critical link between northwestern China and the coast. From Lan-chou another major highway stretches northeastward to Yin-ch'uan, Pao-t'ou, and Hu-ho-hao-t'e in Inner Mongolia. A highway also runs through the Kansu Corridor to Ha-mi and Urumchi. This was the only connection between Sinkiang and the coastal provinces prior to the extension of the railroad between Lan-chou and Urumchi in 1960. A highway also connects Lan-chou with Hsi-ning in Tsinghai Province. The Tsinghai–Tibet Highway further stretches 2,100 kilometers from Hsi-ning through Ko-erh-mu across the Kunlun Mountains to Lhasa, making Ko-erh-mu the new highway center of Kansu, Sinkiang, and Tibet.

In southwestern China, Chungking and Ch'eng-tu in Szechwan are linked by major roads with Hupeh, Hunan, Kweichow, and Yunnan provinces. Ya-an is a new highway node in southwestern China. From this city a highway extends 2,250 kilometers through K'ang-ting to Lhasa, Tibet. Another highway extends south from K'un-ming to the Burmese border, and a road also links western Sinkiang and western Tibet. Finally, a highway stretches 2,000 kilometers southward from An-hsi across the Tsaidam Basin to Ko-erh-mu and Lhasa. At An-hsi this road connects with the railroad from Lan-chou to Urumchi.

AIR TRANSPORT

Air routes play a substantial role in linking the distant regions of the country with the central government in Peking (Map II-13). The national capital is thus the focal point of the air network, which has a total length of 19,000 kilometers. From Peking air routes extend northward to Ch'i-ch'i-ha-erh in Manchuria, southeastward to Shanghai, southward to the island of Hainan, and westward to K'a-shih in Sinkiang. Of China's international air routes, four connect Peking with Pyongyang, Ulan Bator, Irkutsk, and Moscow; and three other air routes join Nan-ning with Hanoi, K'un-ming with Rangoon, and Urumchi with Alma Ata. Six domestic lines link Peking with Shanghai, Nan-ning, Ch'eng-tu, Lhasa, the Tsaidam Basin, and Urumchi. Two domestic routes connect Shanghai with Canton and Lan-chou.

MARINE COMMERCE

Numerous natural harbors and a long coastline— bordering the Gulf of Chihli (Po Hai), the Yellow Sea, the East China Sea, and the South China Sea—have favored the development of marine commerce. This trade is both international and coastal.

The principal international seaports of China are Shanghai, T'ang-ku (for Tientsin), Dairen (Lü-ta), and Canton. From these ports marine trade routes radiate in all directions. The most important of these routes is the shipping lane which links China with Europe by way of the Indian Ocean, the Suez Canal (when open), and the Mediterranean Sea. The main exports carried over this route are soybeans, tobacco, tung oil, animal products, and minerals.

Coastal trade routes extend to the north and south of Shanghai. The northern route connects Shanghai with Tsingtao, T'ang-ku, and Dairen; and the southern route links it with Ning-po, Foochow, Amoy, Swatow, Canton, and Hai-k'ou. The commodities moved include foodstuffs, salt, and coal.

The competitive position of any port with relation to other ports depends upon the size of its hinterland, the volume of its trade, the nature of its harbor facilities, and the length of time, if any, that the harbor is frozen. China's four major ports are well favored with respect to these factors.

T'ang-ku is located 15 kilometers east of Tientsin on the north side of the estuary of the Hai Ho. This port was built to ease the difficulty ocean freighters previously experienced in navigating the Hai Ho; it serves a hinterland with an area of 2 million square kilometers and a population of 100 million. This area's exports include cotton, salt, and handicraft products, as well as animal products from Shensi, Kansu, Tsinghai, and Inner Mongolia. The imports which pass through T'ang-ku are all types of machinery, automobiles, and agricultural implements.

Shanghai is centrally located between northern and southern China and has a hinterland of 2 million

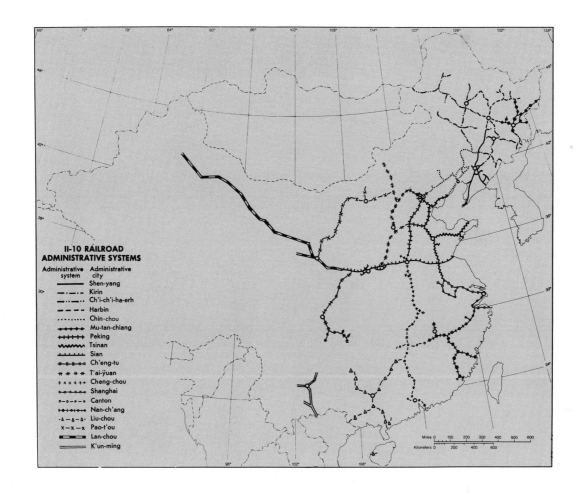

II-10 RAILROAD ADMINISTRATIVE SYSTEMS

Administrative system	Administrative city
——————	Shen-yang
—·—·—	Kirin
—··—··—	Ch'i-ch'i-ha-erh
— — —	Harbin
··········	Chin-chou
━◆━◆━	Mu-tan-chiang
┼┼┼┼	Peking
∿∿∿∿	Tsinan
┴┴┴┴	Sian
╫╫╫╫	Ch'eng-tu
✱✱✱✱	T'ai-yüan
+++++	Cheng-chou
—○—○—○	Shanghai
—⊙—⊙—⊙	Canton
┼○┼○┼○	Nan-ch'ang
—△—△—△	Liu-chou
x—x—x	Pao-t'ou
▬▭▬	Lan-chou
═══════	K'un-ming

Miles 0 100 200 300 400 500 600
Kilometers 0 200 400 600

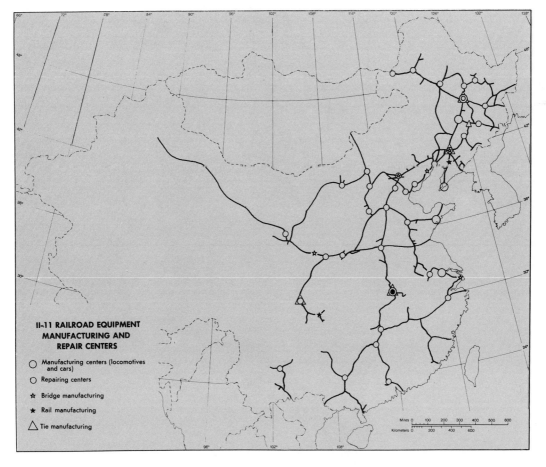

II-11 RAILROAD EQUIPMENT MANUFACTURING AND REPAIR CENTERS

○ Manufacturing centers (locomotives and cars)

○ Repairing centers

☆ Bridge manufacturing

★ Rail manufacturing

△ Tie manufacturing

Miles 0 100 200 300 400 500 600
Kilometers 0 200 400 600

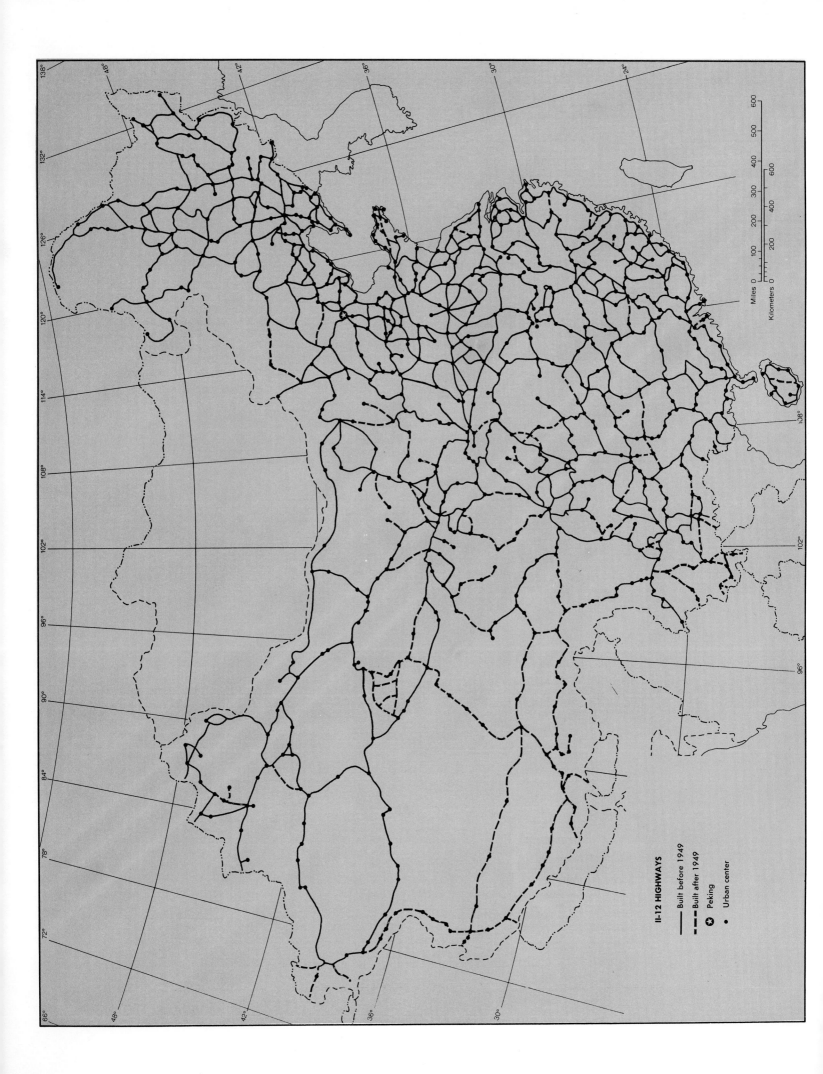

II-12 HIGHWAYS

Built before 1949
Built after 1949
Peking
Urban center

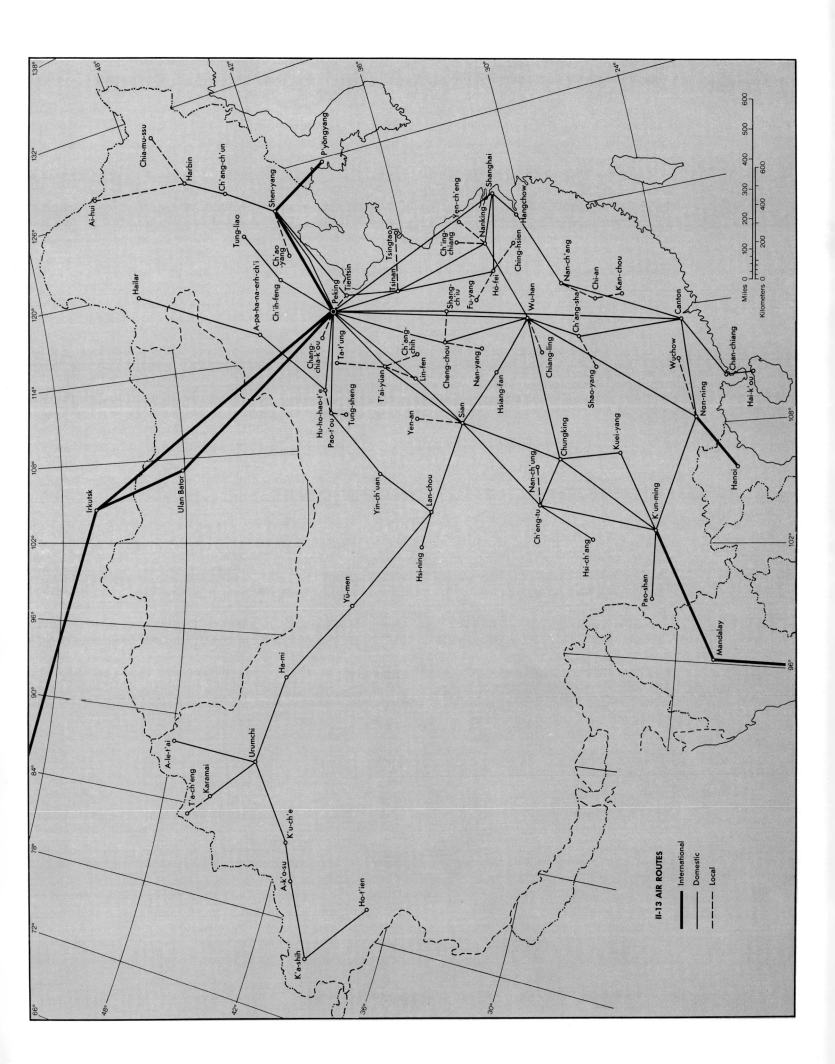

II-13 AIR ROUTES

International
Domestic
Local

square kilometers and 250 million people. Shanghai is also a center for light industry and has a highly trained and experienced labor force. Although it was once China's leading port and accounted for half of the country's international trade and one-third of its domestic trade, the city has declined in relative importance since 1949.

Canton is the principal port of southern China because of its proximity to European trade routes. The city is located at the head of the Pearl River delta, which is the natural outlet for the Tung, Hsi, and Pei rivers. Cantón exports local products such as silk, tung oil, tea, and citrus fruit; it imports automobiles, gasoline, tires, rubber, cotton, dyes, pharmaceuticals, and chemical fertilizers.

Dairen is the most important port of Manchuria, since it not only has a large, deep harbor that is ice-free and capable of accommodating 30,000-ton vessels but also has modern handling and storage facilities. Moreover, it is connected by railroad with a large hinterland encompassing southern Manchuria and the cities of Harbin, Ch'ang-ch'un, and Lung-chiang. It exports soybeans, bean oil, steel, and lumber.

INLAND WATER TRANSPORTATION

China has an extensive network of rivers and tributaries which are a significant element of the country's entire transportation system (Map II-14). Of these inland waterways, 100,000 kilometers are navigable by small craft and 30,000 kilometers by steamboat. The most important arteries of this network are the Yangtze, Hsi Chiang (together with the Pearl River), Amur, Sungari, and Yellow rivers and the major canals.

The Yangtze, the longest of China's rivers, is 5,800 kilometers long and has a drainage area of 2 million square kilometers. Having its headwaters in Tsinghai, the Yangtze flows eastward through the provinces of Yunnan, Szechwan, Hupeh, Hunan, Kiangsi, Anhwei, and Kiangsu. The river is navigable for 2,900 kilometers from its mouth at Shanghai to I-pin.

The Yangtze can be divided into three sections on the basis of navigability. The first section extends 1,100 kilometers from Shanghai to Wu-han. Here the river is wide and has a high volume of flow. During the season of high water level, boats of over 10,000 metric tons can navigate this lower section. The second section of the river stretches from Wu-han to I-ch'ang and can be used by vessels of 2,000 to 3,000 metric tons during the season of high water level and by boats of 1,000 to 2,000 metric tons during the season of low water level. The third

section lies between I-ch'ang and I-pin. Here swift currents and rock-strewn riverbeds make navigation difficult.

The Yangtze flows through one of the most important economic regions of China. The river's watershed encompasses one-fifth of the land area and two-fifths of the total population of the country.

The area adjoining the lower Yangtze is a center of light industry. Shanghai is the principal manufacturing city of the delta, specializing in consumer products for domestic and foreign trade. Wu-han is the metallurgical center of the middle Yangtze. The mineral resources of the river basin include iron ore, coal, salt, and gypsum. The economic importance of this river is underscored by the fact that half of China's inland water commerce is carried on the river, including food, coal, lumber, cement, cotton textiles, and nonferrous metals.

The Hsi Chiang is 2,300 kilometers long and has two important tributaries: the Pei and the Tung. These three rivers flow to the sea via the broad estuary called the Pearl River or Chu Chiang. The Hsi Chiang drainage area receives the highest annual precipitation of any watershed in China. Although the river flows through hilly terrain where there are numerous rapids, the high volume of water permits navigation in this area. Thus the navigable length of the Hsi Chiang is second only to that of the Yangtze. The limit of navigation for vessels larger than junks on the Hsi Chiang is Wuchow, although small craft can travel as far upstream as Liu-chou in Kwangsi Chuang Autonomous Region. The commodities which move over the Hsi include rice, tea, silk, sugar cane, and citrus fruits. The watershed of the Pei Chiang and the Tung Chiang contains significant deposits of tin, antimony, and tungsten. Canton functions as a focal point of river and coastal trade.

The principal rivers of Manchuria are the Amur (Hei-lung Chiang) and the Sungari. The length of the Amur is 4,600 kilometers, of which 3,700 kilometers are in China. It is frozen half of the year, and its use for transport is thus restricted. The area it drains is an economically underdeveloped region.

The Sungari, the fourth most important inland waterway of China, has its headwaters in Ch'ang-pai Shan and flows 1,900 kilometers through Kirin and Heilungkiang provinces before joining the Amur. The Sungari is frozen for a shorter period of time than the Amur is and naviable for a greater length. Moreover, the Sungari flows through an area which is economically better developed. Lumbering is an important activity in its headwater region, and a wide variety of agricultural products is produced in the area through which the river flows, including maize, kaoliang, wheat, beets, and soybeans. Har-

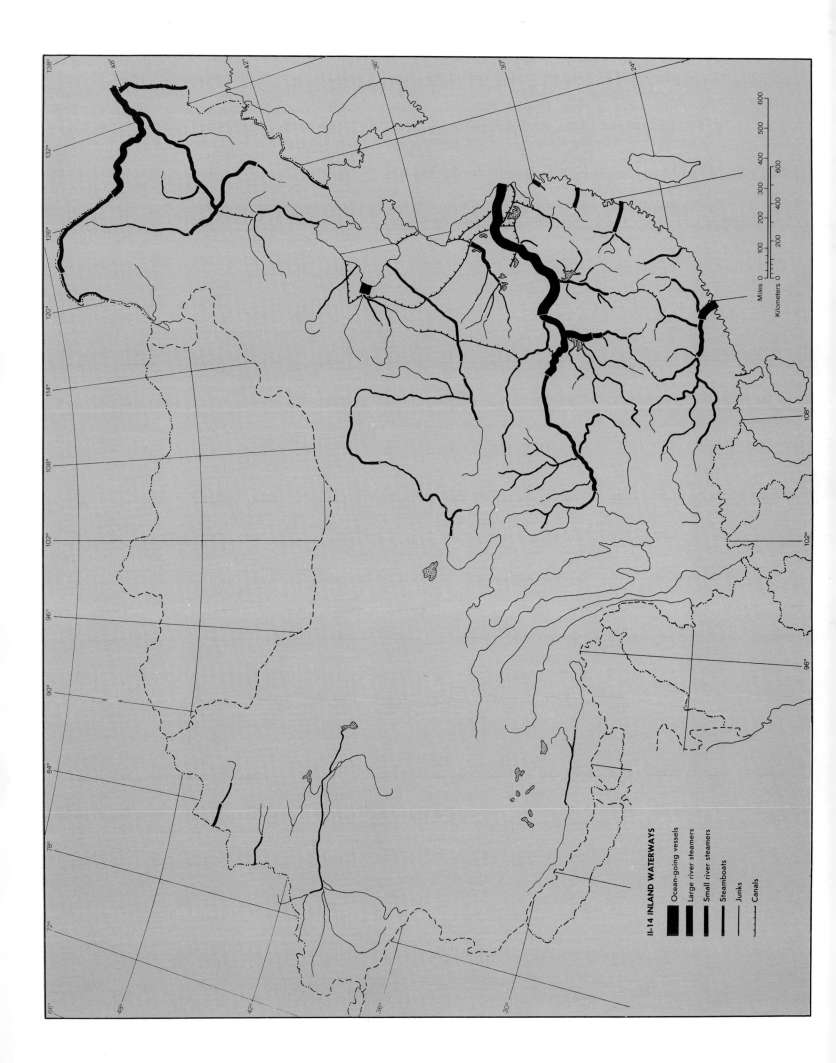

II-14 INLAND WATERWAYS

■ Ocean-going vessels
▌ Large river steamers
▐ Small river steamers
── Steamboats
── Junks
─·─·─ Canals

Miles 0   100   200   300   400   500   600
Kilometers 0   200   400   600

bin is the most important city of the Sungari River Basin and is a center for food-processing and agricultural machinery industries.

The Yellow River (Huang Ho) is the second longest river in China, but the value of the goods shipped on it is less than that of the goods transported on either the Yangtze, the Hsi, or the Sungari. The extension of its navigable course depends upon the success of the Yellow River project, including the San-men Dam. Upon full completion of that project the river will be navigable for 1,500-metric-ton boats as far west as Lan-chou, an important interior city of northwestern China.

Canals are also a critical element of the inland water transportation network of China. The Grand Canal flows through Hopeh, Shantung, Kiangsu, and Chekiang provinces. Other important canals are the Sungari-Liao Canal, which connects the Sungari with the Liao Ho and Gulf of Chihli (Po Hai); the Peking Canal, which links Peking with the Huai Ho; and the Cheng-chou–Nan-yang Canal, which joins the Yellow River and the Han Shui.

Agriculture

Only a little over 36 percent of China's huge land mass is used for agricultural purposes: 11 percent of the total area of China is cultivated, 20.5 percent is used for pasture, and 5.1 percent is forested and partially harvested (Map II-15). Approximately one-third of the land between the Yangtze River and the Great Wall has traditionally been cultivated, but only 15 percent of the land south of the Yangtze is farmland. In that southern region mountains make farming costly and difficult on much of the land. Even north of the Yangtze salt flats still more mountains make a large portion of the land unusable for agriculture.

The Communist regime has made land reclamation one of its major goals, initiating programs of irrigation, afforestation, and soil and water conservation to bring large new areas into agricultural use. Political programs have also been focused on increasing agricultural productivity. Communes and collectives have been organized to reduce inefficiencies associated with small farms and to provide the means for acquiring expensive equipment such as tractors and harvesting machines. Communal organization is also intended to provide large labor forces which can be directed to such tasks as irrigation and afforestation. Units of the army have also been enlisted in these programs, and in the northwest particularly, formerly unusable land has been successfully converted into farmland. At the same time that these massive projects have been carried out, constant experiments at agricultural research stations throughout the country have been directed toward finding improved plant stocks, fertilizers, and methods of cultivation.

About a third of China's cultivated land is "wet land" paddies and irrigated fields. In this atlas, for example, whenever "rice" is included in the legend, it means irrigated rice. South of the Tsinling Shan and the Huai Ho, this kind of farming accounts for more than half of the total land cultivated. North of this divide, the lands of the Yellow River Basin are approximately one-third irrigated.

FOOD CROPS

Food production is the first and most important purpose of agriculture, and small grains are the single most important food product. In China, rice and wheat are the basis of the diet of most of the country's population, with rice generally grown south of the Tsinling Shan and Huai Ho, and wheat grown to the north of the Yangtze. However, there are exceptions, as will be seen below. Map II-16 shows the major crop assemblages, while the following table shows the percentage of acreage planted and the production of the major grain crops:

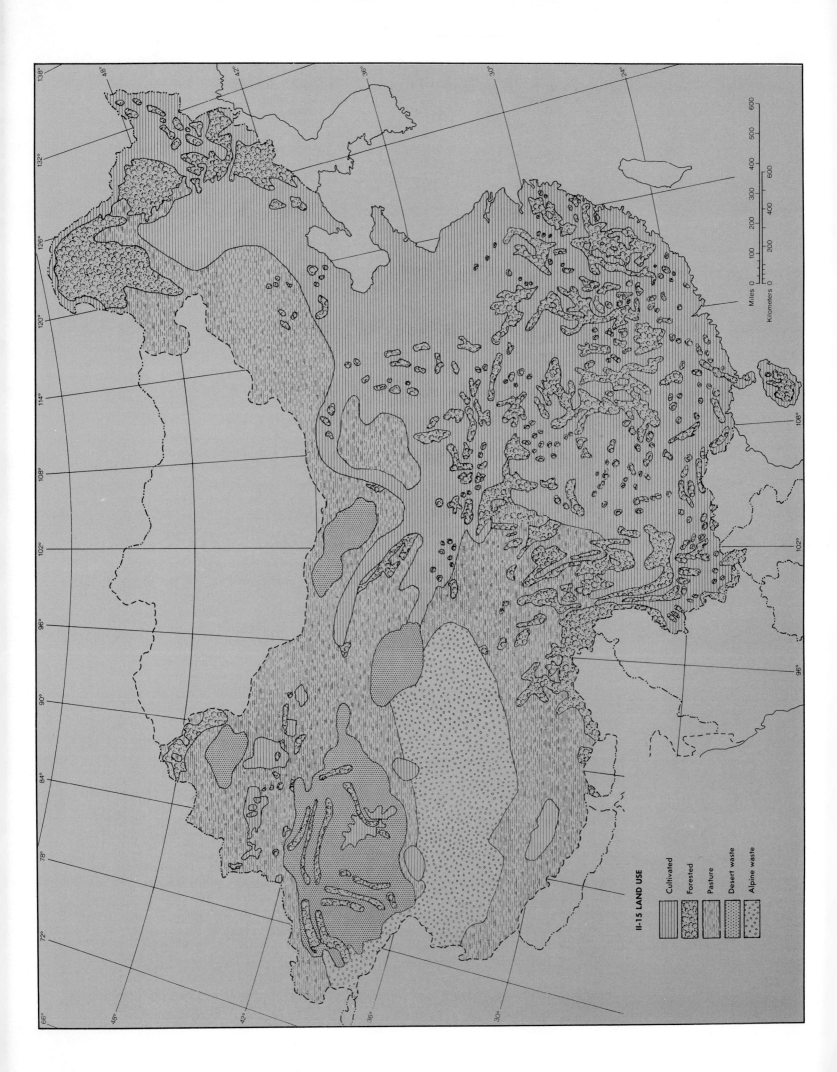

II-15 LAND USE

Cultivated

Forested

Pasture

Desert waste

Alpine waste

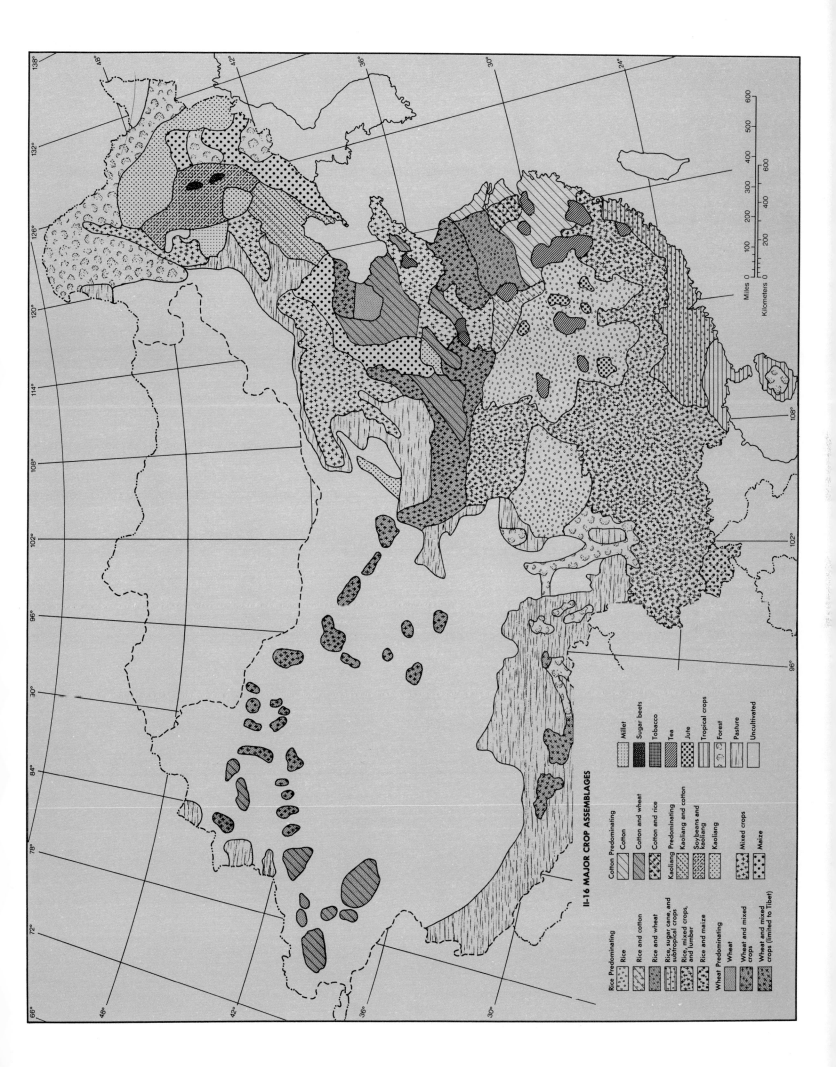

II-16 MAJOR CROP ASSEMBLAGES

Rice Predominating
Rice
Rice and cotton
Rice and wheat
Rice, sugar cane, and subtropical crops
Rice, mixed crops, and lumber
Rice and maize

Wheat Predominating
Wheat
Wheat and mixed crops
Wheat and mixed crops (limited to Tibet)

Cotton Predominating
Cotton
Cotton and wheat
Cotton and rice

Kaoliang Predominating
Kaoliang and cotton
Soybeans and kaoliang
Kaoliang

Mixed crops
Maize

Millet
Sugar beets
Tobacco
Tea
Jute
Tropical crops
Forest
Pasture
Uncultivated

Miles 0   100   200   300   400   500   600
Kilometers 0   200   400   600

Grain crop	Percent of total cultivated land	Percent of total food production
Rice	26.69	45.64
Wheat	22.30	13.52
Other Grains	51.01	40.84

As the table shows, rice accounts for almost half of China's production of grain crops, although less than a third of the total cultivated land in grain is devoted to rice alone. This high rate of productivity is accounted for partly by the high-yielding nature of rice, and partly by double cropping of irrigated rice. Wheat, however, is not double cropped. The most important rice-growing areas are the middle and lower reaches of the Yangtze River, the Canton Delta, the Szechwan Basin, and parts of Hunan, Kwangtung, Kiangsu, and Chekiang provinces. In well-irrigated areas of the north, it is possible to grow one rice crop during the hot summers; and Heilungkiang, Kirin, Hopeh, and Kansu provinces all produce significant amounts of rice. The major wheat-growing areas are the North China Plain, the middle and lower Yangtze plains, the Szechwan Basin, and the Wei and Fen river basins. Winter wheat, planted in the late fall and harvested in the spring, is grown south of the Great Wall, with Honan and Shantung as the great-

est producing centers. Shensi, Kiangsu, Anhwei, Szechwan, and Hupeh also produce a large proportion of the country's wheat. In Manchuria, Sinkiang, and Inner Mongolia spring wheat is the major product (Maps II-17 and II-18).

Other important cereals are maize, kaoliang, and millet (Map II-19). Although maize is distributed throughout the country on land where rice and wheat will not grow productively, the major maize-growing regions are Manchuria, Hopeh, Honan, Shantung, Shensi, Szechwan, and Yunnan. Kaoliang is a hardy grain grown during northern summers. Its deep roots and strong stems make it resistant to dryness, floods, and high winds. It is found chiefly on the southern Manchurian Plain, and in Shantung, Hopeh, Honan, Shansi, and northern Kiangsu. Both maize and kaoliang are used for food, fodder, and wine; kaoliang wine is considered a very high-quality drink. Millet is the food of the poor in the north, since it is a dry crop that will grow in very poor soil and will resist drought. Its distribution is concentrated in the North China Plain, Manchuria, and the loess region, although it is grown only when wheat cannot be grown.

Another important food staple is the potato. Sweet potatoes make up 80 percent of China's potato crop, but white potatoes are also raised, particularly in the cold and relatively dry regions of northern

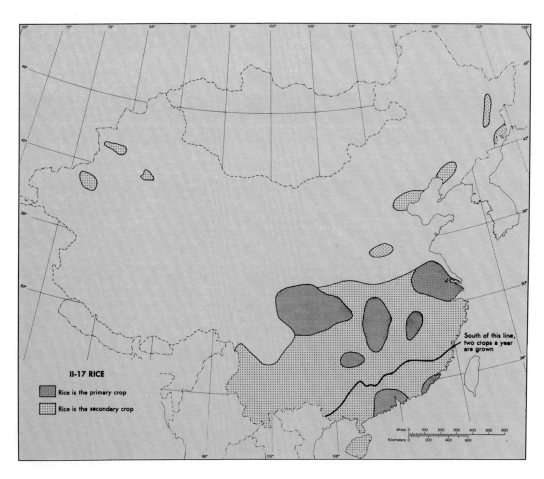

II-17 RICE

Rice is the primary crop

Rice is the secondary crop

South of this line, two crops a year are grown

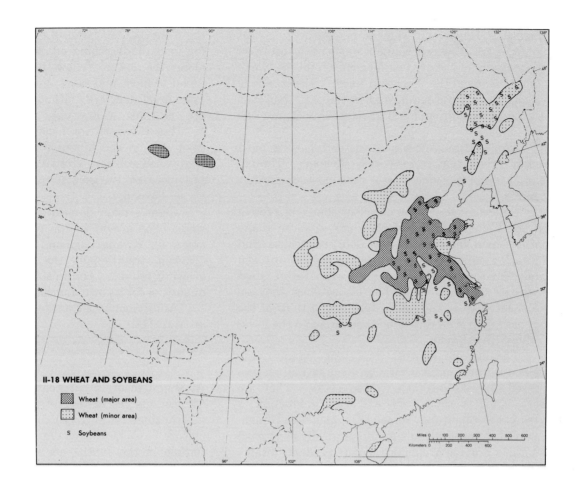

II-18 WHEAT AND SOYBEANS

- ▨ Wheat (major area)
- ▨ Wheat (minor area)
- S Soybeans

Miles 0 100 200 300 400 500 600
Kilometers 0 200 400 600

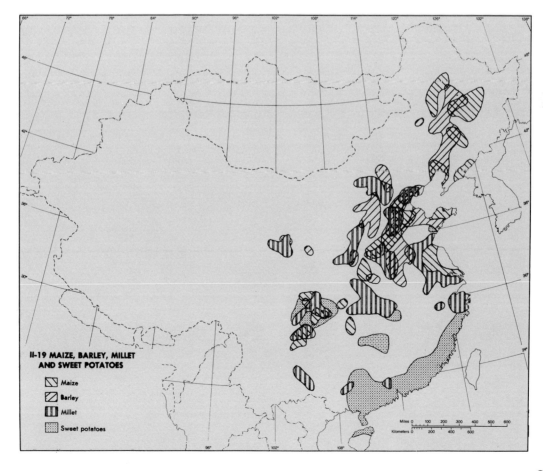

II-19 MAIZE, BARLEY, MILLET AND SWEET POTATOES

- ▨ Maize
- ▨ Barley
- ▨ Millet
- ▨ Sweet potatoes

Miles 0 100 200 300 400 500 600
Kilometers 0 200 400 600

Shantung, Hopeh, and Manchuria. Although sweet potatoes are grown throughout much of the country, the majority of the production comes from the North China Plain and the Szechwan Basin. The economic significance of the potato lies in the fact that it is a productive crop and will grow in almost any soil and climate.

Truck farming occurs on the periphery of most major urban centers, although Chekiang, Hunan, and Anhwei provinces are the most important centers.

Soybeans provide an excellent source of protein in the Chinese diet, and they are eaten in many forms—as a vegetable and as flour, beancakes, and imitation milk. Soybeans grow in almost any soil and climate; they make a good crop for rotation with rice or wheat, since, like all legumes, they restore nitrogen to the soil. More than a third of the soybean crop is produced in Manchuria and the lower Yellow River Basin.

Peanuts are another important legume, consumed in their natural form as food as well as processed to make peanut oil (Map II-20). They are best suited to sandy soil, and thus production is greatest in Shantung, Hopeh, Kiangsu, and Honan.

Other vegetable oils are domestically consumed and also provide a valuable export product. Rapeseed oil, produced in the Szechwan Basin and along

the Yangtze, can be used as a lubricant as well as for food; and sesame oil, produced in Honan and along the lower Yellow River, has a distinctive flavor which makes it an important seasoning. Peanut oil and lard (although not a vegetable oil) are the most widely used for everyday purposes.

Tea is grown for local consumption and as a cash crop in the humid south. Fukien, Kiangsu, Kiangsi, Szechwan, Hunan, Chekiang, and Anhwei provinces are the greatest producers of China's universal beverage.

China's main domestic source of raw sugar is sugar cane grown in the tropical and subtropical areas of Kwangtung and the Szechwan Basin. (Taiwan, traditionally the most productive cane-growing province, continues to produce substantial quantities for its own domestic and foreign markets.)

Additional important food crop areas are located on Map II-21.

ANIMAL HUSBANDRY

Although meat is not nearly as important in the Chinese diet as in that of the Western world, animal husbandry is a critical part of Chinese agriculture. Cattle—oxen in the north and water buffalo in the south—are used primarily as draft animals (Map II-22). The consumption of dairy

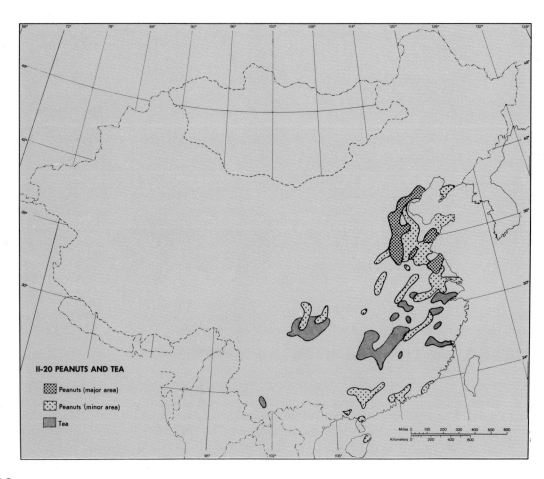

II-20 PEANUTS AND TEA

Peanuts (major area)

Peanuts (minor area)

Tea

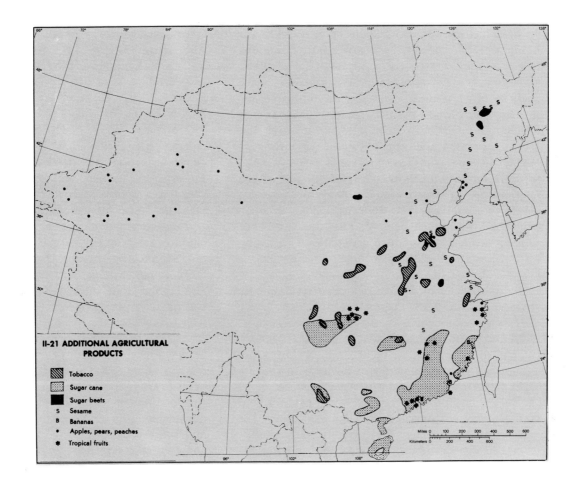

II-21 ADDITIONAL AGRICULTURAL PRODUCTS

Tobacco
Sugar cane
Sugar beets
S Sesame
B Bananas
• Apples, pears, peaches
✳ Tropical fruits

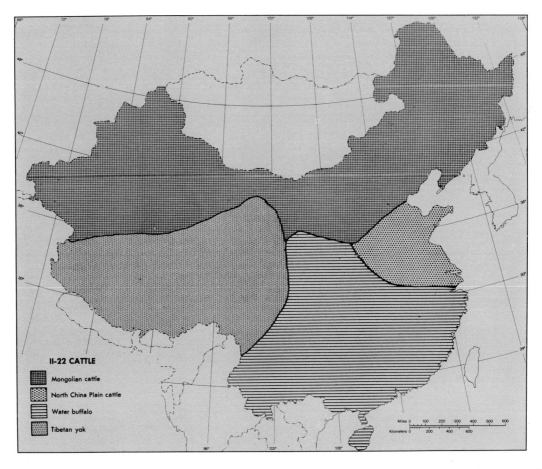

II-22 CATTLE

Mongolian cattle
North China Plain cattle
Water buffalo
Tibetan yak

products has increased markedly since World War II, but only in the northwestern pastoral regions are cattle widely used for meat or milk products. Donkeys serve as work animals in the north, for horses require too much food and care to be practical for many of China's farmers except on the vast Manchurian farms or in the northwestern plains and deserts. Camels are also a significant means of transportation in the desert regions.

Pork forms a much more important part of the diet than beef, partly because pigs do not perform useful labor and are easy to raise. They live on scraps and reproduce quickly, and thus are kept by many farmers whose main occupation is growing rice or wheat. In addition to pork, pig bristles are exported for profit. The greatest centers for pig raising are Szechwan, Hunan, Kiangsu, and Kiangsi provinces (Map II-23).

Like pigs, fowl are raised almost everywhere. Ducks and geese are found most frequently in southern rice areas, and in these areas duck farms are common. The great majority of fowls, however, are raised on farms specializing in other products.

Sheep provide wool for the whole country and meat for the northwest pastoral areas where the open land necessary for sheep grazing is available. Hence the main producers of wool and mutton are Sinkiang, Inner Mongolia, Shensi, and Kansu.

Goats, raised on a small scale, are more widely distributed (Map II-24). Sinkang and Inner Mongolia are also famous for their horses (Map II-25).

ECONOMIC CROPS

In addition to food, agriculture provides the raw material for other products, especially textiles. The two regions with the wet and warm climate necessary for cotton production are the Yellow River and Yangtze basins. The Yellow River Basin, including parts of Hopeh, Shantung, Honan, Shensi, and Shansi, accounts for 62 percent of China's cotton crop, while Kiangsu, Hupeh, Chekiang, Anhwei, and Hunan along the Yangtze account for 23 percent. Cotton is being grown increasingly in Sinkiang as well (Map II-26).

China also has a large hemp crop. Fine-fibered hemp is used to make delicate garment cloth, sailcloth, fishnets, and insulating material for electric wires. This kind of hemp is produced mainly along the Yangtze in Kiangsi, Hupeh, Hunan, and Szechwan; some is also grown in Heilungkiang, Kirin, and Inner Mongolia. Coarse-fibered hemp grows in widely dispersed areas, and is used for burlap bags, rope, and paper.

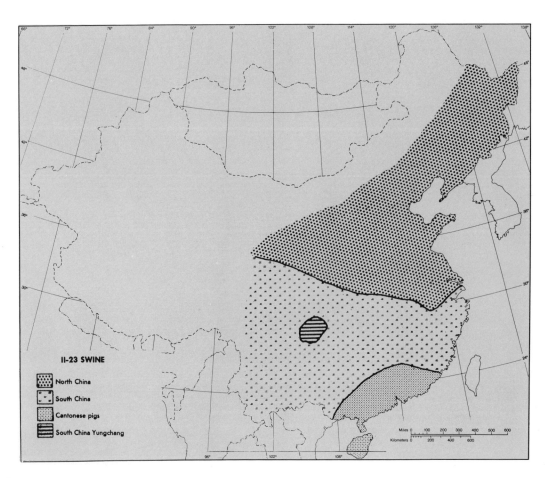

II-23 SWINE

North China

South China

Cantonese pigs

South China Yungchang

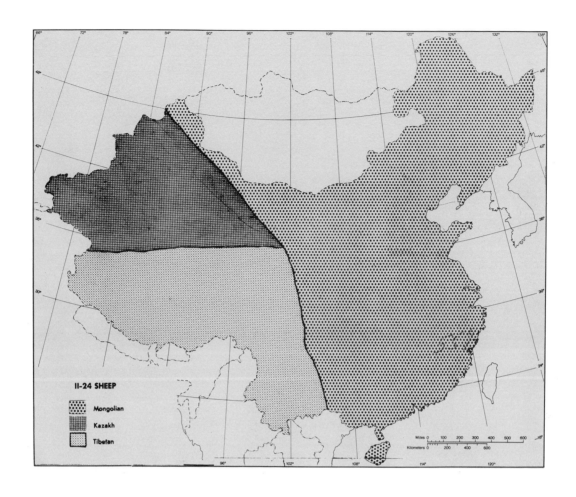

II-24 SHEEP

Mongolian

Kazakh

Tibetan

Miles 0 100 200 300 400 500 600
Kilometers 0 200 400 600

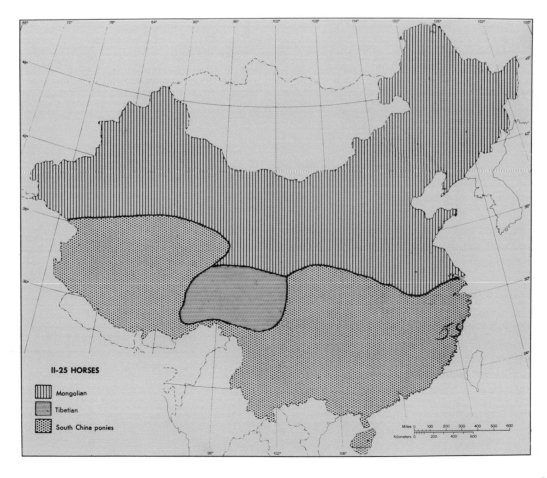

II-25 HORSES

Mongolian

Tibetian

South China ponies

Miles 0 100 200 300 400 500 600
Kilometers 0 200 400 600

Agriculture **89**

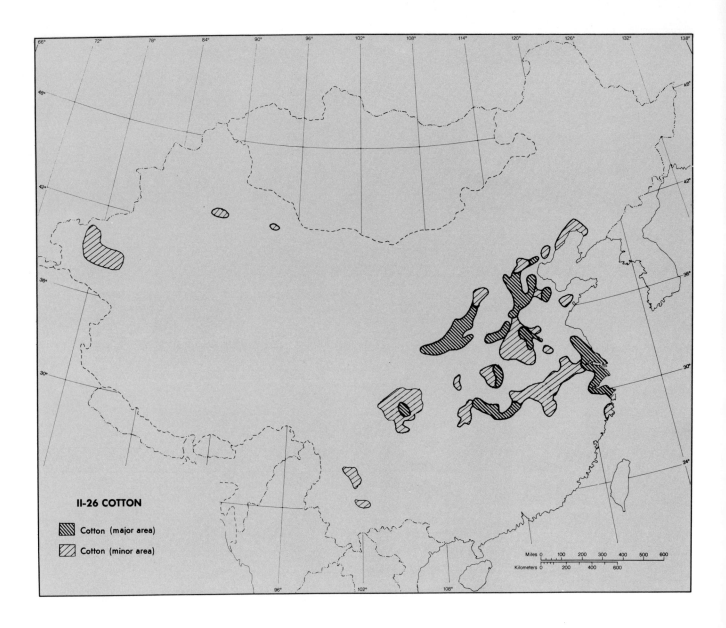

II-26 COTTON

▨ Cotton (major area)

▩ Cotton (minor area)

Miles 0 100 200 300 400 500 600
Kilometers 0 200 400 600

Sericulture continues to be important to the Chinese economy. The mulberry trees on which silkworms feed are found most widely in the T'ai Hu region of Kiangsu, the Szechwan Basin, and the Canton Delta. In these regions, as many as seven or eight generations of silkworms can be raised in a single year (Map II-27).

FORESTRY

Only 5.1 percent of China's agricultural land is devoted to forest; large areas of the country are treeless plains, and the formerly forested plains of the east have long been cleared for farming. Today, natural forests exist primarily in Manchuria, Inner Mongo-

lia, and the southwest. About 60 percent of the forest land is in the Northeast and Inner Mongolia. Efficient transportation makes such forests in the Northeast economically more valuable. Although the forests of Szechwan, Kwangsi, and Yunnan amount to 12 percent of China's total, their remoteness and inaccessibility diminish their economic value. Improved railroads, however, have begun to change this. Today new afforestation projects are steadily improving China's resources.

MARINE RESOURCES

China's rich water resources provide an important supplement to its land resources. Shallow coastal

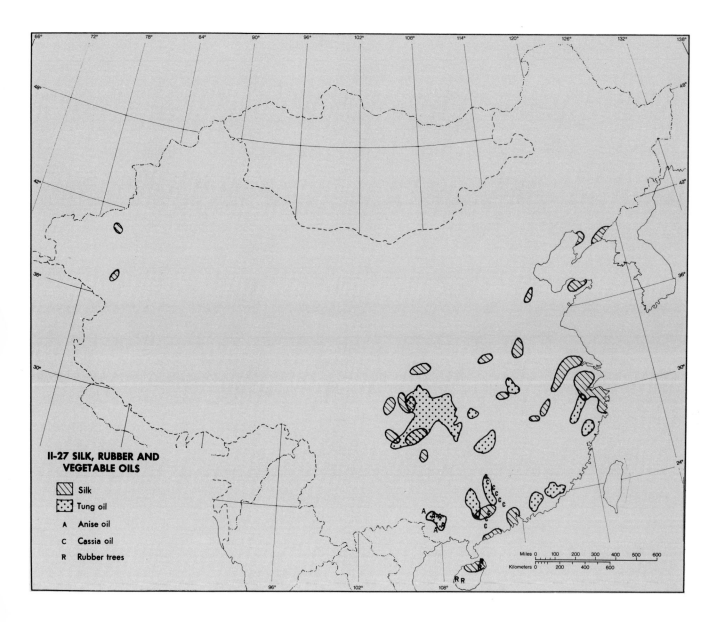

II-27 SILK, RUBBER AND VEGETABLE OILS

- Silk
- Tung oil
- A Anise oil
- C Cassia oil
- R Rubber trees

waters and an abundance of inlets, bays, and islands mean that approximately 23 percent of the world's ocean fishing grounds are easily available to Chinese fisherman (Map II-28). China's many rivers, streams, and ponds provide ample sources of freshwater fish. Salting is still the single most important means of preserving fish, but freezing and industrial processing plants are now being developed for such products as fishliver oil. The greatest processing and marketing centers are in Shanghai, Tsingtao, Chefoo (modern Yen-t'ai), Dairen, Swatow, Canton, and Amoy. These centers reflect the distribution of the major ocean fishing grounds in Kiangsu, Shantung, Liaoning, Kwangtung, and Fukien (Map II-29).

Most of China's freshwater fish come from the Yangtze, the Hsi Chiang and Pearl, and Amur rivers and from large lakes such as Tung-t'ing, P'o-yang, and T'ai. Another significant portion is raised on fish farms, a relatively new form of agriculture especially prevalent in the South, where water is plentiful. Kwangtung accounts for more pisciculture than any other province. The fishing industry still has great potential for development, and programs now under way will contribute to such growth.

Two additional maps which show detailed and generalized patterns of agricultural land use conclude this section: Map II-30 (Detailed Agricultural Regions) and Map II-31 (Generalized Agricultural Regions). See the Appendix for a list of detailed agricultural regions.

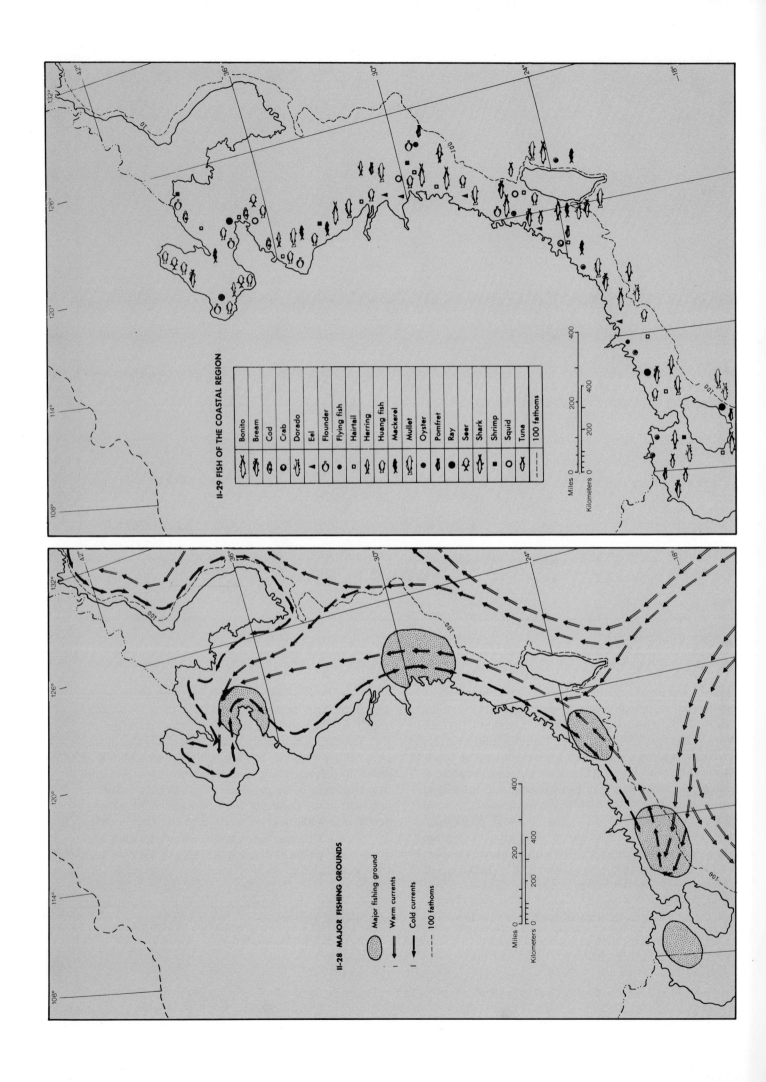

II-29 FISH OF THE COASTAL REGION

Bonito	
Bream	
Cod	
Crab	
Dorado	
Eel	
Flounder	
Flying fish	
Hairtail	
Herring	
Huang fish	
Mackerel	
Mullet	
Oyster	
Pomfret	
Ray	
Seer	
Shark	
Shrimp	
Squid	
Tuna	
100 fathoms	

Miles 0   200   400
Kilometers 0   200   400

II-28 MAJOR FISHING GROUNDS

Major fishing ground
Warm currents
Cold currents
100 fathoms

Miles 0   200   400
Kilometers 0   200   400

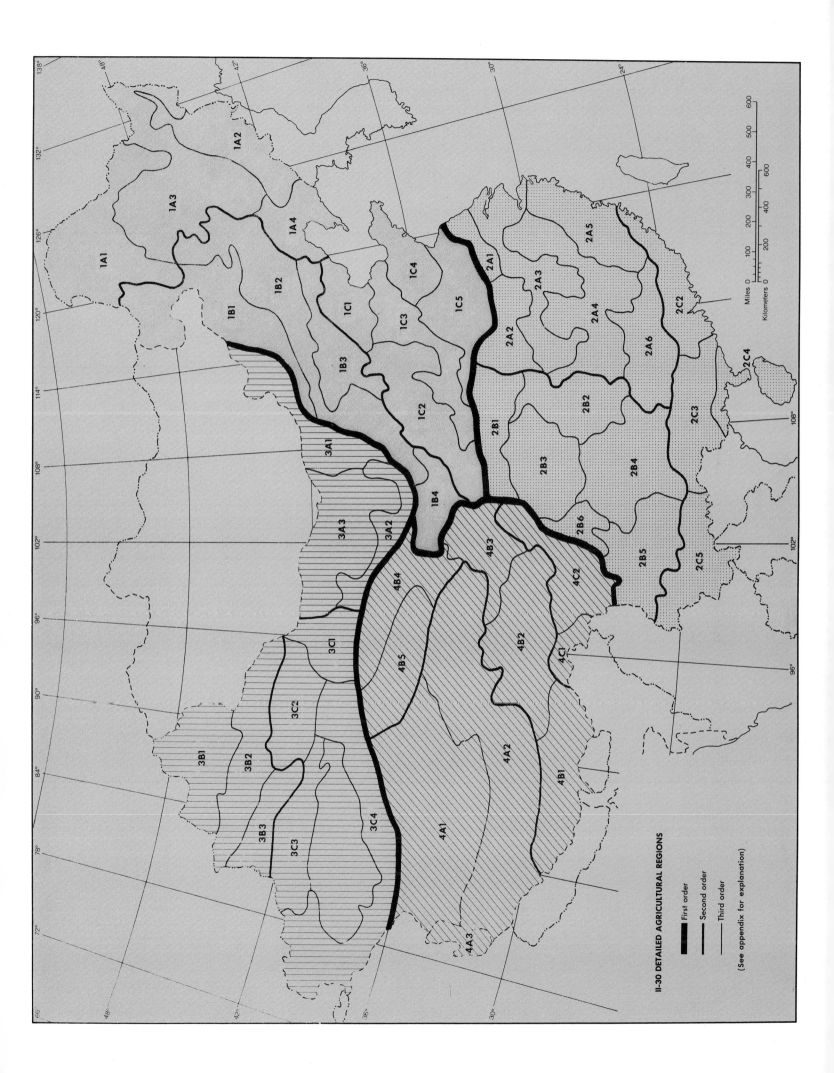

II-30 DETAILED AGRICULTURAL REGIONS

First order
Second order
Third order

(See appendix for explanation)

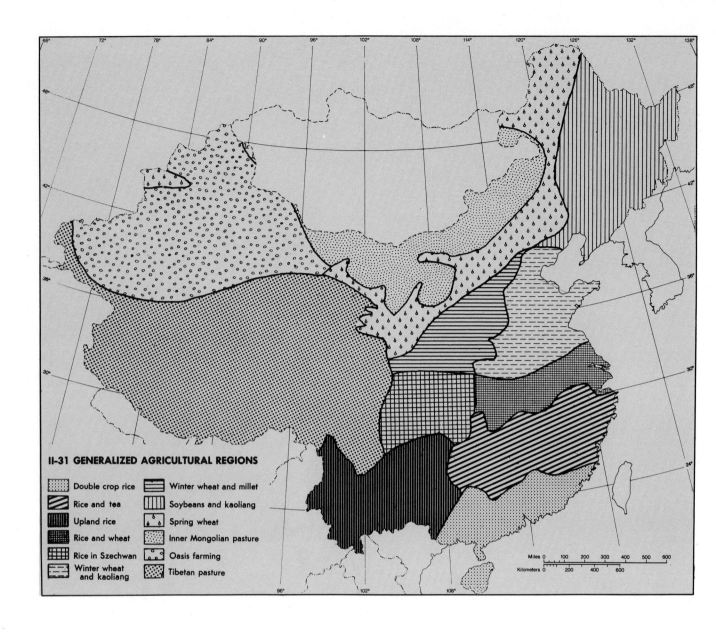

II-31 GENERALIZED AGRICULTURAL REGIONS

- Double crop rice
- Rice and tea
- Upland rice
- Rice and wheat
- Rice in Szechwan
- Winter wheat and kaoliang
- Winter wheat and millet
- Soybeans and kaoliang
- Spring wheat
- Inner Mongolian pasture
- Oasis farming
- Tibetan pasture

Miles 0 100 200 300 400 500 600
Kilometers 0 200 400 600

Mining and Manufacturing

China has traditionally been a world leader in the production of antimony, tungsten, and tin; and today's mainland China is an even more important mineral producer by world standards. In the early 1960s China was one of the three foremost world producers of bituminous and anthracite coal, tin, tungsten, antimony, salt, and magnetite. It also ranked close to fifth or better in bismuth, manganese, mercury, molybdenite, asbestos, fluorspar, and graphite; about seventh in iron and steel; and about tenth in cement, barite, pyrite, and sulfur. Traditional items in which China suffers from an insufficiency include petroleum, chromite, nickel, copper, and phosphates. Continued exploration has shown, however, that unexploited reserves of these minerals may prove to be considerable, except for chromite and nickel.

Coal

Coal is China's most valuable mineral asset, as well as its chief source of energy and fuel (Map II-32). The latest Communist Chinese claim regarding overall coal resources puts reserves at 9.6 trillion metric tons, of which only 100 billion tons are verified. While the amount may be exaggerated, the coal reserve of China definitely does rank among the foremost in the world, along with those of the United States and the Soviet Union. Annual production of coal is between 250 and 350 million tons. Recent exploration has uncovered large coal beds in central, southern, and southwestern China, as well as in the northwest, all of which had hitherto been considered to be lacking in coal for large-scale industrial development. Most of the country's coal is bituminous, and about 30 large coal fields are said to be in existence around the country. There are seven coal-mining centers in China. In order of output, they are Fu-shun, Fu-hsin, K'ai-luan, Pench'i, Huai-nan, Ho-kang, and Ta-t'ung. These account for approximately 30 percent of the national output; each produced more than 10 million metric tons of coal in 1959. Another 20 to 25 mining centers produced between 1 and 10 million metric tons during 1959.

Oil

China may no longer be regarded as having only minor petroleum resources. Productive fields have been discovered in Kansu, Sinkiang, and Heilungkiang. The Chinese Mainland reported their 1962 crude oil output at 7 million tons including 2 mil-

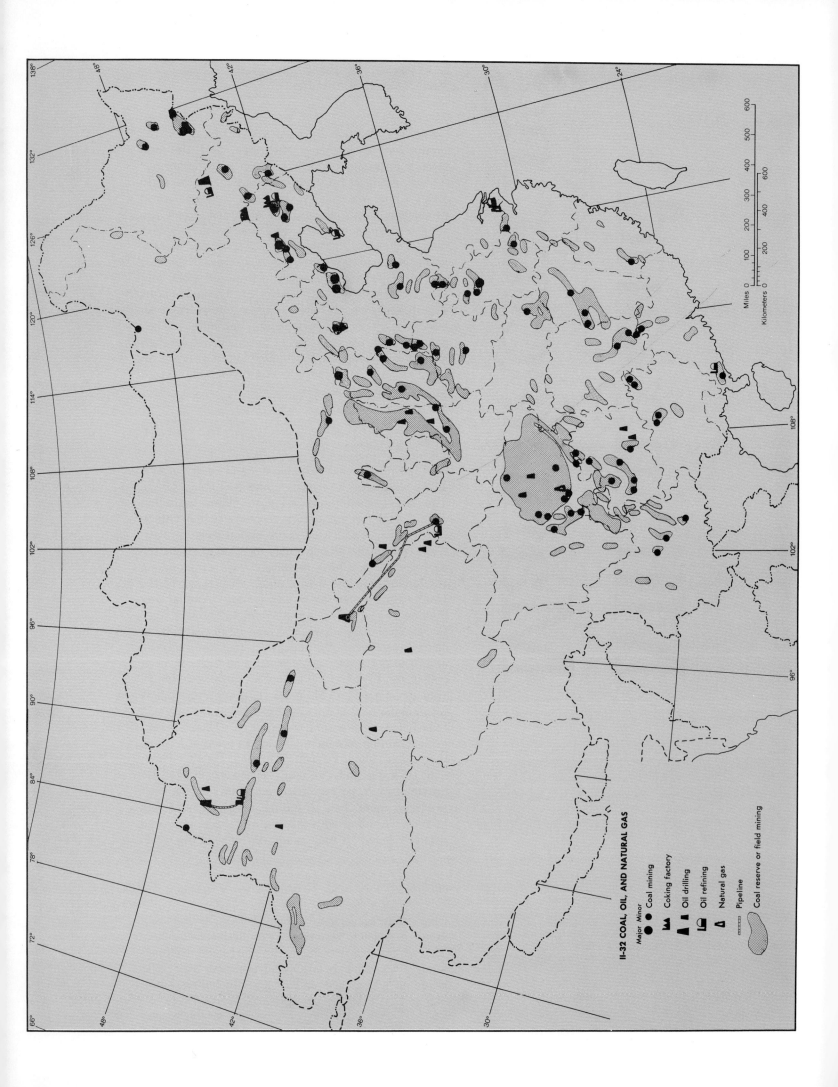

II-32 COAL, OIL, AND NATURAL GAS

Major Minor
● ● Coal mining
◢ ◣ Coking factory
▲ ▲ Oil drilling
◖ ◗ Oil refining
△ △ Natural gas
╍╍╍╍ Pipeline
⬭ Coal reserve or field mining

Miles 0   100   200   300   400   500   600
Kilometers 0   200   400   600

lion tons of oil from shale. The most important producer of oil has been the Yü-men oil field in Kansu, where an oil refinery has been constructed to refine part of the output; the rest of the crude oil is transported to more distant oil refineries, even as far as Dairen in Manchuria. Another refinery for Yü-men oil is in the city of Lan-chou—China's largest oil refinery, constructed with Soviet technical aid. Total known reserves of oil at Yü-men are no less than 500 million tons. The oil production at this site began in 1939, and the output reached 800,000 tons in 1956. By now Yü-men is producing more than 1.5 million tons of crude petroleum products annually. The second most important location of oil reserves is the Sinkiang fields, with the main ones in the Dzungarian Basin, centered near Karamai. Karamai is beginning to surpass Yü-men in production, and will soon produce not less than 3 million tons a year. The third important region in oil output is the Yang-ch'eng oil field in Shansi. Rich oil-producing regions also exist in Ta-ch'ing in Manchuria, the Tsaidam Basin in Tsinghai Province, and central Szechwan (Map II-32).

Iron and Steel

Mainland China has an expanding iron and steel industry with potential annual steel production capacity soon to be 30 million tons (Map II-33). The industrial complexes of An-shan, Pao-t'ou, Wu-han, and Shanghai form the backbone of the Chinese iron and steel industry. An-shan—the steel capital of China in Liaoning Province in Manchuria—produces about a third of the nation's output and is one of the ten largest iron and steel complexes in the world, with an annual capacity of nearly 5 million tons of pig iron, 6 million tons of crude steel, and over 5 million tons of rolled products. An-shan operates over 40 mines, mills, and fabrication plants with a total working force of 170,000 people. The local iron ore deposit alone has 5 billion tons of iron ore. Pao-t'ou in Inner Mongolia is another prominent location of iron ore, with 2 billion tons of reserve. The third important location of iron ore reserves is the Ta-yeh deposit in Central China along the Yangtze, in the vicinity of Wu-han.

Another important steel center is Shanghai. Shanghai has to rely on pig iron from other centers, particularly Ma-an-shan in Anhwei, but nonetheless plays a crucial role in the production of finished steel. Shanghai's steel output in 1961 was between 1.5 and 2 million tons.

In addition, iron ore deposits discovered in 1958 in Kansu and in the Tsaidam are now giving rise to the development of centers there and in Sinkiang.

Other Metals

Mainland China's nonferrous metal industries can be divided into two components, namely the nonferrous base metals—copper, lead, and zinc—and other nonferrous metals which are largely exported—tin, antimony (stibnite), tungsten, mercury, and bismuth (Map II-34). The leading base metal smelters include Shen-yang (copper, lead, and zinc by-products) and Hu-lu-tao in Manchuria (zinc and lead by-products); Chiang-hua in Hunan (lead and zinc); Ma-lung in Yunnan (copper); and Shanghai (scrap metals).

Tin heads the list of nonferrous export metals. Reserves are able to support a 30,000-ton annual output. The Ko-chiu area in Yunnan is still the backbone of the Chinese tin industry, as it supplies about two-thirds of China's total output. Much progress has been made in expanding facilities, streamlining operations, and upgrading products.

In the face of a weakening world market, the Chinese antimony industry, still the largest in the world in terms of output and reserves, is not producing as much as in the past. Hsi-kuang Shan in Hunan remains China's principal center for stibnite: The integrated facilities there produce most of the country's mine output, as well as the high-grade refined products.

China has led the world in the production of tungsten concentrates for many years, much of the output being exported. Production in 1961 was estimated to be 20,000 tons of 68 percent concentrates; however, statistics on actual output in recent years have been a closely guarded secret. Mercury (cinnabar) is another traditional export mineral of China. Mercury deposits are widespread, with the principal centers of production being the T'ung-jen area in Kweichow and Feng-huang in Hunan. China is also one of the leading producers of bismuth—a rank gained by producing in 1961 approximately one-tenth of the world total. Kwangtung is said to be the foremost bismuth-producing area in China. Other areas of production are in Kwangsi and Hunan.

More than 5 percent of the world's manganese ore is produced in China. The deposits are located south of the Yangtze, stretching from Kiangsi westward through Hunan, Kwangtung, and Kwangsi to Kweichow. Little current information is available on Chinese molybdenum. The Chin-chou area in western Liaoning, the largest molybdenum producer in China for many years, formerly accounted for perhaps three-fourths of the national output. Other producing sites exist in Liaoning, and some molybdenum is recovered as a by-product of tungsten mining in Kiangsi, Kwangtung, and Kwangsi. Deposits have also been reported in Fukien, Chekiang, and Sinkiang.

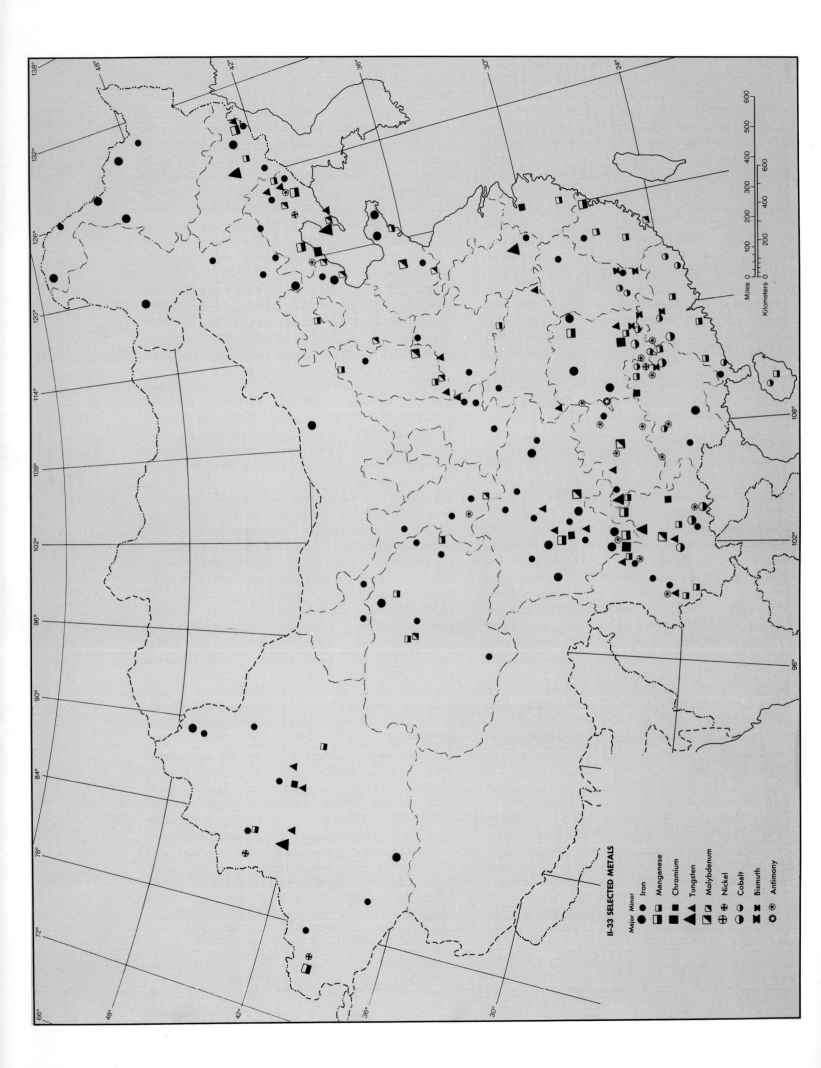

II-33 SELECTED METALS

	Major	Minor	
Iron	●	●	
Manganese	◨	◨	
Chromium	■	■	
Tungsten	▲	▲	
Molybdenum	◩	◩	
Nickel	⊕	⊕	
Cobalt	◖	◖	
Bismuth	✖	✖	
Antimony	✳	✳	

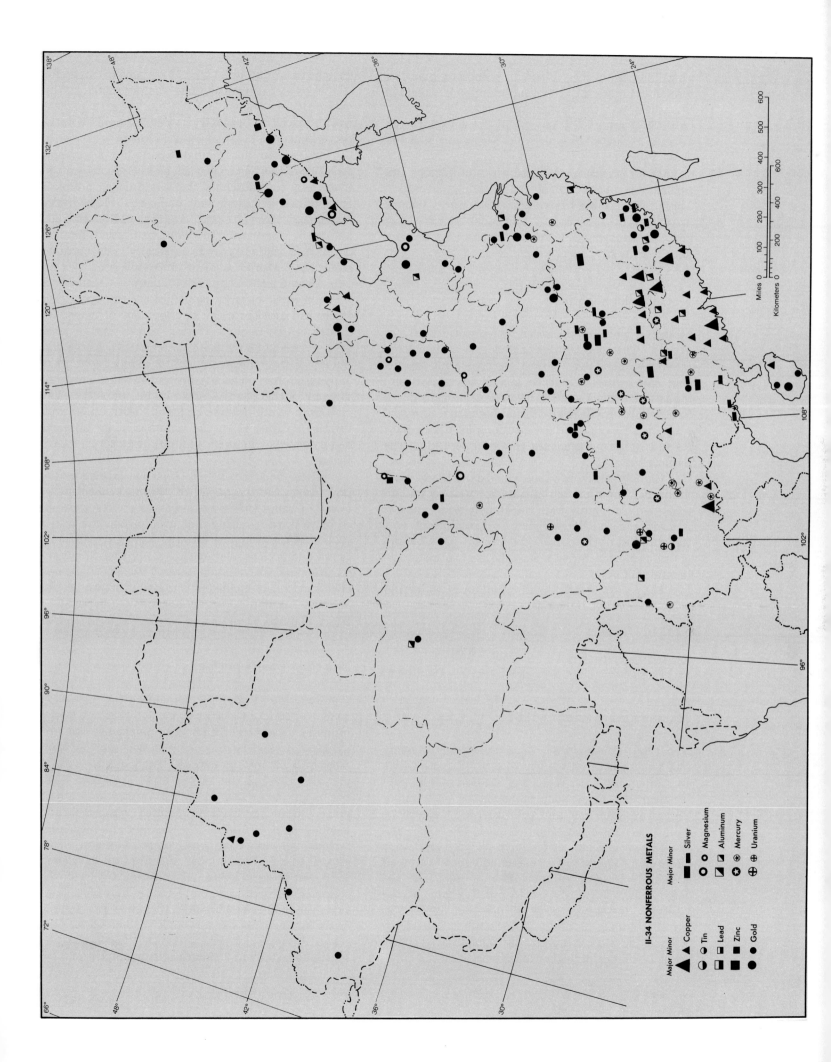

II-34 NONFERROUS METALS

Mainland China has a small integrated aluminum industry. The Fu-shun reduction plant in Manchuria and the Nan-ting aluminum plant in Shantung are the largest producers at present. Other large integrated centers have been constructed at Sian in Shensi Province and Kuei-yang in Kweichow Province.

China produces small quantities of magnesium, presumably at Ying-k'ou in Liaoning Province. Magnesite resources have long been world famous for extensive reserves and high quality. The best deposits are located in the Hai-ch'eng area in Liaoning Province.

Nonmetallic Minerals

Mainland China ranks second as a world producer of salt. Output in 1961 was about 14 million tons. Most salt is still used for food purposes, but production has increasingly been geared to meet future industrial demands. The provinces bordering the Yellow Sea traditionally have been the principal producers. Szechwan has also long been noted for its salt wells and produces about 10 percent of the national total.

China's sulfur raw material base shows some promise. The pyrite output in 1961 was 1.2 million tons, derived mainly from the Hsiang Shan mine in Anhwei and the Ying-te mine in Kwangtung. Although most of the pyrite goes into the manufacture of sulfuric acid, nearly a third is used to make elemental sulfur.

Map II-35 shows the distribution of these and other nonmetallic minerals.

MANUFACTURING

Manufacturing Prior to 1952

The rapid development of an industrial economy has been considered the key to strengthening China to compete with the West, and the Communist government has made such industrialization a major part of its economic and political policy. Socialization, mechanization, improvement of skills, and creation of new industries have all been part of a program of ambitious economic and social transformation. Despite disappointments such as the Great Leap Forward and the dislocations of the Cultural Revolution, progress has been impressive on all fronts. Although China still is considered a lesser developed country, its industrial level has risen dramatically in the last twenty years.

Prior to World War II, China was by no means an industrial nation. Only 17 percent of the value of the gross national product was accounted for by manufactured goods, and of this, only 10 percent was from heavy industry. Furthermore, a large proportion of China's prewar industry was owned by foreign capital. China exported a significant quantity of raw materials such as iron ore and cotton fiber, only to repurchase them as finished products from industrial nations such as Japan. Major heavy machinery, railroad cars, engines, and even rails had to be imported. In addition, China's foreign-dominated industry was spatially concentrated along the eastern coast and in Manchuria.

Although the Japanese occupation of Manchuria was a serious blow to the Chinese, the occupying forces did accelerate the development of heavy industry in that region. During World War II, however, even the heroic feats accomplished in moving industrial equipment inland to escape advancing Japanese forces could not prevent heavy damage to virtually all facets of China's infant industry. The civil war which followed spread destruction even further, so that when the Communist government came to power in 1949, industry was seriously deficient.

The period from 1949 to 1952 was labeled by the government as the period of "People's Reconstruction." During this time intensive efforts were directed toward restoring industrial production to the 1936 levels, the highest prewar standard. Concurrently and in close relationship, the process of nationalization and socialization began. By 1952 all phases of industry had equaled or surpassed prewar levels, and the Communist government was prepared to begin planned economic advances.

The First Five-Year Plan

The First Five-Year Plan, announced for the period 1952 to 1957, emphasized development of heavy industry, decentralization, improvement and expansion of existing industrial bases, and development of basic new industries. Although Soviet aid provided the impetus for the First Five-Year Plan, the most important source of capital was profit gained from government-operated industrial and commercial enterprises. The Soviets provided technicians and industrial plant components and plans, as well as a limited amount of capital through long-term, low-interest loans. A substantial part of the commitment had been completed by mid-1960; however, the final Soviet break at that time was a major crisis for the Chinese, especially in areas where the Soviet advisers not only withdrew their own expertise but also took the plans for plant completion.

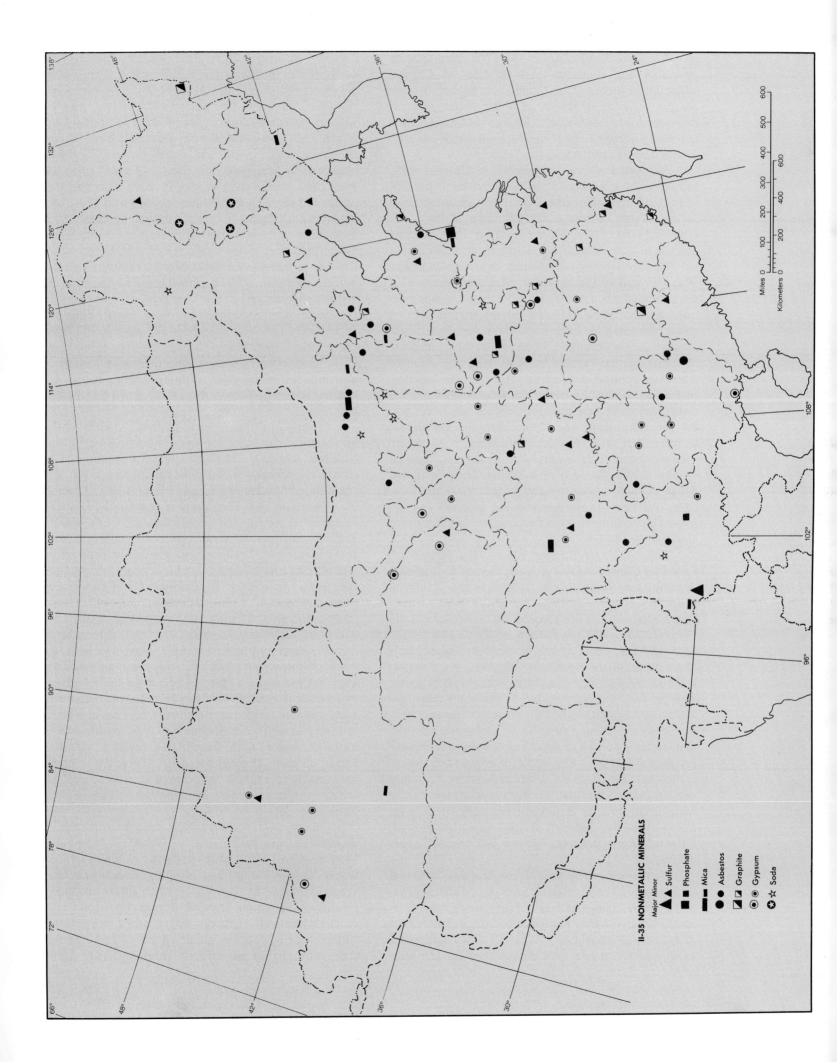

II-35 NONMETALLIC MINERALS

	Major	Minor	
Sulfur	▲	▲	
Phosphate	■	■	
Mica	▬	▮	
Asbestos	●	●	
Graphite	◣	◪	
Gypsum	◉	◉	
Soda	✪	☆	

An important feature of the First Plan was its provision for thorough investigation of China's natural resources. The search proved highly successful, claiming discovery of 88 important mineral deposits distributed widely throughout China. This inventory helped to provide the base for developing new industrial centers in the interior.

As stated above, 70 percent of China's early industrial base had been concentrated in 10 percent of its land area along the coast, located in response to the foreign interests which dominated the country's industry. The First Five-Year Plan pointed out the military vulnerability of this arrangement—so disastrously proven during the Sino-Japanese War—as well as the economic disadvantages of this coastal concentration. Not only were the undeveloped interior areas allowed to stagnate, but in most cases the coastal industries were far from their sources of raw materials. Thus time, labor, and use of scarce transportation facilities were all added to the basic cost of production. One of the primary principles behind the new Plan was to locate industries near their raw material sources and markets. At the same time, the Plan called for systematic coordination of agriculture and industry, to create closely knit industrial-agricultural regions. Special emphasis was placed on the border areas, both because of their mineral resources and strategic location, and because the government planned to integrate the peripheral minority peoples more fully into the Chinese nation.

Following the Russian model, the First Plan called for developing key cities as centers for regional development. Harbin was to become the industrial heart of Manchuria; Tientsin, of the North China Plain; Shanghai, of the Yangtze Delta; Wu-han of the Central Basins Region; Canton, of the Canton Delta; Sian and Lan-chou, of the Northwest Region; and Chungking, of the Southwest Region. Each region was to specialize in the products best suited to its resources and environment, but at the same time, defense requirements called for as much regional economic self-sufficiency as feasible. Defense needs also dictated the location of industrial centers in relatively invulnerable areas. Since 1958, however, this decentralization plan has been de-emphasized in the industrialization process and has been meshed more fully with agricultural development. Since the Great Leap Forward the development of the interior has slowed, although some progress toward the original goals continues.

In planning new capital construction, regional development constituted a keynote, while sources of raw materials and fuel supply, market centers, and national security became the major determinants of industrial locations. As a result of adherence to this policy, a new pattern emerged for the location of China's iron and steel industry, which was designed to provide the nuclei for the regional development programs (Map II-36). In terms of the Plan's regional distribution of industrial plants, Manchuria ranked first, followed by the Southwest, North and Northwest China, Central China, Inner Mongolia, East China, and South China. In these construction programs, the most important projects were the rehabilitation of the An-shan mills and the construction of those now at Wu-han and Pao-t'ou. Thus initiation of the construction of these two latter iron and steel centers during the First Five-Year Plan has often been cited by Communist Chinese authors as an outstanding example of establishing new industry at places close to the supply of fuel, raw materials, and markets while satisfying the locational requirements of national defense. In general, however, in spite of the plan to disperse the iron and steel plants during the First Five-Year Plan, production remained concentrated in Liaoning Province in Manchuria, although there has been healthy growth of iron and steel smelting in the northwest.

Progress in the chemical industry is considered an essential aspect of the development of an industrialized economy, and although China is rich in chemical resources, it depended on imports to supply the bulk of its chemical needs before 1949. During the First Five-Year Plan there were especially significant increases in the production of pure alkali, sulfates, automobile tires, chemical fertilizers, and pesticides. In 1954 China began to export both acids and alkalis. New centers for basic chemical production were developed at Dairen and Kirin, while Shanghai and Nanking became major centers for processing east China's rich chemical resources. The Tientsin–T'ang-ku area in North China was developed to produce consumer goods as well as basic chemical materials. Small-scale plants, which grew up throughout the southwest to manufacture synthetics during World War II, were also modernized. Before 1949 the northwest has no chemical industry at all, but Lan-chou has now grown into a national center, with coordinated plastics and fertilizer plants. During the early 1950s the central and southern regions had no large-scale chemical industry, but even here small-scale fertilizer plants have now developed widely.

One of the most basic light industries is textile production, and in this area too the First Five-Year Plan brought significant changes. China's traditional hand-spinning and weaving crafts were severely damaged by competition with cheap machine-produced, imported textiles during the first half of the twentieth century, and a large portion of China's raw cotton was exported for processing and then repurchased as finished products. By 1960

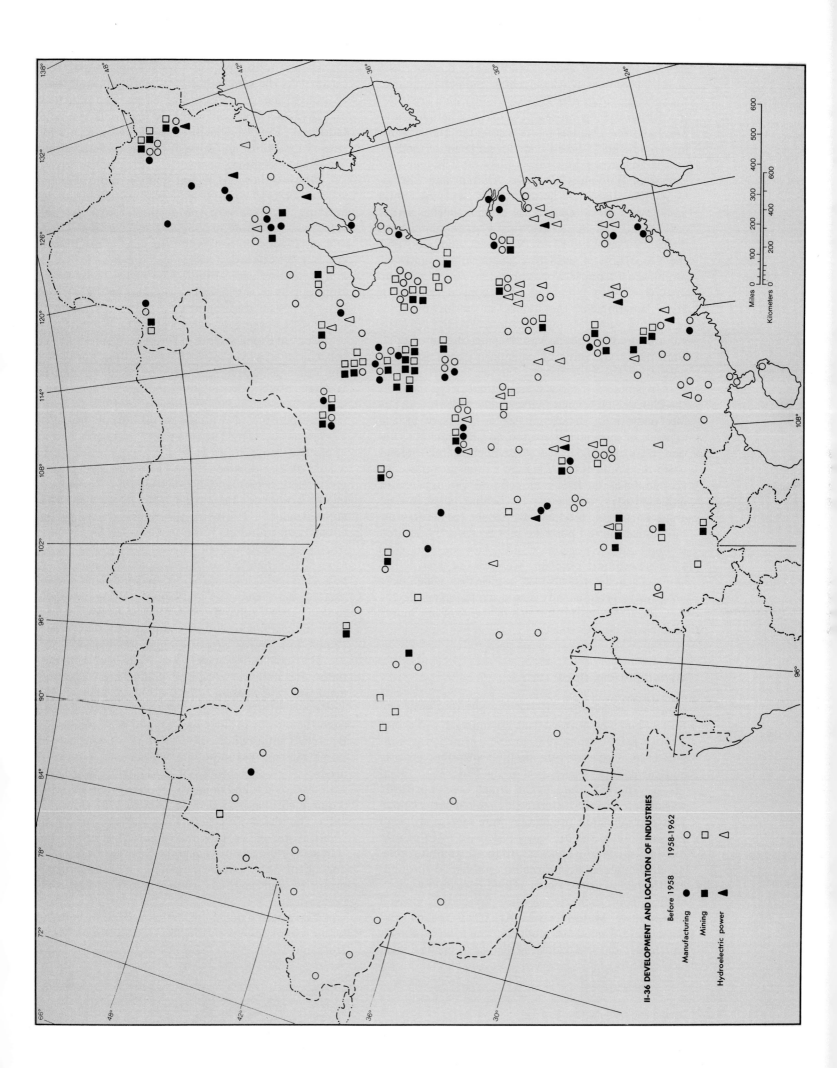

II-36 DEVELOPMENT AND LOCATION OF INDUSTRIES

	Before 1958	1958–1962
Manufacturing	●	○
Mining	■	□
Hydroelectric power	◀	◁

this situation had been altered by the development of textile centers at Cheng-chou, Shih-chia-chuang, Sian, Hsien-yang, and Peking, all of which are close to cotton-growing areas. The older Shanghai and Tientsin mills also increased production and streamlined operation. In addition, development of modern textile industries has taken place at Chi-nan and Tsingtao, Wu-han, Ch'ang-sha, Dairen, and Chungking. Smaller-scale spinning and weaving mills have grown up in most of the cotton-growing areas.

During the First Five-Year Plan economic productivity increased 17 to 18 percent annually, and the proportion of industrial goods in the national product rose from 26.7 percent in 1952 to 39.1 percent in 1956. Heavy industrial goods rose in value from about one-third of the industrial production total in 1952 to just over one-half in 1957. By 1957 the value of producer goods was 290 percent that of 1952, while the 1957 value of consumer goods was 174 percent of the 1952 figure.

In spite of these successes there were flaws in the Plan, which became evident only when it was put into operation. Overemphasis on industry at the expense of agriculture created an unbalanced situation in which agricultural production fell behind basic requirements. A similar criticism applied to the emphasis on heavy industry at the expense of light industry, which fell far behind in such vital areas as textile production. Goals for large-scale mechanization did not take into account the limited training and experience of the workers, and thus serious technical problems were encountered. The emphasis on defense also led to measures which were not always economically sound, as for example the decision not to make full use of the existing industrial bases on the coast.

Manufacturing since 1957

However, encouraged by the overall success of the First Plan, the government announced a Second Plan to extend from 1957 to 1962, which was supposed to accelerate the industrialization process and correct the weaknesses of the First Plan (Map II-37). In 1958, the slogan "Great Leap Forward" was adopted to characterize this movement. In one year coal and iron production were increased by 40 percent, but in the urgency to increase rates of production, much of what was produced was unusable. Small shops and steel furnaces established throughout the countryside, where individuals could work in their leisure time to increase production, proved disastrous. Materials (mostly scrap metal) and labor were wasted on products which were almost worthless, and the sudden attempts to change techniques of production led to inefficiency and confusion. At the same time, 1959 and 1960 were years of drought and crop failure, which resulted in famine and inadequate supplies of raw materials for light industry. Finally, the Russian withdrawal in 1960 caused an additional economic crisis, complicating the whole situation.

Despite these setbacks, some significant gains were made under the Second Plan. Behind the increasing importance of the northwest was the construction, beginning in 1958, of two sizable new iron and steel works in Sinkiang. In view of the discovery in 1958 of extensive iron ore deposits in Kansu and the subsequent organization of the Chiu-ch'uan Iron and Steel Corporation, comparable in scale to Pao-t'ou Steel, the importance of the northwest is likely to increase.

Central China's share of the overall blast furnace capacity increased 30-fold between 1957 and 1961. For this spectacular gain, major credit is due to Wu-han Steel, whose iron-smelting capacity rose from a base of virtually nothing in 1957 to more than 8 percent of China's total output in 1961. There was also considerable growth in the production of electric power (Map II-38).

In 1960 intensive efforts to restore agricultural production began under the heading "Agriculture as the economic foundation; industry as the economic leader." However, the decision to stop the Great Leap in industry was not reached until 1961, when the "backyard industries" were closed down after being publicly recognized as inefficient. A policy of industrial stabilization was then begun. In 1962 the policy was announced as one of simultaneous attention to the coordination of agriculture, light industry, and heavy industry, in that order. Production figures were no longer published.

By 1963 the economy had recovered substantially, and a slower program of industrial advancement was inaugurated. Partially as a result of the experience of the Russian withdrawal, the emphasis from 1963 to the present has been on self-sufficiency. By 1967 China, which used to import two-thirds of its petroleum, was supplying 88 percent of its own needs. A greater variety of high-quality new products, designed to aid domestic sources to fill national requirements, appeared from 1963 to 1967 (Map II-39). The Third Five-Year Plan was announced in 1966 but was never fully implemented because of the "Great Proletarian Cultural Revolution." The impact of that two-year period of restructuring priorities and methods cannot yet be fully comprehended.

The relative degree of industrialization and the broad economic regions of China are shown on Maps II-40 and II-41.

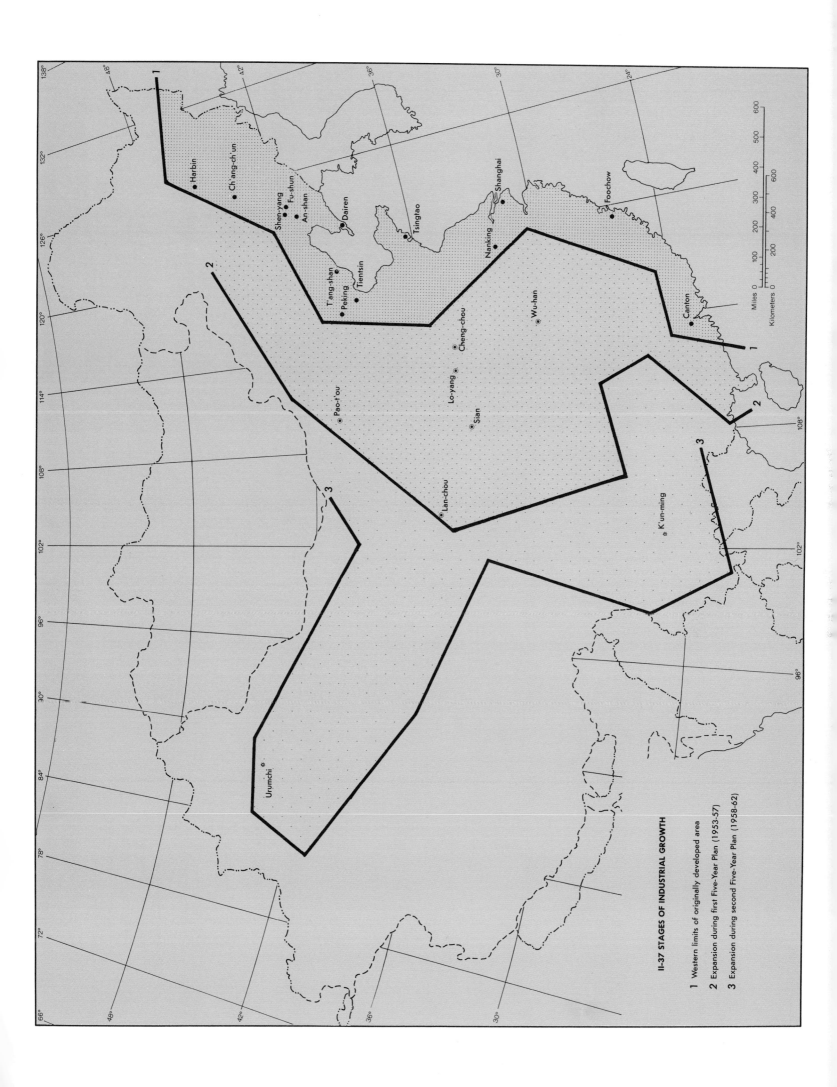

II-37 STAGES OF INDUSTRIAL GROWTH

1 Western limits of originally developed area
2 Expansion during first Five-Year Plan (1953-57)
3 Expansion during second Five-Year Plan (1958-62)

Harbin
Ch'ang-ch'un
Shen-yang
Fu-shun
An-shan
Dairen
T'ang-shan
Peking
Tientsin
Tsingtao
Nanking
Shanghai
Foochow
Wu-han
Cheng-chou
Pao-t'ou
Lo-yang
Sian
Lan-chou
Canton
K'un-ming
Urumchi

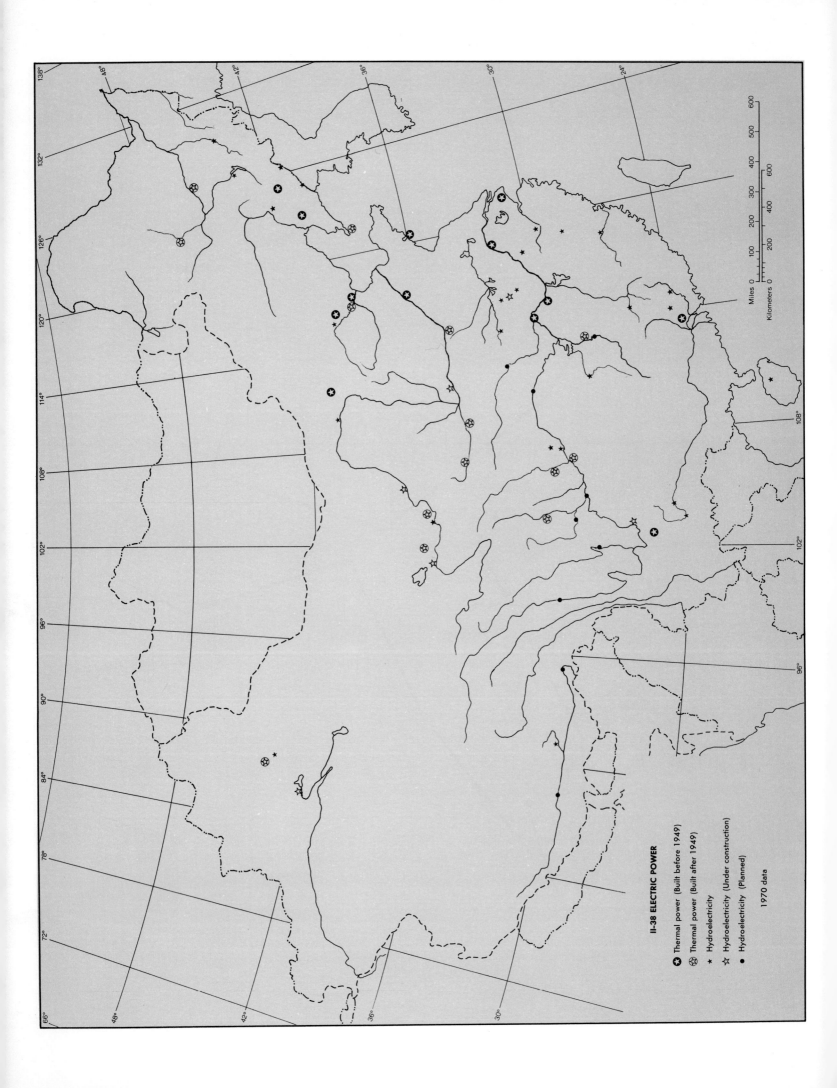

II-38 ELECTRIC POWER

- ⊛ Thermal power (Built before 1949)
- ⊛ Thermal power (Built after 1949)
- ★ Hydroelectricity
- ☆ Hydroelectricity (Under construction)
- ⬤ Hydroelectricity (Planned)

1970 data

Miles 0 100 200 300 400 500 600
Kilometers 0 200 400 600

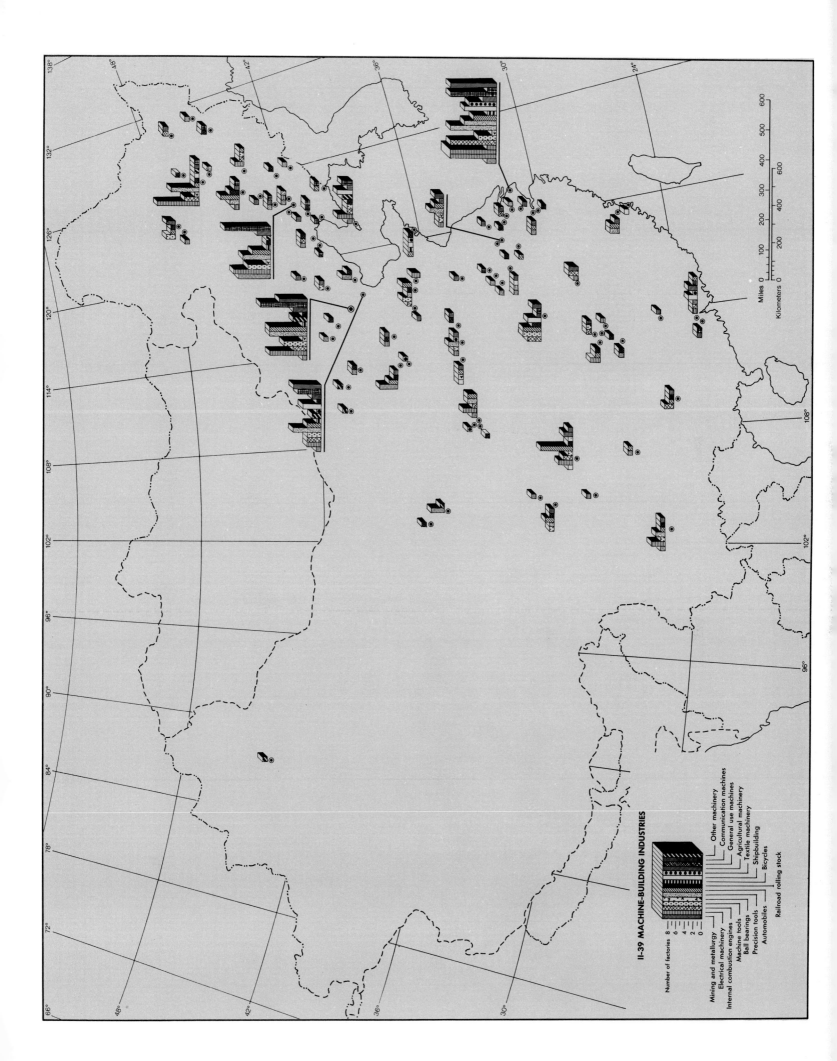

II-39 MACHINE-BUILDING INDUSTRIES

Number of factories
8
6
4
2
0

Mining and metallurgy
Electrical machinery
Internal combustion engines
Machine tools
Ball bearings
Precision tools
Automobiles
Other machinery
Communication machines
General use machines
Agricultural machinery
Textile machinery
Shipbuilding
Bicycles
Railroad rolling stock

Miles 0   100   200   300   400   500   600
Kilometers 0   200   300   400   600

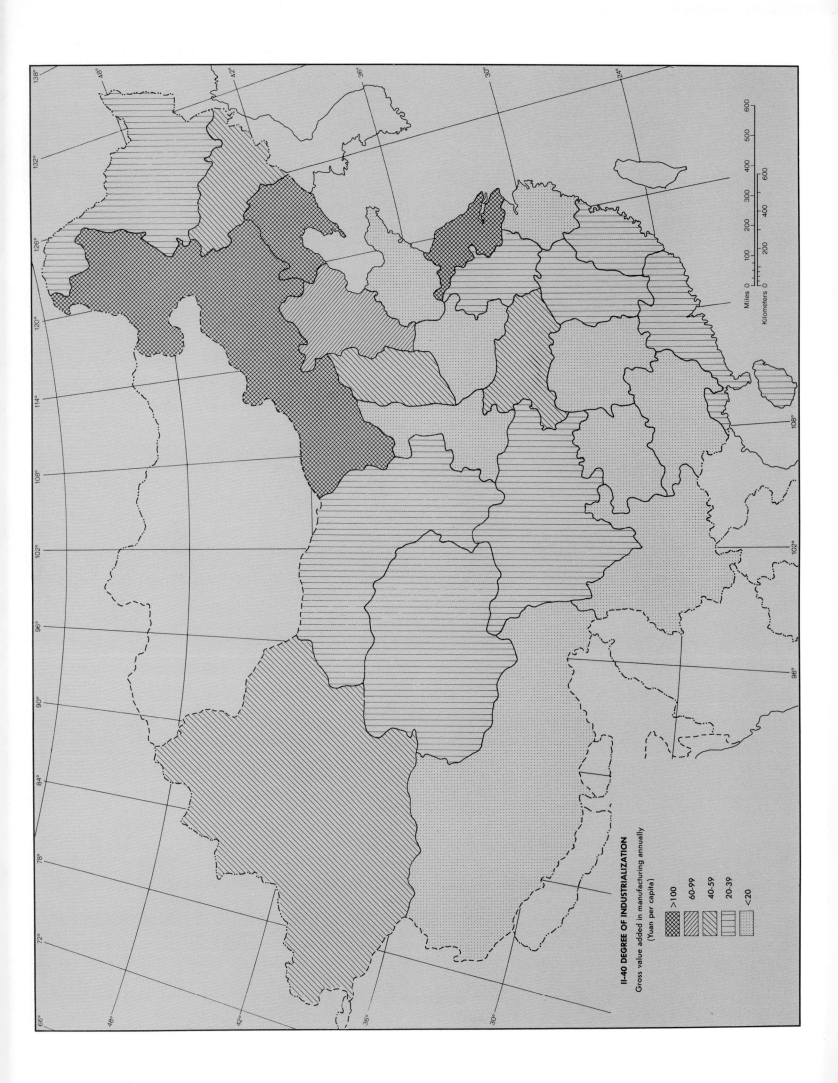

II-40 DEGREE OF INDUSTRIALIZATION

Gross value added in manufacturing annually
(Yuan per capita)

>100

60-99

40-59

20-39

<20

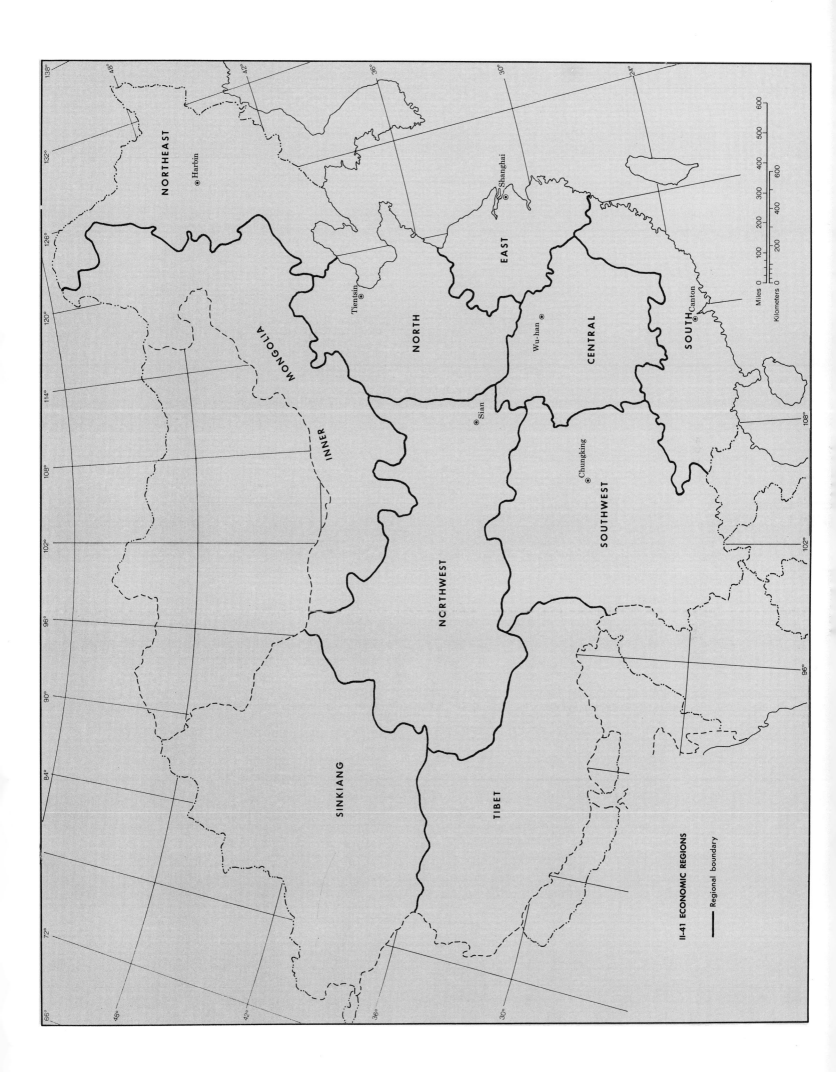

NORTHEAST

⊙ Harbin

MONGOLIA

INNER

Tientsin ⊙

NORTH

EAST

Shanghai ⊙

Wu-han ⊙

CENTRAL

⊙ Sian

SOUTH Canton ⊙

Chungking ⊙

SOUTHWEST

NORTHWEST

SINKIANG

TIBET

II-41 ECONOMIC REGIONS

—— Regional boundary

Miles 0   100   200   300   400   500   600
Kilometers 0 200   400   600

III. REGIONAL

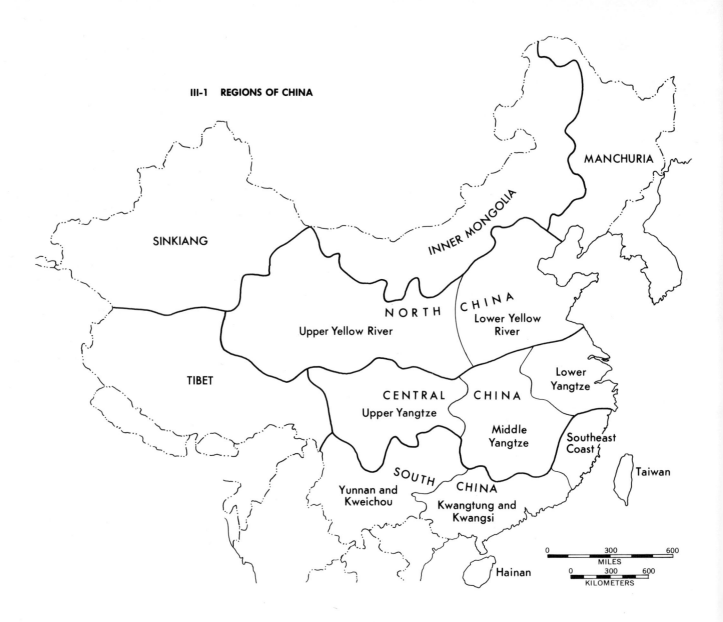

III-1 REGIONS OF CHINA

MANCHURIA

SINKIANG

INNER MONGOLIA

NORTH CHINA
Upper Yellow River

Lower Yellow River

TIBET

Lower Yangtze

CENTRAL CHINA
Upper Yangtze

Middle Yangtze

Southeast Coast

SOUTH CHINA

Yunnan and Kweichou

Kwangtung and Kwangsi

Taiwan

Hainan

0   300   600
MILES

0   300   600
KILOMETERS

North China

North China has been divided into two regions: the Lower Yellow River, including the North China Plain, and the Upper Yellow River (Map III-2).

THE LOWER YELLOW RIVER REGION

The Lower Yellow River Region includes the provinces of Hopeh, Honan, Shantung, and Shansi and the municipalities of Tientsin and Peking, the latter directly under the central government (Map III-3). The region has an area of about 671,000 square kilometers, or 7 percent of the total area of the country. The total population is approximately 171 million, or approximately a quarter of the country's total.

The Lower Yellow River Region is one of the best-defined geographic regions of China. In the west, following the western bank of the Yellow River, is the plateau and mountain area of Shensi Province. The eastern boundary is the coastline of the Yellow Sea and the Gulf of Chihli (Po Hai). The weakly defined watershed of the Huai Ho forms the southern border. To the north, the Great Wall with its mountainous terrain is the border of the region.

There are several passes in the north which have served in the past as invasion routes for the nomads and which today function as major transportation routes. The two best known passes are Shan-hai-kuan in the east and Chu-yun-kuan in the west. *Shan-hai-kuan* means "the mountain-sea pass," and describes the area where mountains underlying the Great Wall meet the sea. In the seventeenth century the Manchus invaded China through this pass, and now the Peking–Shen-yang double-tracked main line passes through here, linking Manchuria to the heart of China. The Chu-yun-kuan (Pass) is located in the mountains just northwest of Peking. During World War II the Japanese army used this pass in one of its invasion thrusts into China from the Manchurian-Mongolian border region. The Peking–Chang-chia-k'ou Railroad today connects North China with Inner Mongolia by way of this pass. Thus Chu-yun-kuan is vital as a link to Inner Mongolia and Shan-hai-kuan plays a similar role for Manchuria.

In the southern margin of the region just south of the Huai Ho, the lower hills are also interrupted by a low pass, through which the Peking-Hankow trunk line extends.

Topographically the region may be divided into three parts: the North China Plain, the Shantung Hills, and the plateau and mountain area of Shansi.

The North China Plain is also called the Yellow River Plain, and owes its existence to the deposi-

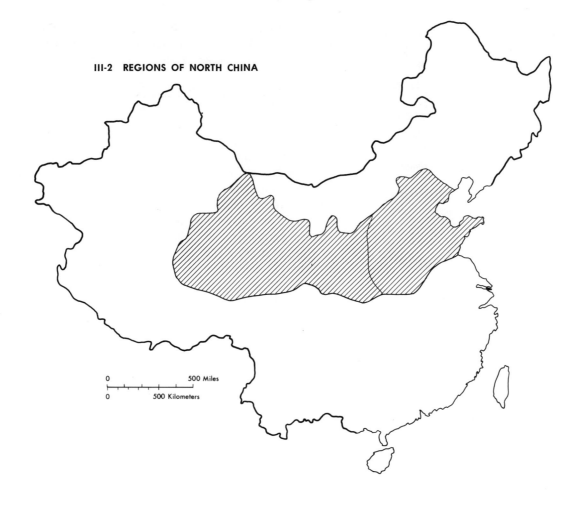

0   500 Miles

0   500 Kilometers

III-3   POLITICAL

tional action of the Yellow River. In earlier geological time this plain was part of a sea, which included the present Gulf of Chihli (Po Hai) and the Yellow Sea, and in which the Shantung Hills rose as isolated islands. The Yellow River brought silt from the loess upland and gradually formed the present alluvial plain. The silt deposition is several thousand feet deep, as revealed by wells drilled in the area. The North China Plain is the most important level region of China, and contrasts sharply with the bordering mountains to the north and west, which rise to more than 1,000 meters above the lowland. The plain can be conceived as a large-scale alluvial fan over which the course of the Yellow River has swept back and forth (Map III-4). Throughout the centuries, the Chinese have labored to contain the river with dikes, which have been raised ever higher as the river bed has been built up by silt deposits. Since the Yellow River now flows at an elevation higher than the surrounding countryside, it receives no tributaries throughout its entire lower course. The North China Plain has an area of approximately 320,000 square kilometers, nearly as large as that of the Manchurian Plain. However, while the former is a depositional plain, the latter is an erosional one (Maps III-5 and III-6).

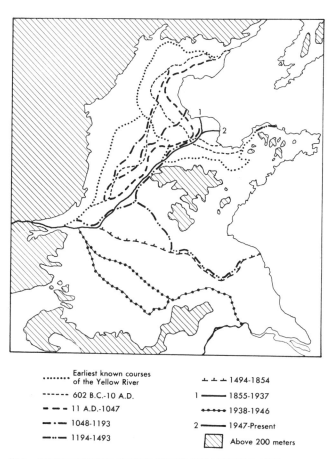

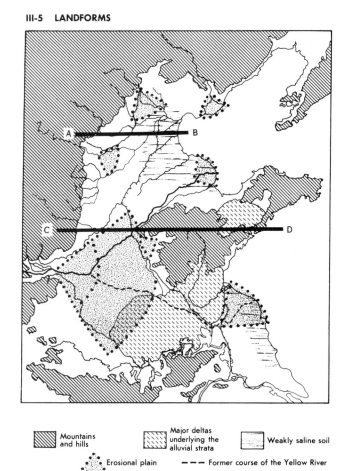

Earliest known courses
of the Yellow River

------ 602 B.C.-10 A.D.

– — — 11 A.D.-1047

— ·— 1048-1193

—··— 1194-1493

⊥ ⊥ ⊥ 1494-1854

1 ——— 1855-1937

•—•—• 1938-1946

2 ——— 1947-Present

▨ Above 200 meters

III-4   CHANGES IN THE COURSE OF THE YELLOW RIVER AND EXTENSION OF ITS DELTA

▨ Mountains and hills

▨ Major deltas underlying the alluvial strata

▨ Weakly saline soil

⦿ Erosional plain

– – – Former course of the Yellow River

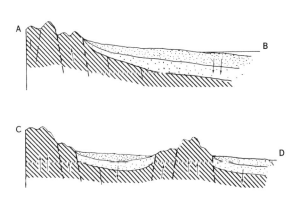

The Shantung Peninsula is composed of ancient metamorphic and igneous rocks that were formerly islands and are now hills which have resisted the forces of weathering.   The highest peak of the peninsula is T'ai Shan, with an elevation of less than 2,000 meters. A basic extrusive rock standing out sharply in fault scarps above the surrounding plain, it has been a famous resort and religious shrine since ancient times.

The Shansi Plateau is bordered by the Yellow River on the west and south, and on the east by the T'ai-hang Shan, which form the edge of the plateau. The rivers which cross the mountain edge and flow eastward onto the plain have made many gaps which have become important communication links. Faulting has produced numerous basins and valleys, notably the valley around the city of T'ai-yüan and along the banks of the Fen Ho, the principal river of the province.

The climate of the region plays an important role in the life of the peasants. Seasonal variations in temperature are primarily a result, during the winter, of air movements from the great continental land mass to the north and east and, during the summer, of cooling air masses from the Pacific Ocean. With high winds, winter temperatures often

drop to − 16°C, whereas summer temperatures may rise to 38°C. The average annual rainfall is less than 750 millimeters, but rainfall varies considerably from year to year. Most of the rain falls from June to August, often in the form of heavy downpours, with periodic droughts in May and June presenting a serious problem for farmers. Moreover, since the plain is so poorly drained, excessive rainfall is very damaging to crops.

The land has been cultivated for so long that natural vegetation is seldom found except in the mountains. In these mountainous areas, most of the trees are deciduous or broadleaf evergreen, and there are very few conifers.

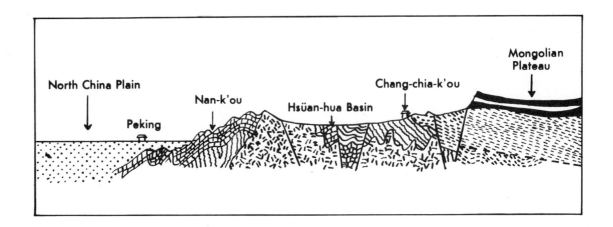

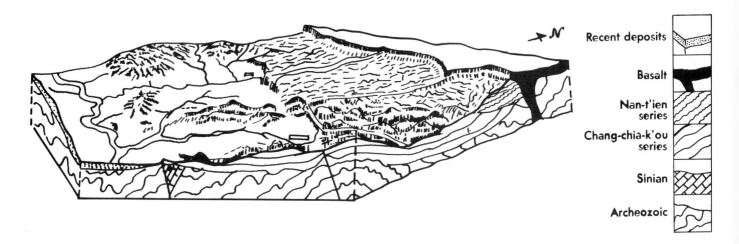

Recent deposits

Basalt

Nan-t'ien series

Chang-chia-k'ou series

Sinian

Archeozoic

The loess soils of the Shansi Plateau contain little organic matter but abundant mineral substances for crop cultivation. Because of a lack of natural vegetation, and because loess is so easily washed or blown away, soil erosion is serious. Much of what has been eroded and carried seaward has come to rest on the North China Plain, leaving it covered by thick, fertile alluvium.

These fertile soils of the Lower Yellow River Region make it an outstanding agricultural area (Map III-7). Wheat is the leading grain; of the country's total output, 43 percent is grown in the Lower Yellow River Region. Wheat, millet, sorghum, soybeans, and maize are grown throughout the area. Cotton is the most important industrial crop, and the region produces 62 percent of the national total (Maps III-8 and III-9). More than a third of the North China Plain is currently irrigated (Map III-10).

A brown forest soil is found in the Shantung Hills. Such a soil is ideal for viticulture and for fruit trees, such as apple, pear, peach, and apricot; and the area is one of China's most important fruit-growing regions.

Hopeh Province is China's principal cotton producer, accounting for one-fifth of the country's output. Tientsin and Tsingtao have long-established textile mills; new centers include Peking, Shih-chia-chuang, Han-tan, and Cheng-chou.

Along the coast of the Shantung Peninsula, fishing is an important activity, with Tsingtao and Chefoo (Yen-t'ai) as its centers.

Rich reserves of both iron ore and coal form the basis of heavy industry in the Lower Yellow River area (Map III-11). The region's coal reserves account for one-half of China's total. The large production of salt—both sea salt along the Gulf of Chihli (Po Hai) and well salt in Shansi—and natural alkali

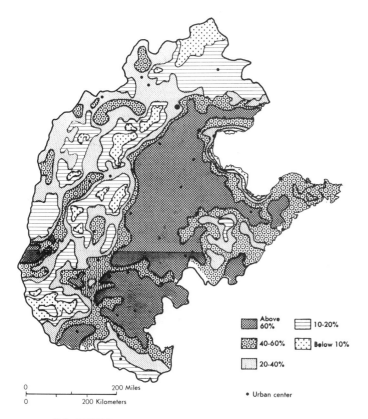

▓	Above 60%	≡	10-20%
⊚	40-60%	⋰	Below 10%
▦	20-40%		

0 ———— 200 Miles
0 ———— 200 Kilometers

• Urban center

III-7   PERCENT OF LAND CULTIVATED

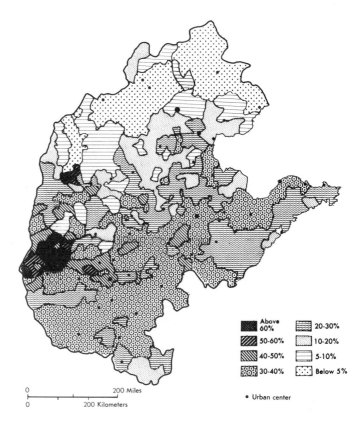

■	Above 60%	≡	20-30%
▨	50-60%	▦	10-20%
▧	40-50%	≣	5-10%
⊚	30-40%	⋰	Below 5%

0 ———— 200 Miles
0 ———— 200 Kilometers

• Urban center

III-8   PERCENT OF CULTIVATED LAND IN WHEAT

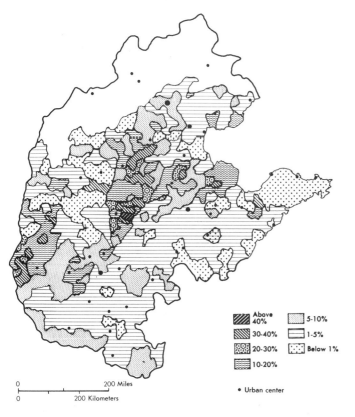

▨	Above 40%	▧	5-10%
▨	30-40%	≡	1-5%
⊚	20-30%	⋰	Below 1%
▦	10-20%		

0 ———— 200 Miles
0 ———— 200 Kilometers

• Urban center

III-9   PERCENT OF CULTIVATED LAND IN COTTON

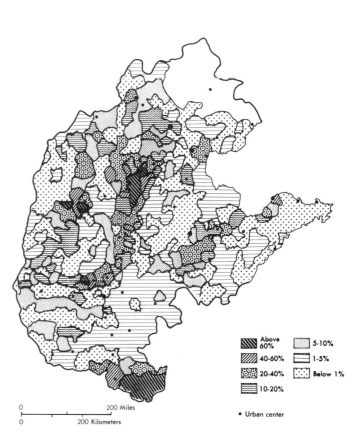

▨	Above 60%	▧	5-10%
▧	40-60%	≡	1-5%
⊚	20-40%	⋰	Below 1%
▦	10-20%		

0 ———— 200 Miles
0 ———— 200 Kilometers

• Urban center

III-10   PERCENT OF CULTIVATED LAND IRRIGATED

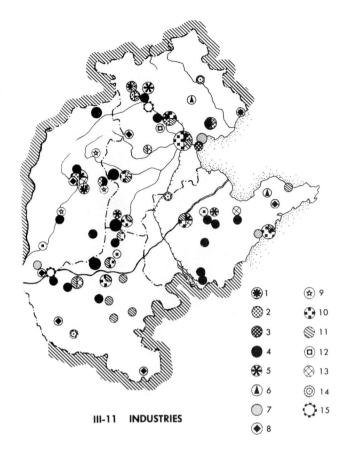

III-11 INDUSTRIES

1.	Machinery
2.	Iron and steel
3.	Chemicals
4.	Coal mining
5.	Iron ore mining
6.	Gold mining
7.	Salt production

8.	Gypsum, asbestos, and graphite mining
9.	Sulfur mining
10.	Textiles
11.	Food processing
12.	Tile and bricks
13.	Diverse industries
14.	Regional economic center
15.	Hydroelectric power station

reservoirs make the region a potential focus of the chemical industry. Coal mining is an important activity, since not only the area's own coal demands, but also those of other regions, have increased. Ta-t'ung and T'ai-yüan are the main coal production centers. The cement industry has also expanded: In addition to the original cement factory at T'ai-yüan, there is a new one at Ta-t'ung.

The Lower Yellow River Region ranks high in terms of railroad mileage; it is second only to Manchuria in the development of its railroad network. Four trunk lines radiate from Peking. (1) The Peking-Shen-yang Railroad extends north along the coastal plain at Shan-hai-kuan. (2) The Tientsin-Nanking Railroad links Peking with the Yangtze delta area. (3) One of the longest railroads in China today is the Peking-Canton Railway, which connects Peking and Canton by way of Cheng-chou on the Yellow River and Wu-han on the Yangtze. (4) The Peking-Pao-t'ou Railroad joins Peking and Inner Mongolia. In addition to these trunk lines, there are the east-west Lung-hai Railroad, and the Shih-chia-chuang-T'ai-yüan, Shih-chia-chuang-Te-chou, Tsingtao-Tsinan, and Ta-t'ung–P'u-k'ou lines.

The most important cities of the Lower Yellow River Region are Peking, Tientsin, Tsinan, Tsingtao, T'ai-yüan, Lo-yang, K'ai-feng, Chefoo, Ta-tung, and Cheng-chou. Peking has been intermittently the seat of China's government for a total of eight hundred years, and is the capital today. The city's population was reported to be 7.5 million in 1970. It lies in a strategically important location between Manchuria, Inner Mongolia, and the North China Plain, and is the historical, political, economic, and cultural center of the country.

THE UPPER YELLOW RIVER REGION

The provinces of Shensi, Kansu, Tsinghai, and Ningsia Hui Autonomous Region comprise this region, which has a land area of 1,610,000 square kilometers and a total population of more than 37 million (Map III-12). Its varied physical geography contributes to the transitional character of the region, which lies between humid, flat lowlands to the east and arid highlands to the west (Map III-13). The divide between the interior and exterior drainage systems of China occurs in the region, and it is also transitional between agriculture and animal husbandry. Many racial groups inhabit the region, including the Han, Tibetan, Hui, Mongolian, and Kazakh peoples. Of special historical importance to the region is the Kansu Corridor, which was served as a natural passage linking China with Central Asia. It was through this corridor in 122 B.C. that Chang-Ch'ien, an explorer who lived during the Han Dynasty, traveled to Central Asia; and in the seventh century A.D. Hsuan-Tsang, a well-known monk of the T'ang Dynasty, journeyed through Kansu to India. Marco Polo followed the same route when he came to China during the Yüan Dynasty (1279 A.D. to 1368 A.D.). As early as the Han Dynasty (206 B.C. to 220 A.D.), Chinese silk goods were sent to Central Asia and Europe through the Kansu Corridor, which became known as "the Silk Route."

The region may be divided into four physiographic regions, the first being the Tsinling-Ta-pa Shan area. The Tsinling Shan range, lying east-west across the lower third of Shensi Province, is broad and rugged; it is roughly paralleled by the Ta-pa Shan to the south, which stretch between Shensi and Szechwan. Between these two mountain systems the Han Shui flows east-southeast. Many low, flat-bottomed intermontane basins and valley plains are found along the banks of this river, the largest being the Han-chung Basin. Resembling the Szechwan Basin in vegetation, the Han-chung Basin is covered with fertile soil, has a warm, humid climate, and is therefore one of the chief agricultural centers of this region (Map III-14).

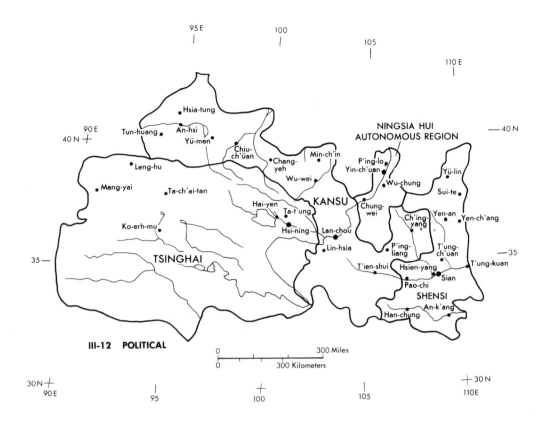

95 E   100   105   110 E

Hsia-tung

90 E   Tun-huang   An-hsi   NINGSIA HUI   40 N
40 N   Yü-men   AUTONOMOUS REGION

Chiu-   Min-ch'in   P'ing-lo   Yü-lin
ch'üan   Chang-   Yin-ch'uan
Leng-hu   yeh   Wu-wei   Wu-chung   Sui-te

Mang-yai   Ta-ch'ai-tan   Hai-yen   Ta-t'ung   KANSU   Chung-   Ch'ing-   Yen-an   Yen-ch'ang
wei   yang

Ko-erh-mu   Hsi-ning   Lan-chou   P'ing-   T'ung-
liang   ch'uan
35   Lin-hsia   T'ung-kuan   35
TSINGHAI   T'ien-shui   Hsien-yang
Pao-chi   Sian
An-k'ang
Han-chung   SHENSI

III-12   POLITICAL

0   300 Miles
0   300 Kilometers

30 N   30 N
90 E   95   100   105   110E

III-13   RELIEF

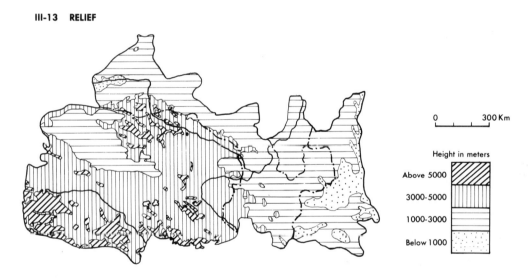

0   300 Km

Height in meters

Above 5000
3000-5000
1000-3000
Below 1000

Another division, the loess plateau, is a typical dissected plateau, although it is dotted with some narrow, elongated mountain ridges which have not been covered with loess. It lies mostly within the great horseshoe bend of the Yellow River north of the Tsinling Shan. There are numerous, intricate loess ravines which have been formed as a result of river erosion, and which vary in depth and width from a few meters to 200 meters (Maps III-15, III-16, and III-17).

A third division of the Upper Yellow River Region is the famous Kansu Corridor, which extends 1,000 kilometers westward from Lan-chou and is flanked by high mountain ranges overlooking its flat floor which lies 1500 meters above sea level. Because it is a natural route to the west of the Yellow River, this area is also known as the Ho-hsi Corridor ("the corridor west of the river"). Though rainfall is not abundant (averaging between 250 mm and 600 mm annually), the base of this structural depression receives considerable snow-melt from the surrounding mountains. When the snow cover melts in summer, the melt water flows down the mountain slopes and forms many streams of varying size,

North China   119

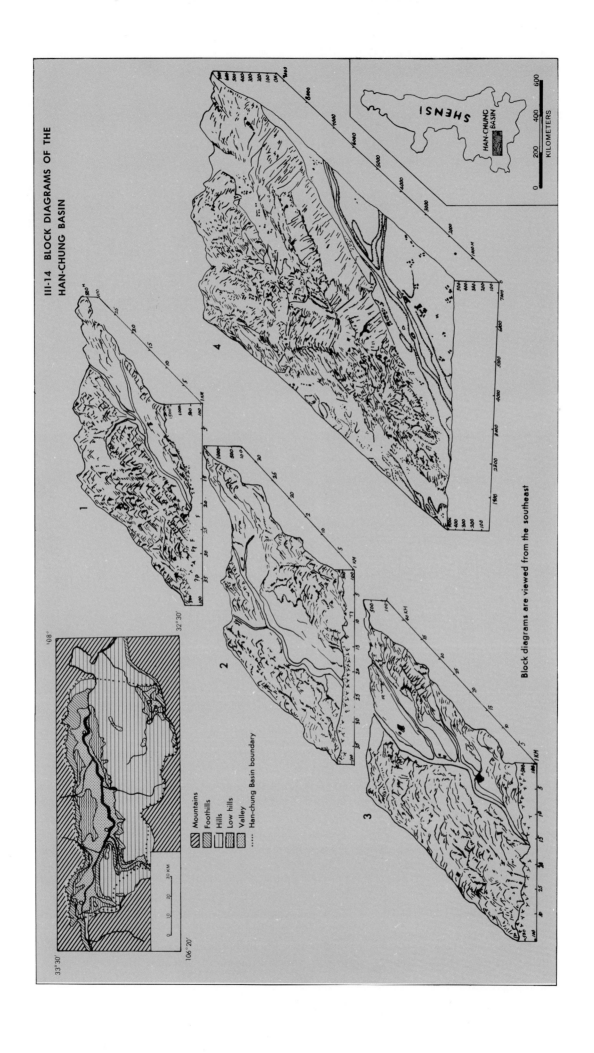

III-14 BLOCK DIAGRAMS OF THE HAN-CHUNG BASIN

Block diagrams are viewed from the southeast

Mountains
Foothills
Hills
Low hills
Valley
Han-chung Basin boundary

SHENSI

HAN-CHUNG BASIN

KILOMETERS
0   200   400   600

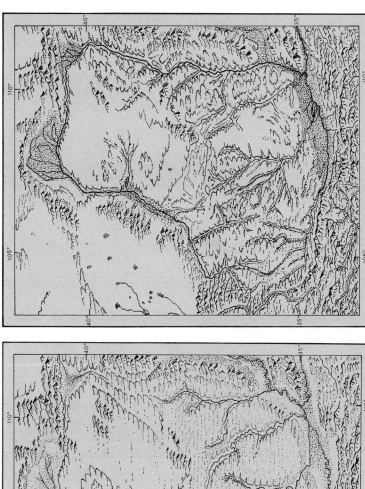

III-15a INITIAL STAGE

Initially streams from the southwest and the northwest flowed into a depression in the southern Shensi Plateau, creating a system of interior drainage.

III-15b LATER STAGE

Subsequently, stream capture from the southeast opened drainage from the eastern portion of the plateau to the east, and the initial relationship between the Wei Ho and the Yellow River was established. Streams to the west of the Shensi Plateau drained from the north and the south into an elongated depression today called the Ningsia Oasis.

III-15c FINAL STAGE

Finally, drainage on the west and the east side of the Shensi Plateau was linked by a north- and northwestward extension of the Yellow River and the stream capture of the interior Ningsia drainage system. Tributaries to the Wei Ho and the Yellow River continue to dissect the plateau.

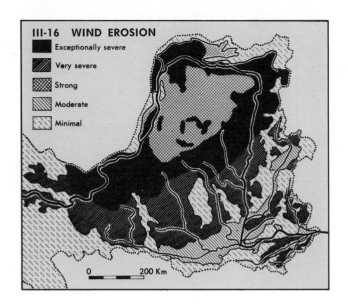

III-16 WIND EROSION

- Exceptionally severe
- Very severe
- Strong
- Moderate
- Minimal

0   200 Km

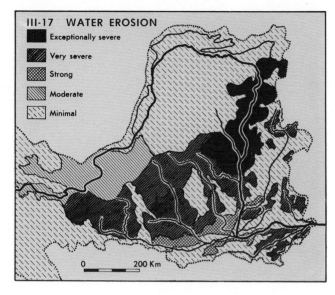

III-17 WATER EROSION

- Exceptionally severe
- Very severe
- Strong
- Moderate
- Minimal

0   200 Km

whose waters are diverted for irrigation when they reach the level land at the base of the mountains. Along the banks of each river are a number of oases of different size which have become agricultural and population centers (Map III-18). The Chinese have expended considerable effort in trying to control these waters (Map III-19). The Lan-chou–Sinkiang Railroad runs through the Kansu Corridor.

A final division is the Tsinghai Plateau, which embraces all of Tsinghai Province and has an elevation of 4,000 meters. At the northern edge of this high tableland are the Ch'i-lien Shan-mo, which form the divide between the interior and exterior drainage systems of China. Through the central part of the plateau extend the Pa-yen-k'a-la Shan, which serve as the watershed for the headwaters of the Yangtze

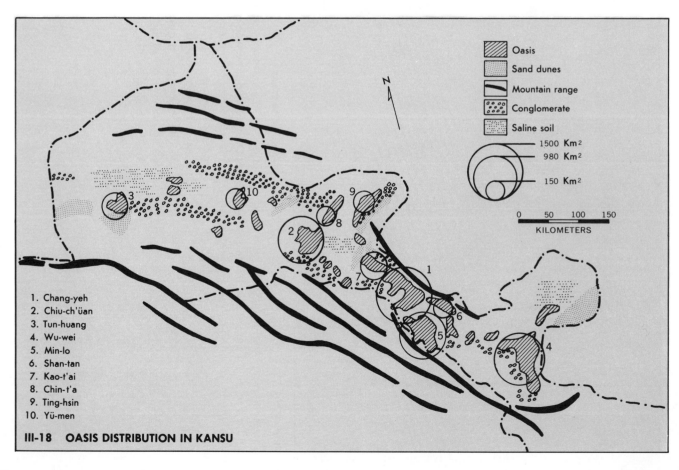

- Oasis
- Sand dunes
- Mountain range
- Conglomerate
- Saline soil

1500 Km²
980 Km²
150 Km²

0   50   100   150
KILOMETERS

1. Chang-yeh
2. Chiu-ch'üan
3. Tun-huang
4. Wu-wei
5. Min-lo
6. Shan-tan
7. Kao-t'ai
8. Chin-t'a
9. Ting-hsin
10. Yü-men

III-18   OASIS DISTRIBUTION IN KANSU

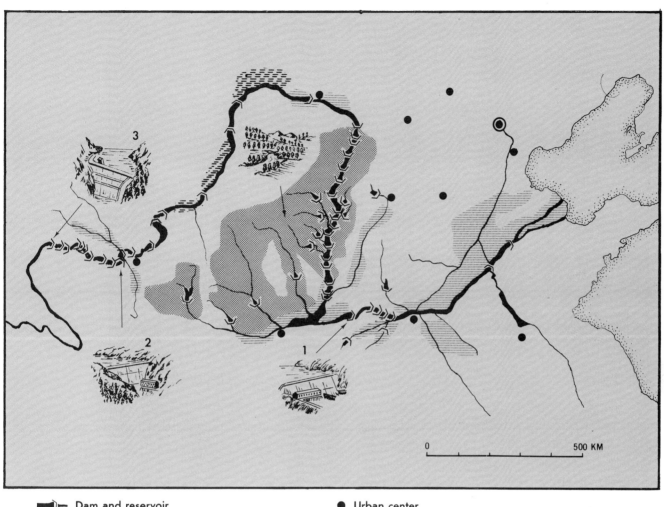

- ◗─ Dam and reservoir
- Principal areas of water and soil conservation
- Irrigated areas by 1967
- Irrigated areas in the final plan when completed

- ● Urban center
- ◎ Peking
- 1. San-men
- 2. Liu-chia
- 3. Kuei-te

0   500 KM

and Yellow rivers. In the southern part of the plateau the Tsinghai-Tibetan boundary parallels the T'ang-ku-la Shan-mo. Between these high mountains are broad valleys, rolling hilly areas, and broad flat tableland. In most places rich grass flourishes, providing extensive alpine pastures. This area is covered with a thick layer of friable fertile loess.

In the northwestern part of the Tsinghai Plateau lies the Tsaidam Basin, an immense, low-lying area between the Pa-yen-k'a-la and Ch'i-lien Shan-mo ranges which rise to 4,000 meters on the north. The basin proper is vast and flat, its lowest point being about 2,700 meters above sea level. There are many fertile spots in the piedmont and lakeside areas of the basin. The southeastern part of the basin is a broad swamp formed by a number of rivers

flowing from the snow-capped Kunlun Range (Maps III-20 and III-21).

The extent and the varied terrain of the Upper Yellow River Region result in great variations in climate, soil, vegetation, and land use (Map III-22). On the whole, the climate of the region is typically continental, being influenced by its remoteness from the sea and by the mountain ranges to the south and east that bar maritime winds. Winter is dry, cold, and windy, while summer is hot. Most of the rainfall occurs during the summer. Such a climate makes it difficult for tall plants to grow, so that most of the region consists of deserts and steppes. High elevations, perpetual snow, and little vegetation give the entire region the appearance of a frigid zone. However, despite the low temperature and

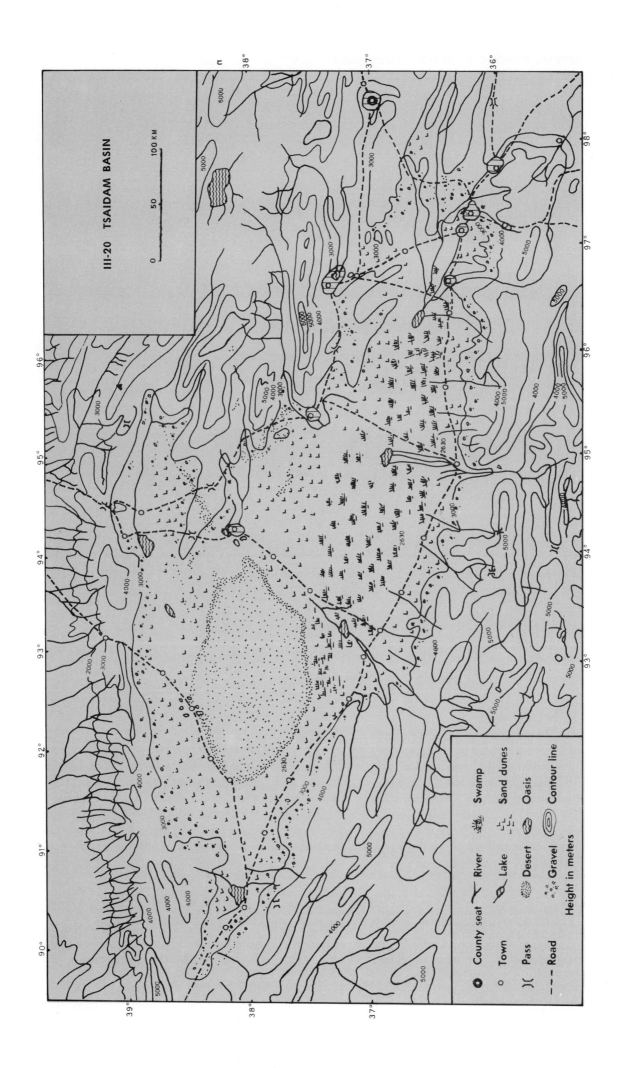

III-20 TSAIDAM BASIN

County seat
Town
Pass
Road

River
Lake
Desert
Gravel

Swamp
Sand dunes
Oasis
Contour line

Height in meters

0   50   100 KM

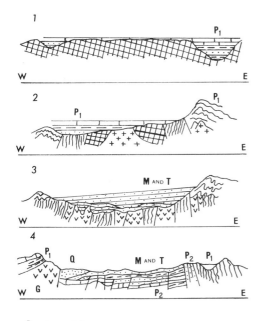

P₁	Lower Paleozoic group
P₂	Upper Paleozoic group
M ᴬᴺᴰ T	Mesozoic and Tertiary groups
Q	Quaternary system
G	Granite

1. Caledonian stage
2. Hercynian stage
3. Alpine stage
4. End of the Quaternary period

scanty rainfall, grass thrives on the vast plateau, providing extensive and reasonably productive pasturelands.

Strong winds from the Inner Mongolian Plateau blanket the otherwise fertile farmland in the Kansu Corridor with a sea of sand. This presents a serious menace to local agriculture. However, the region possesses some of China's best pasturelands for sheep, horses, and yaks. Antelope, wild horses, wolves, foxes, and bears are also found here.

Fed largely by the melting snow of the high mountains, most of the rivers within the internal drainage basin are short, and their flow varies with the seasons. Many of the lakes produce salt in great quantities.

In Shensi Province along most of the large rivers are strips of alluvial land known locally as "brimming granaries." The chief food crops are millet and broom-corn millet. Northern Shensi has also many pasturelands and a large number of livestock farms. Recently, much progress has been made in water and soil conservation, afforestation, and the planting of fodder grasses. By a combination of good practices in farming, forestry, and animal husbandry, the conditions for developing stock raising have been improved.

The Wei Ho Plain (the Wei Ho being the major right bank tributary to the Yellow River) contrasts sharply with northern Shensi. The plain, densely populated, with many towns and villages, extends over 300 kilometers from T'ung-kuan in the east to Pao-chi in the west. A number of irrigation canals have been dug to irrigate the wheat and cotton fields here.

Maize and rice are the chief farm crops of the Han Shui Valley in the southeastern part of the region. The northernmost part of this valley, where subtropical crops are grown, also produces tea and citrus fruit.

Marked fluctuations in annual precipitation in Kansu Province make agriculture marginal at best, since drought is a constant threat. Moreover, there are many ravines and deep valleys which make water conservation practices difficult. Nevertheless an increasing acreage has been brought under irrigation there. Within the Kansu Corridor itself, as we have noted, snow-melt from the Ch'i-lien Shan-mo makes possible a fairly extensive irrigation system. These irrigation works are over two thousand years old, having been constructed when the oases of the corridor were first cultivated. It was at these oases that the first cities and towns of the corridor were established. The southeastern section of Kansu is generally cropped with winter wheat, while the corridor in the west is planted in spring wheat. The rice produced in the corridor is known for its high quality, and the western section of the corridor is suited to cotton growing.

With excellent natural grasslands, the Upper Yellow River Region is a traditional stock-breeding center. Tsinghai horses are known throughout the world, and the chief pastoral products of the region include hides and skins from Tsinghai and wool from Kansu.

Industry is varied in the Upper Yellow River Region and has been actively developed since the First Five-Year Plan (Map III-23). Shensi has abundant coal deposits distributed throughout the province, one of the largest being at T'ung-ch'uan. Rich oil resources are also found throughout the Shensi Plateau. One of the first oil fields to be developed in the region was at Yen-ch'ang, which also has a large machinery industry.

The light industry of the province includes cotton milling, which has been developed on a large scale. All phases of cotton processing are performed here, including spinning, weaving, dyeing, and printing. The larger mills are located in Sian and Hsien-yang on the Wei Ho Plain, which is one of China's major cotton-producing areas. The northwestern provinces provide an easily accessible market for the cotton goods of Shensi.

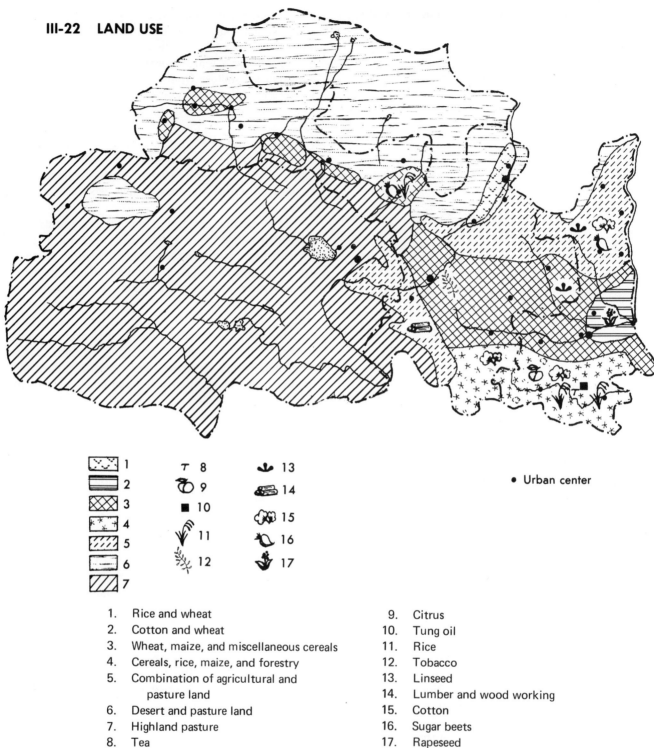

1	⊤ 8	🌿 13
2	🍊 9	🪵 14
3	■ 10	🌸 15
4	🌾 11	🐦 16
5	🌿 12	🌱 17
6		
7		

• Urban center

1. Rice and wheat
2. Cotton and wheat
3. Wheat, maize, and miscellaneous cereals
4. Cereals, rice, maize, and forestry
5. Combination of agricultural and
   pasture land
6. Desert and pasture land
7. Highland pasture
8. Tea

9. Citrus
10. Tung oil
11. Rice
12. Tobacco
13. Linseed
14. Lumber and wood working
15. Cotton
16. Sugar beets
17. Rapeseed

The highway network of the region is well developed and links the Tsinghai Plateau with Sinkiang, Inner Mongolia, Shensi, Shansi, Honan, Szechwan, and Tibet. The railroads of the region include the T'ien-shui-Lan-chou, Pao-chi-Ch'eng-tu, Lan-chou-Sinkiang, and Pao-t'ou-Lan-chou railroads.

The region has the largest proportion of its population concentrated in Shensi and southeastern Kansu. In addition to the Hans found there, there are the Huis, who inhabit southeastern Kansu; the

Tibetans, who live in compact communities on the Tsinghai Plateau and in southwestern Kansu; and the Mongolians and Kazakhs, who are scattered around Koko Nor (Ch'ing Hai) and in the eastern part of the Tsaidam Basin.

Sian, the provincial capital of Shensi, is located in the center of the Wei Ho Plain, and has a population of nearly 2 million. The Wei Ho flows north of the city, while to the south rise the Tsinling Shan. The city, built in the form of a walled rectangle,

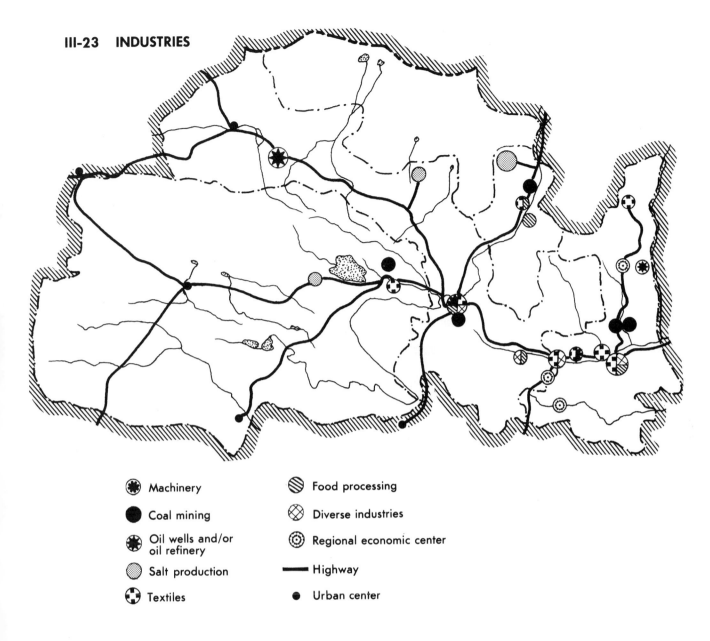

- ✳ Machinery
- ⬤ Coal mining
- ✴ Oil wells and/or oil refinery
- ◎ Salt production
- ✚ Textiles
- ◍ Food processing
- ⊗ Diverse industries
- ◉ Regional economic center
- ▬ Highway
- ● Urban center

has been the provincial capital for about nine hundred years and was China's imperial capital for even longer. On the other hand, though it has many places of historical interest, Sian today is a modern industrial city with a new thermoelectric plant; cotton mills; and electrical equipment, building materials, and meat-processing factories. Most of this new growth lies outside the ancient walls.

Lan-chou, the provincial capital of Kansu, is situated in a mountain-rimmed basin and serves as the industrial and transport center of the province.

With a population of about 1.5 million, the city is becoming a large industrial center; the leading activities are oil refining, manufacturing, and the traditional woolen textile industry.

Hsi-ning is Tsinghai's capital and functions as a trading center for the province's agricultural and livestock products. It is the transport node at the northeastern terminus of the Tsinghai-Tibet Highway which terminates in Lhasa. Motor routes also connect Hsi-ning with the oil wells in the Tsaidam Basin.

Central China

Like North China, the Central China Region has subdivisions and is dominated by one major river, in this case the Yangtze (Maps III-24 and III-25).

THE LOWER YANGTZE REGION

The Lower Yangtze Region is located between the old course of the Huai Ho to the north and Hang-chow Bay to the south; it terminates at Nanking on the west and at the East China Sea on the east (Map III-26). The region is actually a large delta formed by the deposition of alluvium brought down by the great Yangtze River. Lakes and rivers abound in this area; for instance, freshwater bodies in the T'ai Hu Basin occupy 15 percent of the total area of the Lower Yangtze Region. This basin is popularly known as "water country," because travelers here meet a stream every quarter kilometer, and peasants use boats as often as their northern countrymen use carts.

The Yangtze accumulates great amounts of silt and thus causes a continuous building up of land seaward. It has been calculated that the land here is extended toward the sea at an average rate of 25 meters a year naturally, and man has been energetically reclaiming coastal land as well. Research has further revealed that five thousand years ago the sea reached inland to roughly midway between Shanghai and Nanking, a distance of some 150 kilometers, and that T'ai Hu was part of the East China Sea. The present small isolated hills in the T'ai Hu Basin were originally islands. One thousand years ago, most of the present site of the city of Shanghai was under water and Ch'ung-ming Island on the estuary of the Yangtze was only a small sand bar. The intricate stream and canal network in the delta area is shown in Map III-27. Maps III-28 and III-29 show land use and settlement in the same region.

The climate of the Lower Yangtze Region is temperate and humid, with distinctive seasonal differences modified by its coastal location. The average January temperature is always above freezing, and summer temperatures are not as high as at inland stations and do not persist as long.

The region has an annual rainfall of more than 1,000 millimeters in most places, with the heavy rains coming in the summer. In June and July, especially in the Lower Yangtze Valley, there are often rainy periods continuing for several days.

In the inland portion of the delta south of the Huai Ho and north of the Yangtze, rice and wheat are produced in great abundance. However, along the coast there is saline soil, which, when reclaimed and improved, is well suited for the growing of cotton. Because of this, Kiangsu's coastal area north

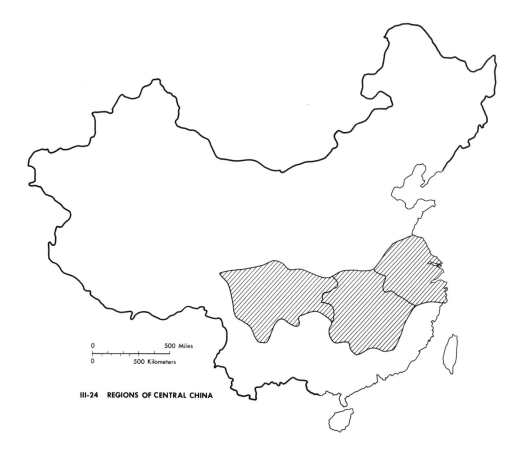

III-24 REGIONS OF CENTRAL CHINA

0   500 Miles

0   500 Kilometers

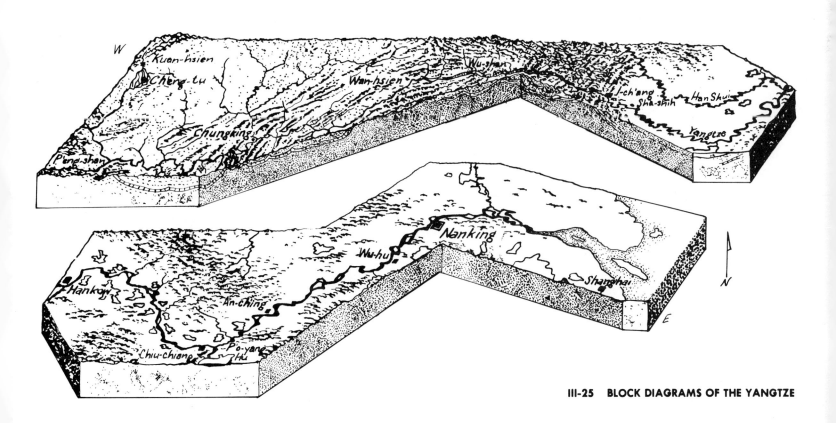

III-25 BLOCK DIAGRAMS OF THE YANGTZE

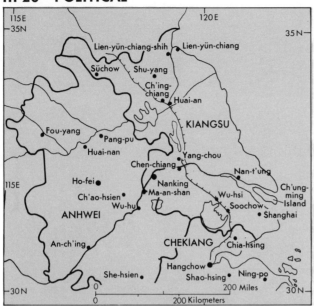

of the Yangtze is one of China's major cotton-producing areas. The greater part of the alluvial plain south of the Yangtze is dominated by paddy fields. Rice is also grown in the numerous river valleys. Around T'ai Hu, mulberry trees are plentiful. In addition, tea is grown on hilly slopes, and broadleaf and coniferous trees and bamboo grow in the steeper areas.

A network of lakes and rivers spreads over the whole Lower Yangtze Region. South of the Yangtze, the largest lake is the beautiful T'ai Hu mentioned above; the Hung-tse Hu and Kao-pao Hu are the two major lakes north of the Yangtze. In addition to the three great waterways—the Yangtze, the Huai, and the Grand Canal—the plains are criss-crossed by countless small canals and rivulets. Most of the canals are tributaries and distributaries of natural waterways and provide facilities for transportation, irrigation, and drainage. Many other benefits

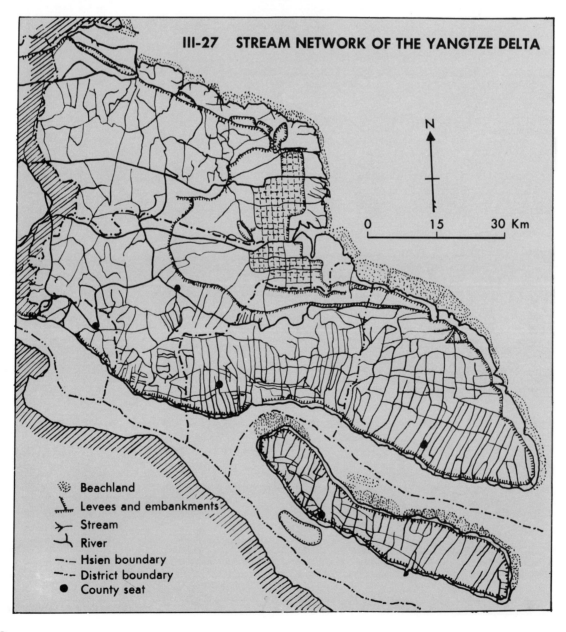

III-27 STREAM NETWORK OF THE YANGTZE DELTA

Beachland
Levees and embankments
Stream
River
-·- Hsien boundary
-··- District boundary
● County seat

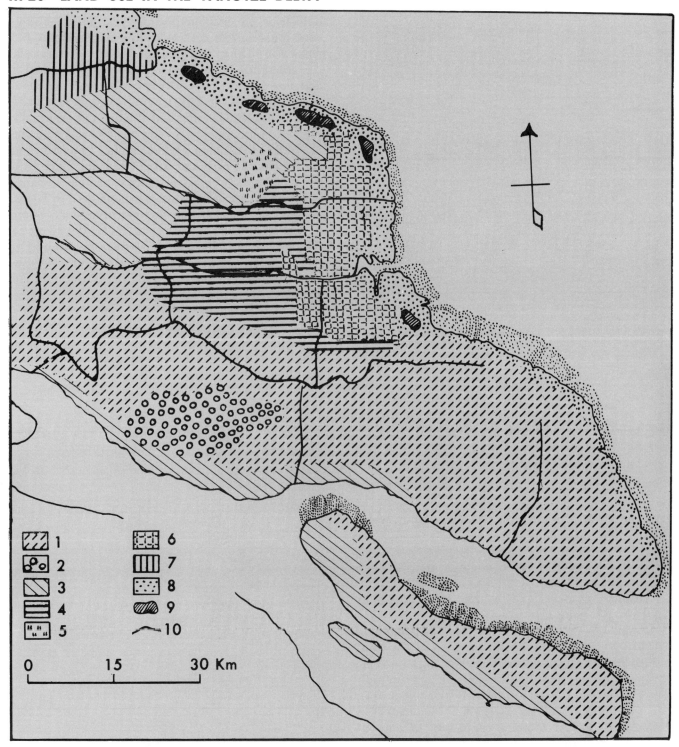

1. Cotton and other crops
2. Special cash crops
3. Rice and wheat
4. Cotton and rice in rotation
5. Marsh
6. Saline soils newly brought under cultivation
7. Mixed crops
8. Alkaline soils with potential for cultivation
9. Salt pans and salt production
10. Main streams

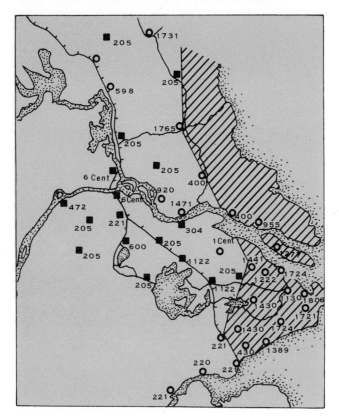

■ County seat (date of origin in years B.C.)
O County seat (date of origin in years A.D.)
/// Land reclaimed in historic times

also are derived from this hydraulic network, which is tens of thousands of miles long. The mud at the canal-bottoms provides fertilizer for countless farms, and the water yields an abundance of fish, water chestnuts, and lotus roots. The region is known as a "country of rice and fish," and this it certainly is.

The Lower Yangtze Region has a population of nearly 87 million, or 13 percent of China's total. With 368 people per square kilometer, it is the most densely settled region in the mainland, and is rapidly becoming one of the most densely populated areas in the world. This delta region is dominated by Shanghai, with a teeming population of approximately 6 million. Here in this delta are more cities with a population of over 100,000 people than in any other region of China.

Shanghai is China's largest city as well as its industrial, commercial, and foreign trade center. It is the center of the textile industry, with more than one-third of the total number of spindles in the country (Map III-30). Shanghai, moreover, is the heart of China's heavy and light machine manufacturing. One-third of the country's production of

machine tools and of forging and pressing equipment is also found here. Additional highly developed industries are shipbuilding, electric power, chemicals, tobacco, and diverse consumer goods. A full one-sixth of Shanghai's people are factory workers.

Shanghai is the delta's center of transportation and communication both by water and by land. Shipping along the Yangtze originates at Shanghai, moves through Nanking and Wu-hu, and eventually reaches as far west as Szechwan. Coastal shipping routes link Shanghai with Tientsin, Tsingtao, and Dairen to the north and with Amoy and Canton to the south. Railway lines northward connect Shanghai with Peking and a southward line goes to Hangchow. Inland navigation likewise serves a large part of this area. The Yangtze, the Huai, the rivers in the T'ai Hu and Kao-pao Hu basins, the Grand Canal, and many other canals form a network of water traffic connecting the towns and the countryside of all the eastern seaboard.

Nanking, the second largest city of the region, is at the intersection of three railway lines, the Shanghai-Nanking, the Tientsin–P'u-k'ou, and the Nanking–Wu-hu. It has a population of approximately 2 million, and is the capital of Kiangsu Province. During several periods in Chinese history it has functioned as the national capital.

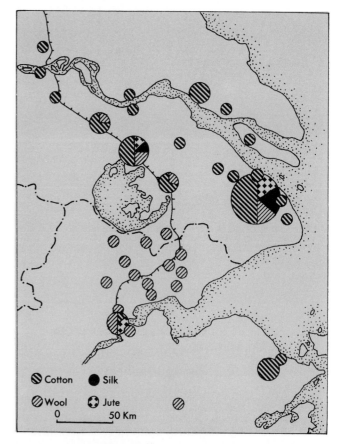

III-30   TEXTILE INDUSTRIES OF THE YANGTZE DELTA

Most of the arable land in this region has already been brought under cultivation. The total area of cultivated land amounts to one-half of the total area of the region (Map III-31). Dense population contributes numerous working hands, and intensive farming has resulted in a high yield per unit of farmlands. The T'ai Hu and Kao-pao Hu basins are well known for rice growing; Wu-hsi and Wu-hu are rice-collecting centers. Sericulture is a popular supplementary occupation of the peasant households in the T'ai Hu area, which produces one-half of the country's silk. Soochow and Wu-hsi likewise are silk-producing centers, and Kiangsu is one of the main cotton-growing regions in the country. Tea is cultivated in great quantities on the hilly slopes. In this region both marine and freshwater fisheries are well developed. The lower Yangtze is a region of both intensive farming and diverse and important manufacture (Map III-32).

THE MIDDLE YANGTZE REGION

The Middle Yangtze Region includes the three provinces of Hupeh, Hunan, and Kiangsi, a total of 550,000 square kilometers or 6 percent of the country's area (Map III-33). Generally speaking, the region is level, with an altitude mostly below 200 meters and in fact below 50 meters in many places (Map III-34).

Roughly dissecting this centrally-located region, the Yangtze provides a great east-west transport route, while the Peking-Canton Railway is the country's major north-south trunk line. The intersection of these thus makes the Middle Yangtze Region a vital land and water communication center. Metropolitan Wu-han's location—almost equidistant from Shanghai to the east, Ch'eng-tu to the west, Peking to the north, and Canton to the south—gives it a marked nodal quality.

Surrounded by mountains, the land slopes downward toward the center of the region. The Yangtze, traversing this region, spills into two big pockets and forms the Tung-t'ing and P'o-yang lakes.

The region is a great basin surrounded by mountains reaching an elevation of 1,000 meters. This vast plain comprises central Hupeh and northern Hunan and includes lakes of all shapes and many meandering rivers. In ancient times there was a huge lake in the flat basin called Yun-meng-tse. Silt was continually carried down by the Yangtze and its tributaries and deposited in the lake, diminishing the lake's area steadily and eventually creating a series of small lakes in the bed of the old large one. The present Tung-t'ing Hu and P'o-yang Hu are the major remnants of the huge ancient lake.

III-31 LAND USE IN THE LOWER YANGTZE

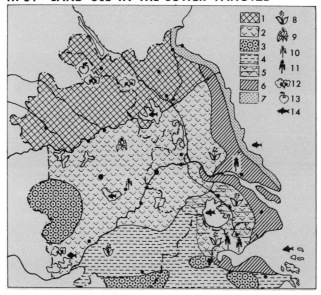

• Urban center

1. Wheat, mixed crops, and oil seeds
2. Rice and wheat
3. Tea
4. Rice and special crops
5. Rice, wheat, and silk
6. Major cotton area
7. Coastal salt industry (land increasingly being brought under cultivation)
8. Rapeseed
9. Tobacco
10. Jute
11. Hemp
12. Secondary cotton area
13. Temperate fruits
14. Fishing

III-32 INDUSTRIES OF THE LOWER YANGTZE

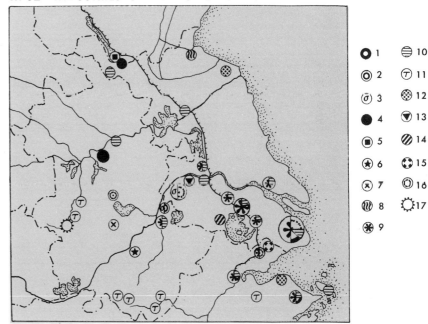

1. Machinery
2. Iron and steel
3. Chemicals
4. Coal mining
5. Iron ore mining
6. Copper mining
7. Alum production
8. Limestone
9. Textiles
10. Food processing
11. Tea processing
12. Salt production
13. Cement
14. Ceramics
15. Tile and bricks
16. Diverse industries
17. Hydroelectric power station

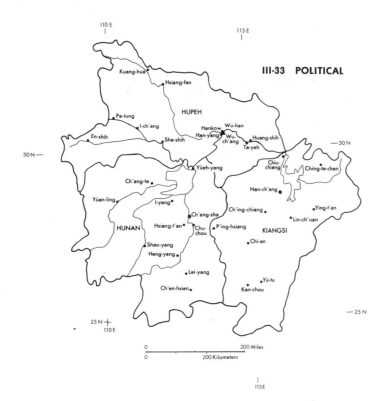

III-33 POLITICAL

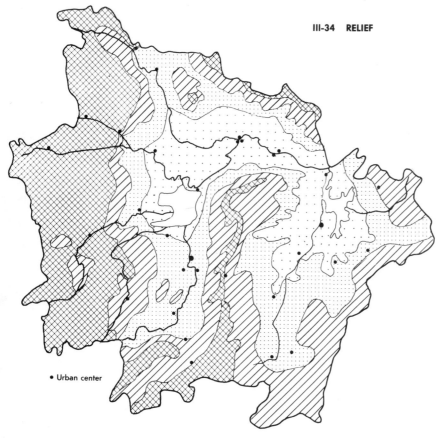

III-34 RELIEF

• Urban center

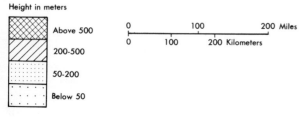

Height in meters

Above 500

200-500

50-200

Below 50

Rich soil and extensive irrigation have made the basin one of the main agricultural areas in the entire country.

The region is one of the warmest parts of China Proper; it has adequate rainfall, an average of about 1,200 millimeters annually; and the soil of the region is primarily alluvial, favoring the productive growing of rice, wheat, and cotton. Mixed forests of evergreen and deciduous trees are found here. Trees of economic value consist mainly of tea, tung, camphor, bamboo, and pine—cultivated tree crops requiring regular replanting practices.

Floods in the Middle Yangtze Region are frequent. Even though the Yangtze characteristically carries less silt than the Yellow River, the shores of Tung-t'ing Hu and the lower reaches of the Han Shui have experienced frequent flooding, with widespread damage to the vast plains of Hupeh and Hunan. Tung-t'ing Hu and the lakes on the Yangtze's north bank were originally natural reservoirs which regulated the water flow of the Yangtze. As they have gradually been reduced in size by silt accumulation, however, they have lost their ability to function as regulators. The massive Sha-shih reservoir project east of I-ch'ang was undertaken in 1954 in an attempt to reduce flood danger by ponding up flood waters before they reached the heavily settled Hupeh and Hunan plains.

The region has a population of over 91 million. The plains along the Yangtze are densely populated, with an average of 280 persons per square kilometer. Mountain flanks and hilly land, however, are sparsely inhabited, averaging 50 persons per square kilometer.

Most of the area's cities are river ports. Wuhan, Hupeh's capital, with a population of approximately 4 million, the largest city in the region, is in reality a union of three cities—Wu-ch'ang, Hankow, and Han-yang. Wu-han is not only a key node for land and water transportation along the middle course of the Yangtze but also one of the most important industrial cities in China. Its huge integrated iron and steel enterpise makes Wu-han the steel center of the region. In the past, Hankow, Han-yang, and Wu-ch'ang were separated by the Yangtze and the Han Shui, preventing the Peking-Hankow and Canton-Hankow (Wu-ch'ang) railways from being able to link up. But with the completion of the bridge across the Han Shui connecting Hankow and Han-yang and the bridge across the Yangtze connecting Wu-ch'ang and Han-yang in 1959, trains can now pass over the bridges to tie together the South and North. Wu-han can also be reached at all times of the year by 10,000- to 15,000-ton ocean freighters (Map III-35).

The Middle Yangtze Region is China's greatest granary (Maps III-36 and III-37). In rice production it ranks first among the regions of the country (Map

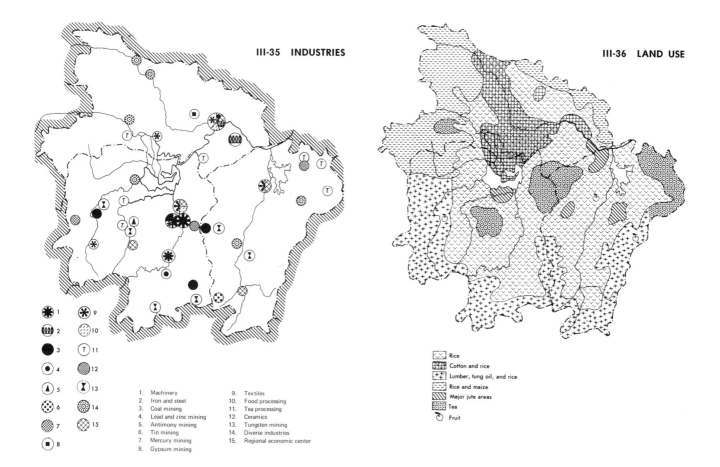

1. Machinery
2. Iron and steel
3. Coal mining
4. Lead and zinc mining
5. Antimony mining
6. Tin mining
7. Mercury mining
8. Gypsum mining
9. Textiles
10. Food processing
11. Tea processing
12. Ceramics
13. Tungsten mining
14. Diverse industries
15. Regional economic center

Rice
Cotton and rice
Lumber, tung oil, and rice
Rice and maize
Major jute areas
Tea
Fruit

III-38). In recent years, per-unit-area yield has been raised significantly as a result of water conservation work, the increased use of fertilizer, improvement of seed, and widespread conversion from single cropping to double cropping. The region produces a surplus of rice, large quantities of which are shipped to North China every year. Wheat also is raised where irrigation is lacking for rice (Map III-39). Industrial crops include cotton, ramie, tea, and tung oil. Cotton is grown mainly in the plains of the middle Yangtze and the valley of the Han Shui, and the region has China's top yields per unit area. Ramie, used in China to make grasscloth, grows in central Kiangsi and eastern Hunan. The hilly area along the southern Yangtze is one of the main tea-growing areas in the country. Tung trees are found mainly in the valley of the Yüan Chiang in Hunan.

This region is also rich in mineral resources, the most important of which are nonferrous metals. Most of China's antimony and tungsten are found here, while China's largest lead-zinc mine is located in Hunan. The abundance of rich coal and iron mines, combined with the convenience of shipping on the Yangtze, provides favorable conditions for the development of the iron and steel industry.

Ching-te-chen, China's porcelain center in Kiangsi Province, has a history of more than a thousand years. Each of the emperors after the

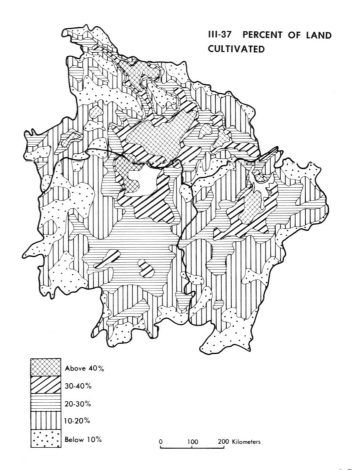

Above 40%
30-40%
20-30%
10-20%
Below 10%

0   100   200 Kilometers

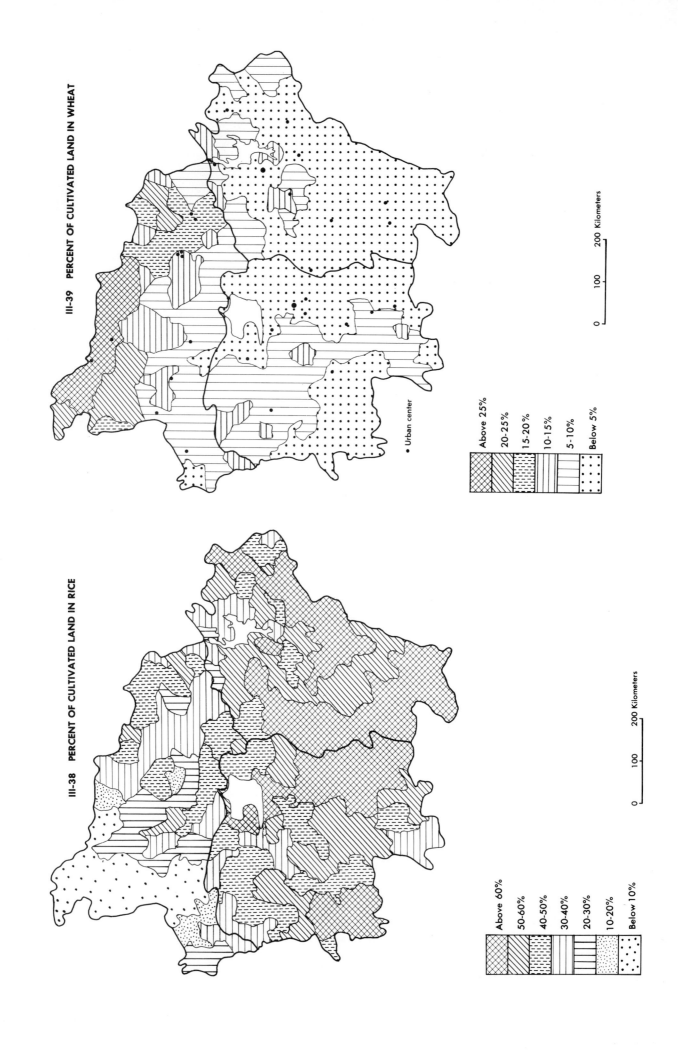

III-39 PERCENT OF CULTIVATED LAND IN WHEAT

Above 25%
20-25%
15-20%
10-15%
5-10%
Below 5%

• Urban center

0   100   200 Kilometers

III-38 PERCENT OF CULTIVATED LAND IN RICE

Above 60%
50-60%
40-50%
30-40%
20-30%
10-20%
Below 10%

0   100   200 Kilometers

Sung Dynasty had in this city his own "imperial kiln," in which were made all kinds of beautiful porcelain to ornament the imperial palaces. China-ware produced here has been exported since the Manchu Dynasty and is still an important article in China's foreign trade today. Grasscloth linen, a well-known handicraft product, is made in Kiangsi and Hunan, and fine embroidery is produced in Ch'ang-sha.

THE UPPER YANGTZE REGION (SZECHWAN BASIN)

Szechwan Province, with a territory of 560,000 square kilometers, borders on Yunnan and Kweichow in the south, and Shensi, Kansu, and Tsinghai in the north (Map III-40). West of Szechwan is the mountain-locked region of Tibet, and toward the east stretch densely populated low hills and plains along the middle Yangtze. As is the case farther east, the Yangtze forms a major connecting link between these diverse areas of Central China. The 2,270-kilometer highway from Ya-an in western Szechwan to Lhasa serves as a second link.

In the Szechwan Basin proper are a number of fertile plains, the biggest of which is the Ch'eng-tu Plain. This latter is traversed by a dense network of waterways (Map III-41). Rice fields in this area are shaped like squares on a chessboard. Everywhere one can hear water gurgling like music as it brings life and growth to the farms. Bridges abound and settlement is as dense as in the T'ai Hu Basin in east China. The industrious Chinese peasants have been cultivating the fertile Ch'eng-tu Plain for more than two thousand years. They forced the often turbulent flow of the Min Chiang into many smaller streams, thus providing both irrigation and power for driving water mills. It is this elaborate control of water that enables the Ch'eng-tu Plain to support such a dense population and produce such an abundance of products. The major portion of the Szechwan Basin other than the Ch'eng-tu Plain, however, is composed of hilly land.

The terraced fields on the slopes are irrigated by water diverted from mountain streams. When filled with water during the growing season, these terraced plots look like innumerable little mirrors dazzling under sunshine. The beauty of these is amplified by the sight of small streams flowing through valleys and of mountains rising in the background. Together they present a rural scene of extraordinary beauty.

The highlands in western Szechwan, which are a part of the Tibetan Plateau, have many mountain peaks that are perennially snowcapped, the highest

of these being above 7,500 meters in the Ta-hsüeh Shan (Map III-42). The torrential current of the rivers found on the flanks of the mountains of western Szechwan provides a good potential source of water power.

The climate of the Szechwan Basin has three clear characteristics: high temperatures, abundant rainfall, and frequent fog and cloud cover (Map III-43). The January average in most cases is above 4°C and the readings often reach 8°C or higher in several places along the Yangtze. July is the warmest month, with a mean temperature of 25°C. The long growing period, which lasts for more than ten months, is very favorable to agriculture. The key to the climate of the basin may be found in its topographic features; for in winter, the high mountains and highlands in the north and northwest serve as effective barriers against the continental arctic cold waves. The terrain, further-

more, tends to slope from north to south, thus forming a vast tract that gets a maximum amount of sunshine.

The basin is likewise blessed by abundant rainfall (Map III-44). Although it is far from the sea, warm moist marine air penetrates the low mountain passes southeast of the basin. In most places the average annual rainfall is 1,000 millimeters. The mountain flanks along the western margin of the basin receive the greatest amount, more than 2,000 millimeters annually. The climate of the Szechwan Basin is thus very damp, with fog and clouds especially common in the southern areas along the Yangtze and the lower Min Chiang. Dense mist is a frequent phenomenon, particularly on winter mornings, when entire areas are enshrouded, causing the sun to appear like a red lantern hung in mid-air. Temperatures and average annual rainfall in western Szechwan are generally lower than in the basin.

III-41 PHYSIOGRAPHY

Province boundaries do not reflect the 1955 enlargement of Szechwan

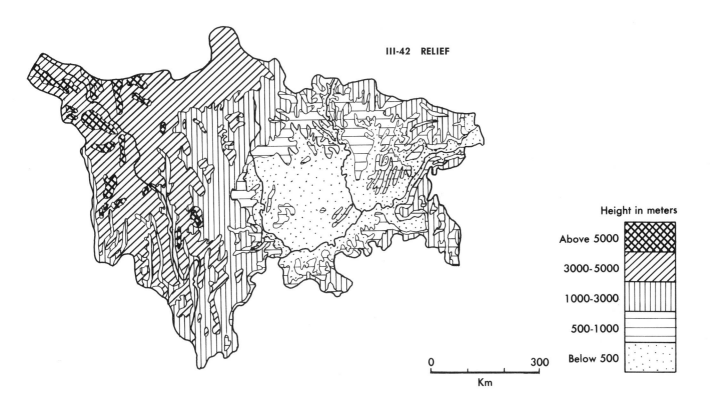

III-42 RELIEF

Height in meters

Above 5000

3000-5000

1000-3000

500-1000

Below 500

0   300
       Km

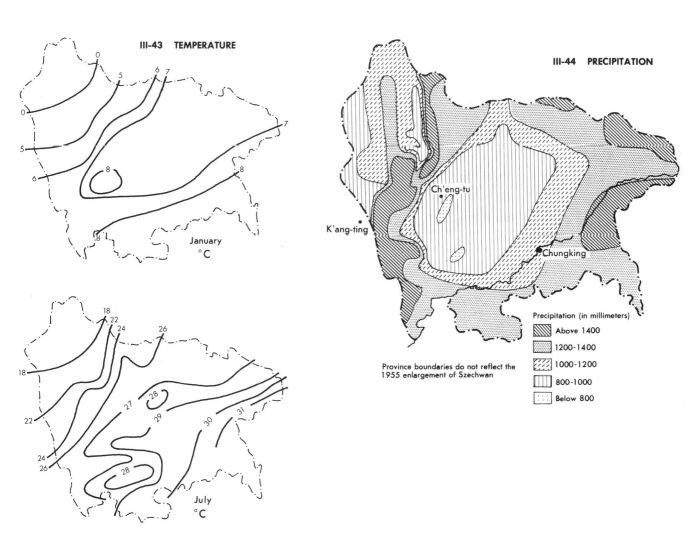

III-43 TEMPERATURE

January
°C

July
°C

III-44 PRECIPITATION

Ch'eng-tu

K'ang-ting

Chungking

Precipitation (in millimeters)

Above 1400

1200-1400

1000-1200

800-1000

Below 800

Province boundaries do not reflect the
1955 enlargement of Szechwan

Central China **139**

The soil of the Szechwan Basin is weathered from a vast foundation of sandstone and shale, the colors of which emerge in a variety of reds and purples, giving the name of the Red Basin to the area. Yellow soils also abound; these are very fertile, loose, and easily plowed.

The warm, humid climate of the basin and its fertile soil make possible the lush growth of natural vegetation which consists mainly of mixed evergreen and deciduous forests. In the mountain areas, however, a different kind of landscape is characteristic. Generally, broadleaf forests are found at the lower elevations, mixed forests in the middle range, and conifers and steppes at the top.

The rivers in Szechwan have three common characteristics: They all join the Yangtze; all have a heavy and relatively stable flow; and most of them have shoals and rapids and form gorges within the flanking mountains, and thus are excellent potential sources of hydroelectricity.

The population of Szechwan ranks first among China's provinces, with 67.9 million reported in 1970. Distribution, however, is somewhat uneven; the overwhelming majority is concentrated in the basin proper, where the density is 500 or more persons per square kilometer. The mountain areas around the basin, however, are thinly settled, especially the highlands in the west, which are inhabited by Tibetans, Yis, and Ch'iangs. Population density in these areas generally does not exceed 15 per square kilometer.

Within Ch'eng-tu, the provincial capital, are a number of places of historical interest. The city is likewise renowned for its light industries, which consist mainly of food processing, textiles, and leather making. Recently, however, industries such as machine building and the manufacture of precision instruments have been developing rapidly (Map III-45).

In addition to being the railway center of Szechwan, Ch'eng-tu is an important motor traffic junction, linking Szechwan with the vital Sinkiang-Tibet Highway. Originating in Ya-an to the west of Ch'eng-tu, passing through K'ang-ting, and terminating in Lhasa, this highway is the most important of the three existing motor roads which connect Tibet with other parts of the country.

Chungking, the second most important city in Szechwan, is situated at the confluence of the Yangtze and the Chia-ling Chiang. Surrounded by water on three sides, this hilly city resembles a peninsula. Chungking functions as the traffic hub for the whole of Szechwan. Steamers of moderate size sail east from it on the Yangtze to Wan-hsien, the trading center of eastern Szechwan, and from Wan-hsien eastward through the Yangtze gorges to Wu-han and Shanghai. Traveling westward along the Yangtze from Chungking, one can reach the important cities of Lu-chou and I-pin in southern Szechwan and, by small steamboat, can go as far as Lo-shan and Ch'eng-tu. A network of highways forms a link between Chungking and the provinces of Hupeh and Hunan. This city also has important connections by air with China's other major cities, including Peking, Wu-han, Shanghai, Canton, and K'un-ming.

The 505-kilometer Ch'eng-tu–Chungking Railway is Szechwan's main rail artery. This railway has been, in large part, responsible for the increasing tempo of the economic development of Szechwan and all the other southwestern provinces. Szechwan's other important railway is the 668-kilometer trunk line of the Pao-chi–Ch'eng-tu Railway.

The province boasts a broad range of agricultural products. Among the major food crops are rice, wheat, maize, highland barley, and sweet potatoes. Rice and wheat are chiefly cultivated in the basin proper, with the most bountiful harvests on the Ch'eng-tu Plain, while maize and sweet potatoes are grown on the plains as well as in the hilly and mountain areas. Szechwan's most important commercial crops include rapeseed, sugar cane, tobacco, and tung trees; its output of rapeseed is the highest in China. Tobacco of an excellent quality is also raised on the Ch'eng-tu Plain. Tung trees dominate the hilly areas in the east, so that Wan-hsien and Chungking serve as collecting and distributing centers of tung oil. Cotton, hemp, tea, citrus fruits, medical herbs, and myriad other crops are cultivated on a smaller scale in Szechwan.

Livestock raising is a substantial activity in Szechwan. Pigs are particularly important, for in

III-45 INDUSTRIES

1. Machinery
2. Iron and steel
3. Chemicals
4. Coal mining
5. Iron ore mining
6. Lead mining
7. Copper mining
8. Zinc mining
9. Mercury mining
10. Asbestos and graphite mining
11. Salt production
12. Textiles
13. Food processing
14. Sugar refining
15. Paper and pulp
16. Tea processing
17. Diverse industries
18. Regional economic center
19. Hydroelectric power station

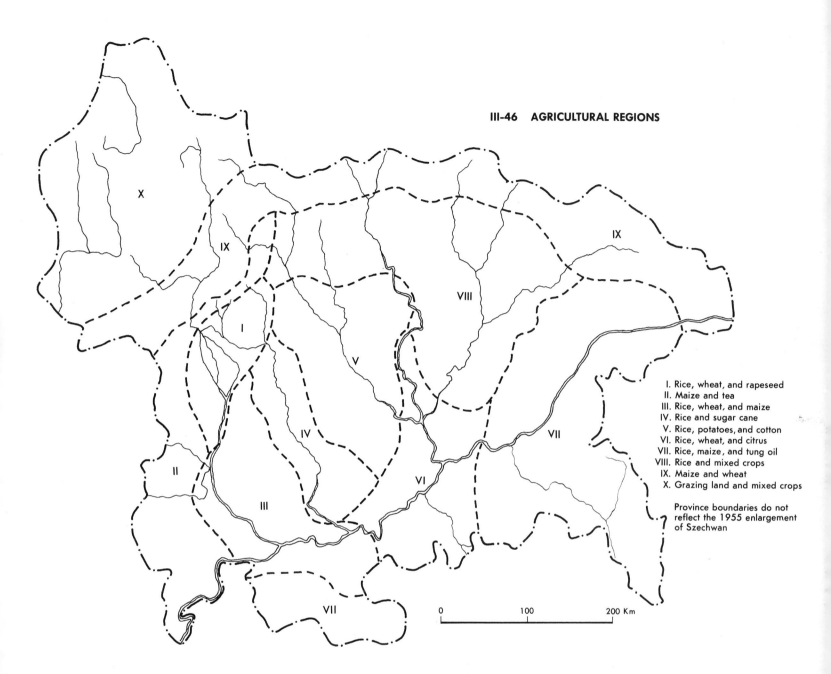

I. Rice, wheat, and rapeseed
II. Maize and tea
III. Rice, wheat, and maize
IV. Rice and sugar cane
V. Rice, potatoes, and cotton
VI. Rice, wheat, and citrus
VII. Rice, maize, and tung oil
VIII. Rice and mixed crops
IX. Maize and wheat
X. Grazing land and mixed crops

Province boundaries do not reflect the 1955 enlargement of Szechwan

0   100   200 Km

addition to their meat, they supply top-quality bristles that constitute one of China's significant export items. Natural mountain pastures in western Szechwan support large numbers of cattle, yaks, sheep, and horses. Hides, skins, and wool are important products. The variety of Szechwan's agricultural activities is shown in Maps III-46, III-47, III-48, III-49, and III-50.

Szechwan has abundant reserves of mineral resources. There is a dependable potential power supply in its water power resources and in its coal, petroleum, and natural gas reserves. Among China's southwestern provinces Szechwan ranks first in coal reserves. The province is also noted for its brine wells, the yield of which meets most of the salt requirements of southwest China; Tzu-Kung is the biggest center, contributing about half of the output. Szechwan, moreover, is richly endowed with iron ore deposits. Chungking is rapidly being developed into a heavy industrial center, with iron and steel, machine-building, electric power, and other plants. There are also rich copper deposits as well as deposits of lead, zinc, and asbestos. The leading light industries are sugar refining and textiles. The brocade made in Ch'eng-tu and the satin produced in Chungking enjoy national fame.

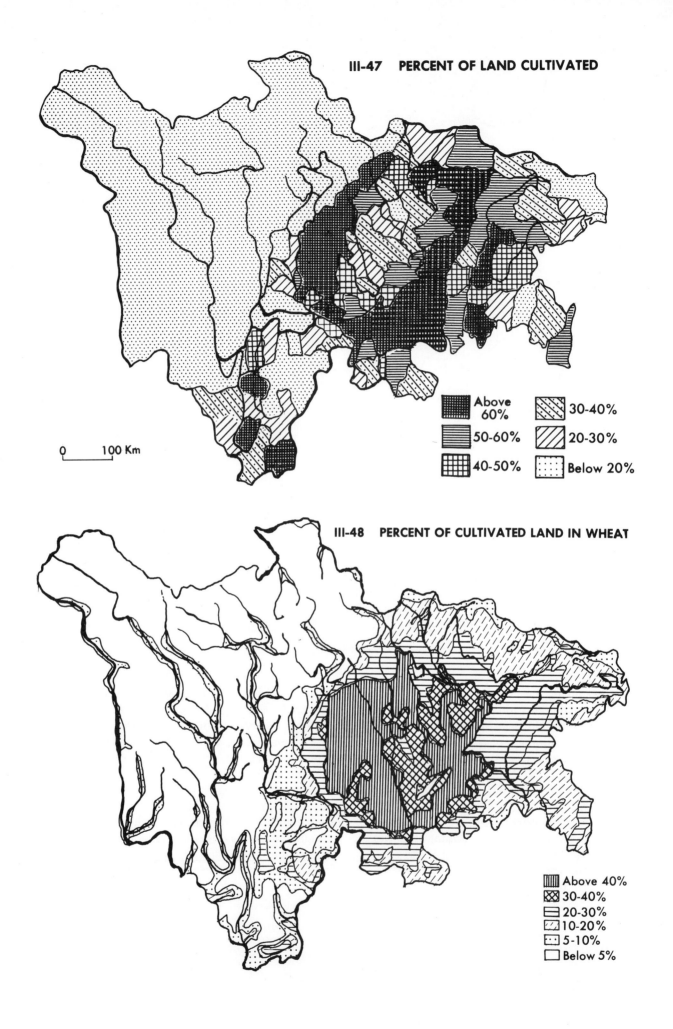

III-47   PERCENT OF LAND CULTIVATED

Above 60%

50-60%

40-50%

30-40%

20-30%

Below 20%

0   100 Km

III-48   PERCENT OF CULTIVATED LAND IN WHEAT

Above 40%

30-40%

20-30%

10-20%

5-10%

Below 5%

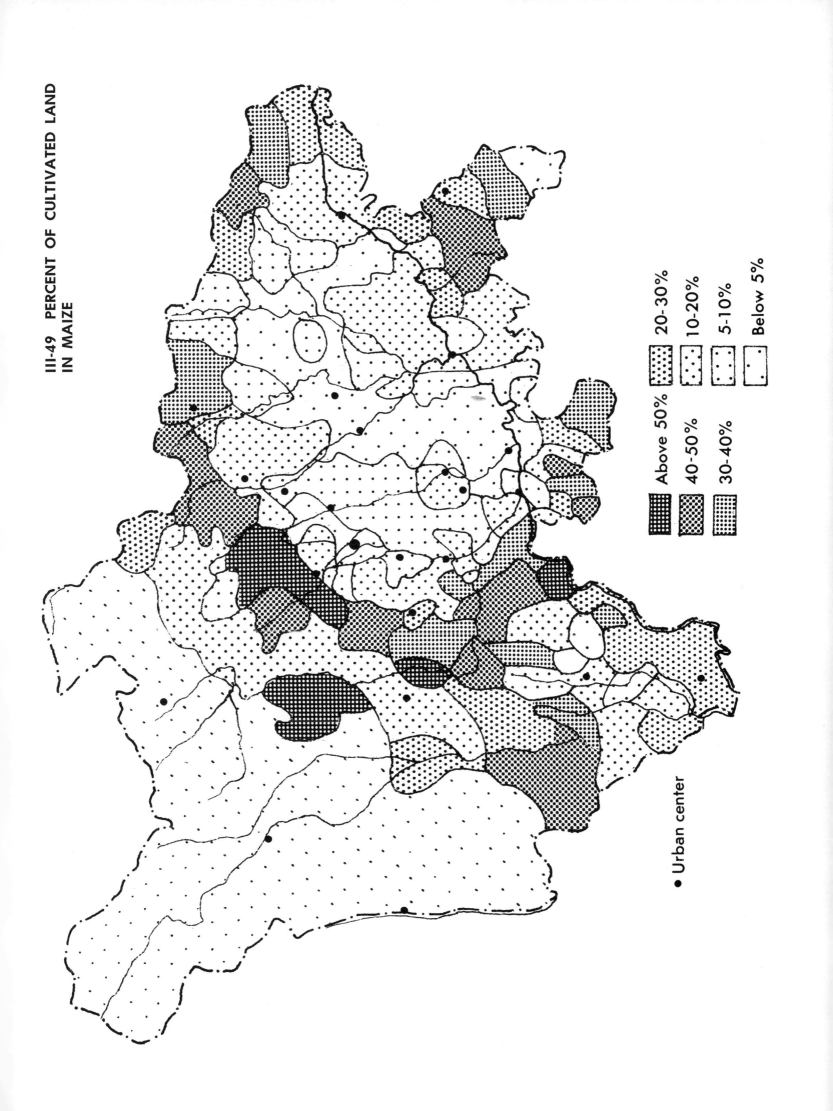

III-49 PERCENT OF CULTIVATED LAND
IN MAIZE

Above 50%   20-30%

40-50%   10-20%

30-40%   5-10%

Below 5%

• Urban center

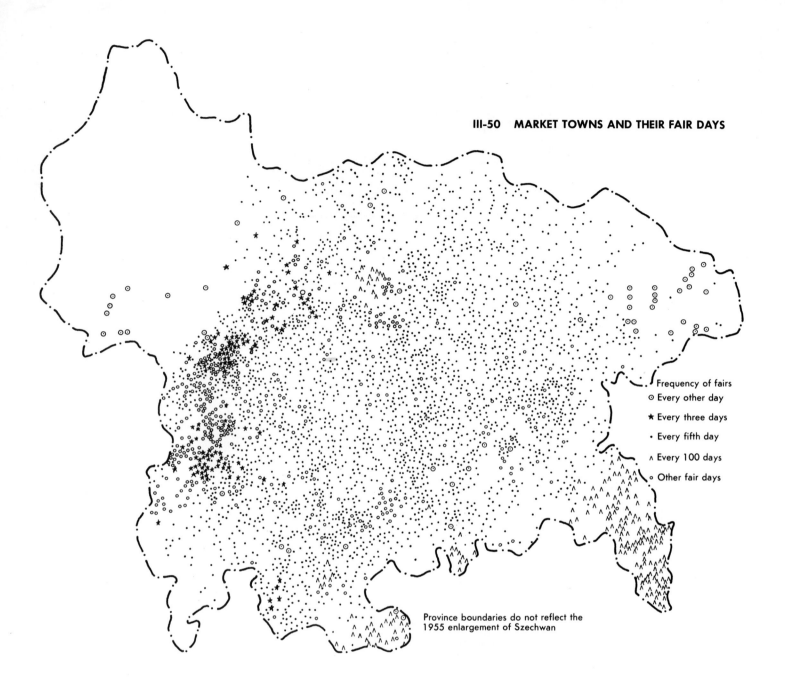

Frequency of fairs
⊙ Every other day
★ Every three days
· Every fifth day
∧ Every 100 days
○ Other fair days

Province boundaries do not reflect the
1955 enlargement of Szechwan

South China

Four subregions comprise South China: the Southeast Coast, the island of Taiwan, the Kwangtung-Kwangsi Region, and the provinces of Yunnan and Kweichow (Map III-51). The general profile of the region is shown by the relief of the land through which the Hsi Chiang flows, as shown by Map III-52.

THE SOUTHEAST COAST REGION

The Southeast Coast Region consists of the eastern portions of the provinces of Chekiang and Fukien (Map III-53). This region is characterized by undulating hills, warm climate, and heavy rainfall. In contrast to other parts of the country, most rivers in this area are short, having steep gradients, and pour directly into the sea. The coast is deeply serrated, and harbors and islands abound.

Hills and mountains are the main physical features of the region; plains are few (Map III-54). In terms of geological age, the area is one of China's oldest land masses, known as the Fukien Massif. The mountain ranges here are the result of eons of weathering and erosion; consequently their altitudes are rather low, generally less than 1,000 meters above sea level. The mountain ranges run from northeast to southwest, roughly parallel to the coast. Erosion of surface rock has produced grotesque mountain ridges, an example of which are the well-known, scenic mountains of eastern Chekiang. Mountains here are also famous for their waterfalls, wreaths of clouds, spring flowers, and autumn leaves, all of which make them enchanting places to visit and to paint.

The jagged coastline is fringed with many good natural harbors, which were coastal lowlands and valleys before the continental mass subsided. Since the lower reaches of the rivers in Chekiang and Fukien are funnel-shaped, they are subject to tidal bores.

This coastal region lies in the subtropical zone. Mountain barriers on the mainland block any cold waves which might sweep down from the north, and winter is relatively warm. Because of proximity to the sea, the temperatures here are lower than directly inland. The region also has the highest rainfall in all China, largely orographic in nature. An additional contributing factor is the occasional heavy precipitation resulting from typhoons. The combined result is an average rainfall of more than 1,500 millimeters throughout most of the area. The rainy season is largely confined to the summer months.

Warm weather and abundant rainfall encourage a luxuriant growth of natural vegetation. In the hilly areas, red and yellow soils predominate. The natural forests on the hills are composed mainly of

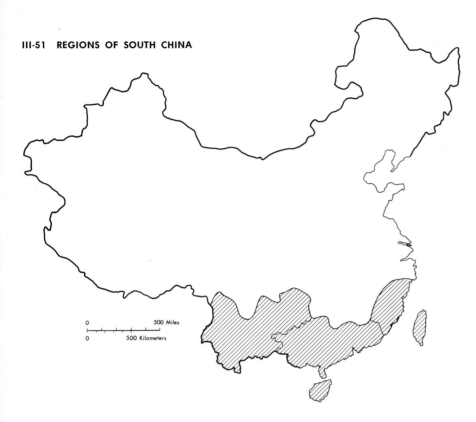

0 ————— 500 Miles
0 ————— 500 Kilometers

subtropical broadleaf evergreens. Camphor, tea, lacquer, wood oil, and tallow trees are cultivated.

The region has many rivers, most of which are short and flow into the sea independently. The longest of these, the Min Chiang in Fukien, is only 480 kilometers long, less than one-tenth the length of the Yangtze. All have steep gradients and swift currents, a combination which provides a potential for the generation of hydroelectricity. Along the lower sections of the rivers small deltas and narrow plains have been built up by alluvial deposits.

The region has uneven distribution of a population in excess of 40 million. Rural population is dense on the deltas along the Chekiang-Fukien coast. Inland mountain areas are thinly populated. Cities are widely scattered and relatively small in size, most major cities being situated on the plains where

the rivers empty into the sea. Hangchow, one of China's famous ancient capitals, has a population of nearly a million and is the provincial capital of Chekiang.

Because of the many good harbors and bays of the Southeast Coast Region and the concentration of inhabitants and major cities along the coast, maritime transportation is of particular local importance. Important seaports are Ning-po and Wenchow in Chekiang, and Foochow and Amoy in Fukien. Chekiang Province had only two railways before 1949: The Shanghai-Hangchow line connects with the Shanghai-Nanking Railway and the river transport of the Yangtze; and the Chekiang-Kiangsi line goes from Hangchow through Kiangsi Province to Chu-chou in Hunan, where it joins the Peking-Canton line. These two railways serve as overland trunk transport lines for the region. Two new railways have been built, one beginning east of Hangchow and running to the coast, near Ning-po. The other lies between Ying-t'an, in Kiangsi, and Amoy; a branch of this line links Nan-p'ing with Foochow.

The Southeast Coast Region is one of China's main producers of subtropical and tropical crops (Map III-55). Irrigated rice is widely cultivated in plains and river valleys, with double cropping in most of the area. Hillside terracing is widely practiced where sweet potatoes, maize, some tea, and other food crops are grown. Other lowland products are sugar cane, silk, and jute. The region is also a major fruit producer. Its tangerines, oranges, pomelos, longans, bananas, pineapples, and lichees are famous throughout China. Large quantities of tea, an important export commodity, are also grown. The area's lacquer trees, oaks, and camphor trees all have great industrial value.

The indented coast, the abundance of harbors, bays, and offshore islands, the vast expanse of shallow sea adjoining the coast, and the plentiful supply of food for fish give the region a position of special importance in China's marine fishing industry.

Hangchow has long been famous for its silk industry, which has now been enhanced by the con-

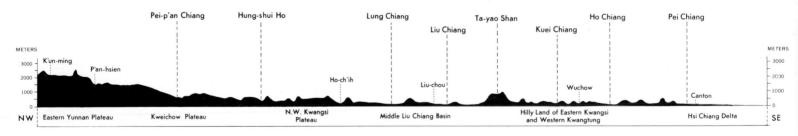

III-52 PROFILE OF THE HSI CHIANG

0   100   200
KILOMETERS

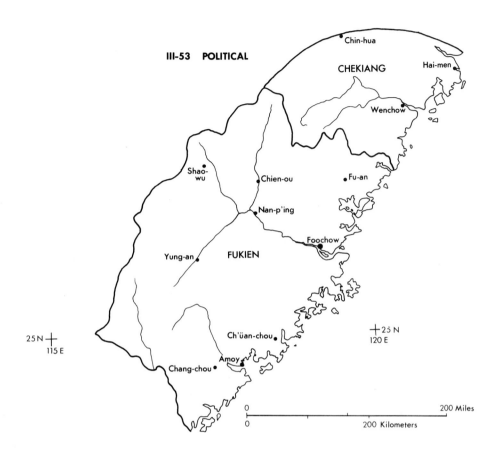

III-53 POLITICAL

CHEKIANG

Chin-hua

Hai-men

Wenchow

Shao-wu

Chien-ou

Fu-an

Nan-p'ing

Foochow

Yung-an

FUKIEN

Ch'üan-chou

Amoy

Chang-chou

115 E
30 N

120 E
30 N

25 N
115 E

25 N
120 E

0   200 Miles

0   200 Kilometers

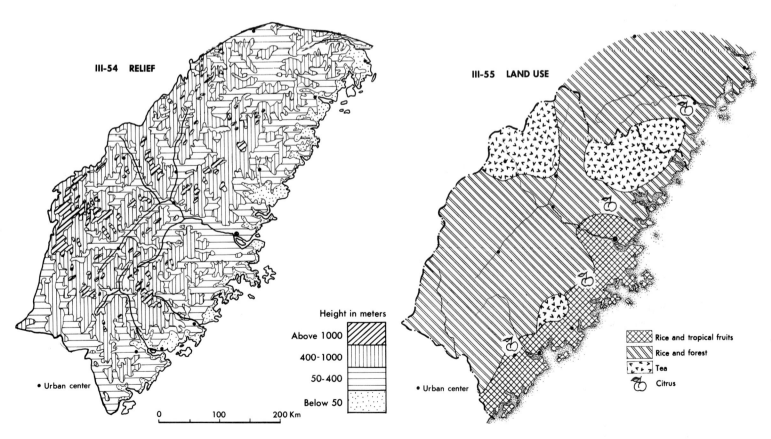

III-54 RELIEF

III-55 LAND USE

Height in meters

Above 1000

400-1000

50-400

Below 50

• Urban center

0   100   200 Km

• Urban center

Rice and tropical fruits

Rice and forest

Tea

Citrus

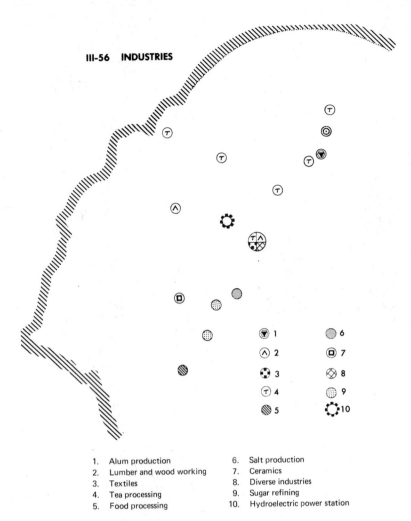

1. Alum production
2. Lumber and wood working
3. Textiles
4. Tea processing
5. Food processing
6. Salt production
7. Ceramics
8. Diverse industries
9. Sugar refining
10. Hydroelectric power station

struction of a large silk-weaving factory. Lacquerwares of Fukien, silk sunshades, sandalwood fans, and other artistic handicraft products of Hangchow are highly treasured both at home and abroad. In general, Chekiang and Fukien are not industrially developed, but they have great potential for light industry because of the hydroelectric power potential and the abundance of good harbors (Map III-56).

TAIWAN

Taiwan lies astride the Tropic of Cancer in a position comparable to that of Cuba and covers an area of 34,263 square kilometers, about the size of Massachusetts or Switzerland. The shape of Taiwan is roughly that of a long oval, approximately 394 kilometers from north to south, and 157 kilometers from west to east at its broadest point, so that no place in Taiwan is more than 80 kilometers from the sea (Maps III-57 and III-58).

It is believed that the island was originally a part of the China mainland mass in early geological periods. This assumption is based on a variety of evidence—contrasting curvature between the Ryukyu arc, the Philippine archipelago, and Taiwan;

the structural alignment and rock correlation between Fukien, mainland China, and Taiwan; the character of the Formosa Strait's submarine configuration; the simple and smooth coast line of the island, and the existence of extensive basalt mesas formed through fissure eruptions. Not until the Pleistocene epoch when the land beneath the present Strait sank and formed a rift valley, was Taiwan separated from the continent and isolated as an island.

About two-thirds of the island of Taiwan consists of rugged mountains (Map III-59). The most prominent topographic feature is a tilted block which forms a backbone traversing from northeast to southwest, with precipitous slopes on the east side and gentler relief toward the Formosa Strait. The central part of the island is made up of four parallel anticlinal ranges, lying close to the eastern coast, which thrust up 48 peaks of approximately 3,000 meters in height. Below these sharp elevations the sea cliffs drop perpendicularly on the east for 90 meters. On these slopes, streams are few in number, with short, steep watercourses. It is on the western part of the island that rivers cut the land into successive terraces and, further downstream, build the alluvial plains sloping to the sea. Even here, most of the streams which originate in the mountain region are short and swift, deeply incising their valleys and giving the island a radial drainage pattern. Most of these streams are not navigable and flood frequently during the rainy season with their debris building up alluvial fans on the coastal plain (Map III-60).

Taiwan's climate is characterized by high temperatures, heavy rainfall, and strong winds. Summer in Taiwan is long and hot; winter is very short and mild. Throughout the island, the annual mean temperature is more than 21°C. During most of the year, as one travels from north to south in Taiwan, with each degree of latitude one finds an increase of 0.8°C in temperature. However, during July, Taiwan's hottest month, the heat is practically as great in the north as in the south: For that month the average temperature at Chi-lung is 28.2°C, while at the southern tip of the island it is 27.4°C, a difference of only 0.8°C. In January and February, the coldest months, the temperature variance between north to south is greater, Chi-lung having a monthly average of 15.2°C and Heng-chun, 20.5°C, a difference of 5.3°C. Snow is rarely seen in the lowland areas of the island although the summits of the lofty mountains are covered with snow for a short time.

Taiwan has abundant rainfall throughout the year. Many stations have an average annual rainfall of almost 2,500 mm. But the rainfall is by no means evenly distributed. In general, the eastern coast has more rain than the west, and lowlands receive less rain than mountain slopes. The most striking

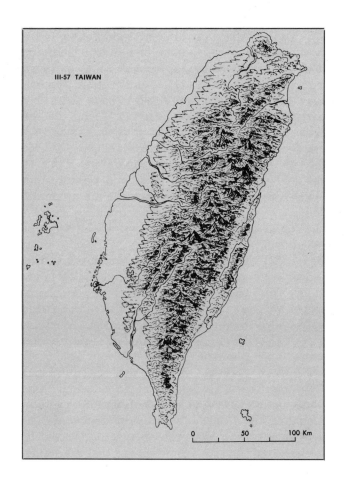

III-57 TAIWAN

0   50   100 Km

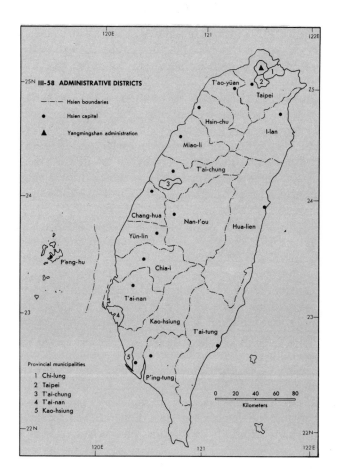

III-58 ADMINISTRATIVE DISTRICTS

— · — Hsien boundaries
● Hsien capital
▲ Yangmingshan administration

25N

T'ao-yüan
Taipei
Hsin-chu
I-lan
Miao-li
T'ai-chung
Chang-hua
Nan-t'ou
Hua-lien
Yün-lin
P'eng-hu
Chia-i
T'ai-nan
Kao-hsiung
T'ai-tung
P'ing-tung

Provincial municipalities

1 Chi-lung
2 Taipei
3 T'ai-chung
4 T'ai-nan
5 Kao-hsiung

0   20   40   60   80
Kilometers

22N

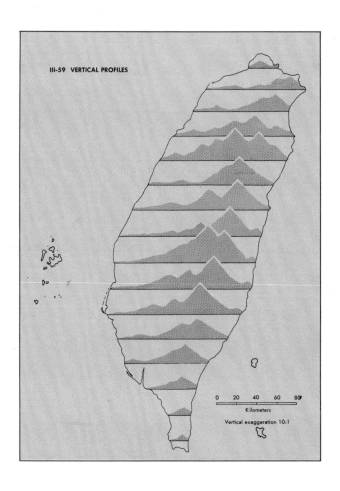

III-59 VERTICAL PROFILES

0   20   40   60   80
Kilometers

Vertical exaggeration 10:1

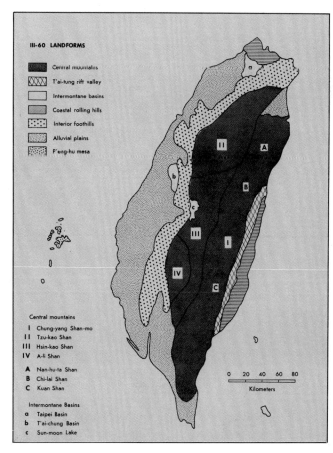

III-60 LANDFORMS

Central mountains
T'ai-tung rift valley
Intermontane basins
Coastal rolling hills
Interior foothills
Alluvial plains
P'eng-hu mesa

Central mountains

I Chung-yang Shan-mo
II Tzu-kao Shan
III Hsin-kao Shan
IV A-li Shan

A Nan-hu-ta Shan
B Chi-lai Shan
C Kuan Shan

Intermontane Basins

a Taipei Basin
b T'ai-chung Basin
c Sun-moon Lake

0   20   40   60   80
Kilometers

feature of Taiwan's rainfall is that the dry season at one end of the island is concurrent with the rainy season at the opposite point: In the north the rains fall from October to March; during this period Chilung has a precipitation of 1,600 mm, or 56 percent of its total rainfall of 2,850 mm. On the other hand, during the fall and winter months, the south enjoys continually fine and delightful weather and irrigation is a necessity for farming. In the south the rainy season lasts from April to September; during these months Heng-chun has a rainfall of 1,980 mm, 88 percent of its total rainfall of 2,250 mm.

As a result of its location on the eastern side of the great land mass of Asia and in the western sector of the Pacific Ocean, Taiwan's wind patterns are determined by the monsoons. Typhoons plague the island each year, usually in August and September. Taiwan has a variety of climates, ranging from the subhumid and cold type in the high central mountains to the hot tropical climate found in the coastal area. On the basis of the Köppen system of climatic classification, Taiwan has an A climate, with high temperature and abundant rainfall throughout the year, found in the southern tip of Taiwan; and C climates, with moderate temperature, adequate rainfall, but long, very warm summers and mild winters, which cover most of the remainder of Taiwan (Map III-61). The high mountains, of course, modify these generalizations.

The interplay of different soil-forming factors (including climate, parent materials, landforms, and vegetation cover), gives the soils in Taiwan a great diversity (Maps III-62 and III-63). However, as a result of the island's relief, soils show more vertical than horizontal zonation. Along the west coast salines and paddy soils, then alluvial soils are found. Next come the hills and terraces with lateritic soils. Eastward at higher elevations the red and yellow soils are seen, and on the upper slopes the gray-brown podzolic soils are prominent. Mountain podzolic soils and lithosols are found at the top of the ranges. Land use, of course, varies as a result of these differences in soils and topography. Salt fields and pisciculture are important in the landscape along the coast; proceeding inland, sugar cane, paddy fields, citrus fruits, and barren slopes are encountered; in the high mountains one is surrounded by huge forests or wasteland.

With moderately high mountains, high temperature, and abundant rainfall, Taiwan has a rich flora (Map III-64). The vertical distribution of Taiwan's forests demonstrates an unusually large variety and distinct zonations of natural vegetation including the tropical, subtropical, temperate, and cold temperate. However, this natural cover has been cleared from all western plains that are suitable for agriculture (Map III-65). Four main types of vegetation are now dominant in different regions,

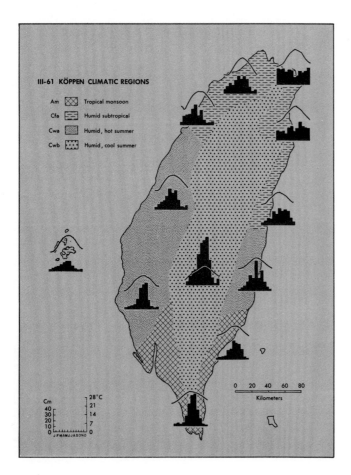

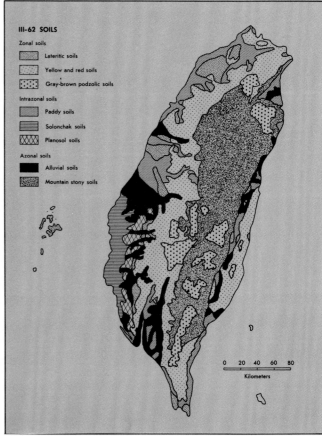

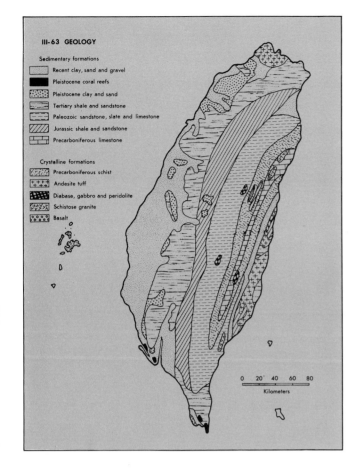

III-63 GEOLOGY

Sedimentary formations

Recent clay, sand and gravel
Pleistocene coral reefs
Pleistocene clay and sand
Tertiary shale and sandstone
Paleozoic sandstone, slate and limestone
Jurassic shale and sandstone
Precarboniferous limestone

Crystalline formations

Precarboniferous schist
Andesite tuff
Diabase, gabbro and peridolite
Schistose granite
Basalt

0 20 40 60 80
Kilometers

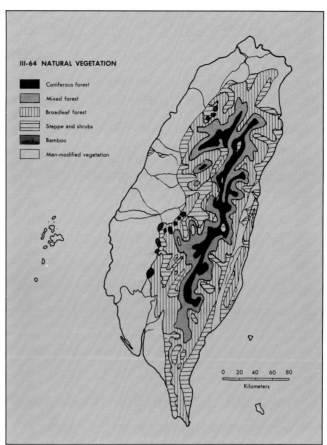

III-64 NATURAL VEGETATION

Coniferous forest
Mixed forest
Broadleaf forest
Steppe and shrubs
Bamboo
Man-modified vegetation

0 20 40 60 80
Kilometers

namely, broadleaved evergreen forests, mixed forests, coniferous forests, and a mixture of steppe shrub and grasses including bamboo. The total number of species of commercial importance is about 100, ranging from tropical hardwood growing at sea level to spruce, hemlocks, and firs growing at higher elevations.

Taiwan's historical geography and contemporary demography are complex and interesting facets of the island's nature (Maps III-66 and III-67). Today it is one of the most densely populated regions in the world. Nearly 15 million people live on its 34,263 square kilometers. The population density (more than 440 persons per square kilometer) is higher than that of the Netherlands (356 per square kilometer). It also is higher than that of Belgium (314), Japan (264), South Korea (240), and even of Puerto Rico (270). Taiwan's population density is greater than that of any province in mainland China except Kiangsu, which has 445 persons per square kilometer.

The uneven distribution of the population in Taiwan (Map III-67) is closely related to the physical conditions of the island. A comparison of the rainfall and population distribution maps will show in general a negative correlation between population density and amount of precipitation: The heavy rainfall regions in the central part of the island are the most sparsely populated areas. Areas with an annual rainfall of 1,880 mm or more have a population

density of fewer than 26 persons per square kilometer. On the other hand, the western coastal region where annual rainfall averages less than 1,880 mm, is the most densely populated area; here efficient utilization of the rainfall and careful irrigation of the land have made the region the most important agricultural area in Taiwan.

A close relationship between surface configuration and population density can also be seen: The plains are crowded, while the mountain regions are sparsely inhabited. In particular, the western coastal plains, which are ideal for paddy cultivation, have an average population of more than 800 persons per square kilometer and comprise the most densely populated part of the island. The total area of Taiwan's western coastal plains is about 7,680 square kilometers, approximately 22 percent of the total area of the island; the population of this plain however, amounts to more than two-thirds of the total population of Taiwan. In the central and eastern parts of the island, the mountains are less suitable for agriculture; thus, the mountainous counties have the lowest population density. In the hilly areas the population density varies from 259 to 520 persons per square kilometer; while in the higher mountains where the heavy rainfall has not been well managed, the density decreases to 52 persons per square kilometer, and in some places to less than 26. Population on the western coastal plains is

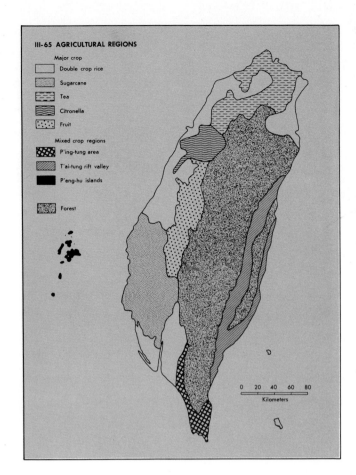

III-65 AGRICULTURAL REGIONS

Major crop
- Double crop rice
- Sugarcane
- Tea
- Citronella
- Fruit

Mixed crop regions
- P'ing-tung area
- T'ai-tung rift valley
- P'eng-hu islands

- Forest

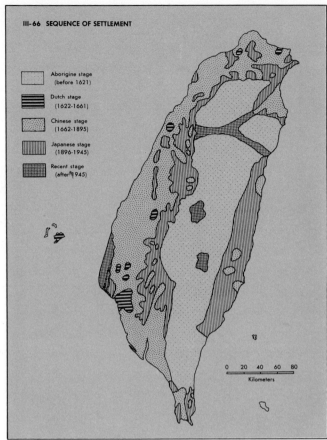

III-66 SEQUENCE OF SETTLEMENT

- Aborigine stage (before 1621)
- Dutch stage (1622-1661)
- Chinese stage (1662-1895)
- Japanese stage (1896-1945)
- Recent stage (after 1945)

relatively evenly distributed, while landforms have imposed more limits on settlement in the less advanced eastern areas, with the result that here the people are concentrated either along the transportation lines or in valleys and basins.

Taiwan's colonial history has affected the composition of its population. The island lies close to the mainland, halfway between Shanghai and Hong Kong, halfway between the Philippines and Japan. This location has attracted travelers and colonists from mainland China and Japan; traders from Portugal, Holland, and Spain; and aboriginal seafarers from other parts of Southeast Asia. These various influences have left their mark on the landscape of Taiwan, and even today one can still find remnants of each of these cultures.

In the aboriginal period prior to the fifteenth century, settlement was probably distributed more or less evenly over the plains of the island. The Malayans settled in villages under the control of native chiefs and held the land in common under a usufruct system. They were a society of hunters and fishermen who also engaged in shifting agriculture, with millet and sweet potato as the main crops. Farm implements were primitive, and fertilizer was not used. A simple division of labor dictated that women cultivate the land while the men hunted; the crafts were generally the province of men and the raising of animals was carried on by women. Self-sufficient

until the arrival of outsiders, the aborigines were finally driven into the mountains in the seventeenth and eighteenth centuries; there they conducted a subsistence economy which persists to this day. At present, aborigines still live in the central mountains, occupying about half of the island, with a population that constitutes less than 2 percent of the island's total.

The Dutch went into Taiwan in the seventeenth century under the auspices of the East India Company which occupied the southern part of the island and established a colonial government. All cultivated land was owned by the company, which rented land and farm implements to the tenants. In their pursuit of commercial enterprise, the Dutch introduced oxen and encouraged the cultivation of sugar cane; they also made a survey of the land and introduced the technique of well-digging.

The Dutch were interested not only in the profits to be gained from commerce, but also in the spread of their religion. They left their mark on the landscape of Taiwan in the form of castles, churches, wells, and land survey units. They also romanized the alphabets of the aboriginal languages. However, despite their technological advancement and their industry and enterprise, their tenure in this island was short.

Chinese settlement in Taiwan dates back as far as the twelfth century A.D., but it was not until

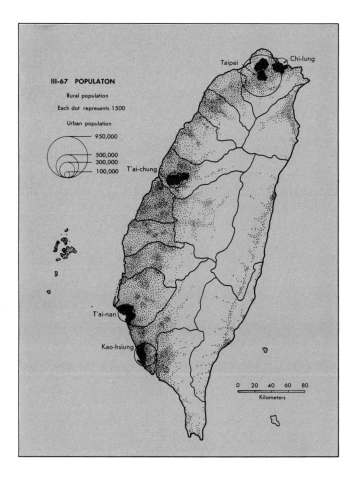

III-67 POPULATON

Rural population

Each dot represents 1500

Urban population

950,000
500,000
300,000
100,000

Taipei
Chi-lung
T'ai-chung
T'ai-nan
Kao-hsiung

0 20 40 60 80
Kilometers

conservatism was in marked contrast to the bustling commerce developing nearby in South China.

The landmarks made by the Chinese in Taiwan include not only paddy fields, irrigation ponds and ditches, and tea gardens, but also brick walls and sun-dried tiles of rural houses, city walls, Confucian temples, and arcades. Arcades were a prominent urban feature brought in from southern China.

When the Japanese took over the island from China in 1895, they began a new stage in the sequent occupance of Taiwan—the industrial era. Modern transportation was introduced, harbors were built, industries were established, and agriculture was intensified by the introduction of a new kind of rice. Many fruits, especially pineapple, had previously been cultivated in Taiwan, but it was only after the coming of the Japanese that the canning process was introduced. Thus the processing and export of food products became an important island industry.

The Japanese rule differed from the Dutch and the Chinese in that it was a military administration designed to further the Japanese goal of expansion: Taiwan was designed and used as a stepping stone for the Japanese southern expansion during the Sino-Japanese War. Under this military rule and the consequent economic policy, the people of Taiwan became Japanese subjects in obligation, enjoying few civil rights.

At the conclusion of World War II, Taiwan was returned to China, and the economy of the island changed from a colonial state to a provincial state. In 1949 the Chinese Nationalist Government was driven to Taiwan by the Communist armies, and with them came civilians, officials, and soldiers who increased the island's population by nearly 2 million.

The high temperature, abundant rainfall, and fertile alluvial soils make Taiwan, especially the western region, almost ideal for agriculture. Rice is predominant, accounting for over half of the total value of agricultural production. It is grown chiefly as paddy (wet fields) in the northern part of the island. The southern part generally produces sugar cane, sweet potatoes, and tropical fruits. Sugar is the second most important cash crop for the farmers of Taiwan. The sweet potatoes are indispensable in the diet of the people and the plant is widely cultivated over the island throughout the year. Tea, produced mainly in the north, forms an important article of trade. Tropical fruits such as pineapples, bananas, and oranges are extensively grown.

In recent years, the economy of Taiwan has developed greatly; farming, forestry, manufacturing, and mining have expanded, as well as foreign trade (Maps III-68 and III-69). All this growth has demanded coordinated improvements in transportation (Map III-70). As part of the legacy of the Japanese occupation, Taiwan has a well-developed rail system.

the seventeenth century that large groups of Chinese began to cross the Taiwan Strait and drive the Dutch out of the island. The waves of Chinese immigrants, most of them from Fukien and Kwangtung, also pushed the aborigines back into the mountains and occupied the plains.

The period of Chinese dominance (roughly from the late seventeenth to the late nineteenth century) was characterized by a new form of land use. Both the aboriginal shifting agriculture and the more highly developed sugar plantations of the Dutch gave way to the traditional Chinese rice culture; and the landscape was soon dotted with small farms, terraces and paddy fields, with the dense population settled in small nucleated villages. As on the mainland, there was intensive use of human labor, and water buffalo and oxen were the only beasts of burden. Tea culture was also introduced to the island in this period, but the basis of the economy was rice, with sugar cane secondary.

As the Chinese economy supplanted the island's earlier forms, so, in time, the traditional Chinese culture also prevailed. A form of private enterprise developed, with relatively little formal governmental regulation; economic as well as social sanctions were applied by the clan or village elders rather than by officialdom, and even tax obligations were modest. However, this informal structure proved inefficient in many ways; furthermore, its extreme agrarian

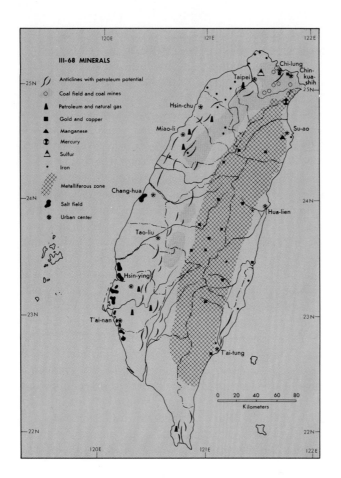

III-68 MINERALS

- ∫∫ Anticlines with petroleum potential
- ○ Coal field and coal mines
- ▲ Petroleum and natural gas
- ■ Gold and copper
- ▲ Manganese
- ☿ Mercury
- △ Sulfur
- • Iron
- Metalliferous zone
- ◗ Salt field
- ✳ Urban center

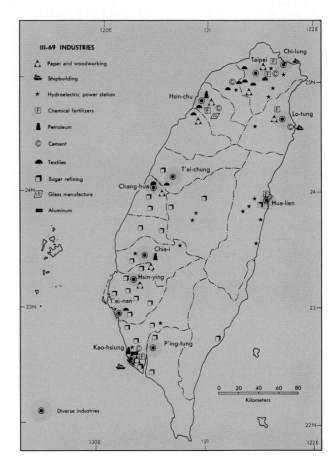

III-69 INDUSTRIES

- △ Paper and woodworking
- ⚓ Shipbuilding
- ★ Hydroelectric power station
- Ⓕ Chemical fertilizers
- ▮ Petroleum
- Ⓒ Cement
- ▲ Textiles
- ▢ Sugar refining
- ▽ Glass manufacture
- ▬ Aluminum

◉ Diverse industries

The most important railroad is the main line between south and north Taiwan, connecting Chi-lung, and Kao-hsiung, a port of primary importance in the south. This line has a length of 406 kilometers with 79 stations; indeed, most of the principal cities of the island are along this line where the greater portion of staple products accumulate for transportation. The line forms a main artery of passenger as well as freight traffic. Besides the public railroads, there are private railways which were started by sugar refineries and formerly used largely for cane transport; these are now open to the general public. The highways of Taiwan are also well developed, the most important ones being concentrated in the western coastal plains of the island and running parallel to the north-south railroad. The highway network has the average ratio of 50 kilometers per hundred square kilometers.

The main resources of Taiwan are its soils and climate rather than minerals. The low mineralization in Taiwan is chiefly due to a lack of widespread igneous intrusion, which is usually associated with mineral-forming processes. However, some metallic minerals are mined in the extreme north, in the central mountain area, and along the eastern coast. In addition, the northern lowland contains the island's principal coal field, and petroleum is pro-

duced in the central and southern parts. Mineral production in the island also includes gold, copper, mercury, sulfur, silver, manganese, and phosphates. Of these minerals, coal, gold, copper, petroleum, and sulfur are most significant.

Taiwan has several favorable factors contributing to industrial development; these include cheap hydroelectric power, excellent transportation in the heavily settled areas, abundant labor supply, social stability, and an industrial foundation. But like other underdeveloped countries, Taiwan suffers a shortage of capital, a lack of entrepreneurs, and a lack of technical know-how. Also, its mineral resources are quite limited, especially those most useful to Taiwan's industry, such as iron ore and bauxite.

The location of Taiwan's industries is influenced by availability of raw materials, labor, transportation facilities, and markets. Since two-thirds of Taiwan's land is mountainous, its agriculture, manufacturing, and commerce are concentrated on the fertile coastal plain. On this plain are located two seaports, Kao-hsiung in the south and Chi-lung in the north. Most of the island's basic or heavy industries—iron and steel, aluminum, machinery, petroleum, acids and alkalis—are located in Kao-hsiung. Most of the light industries, producing

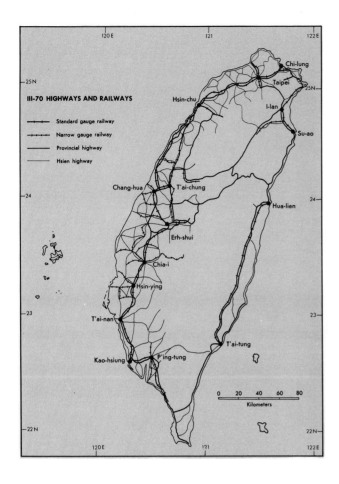

III-70 HIGHWAYS AND RAILWAYS

—·—·— Standard gauge railway
—·—·— Narrow gauge railway
———— Provincial highway
———— Hsien highway

condiments. Processing of marine products, including fish canning, is done on the northeast and southwest coasts. The solar salt industry is located on the southwest coast, which is also the location of the cement plants near the limestone-producing area in the south. The forested mountain areas in the central part of the island are the home of the lumber industry, while on the northwestern hills are many tea plantations. Maps III-71 through III-77 show the specific interplay of various types of land use for seven important cities in Taiwan. The combination of the urban maps and the oblique sketches provide a good sense of function and setting.

Though Taiwan has considerable hydroelectric potential, much of this remains underdeveloped. Electric power is greatly needed in the southwest, where metal and machinery-manufacturing industries, food processing, the cement industry, and irrigation projects are located. Next in consumption of electric power are the northwestern areas, where coal, gold, and copper are mined and where the fertilizer, textile, and metal industries are situated.

As can be seen from this short summary of the physical, social, and economic characteristics of Taiwan, the island is rich in diversity and potential.

In future industrial expansion, development of basic industries besides those producing fertilizer, food, textiles, and power should be emphasized. The chemical industries especially stand out as having favorable conditions—an abundant supply of power; a steady supply of basic resources such as natural gas, oil, salt, limestone, and coal; and some experience with industries such as sugar-refining, paper manufacturing, salt-electrolysis, petroleum refining, and camphor distilling. Finally, its good location between Japan and Hong Kong, its beautiful scenery, and its excellent transportation facilities should be favorable factors in further developing the tourist industry.

It should be noted that several of the maps in this section were based on those appearing in *Taiwan-Ilha Formosa,* by Chiao-min Hsieh (Butterworths, 1964). They have been used with the permission of the publisher.

consumer goods, are located near the capital, Taipei, which uses the facilities of Chi-lung Harbor to bring in imported raw materials. Some industries, such as textiles, are especially dependent on the labor supply, as well as on imported raw materials, and therefore are located in or near cities with port facilities. Other consumer goods produced in the cities are soap, and articles made of leather, wool, and rubber. The printing industry is also located in the cities. Some food industries have been established near agricultural areas, where seasonal laborers are numerous. Among these food industries are sugar refining, rice hulling, grain milling, pineapple canning, and the production of edible oil, bean curd, and

TAIPEI

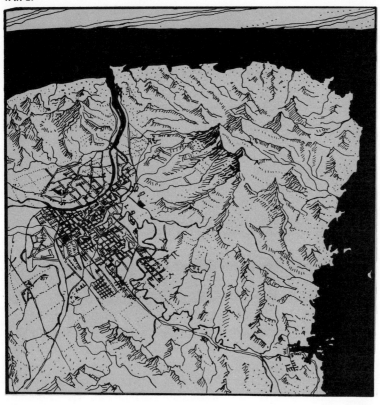

III-71 TAIPEI

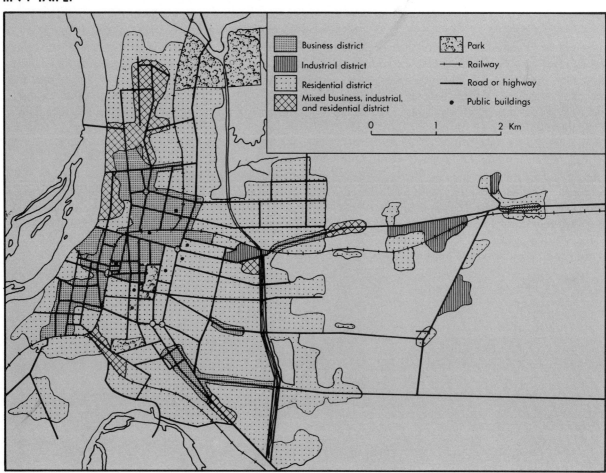

Business district

Industrial district

Residential district

Mixed business, industrial, and residential district

Park

Railway

Road or highway

Public buildings

0   1   2 Km

T'AI-CHUNG

T'AI-NAN

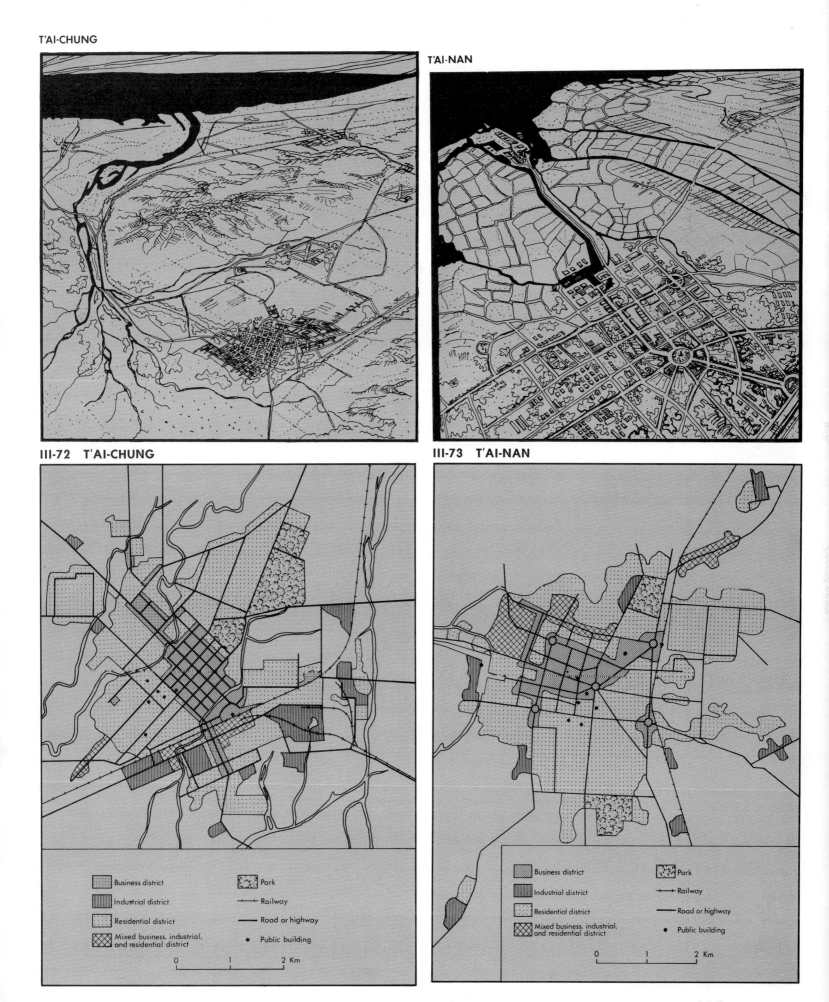

III-72   T'AI-CHUNG

III-73   T'AI-NAN

Business district

Industrial district

Residential district

Mixed business, industrial,
and residential district

Park

Railway

Road or highway

Public building

0   1   2 Km

Business district

Industrial district

Residential district

Mixed business, industrial,
and residential district

Park

Railway

Road or highway

Public building

0   1   2 Km

HSIN-CHU

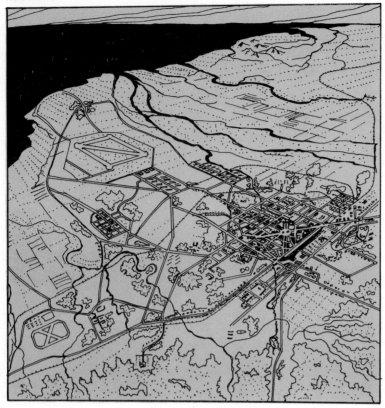

III-74 HSIN-CHU

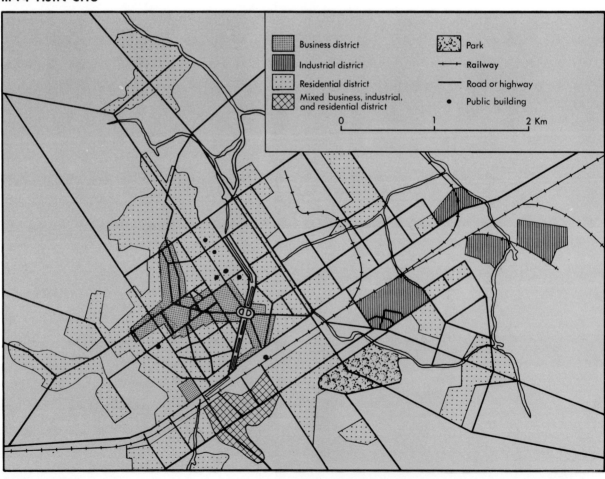

Business district

Industrial district

Residential district

Mixed business, industrial, and residential district

Park

Railway

Road or highway

Public building

0   1   2 Km

CHIA-I

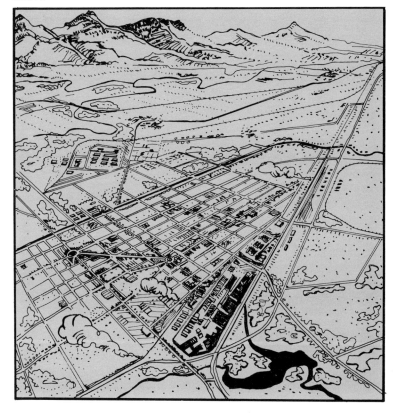

III-75 CHIA-I

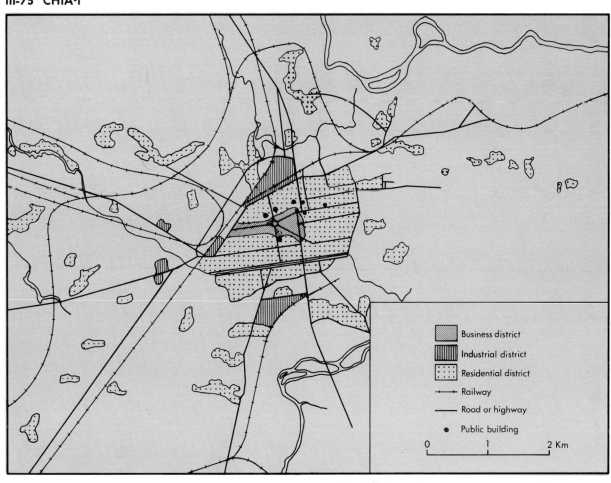

Business district

Industrial district

Residential district

Railway

Road or highway

Public building

0   1   2 Km

HUA-LIEN

III-76 HUA-LIEN

Business district

Industrial district

Residential district

Mixed business, industrial, and residential district

╾╼╾ Railway

───── Road or highway

● Public building

0   1   2 Km

T'AI-TUNG

III-77 T'AI-TUNG

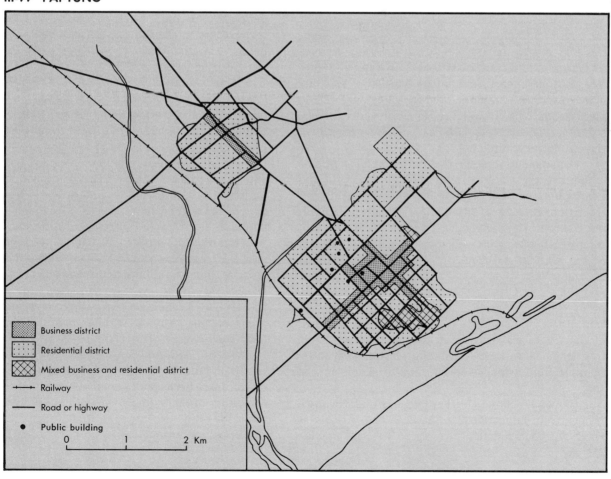

Business district

Residential district

Mixed business and residential district

+—+— Railway

——— Road or highway

● Public building

0   1   2 Km

THE KWANGTUNG AND KWANGSI REGION (INCLUDING HAINAN ISLAND)

Kwangtung Province and the Kwangsi Chuang Autonomous Region have a combined total area of 450,000 square kilometers (Map III-78). This region is bisected by the Tropic of Cancer. In the north, the region is separated from the Middle-Yangtze Region by the Nan Ling range; in the northeast, it is sheltered by the Fukien Massif. It borders on the Yunnan-Kweichow Plateau in the northwest and adjoins Vietnam in the southwest. Its southern coast is washed by the South China Sea. Just south of Kwangtung's Luichow Peninsula between this sea and the Gulf of Tonkin lies Hainan Island. Administratively a part of Kwangtung Province, this island is only slightly smaller than Taiwan. The people in Kwangtung and Kwangsi are marine-minded, and the early development of navigation has long since brought the region into close contact with the outside world.

The two provinces are studded with low hills, and level land can be found only in narrow strips along the deltas at the lower courses of the rivers and along the seaboard (Map III-79). Kwangsi, particularly in the western part, is characterized by karst topography. Limestone predominates as the bedrock, and, having undergone erosion by solution for centuries, this limestone has created a forest of pinnacles and spires, sinkholes and caverns. Rivulets and creeks disappear midway in their courses to become subterranean streams. Kwangsi, therefore, may be likened to a natural garden of spectacular limestone scenery. Everywhere one finds picturesque hills, residual columns of vertical limestone spires, intricate caverns, and bizarre stalactites and stalagmites.

Conspicuous among the narrow plains of the region are the Canton Delta at the estuary of the Pearl River, and the delta of the Han Chiang, where the city of Swatow is situated. The delta surrounding Canton is by far the larger, with a total area of roughly 10,000 square kilometers. It is composed of the alluvial sediments of three rivers: the Hsi Chiang (West River), the Pei Chiang (North River), and the Tung Chiang (East River), which combine in one estuary known as the Pearl River. The terrain of the Canton Delta is interlaced by a network of distributaries, cutting it into numerous pieces in a trellised pattern. It is also dotted with innumerable hills, which were originally islands in the sea.

Since the climate of Kwangtung and Kwangsi ranges from subtropical to tropical, the weather is warm all year round. The region has an average annual rainfall of 1,200 millimeters, the rainy season starting as early as April or May and lasting until October. From May to October there is the additional probability of typhoons, which are frequently accompanied by torrents of rain.

The region has mostly red soils in the hilly areas, and fertile noncalcareous alluvial soil in the flood plains and deltas. Vegetation is both tropical and subtropical. Mangroves abound in the shallow portions of the estuaries, while on Hainan Island and in the Luichow Peninsula coconut palms and banyan trees cover a wide area. Vegetation in the mainland hills of Kwangtung and Kwangsi is less luxuriant and smaller in size than on Hainan Island because winters here are somewhat drier and cooler. Most of the rivers of the two provinces pass through hilly areas, and their flow is swift. Heavy rainfall, particularly during the summer, swells these rivers; in point of volume, the Pearl (to which the Hsi Chiang is the major contributor) is second only to the Yangtze. Its drainage area is only about half that of the Yellow River, yet every year it sends six and a half times as much water to the sea. Most of the rivers of the area, furthermore, have a low silt content because they flow through hilly areas covered with lush vegetation. Rapid currents and the large volume of water bring to the region enormous hydroelectric potential—especially significant for industrial development in the area in view of its deficiency of coal. Such silt as these rivers carry is deposited in the Canton Delta, which is gradually being extended seaward; shifting sand bars are a handicap to navigation here.

The combined population of Kwangtung and Kwangsi was approximately 63 million in 1970, the greatest concentration being found in the Canton Delta. With an average of more than 500 persons per square kilometer in the delta, this area is among China's most densely populated areas. Like all the southeast coastal areas, Kwangtung Province is a major departure point for emigration. Most of the people have gone to Southeast Asia, but some to places as far away as Europe and America.

Canton, the provincial capital of Kwangtung, is the largest city in the region, with a population of more than 2.3 million, and is the largest seaport in the South. Industry in present-day Canton, and in the area as a whole, is expanding, especially in the areas of silk weaving, rubber manufacturing, and food processing (Map III-80). This southern metropolis is connected by railroad with many parts of the mainland. Although it is not accessible to ocean liners because of the shallowness of the Pearl, dredging and port improvements have made it possible for ships as large as 10,000 tons to call at Whampoa, Canton's outer port 15 kilometers dis-

III-78 POLITICAL

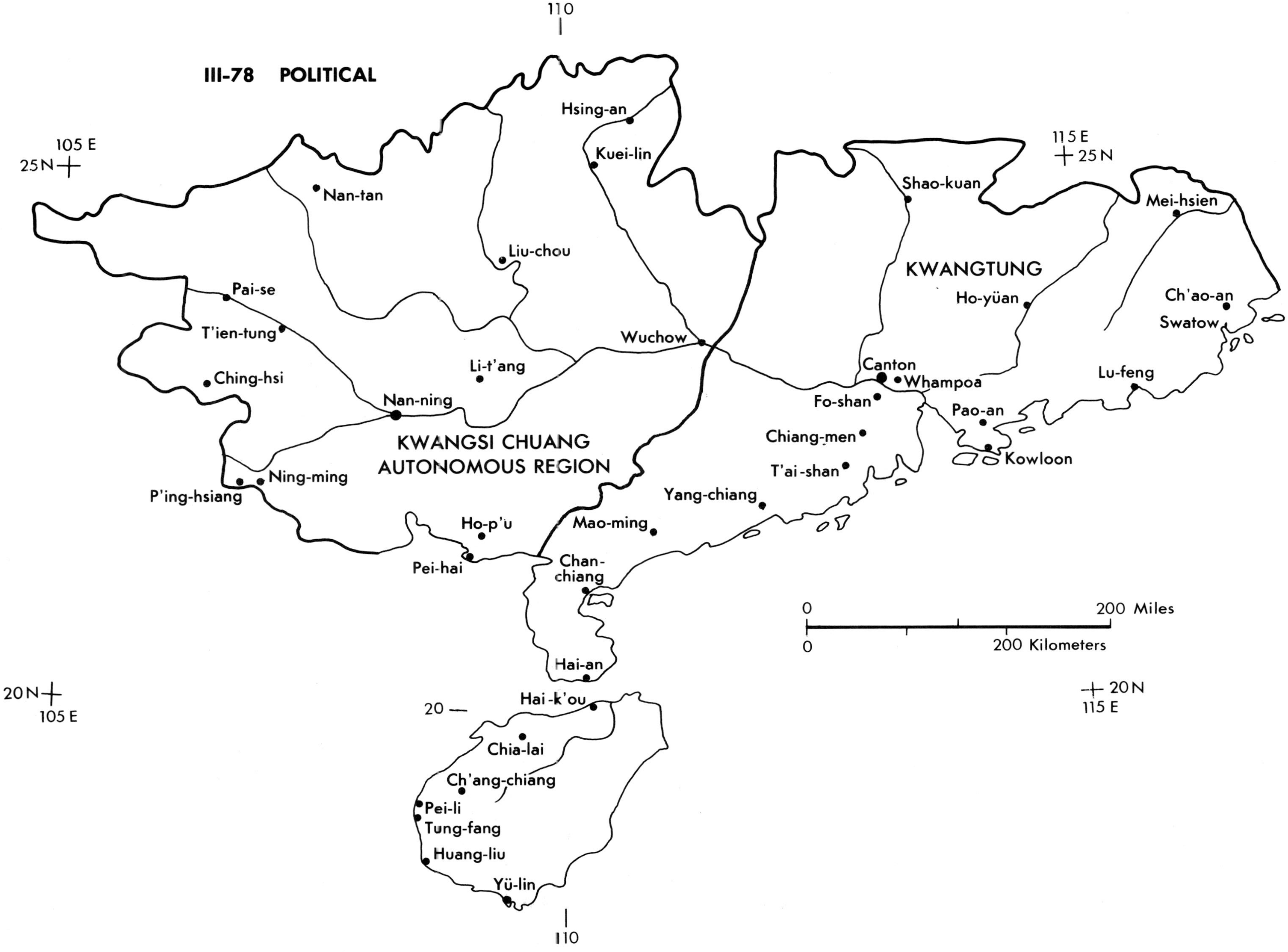

KWANGTUNG

KWANGSI CHUANG
AUTONOMOUS REGION

Mei-hsien

Ch'ao-an
Swatow

Lu-feng

Shao-kuan

Ho-yüan

Canton
Whampoa
Fo-shan

Pao-an
Kowloon

Chiang-men
T'ai-shan

Yang-chiang

Wuchow

Hsing-an
Kuei-lin

Liu-chou

Li-t'ang

Mao-ming

Chan-
chiang

Hai-an

Ho-p'u

Nan-tan

Nan-ning

Pei-hai

Hai-k'ou

Chia-lai

Ch'ang-chiang

Pai-se
T'ien-tung

Ning-ming

Ching-hsi

Pei-li
Tung-fang
Huang-liu

Yü-lin

P'ing-hsiang

115 E
25 N

110

105 E
25 N

200 Miles

200 Kilometers

20 N
115 E

110

20

20 N
105 E

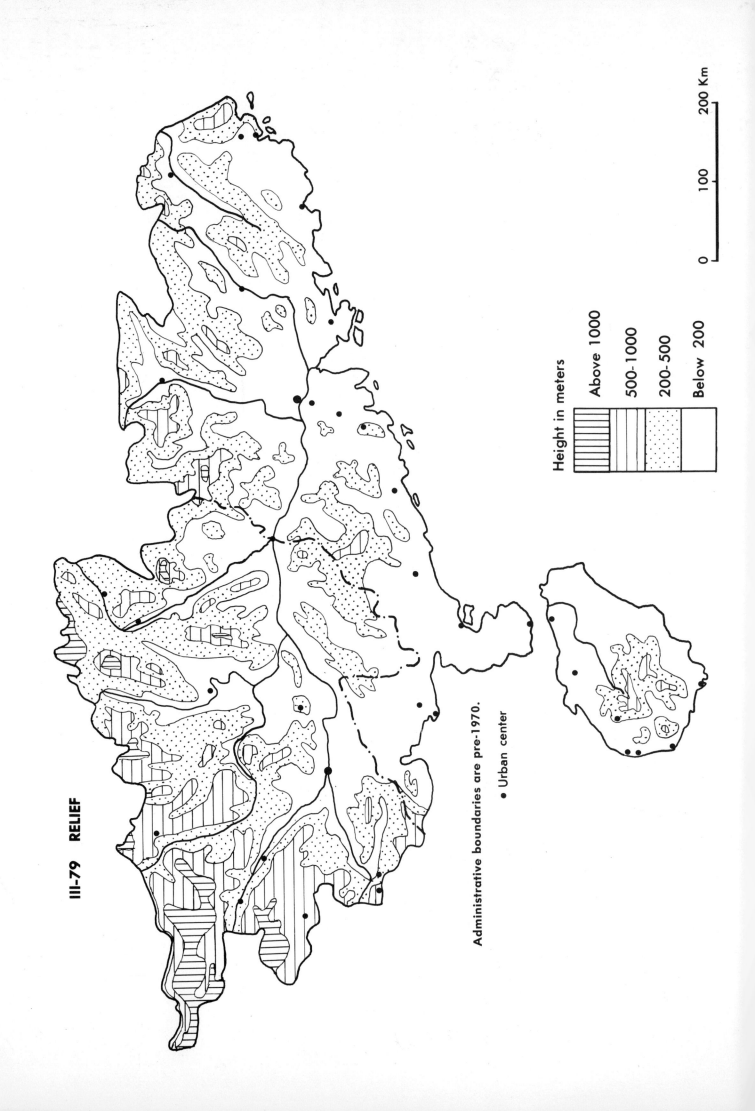

III-79 RELIEF

Height in meters

Above 1000

500-1000

200-500

Below 200

Administrative boundaries are pre-1970.

• Urban center

200 Km

100

0

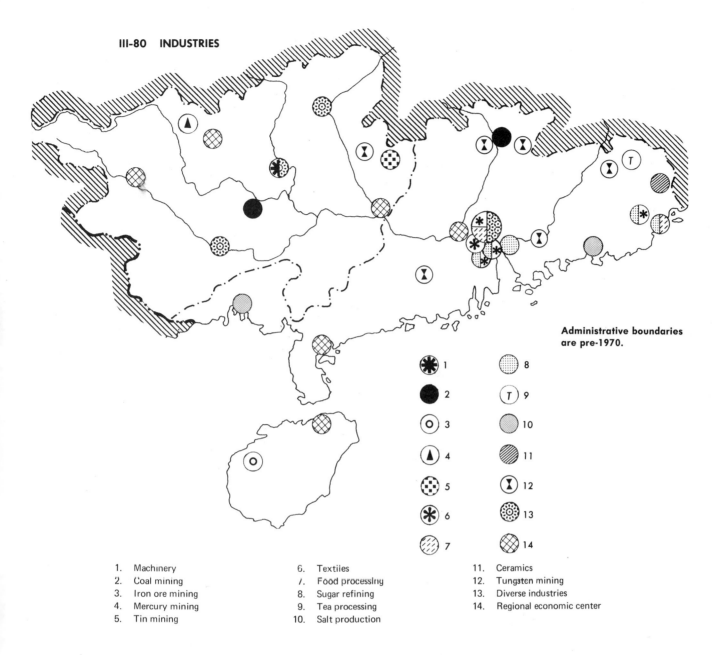

Administrative boundaries are pre-1970.

⊛ 1		⊙ 8	
● 2		Ⓣ 9	
◉ 3		◓ 10	
◮ 4		◪ 11	
⊞ 5		ⓧ 12	
✳ 6		⊛ 13	
◿ 7		⊗ 14	

1. Machinery
2. Coal mining
3. Iron ore mining
4. Mercury mining
5. Tin mining
6. Textiles
7. Food processing
8. Sugar refining
9. Tea processing
10. Salt production
11. Ceramics
12. Tungsten mining
13. Diverse industries
14. Regional economic center

tant. Canton also has the largest airport in the South, with direct flights to Peking, Chan-chiang, Chungking, and Hanoi.

Agriculture is largely restricted to the deltas and plains, though terracing is a common practice, making cultivation possible on the lower hills (Maps III-81 and III-82). The proportion of cropland acreage to the total area is comparatively small, with only 15 percent of Kwangtung and 12 percent of Kwangsi under permanent cultivation. The region, due to its uniformly high temperatures and abundance of rainfall, is an important rice-producing area; irrigated rice fields here yield two or even three crops a year (Map III-83). While rice is the dominant food grain of the lowlands, corn and sweet potatoes are staple crops in hilly areas. Sugar cane is widely grown, with the biggest harvests in the Canton Delta (Map III-84). Sericulture is also important here. Ranking next to the T'ai Hu area

and the Szechwan Basin, the Canton Delta is the country's third largest silk producer. The Canton lowlands are also a major source of tropical and subtropical fruits. Bananas, pineapples, oranges, tangerines, pomelos, lichees, and longans are widely grown and exported to other parts of the country. The delta is also characterized by a relatively high density of draft animals per unit of farm land (Map III-85).

The island of Hainan is also part of this region and has several tropical products peculiar to it. These include coconuts, betel nuts, coffee, and cinchona. The cultivation of natural rubber has recently become highly successful, giving rise to the possibility that the island may eventually become China's largest rubber plantation region.

The output of marine products of the Kwangtung and Kwangsi Region ranks first in the nation. Freshwater fisheries are highly developed, and the

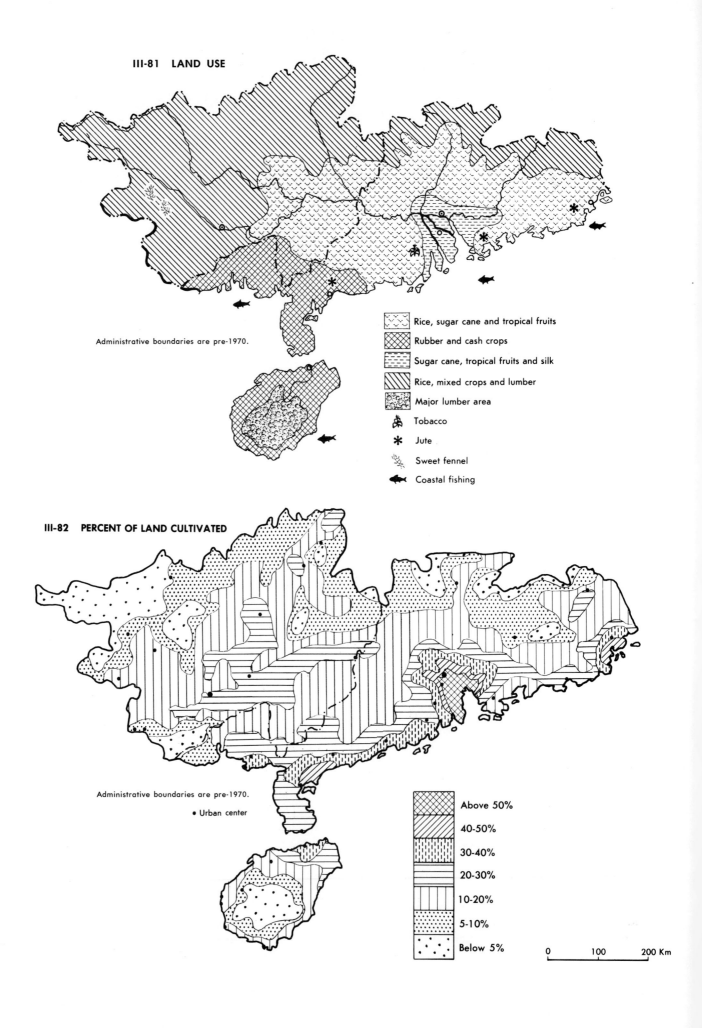

III-81 LAND USE

Administrative boundaries are pre-1970.

Rice, sugar cane and tropical fruits
Rubber and cash crops
Sugar cane, tropical fruits and silk
Rice, mixed crops and lumber
Major lumber area
Tobacco
Jute
Sweet fennel
Coastal fishing

III-82 PERCENT OF LAND CULTIVATED

Administrative boundaries are pre-1970.

• Urban center

Above 50%
40-50%
30-40%
20-30%
10-20%
5-10%
Below 5%

0   100   200 Km

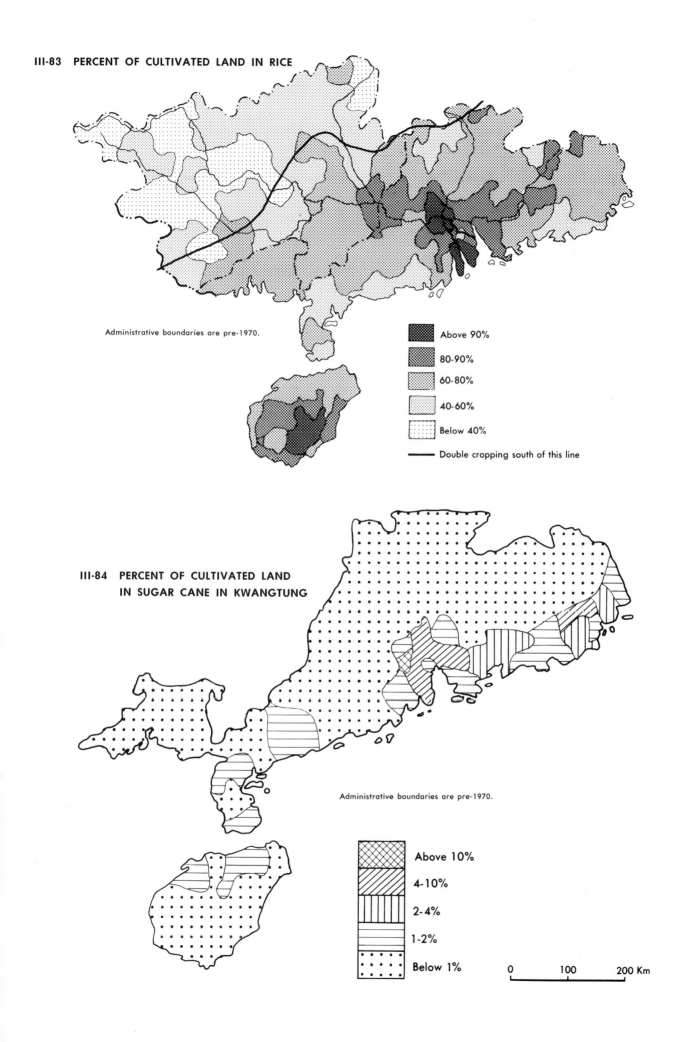

III-83 PERCENT OF CULTIVATED LAND IN RICE

Administrative boundaries are pre-1970.

Above 90%
80-90%
60-80%
40-60%
Below 40%
Double cropping south of this line

III-84 PERCENT OF CULTIVATED LAND
IN SUGAR CANE IN KWANGTUNG

Administrative boundaries are pre-1970.

Above 10%
4-10%
2-4%
1-2%
Below 1%

0   100   200 Km

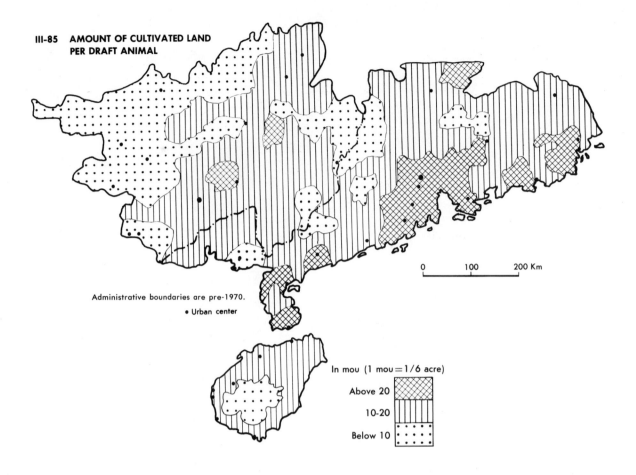

III-85 AMOUNT OF CULTIVATED LAND
PER DRAFT ANIMAL

0   100   200 Km

Administrative boundaries are pre-1970.

• Urban center

In mou (1 mou = 1/6 acre)

Above 20

10-20

Below 10

Hsi Chiang is famous for its fry, the abundance of which helps to make pond fisheries common in the Canton Delta. Though the region is not heavily endowed with coal, it is rich in nonferrous metals. Tungsten deposits in northern Kwangtung rank second in the country, after those in Kiangsi. China's second largest tin mine is located in eastern Kwangsi, where production levels are second only to those of the Ko-chiu mine in Yunnan.

The region possesses a network of highways and waterways and has long been China's southern gateway to the sea. The main railways in Kwangtung are the Peking-Canton and Canton-Kowloon lines. Kwangsi is traversed diagonally by a trunk line which extends to Hunan in the northeast and to the Vietnam border in the southwest.

THE YUNNAN-KWEICHOW REGION

The southwest provinces of Yunnan and Kweichow have a combined area of 550,000 square kilometers (Map III-86). The Yunnan-Kweichow Region is largely a limestone plateau. Here the elevation gradually decreases from about 3,000 meters in the west to less than 1,000 meters in eastern Kweichow. Scattered throughout the plateau are small, upland plains (locally called *pa-tze*), flood plains, and valleys (Map III-87). Like Kwangsi, the plateau has a spectacular karst landscape, with precipitous slopes, overhanging cliffs, spires, circular sinkholes, caverns, and subterranean channels. Clear streams suddenly disappear underground only to re-emerge some distance away. Natural limestone bridges span many rivers, which flow through gorges flanked by high cliffs.

Yunnan Province occupies a strategic position adjacent to Vietnam, Laos, and Burma. In western Yunnan, several parallel chains of high mountains run from north to south; these are collectively known as the Heng-tuan ("horizontally cut" mountains). The altitudes of these mountains range from 4,000 meters in the north to less than 2,000 meters in the south; they are so high and the river-cut valleys so deep that the distance between mountain peak and valley floor often exceeds 2,000 meters. Where river valleys are the narrowest, two people standing on opposite summits can nearly hear each other, but if one wished to meet the other, it would take a day to climb down one scarp and up the other. The currents are so swift that rivers are not navigable. Rope suspension bridges are common for passage. These rivers are potential sources of enormous hydroelectric power for economic development of southwest China.

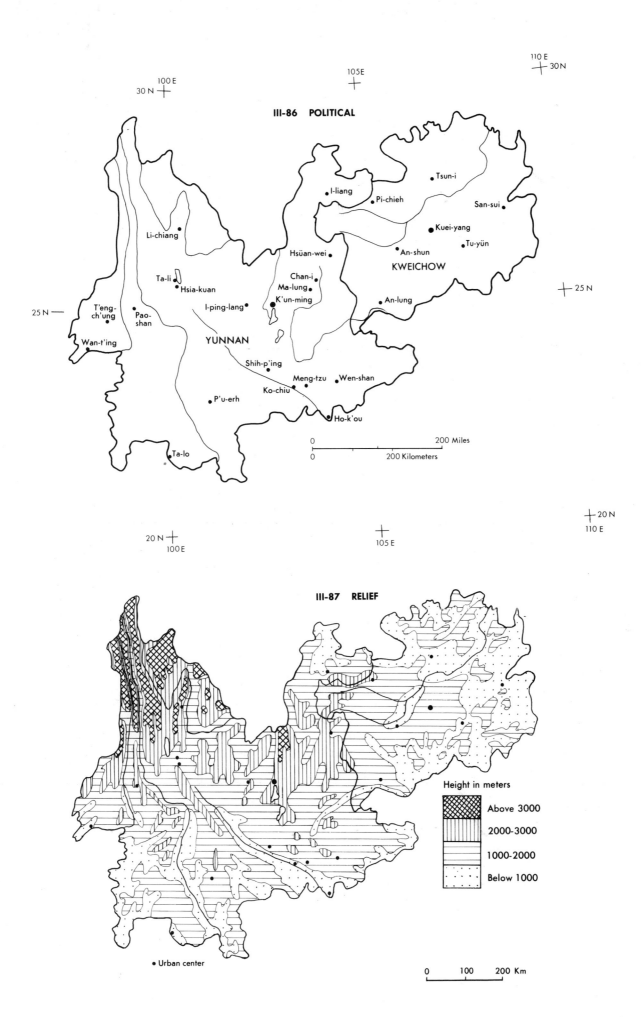

III-86 POLITICAL

100 E
30 N

105E

110 E
30 N

Tsun-i

I-liang
Pi-chieh

San-sui

Li-chiang

Kuei-yang

Hsüan-wei

Tu-yün

An-shun

KWEICHOW

25 N

Ta-li
Hsia-kuan

Chan-i
Ma-lung

I-ping-lang
K'un-ming

An-lung

T'eng-
ch'ung

Pao-
shan

25 N

YUNNAN

Wan-t'ing

Shih-p'ing

Meng-tzu
Wen-shan

Ko-chiu

P'u-erh

Ho-k'ou

0   200 Miles
0   200 Kilometers

Ta-lo

20 N
100 E

105 E

20 N
110 E

III-87 RELIEF

Height in meters

Above 3000

2000-3000

1000-2000

Below 1000

• Urban center

0   100   200 Km

Fault traces are common in Yunnan. Some places have been faulted into grabens, and where these have become filled with water, they have become lakes, as is the case with Tien Ch'ih at K'un-ming. These rippling lakes, surrounded by high mountains, are noted for their scenic beauty. Mountain ranges in Yunnan are the result of tectonic action: Earthquakes causing faulting and folding are recurrent in this unstable area.

The region is neither cold in winter nor hot in summer. Because of its low latitude and because it is shielded by mountain barriers in the north, the weather is relatively mild in the winter, and as a consequence of its high altitude, it is cool in the summer. Temperature variations throughout the year are relatively slight. Average January temperatures for the region range from 4°C to 10°C. July temperatures average only 25°C in Kuei-yang, and 20°C in K'un-ming. The average annual rainfall in most locations ranges between 1,000 and 1,200 millimeters, with the largest concentration falling in summer.

In a strict sense, K'un-ming in Yunnan has no summer season, but rather a very long spring leading directly into autumn, a sequence lasting in all approximately ten months. In Yunnan, moreover, there is little cloudiness in winter and thick fog is found only in the upland plains at night. The weather is balmy and fair, with plenty of sunshine. On the other hand, Kweichow has the largest number of overcast and rainy days a year of any of the provinces in China. It is cloudy or foggy on an average of seven or eight days out of ten. "The province rarely has three successive sunny days," as a local saying goes.

Western and northern Kweichow are primarily covered with yellow soil due to the great humidity, relatively low temperatures, and the consequent incomplete oxidation of the iron in the soil. Topsoil in Kweichow is generally very thin, with many rock outcrops; only on the upland plains are there thicker layers of soil. Most of eastern Yunnan and southeastern Kweichow is characterized by red soil.

Natural vegetation in the region is primarily composed of mixed coniferous and broadleaf deciduous forests, intermingled with a small number of evergreen broadleaf trees. These mountains and their river valleys are covered with luxuriant vegetation.

Because this region's topography is very rugged with high local relief, the canyons of western Yunnan are characterized by a vertical zonation of climate, soils, and vegetation. They have become known as a national botanical garden because of this rich variety. Everywhere, including the mountainsides and wilderness areas, there is a virtual sea of beautiful flowers. Notable varieties include azaleas, camellias, roses, and fairy primroses. In the tropical forests wild animals including monkeys, bears, elephants, and porcupines abound; in fact, they often make unwelcome intrusions into the settled areas where crops are turning ripe.

Most of the region's population, totaling approximately 38 million, is concentrated in compact agricultural communities in the *pa-tze,* or small, upland plains, and in the flood plains of the plateau, while the canyon section of western Yunnan is sparsely settled. A number of ethnic minorities live on the plateau and in the canyons, the more populous among them being the Miao, Puyi, Yi, T'ai, Hani, and Lisu.

K'un-ming, the provincial capital of Yunnan, is also a communication center, with highways leading to Szechwan Province in the north, to Kuei-yang in the east, and, through Ta-li and Hsia-kuan in western Yunnan to the important frontier town of T'eng-ch'ung in the west. Three railroad lines originate at K'un-ming, one connecting with Ho-k'ou on the China-Vietnam border in the south, a shorter one connecting with Chan-i in the east, and a third line running west to I-ping-lang. Planes leave regularly from the provincial capital for Mandalay and Rangoon in Burma, and also for domestic terminals at Chungking, Canton, and Nan-ning. Situated on the north shore of the Tien Ch'ih, K'un-ming is blessed by nature with both splendid scenery and a perpetually gentle climate.

Kuei-yang, the provincial capital of Kweichow, is located in the heart of the province. From here highways radiate in many directions, the most important being the Kuei-yang-Chungking and the Kuei-yang–Ho-ch'ih roads. Tsun-i in the north is the second most important city of the province.

In general, however, communications in these two remote provinces have remained underdeveloped. Railways are relatively few and only the K'un-ming–Ho-k'ou section of the Yunnan-Vietnam Railway has been of any significance. Two rail lines have been planned to connect Kuei-yang with Chu-chou in Hunan and K'un-ming with Ch'eng-tu via Hsi-ch'ang in Szechwan. Once these new lines are completed, the southwest will be equipped with a comprehensive rail network. Through train traffic may eventually reach K'un-ming from Peking and major coastal ports. With only a few exceptions, all rivers in the region are unnavigable because of the rocks and treacherous rapids.

The Yunnan-Kweichow Region is a predominantly agricultural area, with little noteworthy industry (Maps III-88 and III-89). There is much virgin land; that which is already under cultivation is mostly located in the upland plains. Rice constitutes the major crop on permanent fields (Map III-90). Wheat, soybeans, maize, and sweet potatoes are raised in mountain areas (Maps III-91 and III-92).

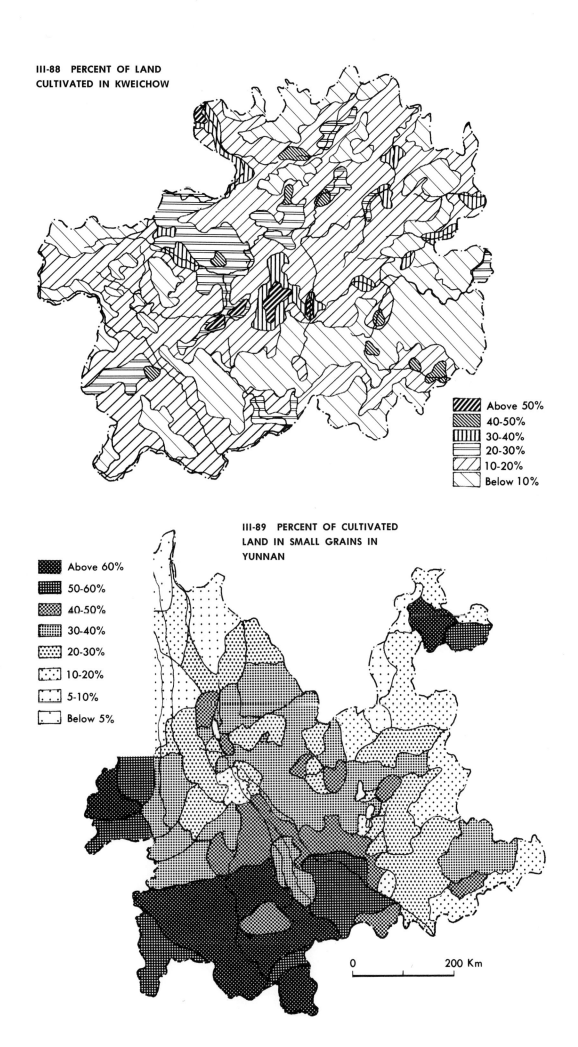

III-88 PERCENT OF LAND
CULTIVATED IN KWEICHOW

Above 50%
40-50%
30-40%
20-30%
10-20%
Below 10%

III-89 PERCENT OF CULTIVATED
LAND IN SMALL GRAINS IN
YUNNAN

Above 60%
50-60%
40-50%
30-40%
20-30%
10-20%
5-10%
Below 5%

0   200 Km

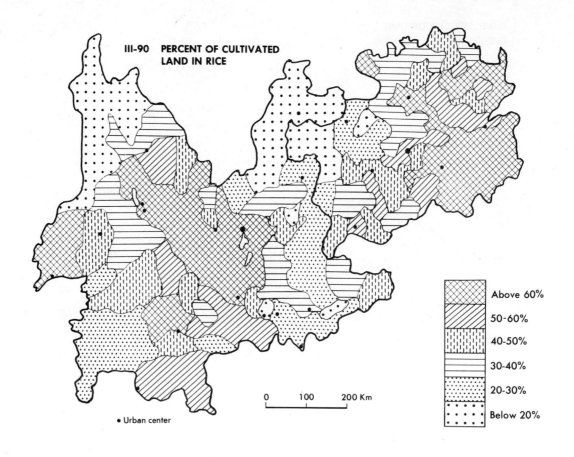

III-90   PERCENT OF CULTIVATED
LAND IN RICE

Above 60%
50-60%
40-50%
30-40%
20-30%
Below 20%

0   100   200 Km

• Urban center

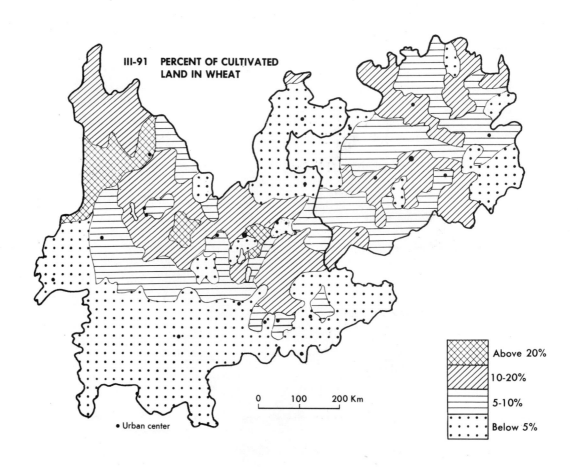

III-91   PERCENT OF CULTIVATED
LAND IN WHEAT

Above 20%
10-20%
5-10%
Below 5%

0   100   200 Km

• Urban center

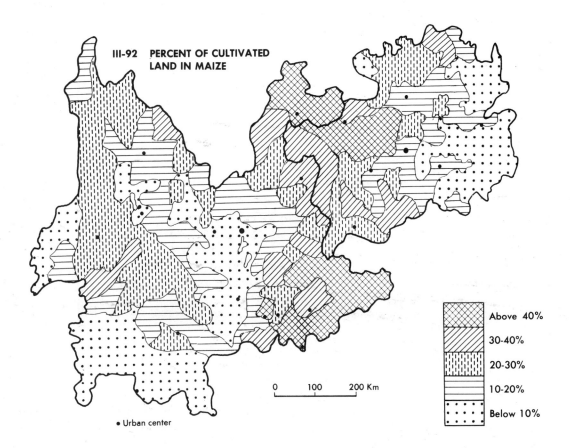

III-92 PERCENT OF CULTIVATED LAND IN MAIZE

Above 40%
30-40%
20-30%
10-20%
Below 10%

0   100   200 Km

• Urban center

Tobacco is produced in Kweichow, and the best variety is that from the area east of Kuei-yang. P'u-erh in Yunnan enjoys a national reputation for its tea. Tung trees are cultivated widely in eastern Kweichow. In western Yunnan are located some of China's major timber stands, many of which are as yet untouched. Tropical forests in southern Yunnan yield an abundance of teak.

The region's principal mineral resources are tin, copper, mercury, sulfur, phosphorus, manganese, and coal (Map III-93). Tin is produced chiefly in Yunnan's Ko-chiu, which is known as China's "tin city"; that locality has both the largest reserves and the largest output in the country. The copper mine of Ma-lung in Yunnan Province is one of the biggest in China; in addition, the country's largest phosphorus mine is located near K'un-ming. The vast coal fields recently discovered in Kweichow Province are of paramount importance to the industrial development of the region and a significant factor in the growth of Tsun-i (Map III-94). Ta-li in Yunnan is noted for its beautiful marble, which is used principally as a highly decorative building material.

The mountains where these mines are situated are also home to a number of scenic lakes, the most notable of which is Tien Ch'ih meaning "heavenly pool," which is treated in Maps III-95 through III-99.

III-93 INDUSTRIES

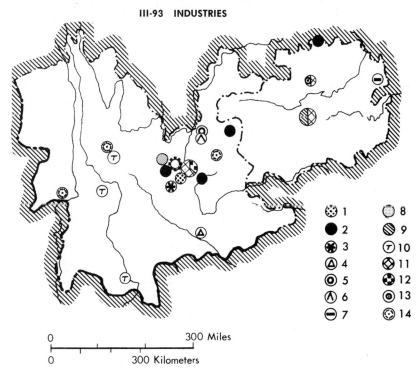

1
2
3
4
5
6
7
8
9
10
11
12
13
14

0   300 Miles

0   300 Kilometers

1. Iron and steel
2. Coal mining
3. Iron ore mining
4. Lead mining
5. Copper mining
6. Zinc mining
7. Mercury mining
8. Salt production
9. Food processing
10. Tea processing
11. Diverse industries
12. Textiles
13. Manganese mining
14. Regional economic center

South China **173**

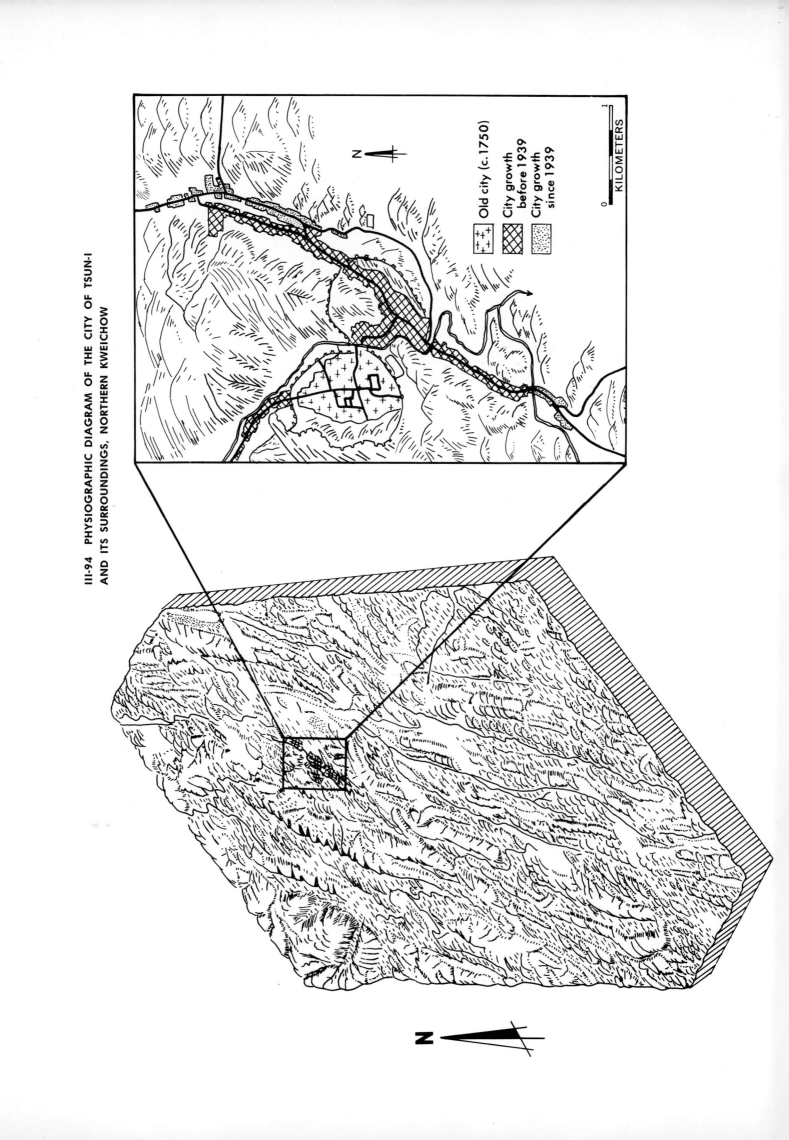

III-94 PHYSIOGRAPHIC DIAGRAM OF THE CITY OF TSUN-I
AND ITS SURROUNDINGS, NORTHERN KWEICHOW

Old city (c.1750)

City growth
before 1939

City growth
since 1939

KILOMETERS

N

III-95 BLOCK DIAGRAM OF TIEN CH'IH

III-96 THE DEVELOPMENT OF TIEN CH'IH

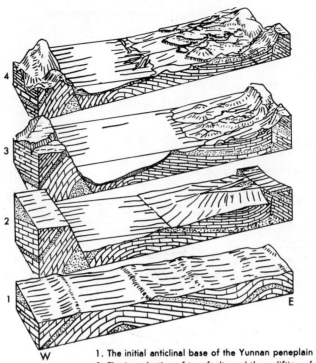

1. The initial anticlinal base of the Yunnan peneplain
2. The introduction of two faults and the uplifting of a dome
3. Erosion wears away the western portion of the plain
   and the eastern section is differentially eroded to
   100 meter relief
4. The present Tien Ch'ih Basin

III-97 LAND FORMS OF THE TIEN CH'IH AREA

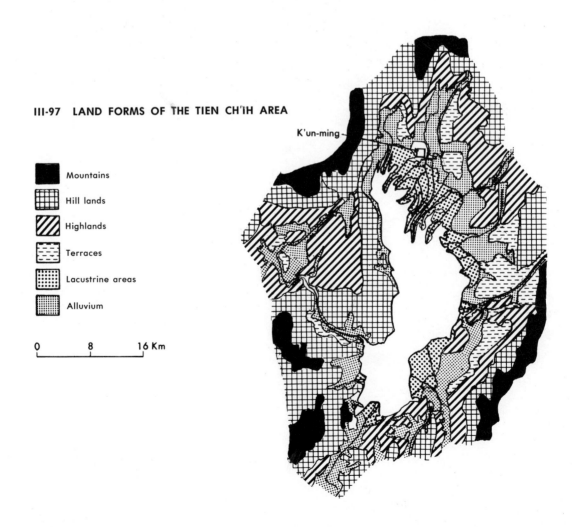

Mountains

Hill lands

Highlands

Terraces

Lacustrine areas

Alluvium

0   8   16 Km

K'un-ming

III-98 LAND USE IN THE TIEN CH'IH AREA

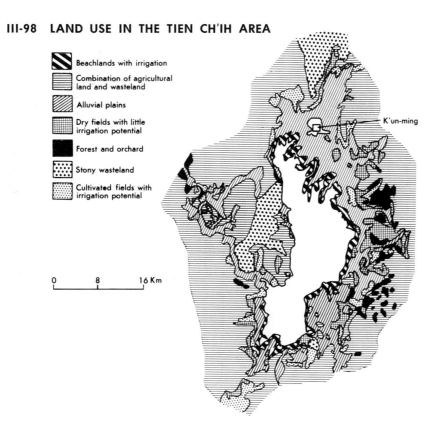

Beachlands with irrigation

Combination of agricultural land and wasteland

Alluvial plains

Dry fields with little irrigation potential

Forest and orchard

Stony wasteland

Cultivated fields with irrigation potential

0   8   16 Km

K'un-ming

III-99   IRRIGATION OF THE TIEN CH'IH AREA

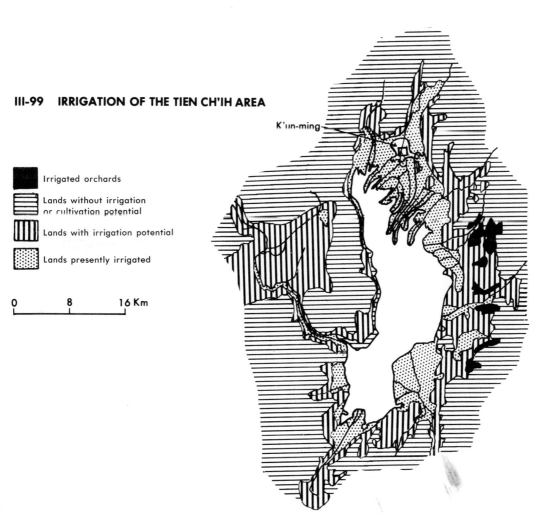

Irrigated orchards

Lands without irrigation or cultivation potential

Lands with irrigation potential

Lands presently irrigated

0   8   16 Km

K'un-ming

The Northeast (Manchuria)

Manchuria, the Western name for Northeast China, comprises the three provinces of Liaoning, Kirin, and Heilungkiang (Maps III-100 and III-101). It is located proximate to the North China Plain, Soviet Siberia, and Japan—all areas of relatively high population density. During the nineteenth century, Manchuria was seen as an outlet for expansion by China Proper, Czarist Russia, and Japan. The region borders the Soviet Union along the Amur and Ussuri rivers and Korea along the Tumen and Yalu rivers. Although Manchuria is isolated from China Proper, this isolation does not interfere with Manchuria-North China relations, for Manchuria's transportation facilities enable it to maintain efficient contact with the Chinese central government. Dairen (Lü-ta) on the Liaotung Peninsula is Manchuria's main port. A narrow strip of coastal lowland in western Liaoning joins the Manchurian Plain with the North China Plain at Shan-hai-kuan and this provides a land link between the two regions.

Manchuria has about 8 percent of China's total population and area. It has been and continues to be essential to the protection of northern China, where Peking, the national capital, is located. It is today a most vital region, producing about half of the country's steel. Moreover, Manchuria has a significant hydroelectric power potential, as well as rich forest and mineral resources, and produces a grain surplus.

Topographically, Manchuria consists of three semicircular belts (Map III-102). The outer belt is defined by the major navigable rivers—the Amur (Hei-lung Chiang), the Ussuri, the Tumen, and the Yalu. The middle belt consists of a group of mountains including the Greater Khingan Range in the west, the Lesser Khingan Range in the north, and the Ch'ang-pai Shan and associated ranges in the east. The inner belt is occupied by the Manchurian Plain, which is surrounded on three sides by the mountains of the middle belt. It is an immense, flat basin drained by the north-flowing Sungari, and the south-flowing Liao Ho; thus this plain is also called the Sungari-Liao Plain. Formed primarily by erosion but also by some alluvial deposits of the rivers, the Manchurian Plain is about 350,000 square kilometers in area—the largest plain in China, accounting for one-third of the country's total area of plains.

The central mountain belt contains China's richest timber reserves, while in the south the coast, bays, and islands adjoining the Gulf of Chihli (Po Hai) provide excellent facilities for shipping, fishing, and salt distillation.

Most of Manchuria lies between 40° and 50° north latitude. Its northern location on the eastern margin of the Eurasian continent explains its short, hot, moist summers and long, cold winters (Map III-103).

The winter is indeed cold, with prevailing winds blowing southward from Siberia and eastward from the Mongolian Plateau. The average January temperature ranges from $-6°C$ in the south to $-25°C$ in the north. These are lower readings than are found at the same latitudes elsewhere in the world. Consequently, even in southern Manchuria, the rivers are frozen for about six months; only the harbors at Dairen, Lü-shun (Port Arthur), and Hu-lu-tao remaining ice-free. During these winter months, snow and ice cover the ground, accounting for the regional proverb that "small snow freezes the land, while big snow freezes the river." Horsecarts and motor vehicles travel safely on the frozen rivers, while on the snow-covered plains, sleds are used as a common means of transport (Map III-104).

III-100 MANCHURIA

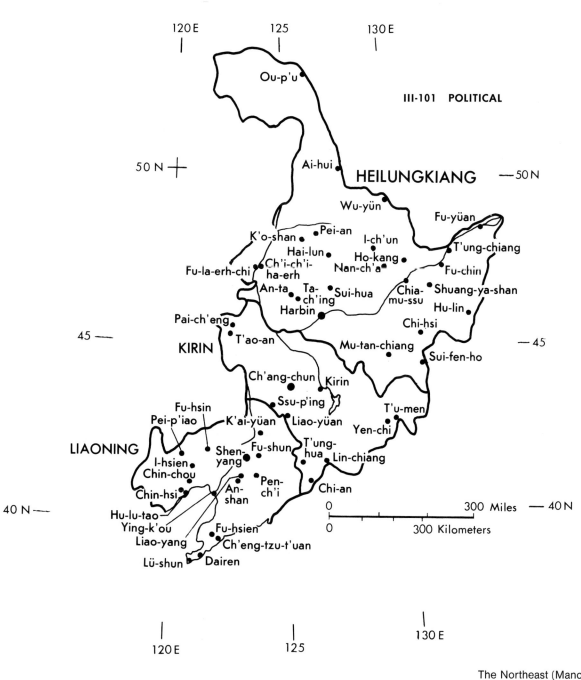

III-101 POLITICAL

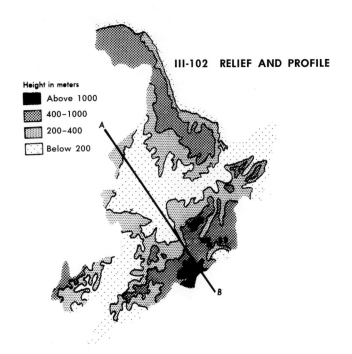

III-102 RELIEF AND PROFILE

Height in meters
■ Above 1000
▨ 400-1000
▩ 200-400
░ Below 200

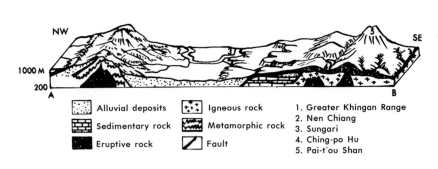

Alluvial deposits   Igneous rock   1. Greater Khingan Range
Sedimentary rock   Metamorphic rock   2. Nen Chiang
Eruptive rock   Fault   3. Sungari
   4. Ching-po Hu
   5. Pai-t'ou Shan

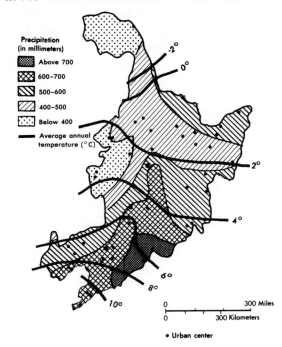

Precipitation
(in millimeters)
▨ Above 700
▩ 600-700
▨ 500-600
░ 400-500
░ Below 400
— Average annual
temperature (°C)

• Urban center

III-104 ANNUAL NUMBER OF DAYS WITH SNOW

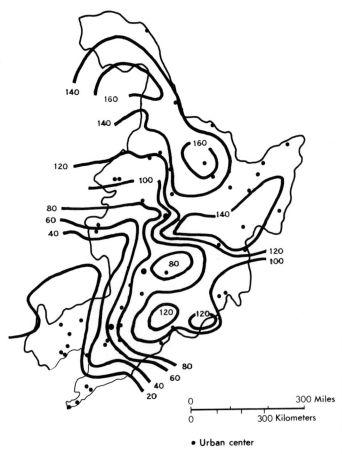

• Urban center

The duration of frost in Manchuria is long, ranging from 143 days in Dairen in the south to 212 days in Shen-yang (Mukden) and 220 days in Ch'i-ch'i-ha-er; thus winter cultivation is basically impossible (Map III-105).

Summer temperatures are fairly high throughout the region. The average July temperature ranges from 27° C in the south to 21° C in the north. Summer lasts about three months in the south and less than one month in the extreme north. As a result, the growing period for plants is confined to five or six months a year even in the south, and only one crop can be raised a year. This wide range between winter and summer temperatures reflects the influence of continentality upon Manchuria's climate, even though the region itself lies on the margin of Asia.

The annual precipitation in Manchuria ranges from 950 millimeters in the southeast to 275 milli-

meters in the northwest; it is highest in the mountain areas and relatively low in the plains, but most of it occurs during the growing season. Half of the annual precipitation occurs during July and August.

The natural vegetation of most of Manchuria is grassland or mixed grassland and forest. The

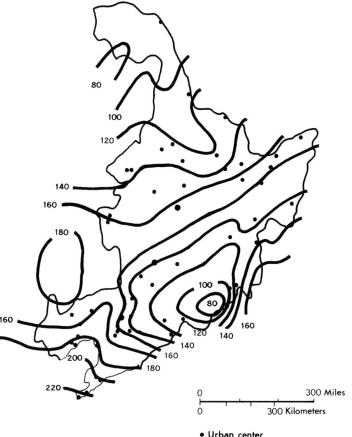

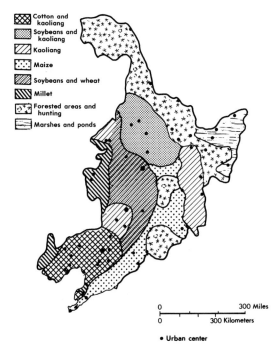

Cotton and kaoliang
Soybeans and kaoliang
Kaoliang
Maize
Soybeans and wheat
Millet
Forested areas and hunting
Marshes and ponds

0   300 Miles
0   300 Kilometers

• Urban center

0   300 Miles
0   300 Kilometers

• Urban center

III-107   LAND USE

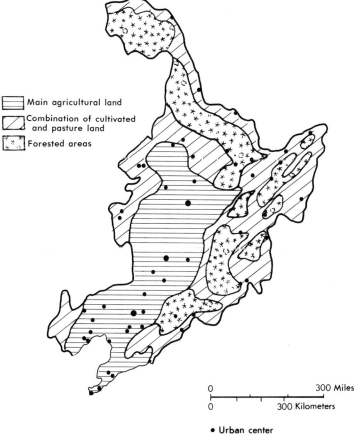

Main agricultural land
Combination of cultivated and pasture land
Forested areas

soils which have developed here are among the most fertile in China. There is extensive chernozem in the Sungari-Liao Plain, which makes Manchuria one of the outstanding agricultural regions of China, despite its short growing season.

The development of this region is a two-pronged effort, with emphasis on both large-scale agriculture and industry. The rich soils, the relative under-population, the vast area of plain, and the climate with rain concentrated in the warm season make large parts of the Northeast ideal for highly productive mechanized agriculture (Maps III-106 and III-107). Main crops include soybeans, kaoliang, wheat, sorghum, flax, hemp, sugar beets, and fruits. In value of total production, in acreage, and in export value, soybeans are the most important. Timber is also a major product, for the rich forest lands of this region account for 60 percent of China's total forests. Both saltwater and freshwater fishing rank as significant aspects of the economic base of the Northeast, and saltbeds are also plentiful along the long coastline.

The Northeast is the most intensively developed industrial region of China (Map III-108). Several factors have favored Manchuria's industrial development. First, the area is endowed with rich mineral resources: Manchuria's iron ore, coal, oil shale, and hydroelectric resources are among the most valuable in China. Second, the area has long had a good foundation for heavy industry. Fu-shun coal mining, An-shan steel production, and hydroelectricity

0   300 Miles
0   300 Kilometers

• Urban center

have aided the growth of heavy industry. Third, the transportation network of the region is well developed. For example, the Northeast leads the country in total length and density of railroads.

The major heavy industrial centers in the south of Manchuria are An-shan, Fu-shun, Shen-yang,

The Northeast (Manchuria) **181**

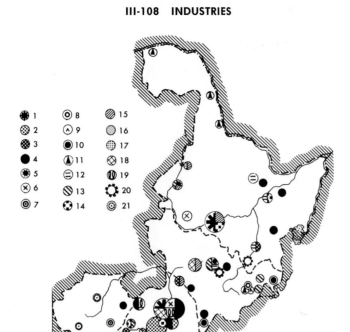

1 8 15
2 9 16
3 10 17
4 11 18
5 12 19
6 13 20
7 14 21

1. Machinery
2. Iron and steel
3. Nonferrous metallurgy
4. Chemicals
5. Coal mining
6. Petroleum refinery
7. Fuel extraction from oil shale
8. Manganese mining
9. Copper mining
10. Lead and zinc mining
11. Magnesite mining
12. Gold mining
13. Lumber and wood working
14. Paper and pulp
15. Textiles
16. Food processing
17. Salt production
18. Sugar refining
19. Thermal power station
20. Hydroelectric power station
21. Regional economic center

Pen-ch'i, Lü-shun, and Dairen (Lü-ta); those to the north are Ch'ang-ch'un, Harbin, and Ch'i-ch'i-ha-erh. An-shan leads all other cities in China in steel produc-

tion; Pen-ch'i is another important steel producer. The open pit coal mine in Fu-shun is equipped with modern excavators, and its annual output is the highest in the country. Shen-yang is a center for the refining of copper, aluminum, and zinc, and also for the manufacture of machinery. Dairen is noted for shipbuilding and is the center of Manchuria's chemical fertilizer industries. Ch'ang-ch'un is the site of the leading motor works in China. In the north, woodworking and agricultural machinery factories, as well as a cement plant, are located in Harbin. Ch'i-ch'i-ha-erh is the center for the processing of soybeans and grains. Salt production and timber production have also been expanded as part of Manchuria's healthy economic growth. Other industries in the Northeast include papermaking, flour milling, oil refining, and sugar refining.

Transportation has played a vital role in Manchuria's industrial development. The railroad system, primarily built by Russian and Japanese interests, was virtually nonexistent prior to 1900 but today includes more than 12,800 kilometers of track, or approximately a third of the national total. Three main rail lines cross Manchuria in east-west directions, and three lines run north and south. Harbin, the capital of Heilungkiang Province, is the railroad hub of northern Manchuria, as well as the center of water transport. The capital of Liaoning Province, Shen-yang, with a population of more than 2 million, is the center of Manchuria's railroad system.

There is also a highway system of approximately 24,000 kilometers; and the Sungari, Amur, Liao, and Ussuri rivers are all navigable. Dairen, Lü-shun, Hu-lu-tao, and Ying-k'ou are all good ocean ports, providing access to ocean transportation. Three airlines also cross the Northeast on routes connecting China Proper and the Soviet Union.

Inner Mongolia

Inner Mongolia is situated between the North China Plain, the Manchurian Plain, and the Mongolian Plateau (Maps III-109 and III-110). The transitional nature of the region is also reflected in its drainage pattern, both interior and exterior; in landforms, a combination of plains and plateaus (Map III-111); in climate, both dry and semihumid; in races, both Han and Mongolian peoples;. and in economy, both agriculture and pastoralism (Map III-112).

Inner Mongolia was the first autonomous region to be established by the Chinese Communists. It has a total area of 1,170,000 square kilometers, and so is surpassed in size only by Sinkiang and Tibet among China's administrative units. According to the new territorial boundaries defined by the Communists, the Inner Mongolian Autonomous Region— a long, narrow, landlocked strip of land—extends 2,700 kilometers from the pine forests of northern Manchuria to the area north of the Kansu Corridor.

The total population of the region is now close to 11 million, with the highest densities occurring in the southeastern agricultural region and along the railroads, where it is between 10 and 100 persons per square kilometer. In the pasture and forest lands the density decreases to less than 10 persons per square kilometer. Han Chinese, who are settled mostly in the agricultural areas, number nearly 9 million and therefore account for the great majority of the total population. In addition, there are more than 1 million Mongols distributed throughout the region, and a somewhat lesser total of Oronchons, Evenki, and Koreans (Map III-113b).*

The greater part of Inner Mongolia is plateau at an elevation of about 1,000 meters above sea level. In the central part of the region the Yin-shan Shan-mo extend from east to west, while the Ala Shan in the southwest run from north to south. The highest mountains are the Greater Khingan which run north-south and divide the plateau from the Manchurian Plain to the east. South of the Yin-shan Shan-mo, along the northwest corner of the bend of the Yellow River, are several alluvial plains, formed by silt deposited by the river. Lying within the Great Bend of the river is the arid Ordos Plateau.

Inner Mongolia is characterized by extreme continentality, which is clearly shown by a wide annual temperature range. During the winter the region is windy, dry, and cold; the mean January temperature is $-13\,°C$. Summer temperatures are fairly uniform throughout the region; averages in July range from $20\,°C$ to $22\,°C$. Rainfall decreases toward the west (with increasing distance from the sea) and the region's highest annual rainfall (500

---

*Author's note added in proof: In 1970 according to the China Cartographic Institute's world atlas, the Inner Mongolia Autonomous Region has been reduced to 450,000 square kilometers. Because of the boundary change, the population was then reduced to 6.2 million.

III-109 INNER MONGOLIA

0 ____ 500 Miles
0 ____ 500 Kilometers

millimeters) occurs in the Greater Khingan Range. Luxuriant pine forests make these mountains one of the important timber-producing regions of the north. The western part of the plateau, where rainfall is less than 200 millimeters in most locales, has a dry climate, with broadly scattered deserts. Throughout most of Inner Mongolia, rainfall is inadequate for farming, and irrigation is essential for permanent field agriculture. Annual rainfall varies greatly from year to year—a characteristic of continental interiors (Map III-113a).

Climate and landforms combine to restrict agriculture to a few areas (Map III-113c). Irrigated farming is practiced on the fertile plains near the Yellow River bend. The leading crops here are spring wheat, kaoliang, millet, oats, corn, linseed, soybeans, and sugar beets. Wheat and oats have the highest yields on irrigated land. Millet and kaoling, which are drought-resistant crops, are cultivated on nonirrigated land. Eighty percent of the agricultural produce is exported to other parts of the country (Map III-113f).

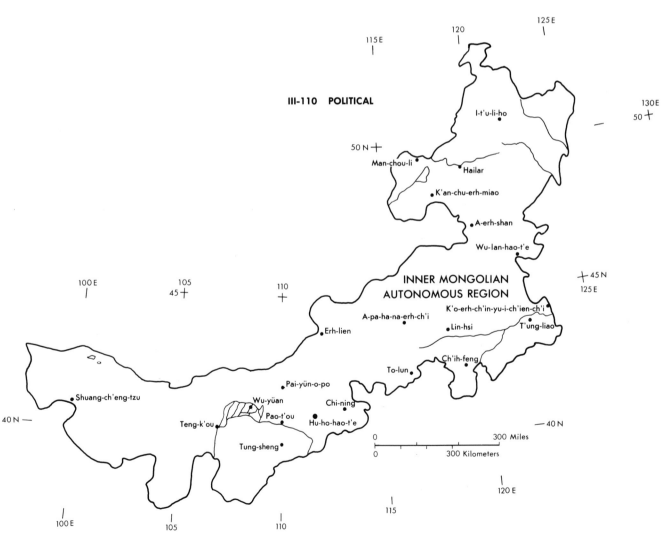

III-110 POITICAL

INNER MONGOLIAN AUTONOMOUS REGION

0 ____ 300 Miles
0 ____ 300 Kilometers

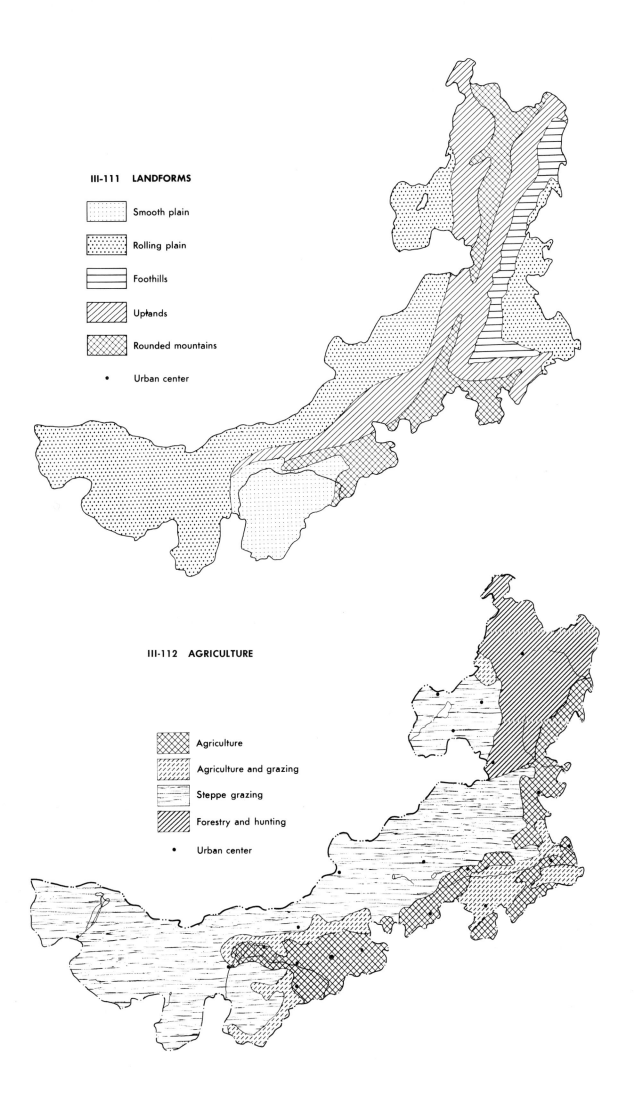

III-111 LANDFORMS

- Smooth plain
- Rolling plain
- Foothills
- Uplands
- Rounded mountains
- • Urban center

III-112 AGRICULTURE

- Agriculture
- Agriculture and grazing
- Steppe grazing
- Forestry and hunting
- • Urban center

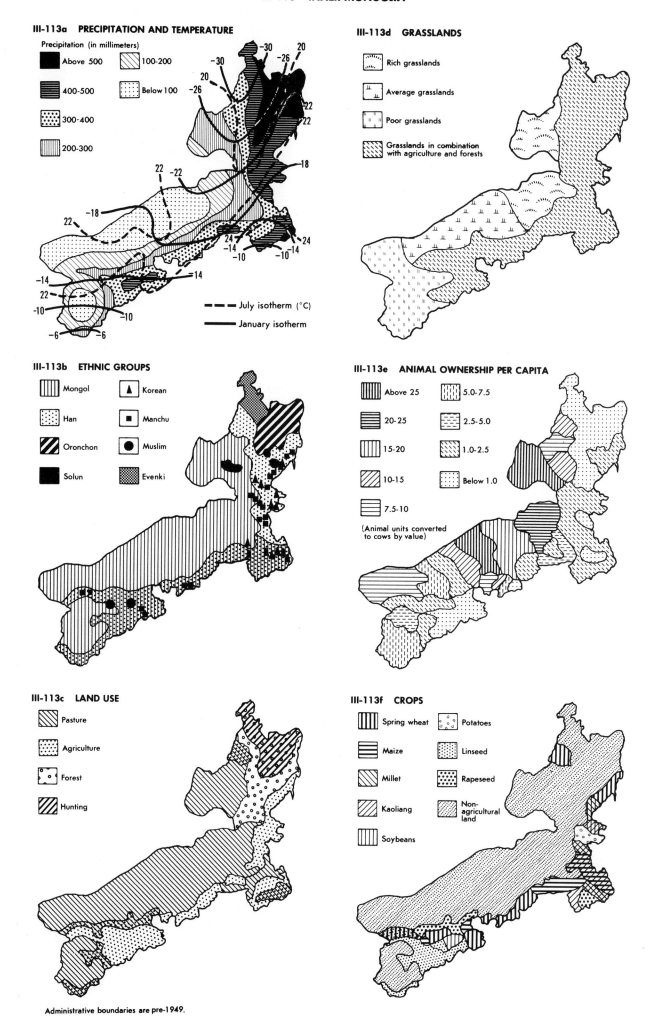

III-113a   PRECIPITATION AND TEMPERATURE

Precipitation (in millimeters)

- Above 500
- 400-500
- 300-400
- 200-300
- 100-200
- Below 100

- - - July isotherm (°C)
——— January isotherm

III-113d   GRASSLANDS

- Rich grasslands
- Average grasslands
- Poor grasslands
- Grasslands in combination with agriculture and forests

III-113b   ETHNIC GROUPS

- Mongol
- Han
- Oronchon
- Solun
- Korean
- Manchu
- Muslim
- Evenki

III-113e   ANIMAL OWNERSHIP PER CAPITA

- Above 25
- 20-25
- 15-20
- 10-15
- 7.5-10
- 5.0-7.5
- 2.5-5.0
- 1.0-2.5
- Below 1.0

(Animal units converted to cows by value)

III-113c   LAND USE

- Pasture
- Agriculture
- Forest
- Hunting

Administrative boundaries are pre-1949.

III-113f   CROPS

- Spring wheat
- Maize
- Millet
- Kaoliang
- Soybeans
- Potatoes
- Linseed
- Rapeseed
- Non-agricultural land

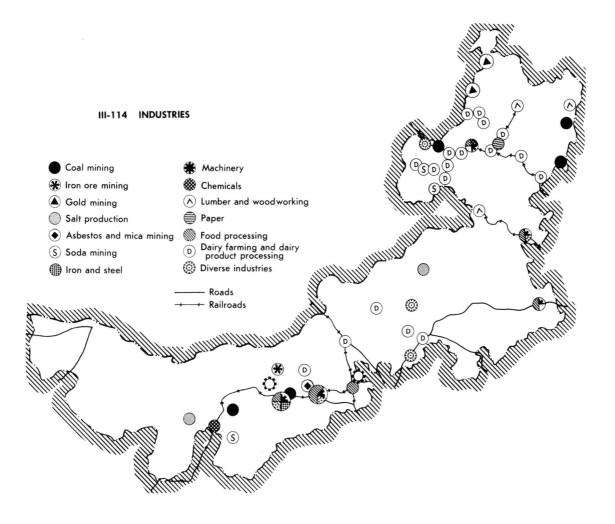

III-114 INDUSTRIES

- ● Coal mining
- ✳ Iron ore mining
- ▲ Gold mining
- � Salt production
- ◆ Asbestos and mica mining
- Ⓢ Soda mining
- ▦ Iron and steel
- ✱ Machinery
- ✿ Chemicals
- ⋀ Lumber and woodworking
- ▤ Paper
- ▥ Food processing
- Ⓓ Dairy farming and dairy product processing
- ✤ Diverse industries
- —— Roads
- —+—+— Railroads

Pastoral areas constitute a large part of Inner Mongolia, with animal husbandry especially well developed there (Map III-113d). Sheep, cattle, horses, and camels are included among the livestock, sheep being the most numerous. Hundreds of thousands of square kilometers of natural pastures and the long experience of the people in livestock raising have made Inner Mongolia the most important exporter of animal products in China (Map III-113e).

However, although herding is of historic economic importance, the highly developed agriculture is still the single most important component of the area's economy, and industrial development will eventually change the entire balance. Of the usable land area, 65 percent is devoted to herding, 14 percent to forests, 12 percent to mixed agriculture and herding, and 9 percent to sedentary agriculture. The area under cultivation is steadily increasing, and new techniques are raising production levels.

Fishing and forestry are two additional elements of the economy of Inner Mongolia. Freshwater fish provide an important trade item with China Proper, while timber resources have been estimated at 986 million cubic meters, or one-fifth of China's total.

The most important forests are in the Greater Khingan Range, with conifers providing the major stands.

Although little industrial development has yet taken place, significant resources are available. Minerals include sodium sulfate, gold, iron, coal, natural alkalis, mica, and asbestos; so far, only coal has been mined to any extent. Small-scale industries include sodium sulfate, leather, meat and fish packing and processing, dairying, canning, hemp, lumber, tobacco, and iron- and steel-fabricating plants. Future plans include breweries and birch oil plants, and possibly rope and chemical industries (Map III-114).

On the extensive grasslands, horses, camel caravans, and bullock carts are the principal means of transport, although highways and railroads are being developed.

The main railroads are concentrated in the eastern area and include lines from Harbin to Manchou-li (on the U.S.S.R. border) as well as to Tung-liao in southeastern Inner Mongolia. In addition to railroads, there are highways connecting Inner Mongolia with Mongolia, the Northeast, and the northern regions of China Proper.

In a region as large and sparsely populated as this, it is not surprising that there are few cities. Hu-ho-hao-t'e and Pao-t'ou are the two ranking cities of Inner Mongolia. Hu-ho-hao-t'e, the capital of the region, is one of China's famous ancient cities; it was once a trade center to which the wool, hides, food, and medicine from the surrounding grasslands were brought. The city formerly had a small population which fluctuated seasonally; the present level is more stable, at approximately 150,000–200,000. Pao-t'ou, with the rich iron ore and abundant coal deposits in its vicinity, has now become one of the three metallurgical centers in China, the other two being An-shan and Wu-han. Other urban centers are *meng* (subprovince) capitals, railheads, and agricultural market centers, in addition to the religious centers where there are many Lamaist temples.

Sinkiang

The Sinkiang Uighur Autonomous Region is located in the northwestern part of China, bordered by the Mongolian People's Republic, the Soviet Union, Afghanistan, Pakistan, and India. It is China's largest political unit, occupying one-sixth of China's total area, and is larger than the combined areas of Britain, France, Germany, and Italy (Maps III-115 and III-116). The population of Sinkiang is approximately 7.2 million, or less than 5 people per square kilometer. Most of the population is concentrated in the southern oases or in the valleys of northern Sinkiang.

The total region is inhabited by more than a dozen ethnic groups. The Uighurs, most of whom live in southern Sinkiang, are the most numerous and most widely distributed of these groups, and account for two-thirds of the total inhabitants of Sinkiang. The Han Chinese and the Kazakhs each account for one-tenth of the total population. Other ethnic groups include the Hui, Kirghiz, Mongol, Russian, Uzbek, Tadzhik, Sibo, and Manchu (Map III-117).

The Tien Shan range cuts across the central part of Sinkiang, with a great basin on either side—the Tarim Basin to the south and the Dzungarian Basin to the north.

High ranges fringe the Tarim Basin: the Tien Shan to the north, the Kunlun to the south, and the Pamirs to the west, with the Kansu Corridor opening to the east (Map III-118). The basin has a length of 1,500 kilometers from west to east and a width of 500 kilometers from north to south; it occupies 55 percent of the land area of Sinkiang. The basin is higher in the west than in the east, with an average elevation of 1,100 meters above sea level. The lowest part of the basin is the Lop Nor area, which has an elevation of 760 meters. Many rivers descend into the basin from the mountains in the north and south. They form a string of oases and salt lakes—features which reflect the interior drainage pattern of the Tarim Basin (Map III-119). The enclosed basin consists of concentric rings. Adjoining the outer mountain barriers is a belt of foothills and alluvial fans with widths of a few kilometers up to about 40 kilometers. Within this is a string of oases, where irrigation is possible. The central area is Takla Makan, a desolate sandy desert with numerous dunes and playa lakes.

The principal oases of the Tarim Basin are Ho-t'ien, So-ch'e, K'a-shih, and A-k'o-su. The basin's main river, the Tarim, is fed by the melting snow and ice from the Kunlun, the Pamirs, and the Tien Shan. It is the longest river in China's region of interior drainage.

The Dzungarian Basin is located to the north between the Tien Shan and the Altai Mountains. It has a triangular shape, the south being wide and the north narrow, and its floor is 500 meters above

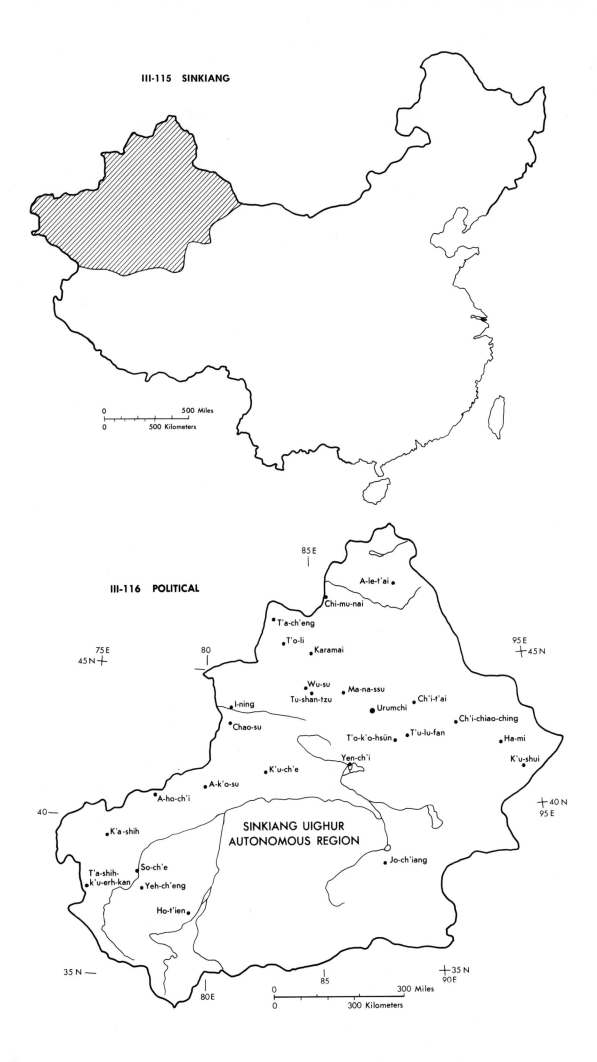

III-115 SINKIANG

0 _____ 500 Miles
0 _____ 500 Kilometers

III-116 POLITICAL

85 E

• A-le-t'ai

Chi-mu-nai

• T'a-ch'eng

• T'o-li
• Karamai

75 E
45 N +   80

95 E
+ 45 N

• Wu-su
Tu-shan-tzu •   • Ma-na-ssu

• I-ning   • Urumchi   • Ch'i-t'ai

• Chao-su   • Ch'i-chiao-ching

T'o-k'o-hsün •   • T'u-lu-fan   • Ha-mi

Yen-ch'i   • K'u-shui

• K'u-ch'e

40 —   • A-k'o-su   + 40 N
• A-ho-ch'i   95 E

• K'a-shih   SINKIANG UIGHUR
AUTONOMOUS REGION

T'a-shih-   So-ch'e •   • Jo-ch'iang
k'u-erh-kan •   • Yeh-ch'eng

Ho-t'ien •

35 N —   + 35 N
90 E

80 E   0 _____ 300 Miles
85   0 _____ 300 Kilometers

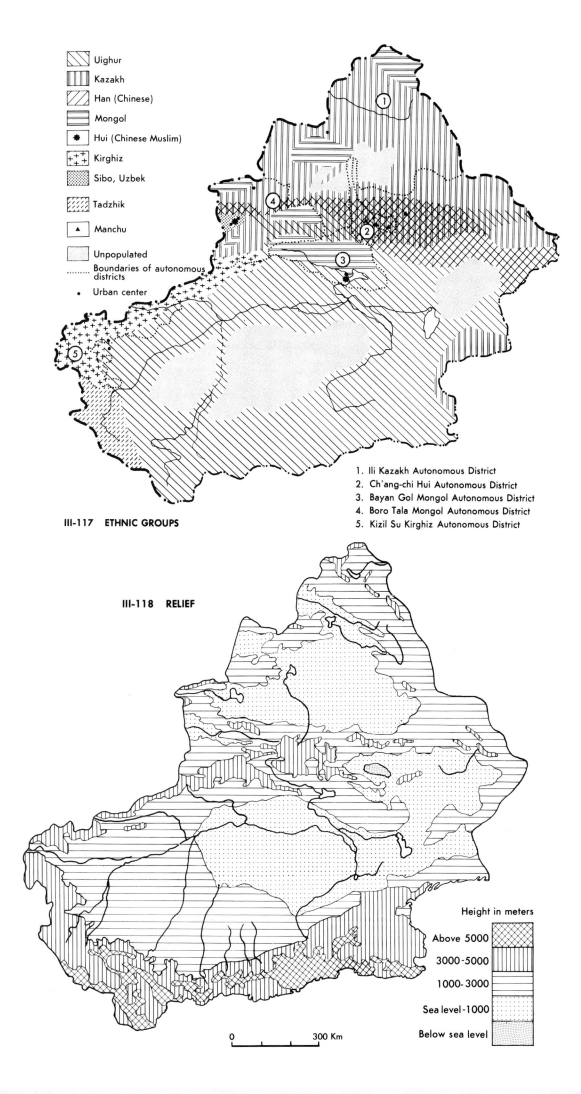

Legend (III-117 ETHNIC GROUPS):

- Uighur
- Kazakh
- Han (Chinese)
- Mongol
- Hui (Chinese Muslim)
- Kirghiz
- Sibo, Uzbek
- Tadzhik
- Manchu
- Unpopulated
- ·········· Boundaries of autonomous districts
- • Urban center

III-117 ETHNIC GROUPS

1. Ili Kazakh Autonomous District
2. Ch'ang-chi Hui Autonomous District
3. Bayan Gol Mongol Autonomous District
4. Boro Tala Mongol Autonomous District
5. Kizil Su Kirghiz Autonomous District

III-118 RELIEF

Height in meters

- Above 5000
- 3000 - 5000
- 1000 - 3000
- Sea level - 1000
- Below sea level

0   300 Km

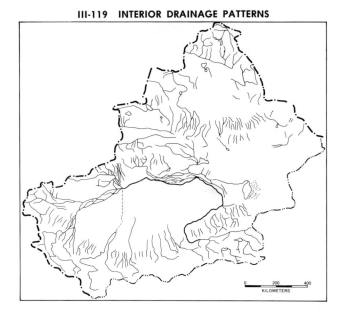

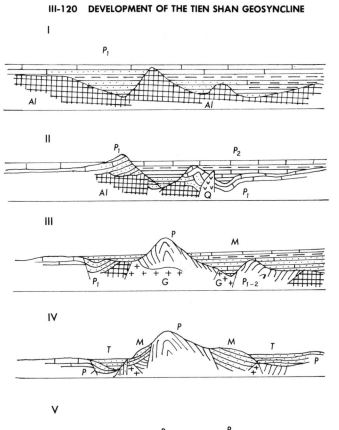

AI	Pre-Sinian metamorphic rock formation	I. Caledonian stage
P	Paleozoic	II. Hercynian stage
P_1	Lower Paleozoic	III. Mesozoic era
P_2	Upper Paleozoic	IV. Early Tertiary period
M	Mesozoic	V. Present
T	Tertiary	
Q	Quaternary	
G	Granite	

sea level. It is higher in the south and east than in the north and west; as a result, all the rivers flow from east to west. To the northwest are massive mountains interspersed with depressed valleys. These valleys are natural passages between China and the Soviet Union and also permit moist air from the western reaches of Asia to penetrate northern Sinkiang. The longest river of the basin is the O-erh-ch'i-ssu Ho (Kara Irtish), which flows into the Soviet Union and joins the Ob River. It is the only stream in Sinkiang that has an outlet to the sea and the only one of China's rivers that empties into the Arctic Ocean.

The Dzungarian Basin has a varied landscape characterized by high mountains, desert, steppes, salt lakes, and swamps. The desert is confined to the central and eastern parts of the basin and is much smaller in area than the Takla Makan desert of the Tarim Basin. As in the Tarim Basin, there is a zone of oases, the major ones along the northern base of the Tien Shan found at Ch'i-t'ai, Urumchi, and Wu-su.

The Tien Shan system consists of a series of east-west parallel ranges and valleys interrupted by a broad pass where the provincial capital, Urumchi, is situated (Map III-120). West of Urumchi the Tien Shan are higher than to the east; here the average elevation is 3,000 meters above sea level, and there are numerous snow-capped peaks and glaciers. Among the many narrow valleys the best known is the I-li Valley, centered on the city of I-ning and oriented toward the Soviet Union. The valley owes its prosperity to its relatively moist climate, which favors agriculture and animal husbandry. East of the capital, the Tien Shan have an average elevation of 2,000 meters above sea level. Just south of this portion of the range lie the Turfan and Ha-mi basins, formed by a pronounced fault depression. The bot-

tom of the Turfan Depression is the lowest land point in China, 154 meters below sea level (Map III-121).

Located within the interior of Asia and enclosed by mountain ranges, Sinkiang is far removed from ocean influence, and thus has an arid continental climate. The entire province has a long cold winter and a short hot summer. The southern part of Sinkiang has 210 frost-free days, the northern part 150. With a maximum temperature of 38°C, the Turfan Depression is the hottest place in China during the summer. The Tarim Basin has an average, but highly variable, annual rainfall of less than 100 millimeters, the Dzungarian Basin 250 millimeters. However, with the arrival of spring, mountain snow begins to thaw, and the water reaching the plains is diverted by farmers for irrigation.

Aside from the rugged mountains and valleys, in Sinkiang there are four kinds of natural surface—mountain plateau, gravel, oasis, and desert—and a distinctive type of vegetation is associated with each. The high plateaus are well watered and rich in grass-

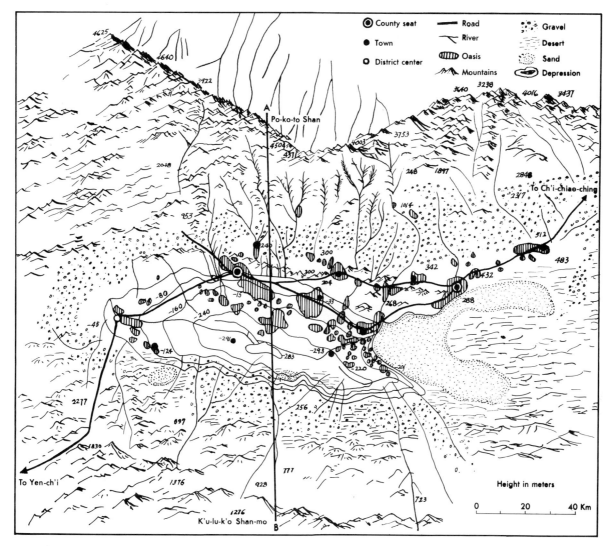

III-121 TURFAN DEPRESSION AND PROFILES

County seat · Road · Gravel
Town · River · Desert
District center · Oasis · Sand
Mountains · Depression

Height in meters

0   20   40 Km

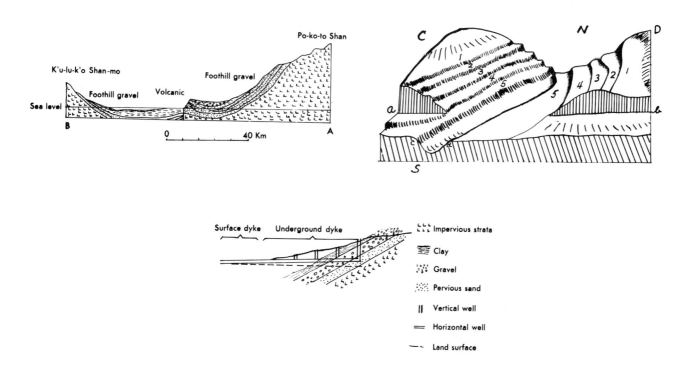

Surface dyke · Underground dyke

⌐⌐⌐ Impervious strata

≋ Clay

Gravel

Pervious sand

‖ Vertical well

= Horizontal well

- - - Land surface

es. However, when water flows from the melting snow of the mountains to the gravel area of mountain foothills, it disappears underground and vegetation consists of a very few scanty grasses. In the oasis areas, at a lower elevation than the gravel zone, are found fertile alluvial soils and a natural vegetation of grass, tamarisk, and scrub. Alkali soils occur in the desert areas and vegetation is sparse or absent.

Since most of Sinkiang has a dry climate, over 90 percent of its cultivated land has to be irrigated throughout the year. Oasis agriculture is a characteristic feature of this region. It is estimated that over 153,000 square kilometers of wasteland can be turned into farmland if more effective use is made of water from surrounding mountains, glaciers, rivers, and underground streams. A variety of food and cash crops are grown in Sinkiang such as wheat, maize, rice, and cotton. The abundant sunshine of the basins, especially the Tarim Basin and Turfan Depression, makes the area ideal for cotton cultivation. Owing to its climate, Sinkiang is also one of China's major fruit-growing regions. Sweet Ha-mi melons, seedless Turfan grapes, and I-li apples are known throughout China (Map III-122).

Sinkiang has abundant deposits of oil, coal, iron ore, gold, sulfur, and salt. Oil is found chiefly in Karamai in the Dzungarian Basin and along the northern and southern piedmont of the Tien Shan. Sinkiang's coal reserves are also a significant part of China's resource base. An iron and steel works and a cement factory have been built in Urumchi and a farm tool plant in K'a-shih. In addition, cotton mills and a hydroelectric plant have been built in Urumchi, and a mechanized filature has been set up in Ho-t'ien (Map III-123).

For transportation Sinkiang depends primarily upon highways, which total 20,000 kilometers. There are four main routes: east to Kansu, east-northeast to Mongolia, southeast to Tsinghai, and south to Tibet. All the main highways radiate from the capital at Urumchi, which also has scheduled airline service east to Lan-chou and Peking, south to K'a-shih, and west to the Soviet Union. Sinkiang is linked with Tibet by the Sinkiang-Tibet Highway, which begins at Jo-ch'iang (Char-khlik) in southern Sinkiang. Crossing northwestern China, the Lan-chou–Sinkiang Railroad now extends to Urumchi, and was planned to connect ultimately with the railroads of the Soviet Union. But construction toward that goal has been indefinitely suspended, as far as is presently known.

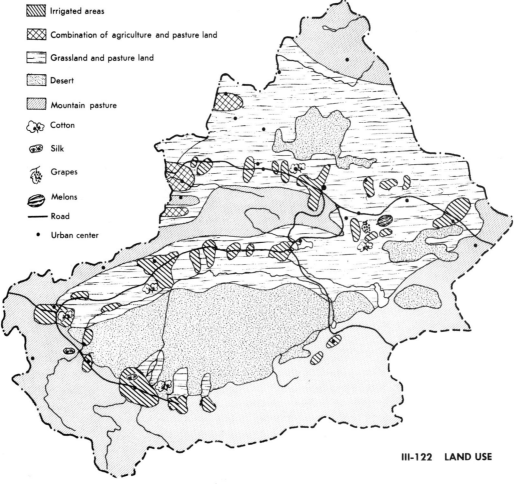

Irrigated areas

Combination of agriculture and pasture land

Grassland and pasture land

Desert

Mountain pasture

Cotton

Silk

Grapes

Melons

Road

Urban center

III-122 LAND USE

- ◉ Iron and steel
- ● Coal mining
- ✸ Petroleum wells and/or refinery
- ▲ Gold mining
- ✦ Textiles
- ▨ Food processing
- ⊗ Diverse industries
- ❀ Regional economic center
- • Urban center

III-123   INDUSTRIES

Tibet

The Tibetan Autonomous Region, a unique part of China, embraces the largest portion of the world's highest plateau (called "the roof of the world") with an average elevation of over 4,000 meters (Maps III-124 and III-125). The region is encircled by the Heng-tuan Range on the east, the Great Himalaya Range on the south, the Pamirs on the west, and the Kunlun Range and T'ang-ku-la Shan-mo on the north. In the southern third of the plateau the Nien-ch'ing-t'ang-ku-la Shan run from east to west. The Himalaya Range contains 40 peaks with elevations greater than 7,000 meters; the highest of these is Mt. Chomolungma (Everest), the highest mountain in the world (8,880 meters), located between China and Nepal. As a whole, Tibet's snow-covered mountains, the dazzling glaciers, the green forests in the southern valleys, and the vast grasslands, interspersed with salt lakes, present a picturesque landscape (Maps III-126 and III-127).

The Tibetan region has a land area of 1,200,000 square kilometers and a population of approximately 1.3 million, or barely more than 1 person per square kilometer. It is the most thinly populated region in China. On its desolate plateau the inhabitants lead a precarious existence, depending upon animal husbandry and marginal agriculture for their livelihood.

The Nien-ch'ing-t'ang-ku-la Shan, running through the southern part of the region, form the major divider between the plateau of northern Tibet and the valleys of southern Tibet. The high mountains and deep valleys of eastern Tibet comprise the Heng-tuan region.

The valleys of southern Tibet are long and narrow and slightly lower in elevation than those of eastern Tibet; here in the south the Brahmaputra flows through such a valley, where the climate is relatively warm, and the annual rainfall is more than 500 millimeters. Along the banks of the Brahmaputra and its tributaries the valleys are broad, the soil is fertile, and irrigation is easy. This is Tibet's principal farming area.

Tibet has more snow-covered peaks than any other region of China. There is as great a variation in temperature between the summits and the foothills of southern Tibet as there is between polar regions and the subtropics.

Northern Tibet consists of a broad plateau with an average elevation of approximately 4,000 meters, tilting somewhat downward toward the north. It is a region of numerous lakes, the largest of which is the Na-mu Hu (Tengri Nor), or "the heavenly lake," 4,627 meters above sea level. Surrounded as the region is by high mountains which allow penetration of very little moisture, the climate here is cold and dry, with rarefied air and strong winds. Vegetation consists largely of grasses, and the sunny

III-124 TIBET

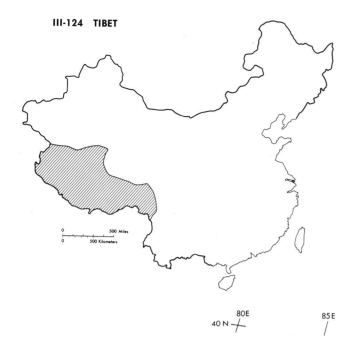

slopes and lakeside steppes provide excellent pastures (Map III-128).

Animal husbandry is an important occupation in Tibet, the yak being the chief draft animal. Adapted to a cold climate, it serves as a means of transport, and its long hair, milk, flesh, and hide make it a very useful animal in the region. Sheep and goats are also important.

The high altitude, deep canyons, and cold climate of Tibet have impeded the development of a transportation network. The Chinese government has expended much energy in an attempt to provide better links between Tibet and China Proper. Roads which have been completed so far are the Szechwan-Tibet Highway (from Ya-an in Szechwan to Lhasa), the Tsinghai-Tibet Highway (from Hsi-ning in Tsinghai to Lhasa) and the Sinkiang-Tibet Highway (from

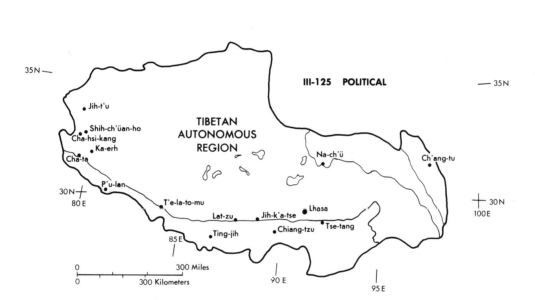

III-125 POLITICAL

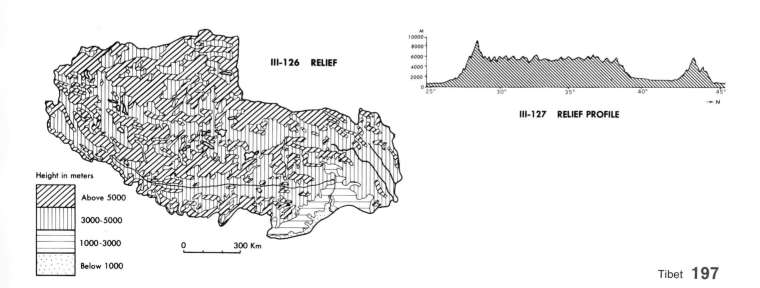

III-126 RELIEF

III-127 RELIEF PROFILE

Tibet **197**

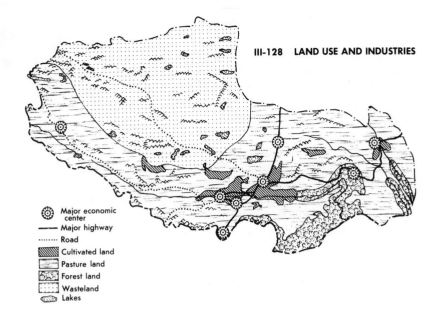

III-128   LAND USE AND INDUSTRIES

- ◉ Major economic center
- —— Major highway
- ········ Road
- Cultivated land
- Pasture land
- Forest land
- Wasteland
- Lakes

Jo-ch'iang in Sinkiang to P'u-lan in western Tibet). Air service between Peking and Lhasa has been established on a regular basis.

Tibet has abundant potential for the development of hydroelectric power and other industries. Hydroelectric stations, thermal power plants, motor vehicle repair works, an iron-smelting plant, farm implement factories, and a leather works have been built in the past two decades.

The political, religious, cultural, and economic center of the region is Lhasa; it is also the communications hub with highways radiating outward from it. A city with a long history, it has towers, palace halls, temples, and forts which can be seen from 20 kilometers away. The impressive Potala Palace was built here thirteen hundred years ago, during the T'ang Dynasty.

Jih-k'a-tse, Tibet's second largest city, is located on the Brahmaputra southwest of Lhasa, in Tibet's major grain-producing area, with highland barley as the major grain. Handicrafts are well developed in this region, especially Tibetan carpets and wooden bowls.

Cities

A more detailed view of various urban centers in China is afforded by Maps III-129 through III-156. Although these maps are not a replacement for knowing the cities firsthand—indeed no cartographic representation can replace the reality of being in a certain place—they do add a dimension of imagery for the reader. The placement of the traditional city wall, the relationship of major and minor lines of transport and physical features, or the location of temples and municipal buildings of special significance are new elements of the landscape available in these large-scale maps. They are arranged in a sequence parallel to the regions in the earlier pages of this section of the atlas.

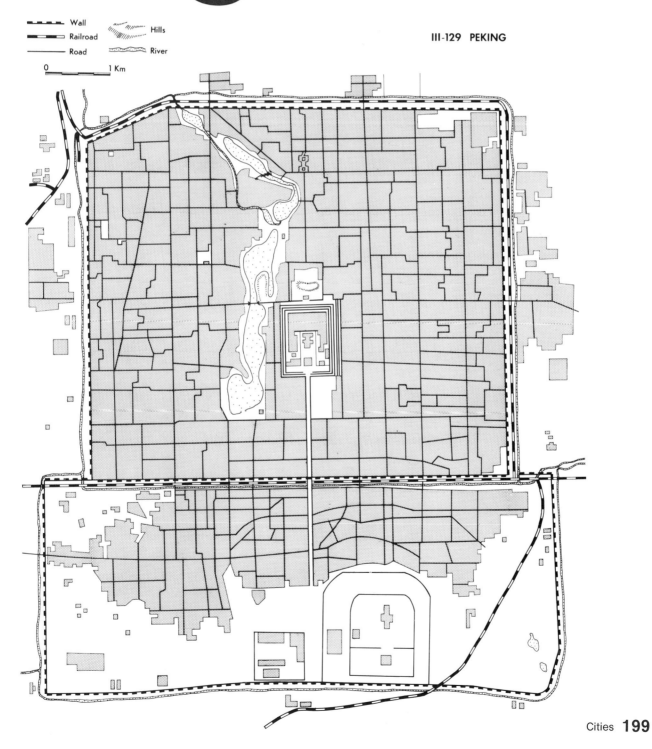

Wall
Railroad
Road

Hills
River

0   1 Km

III-129 PEKING

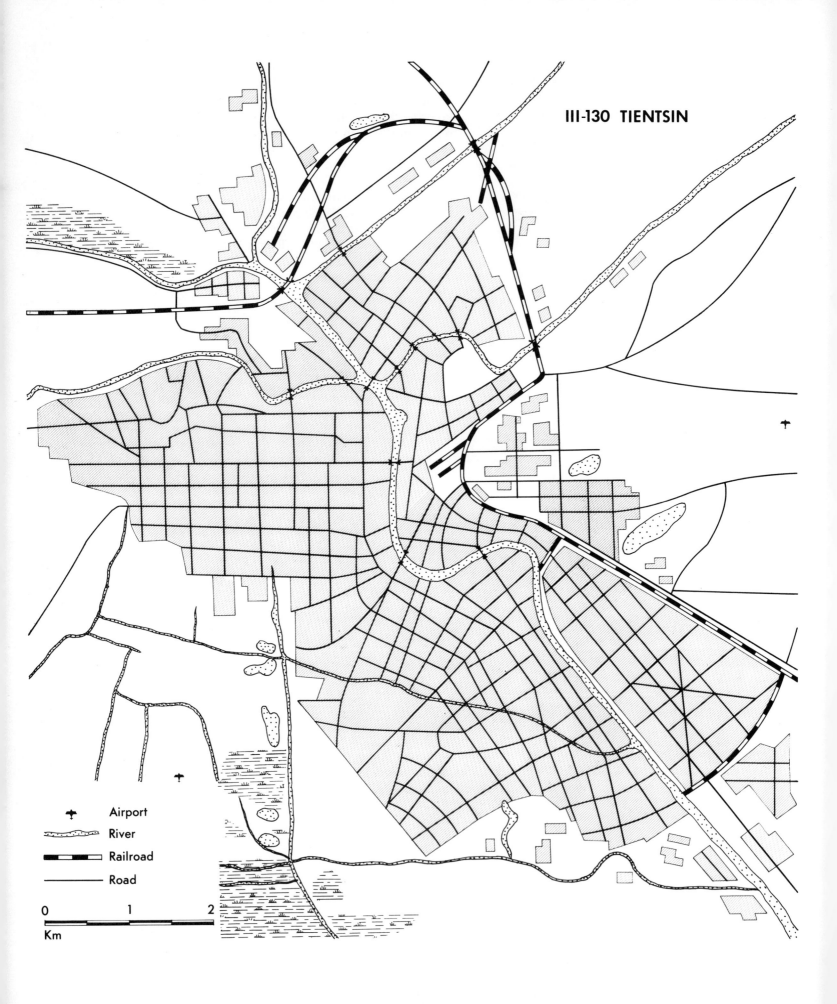

III-130 TIENTSIN

Airport
River
Railroad
Road

0   1   2
Km

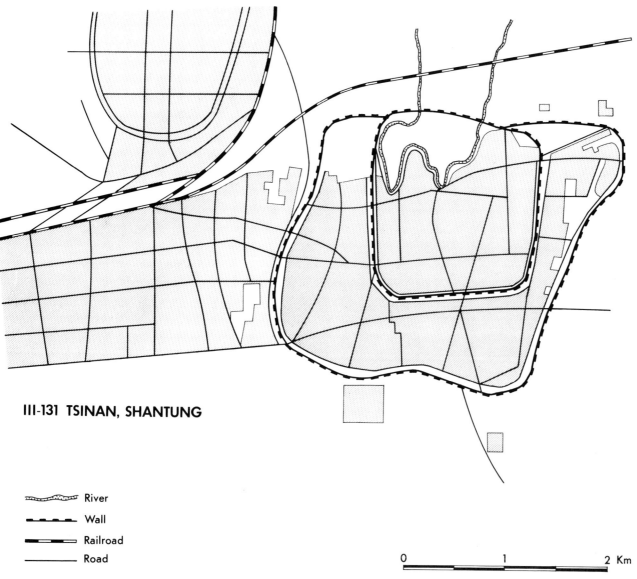

III-131 TSINAN, SHANTUNG

~~~~~ River
- - - Wall
▬▬▬ Railroad
──── Road

0   1   2 Km

III-132 CHENG-CHOU, HONAN

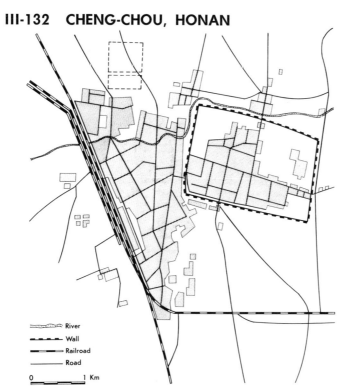

~~~~~ River
- - - Wall
▬▬ Railroad
── Road

0 ──── 1 Km

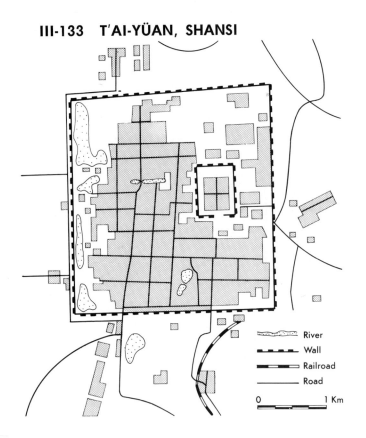

III-133   T'AI-YÜAN, SHANSI

River
Wall
Railroad
Road

0   1 Km

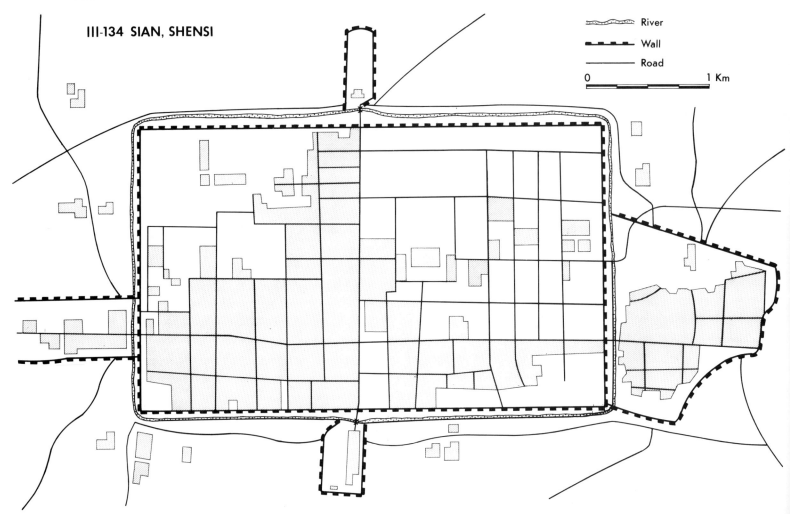

III-134 SIAN, SHENSI

River
Wall
Road

0   1 Km

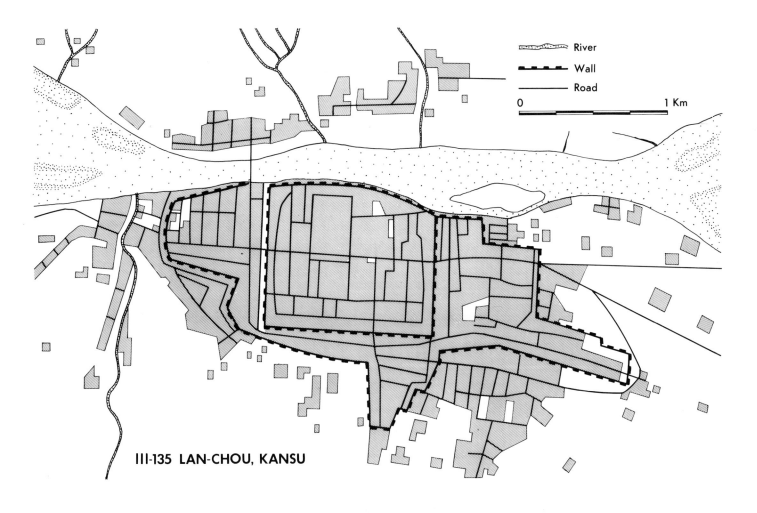

III-135 LAN-CHOU, KANSU

River
Wall
Road

0   1 Km

III-136   HSI-NING, TSINGHAI

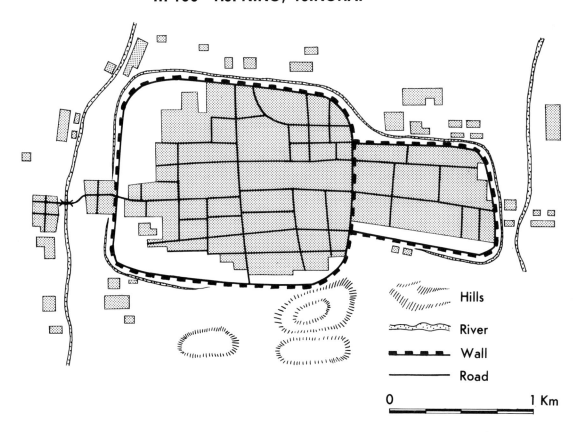

Hills
River
Wall
Road

0   1 Km

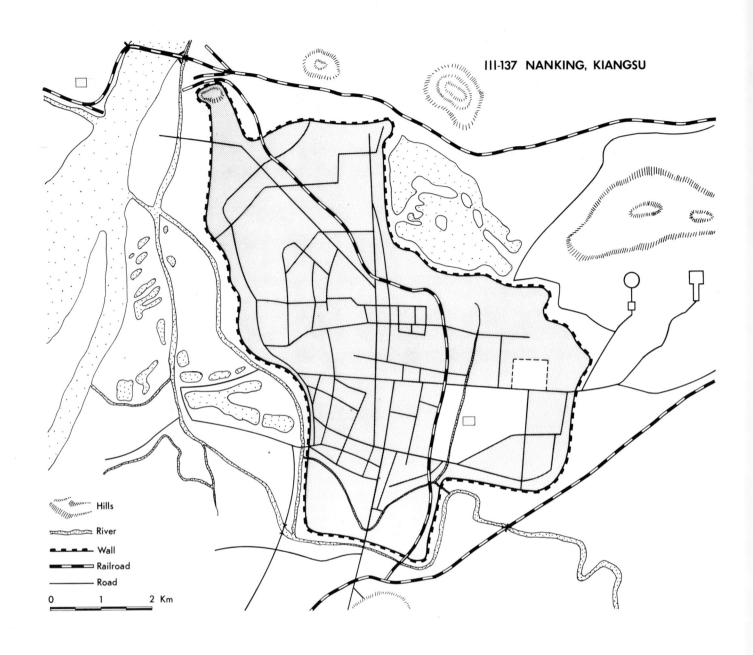

III-137 NANKING, KIANGSU

Hills
River
Wall
Railroad
Road

0   1   2 Km

III-138 SOOCHOW, KIANGSU

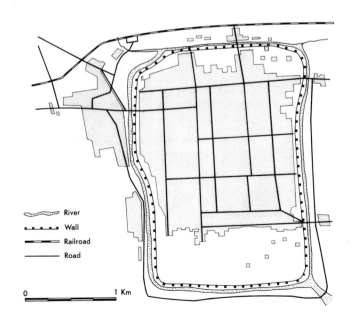

River
Wall
Railroad
Road

0   1 Km

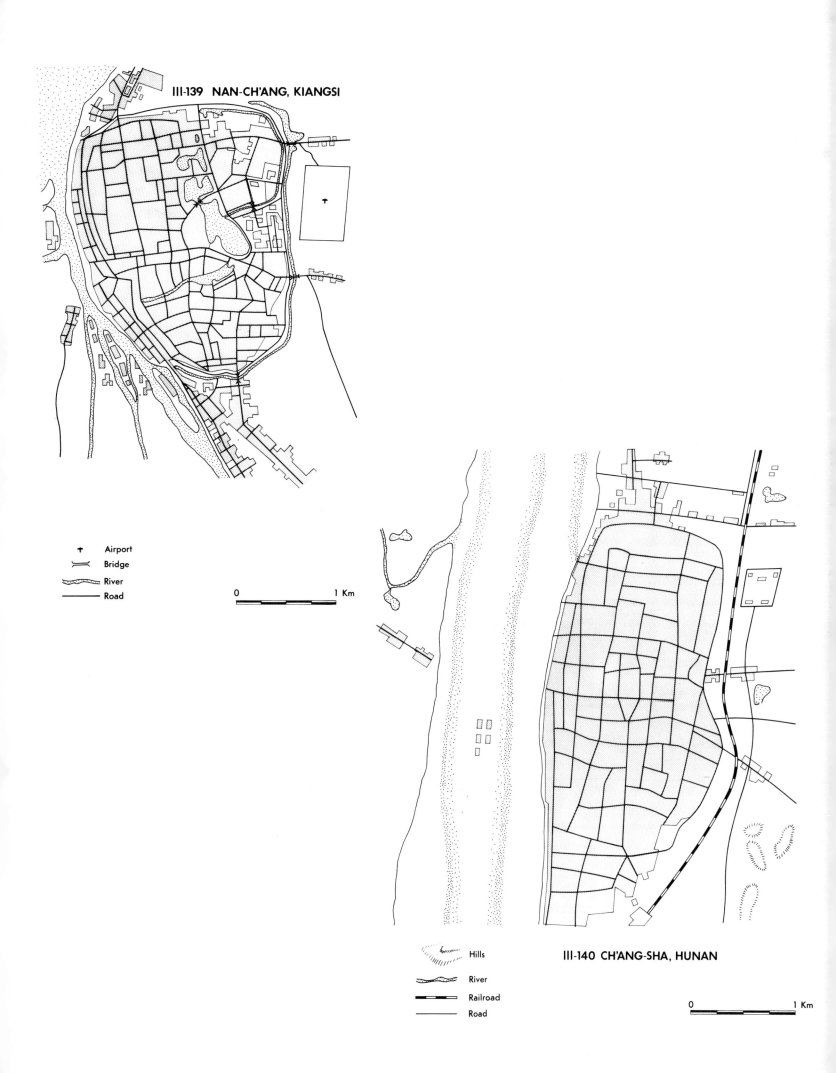

III-139 NAN-CH'ANG, KIANGSI

† Airport
⊨ Bridge
〰 River
— Road

0   1 Km

Hills

〰 River

▬ Railroad

— Road

III-140 CH'ANG-SHA, HUNAN

0   1 Km

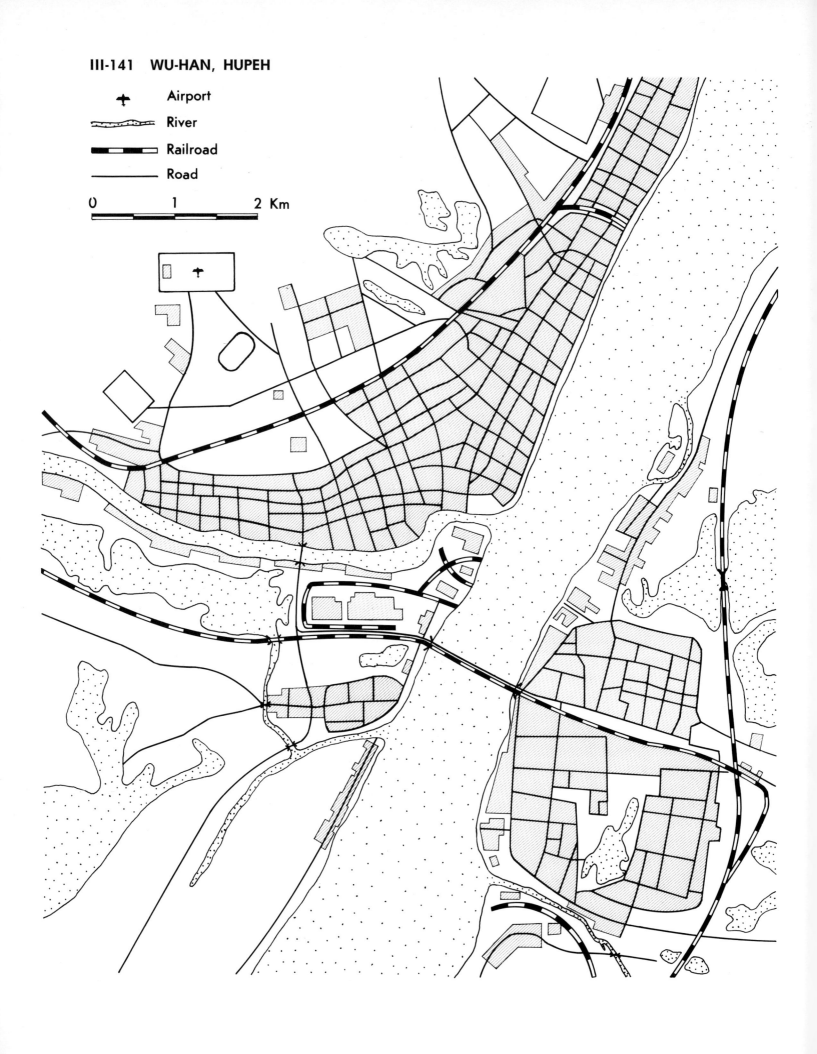

III-141 WU-HAN, HUPEH

Airport

River

Railroad

Road

0   1   2 Km

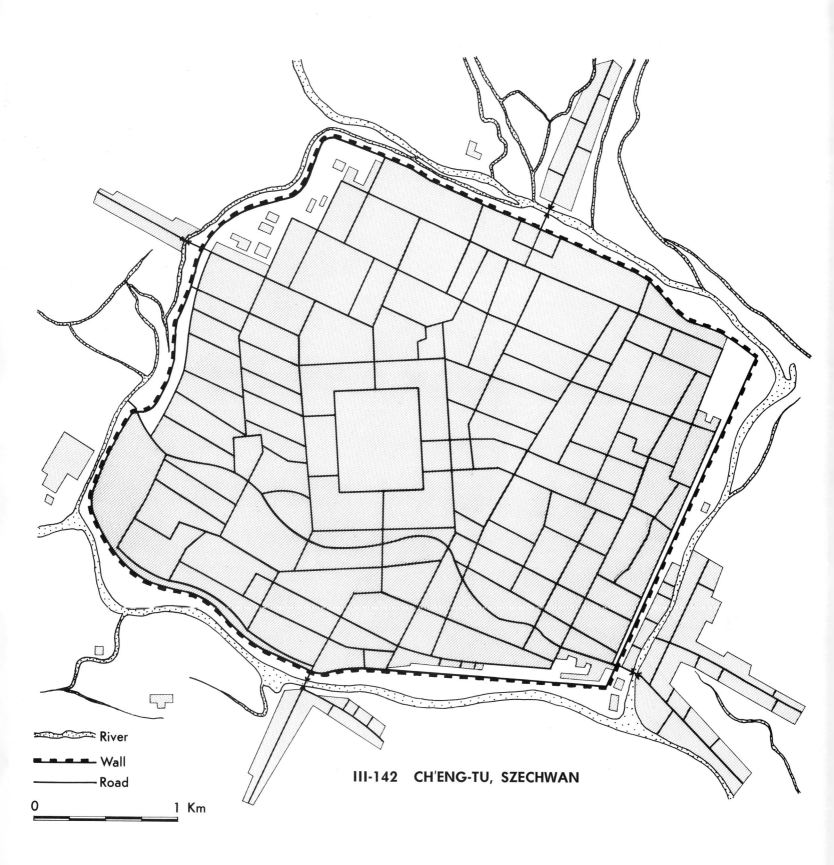

River

Wall

Road

0   1 Km

III-142   CH'ENG-TU, SZECHWAN

III-143 CHUNGKING, SZECHWAN

▬▬▬ Wall	〰〰 Hills
▬▬▬ Railroad	〰〰 River
─── Road	

0 ▭▭▭▭ 1 Km

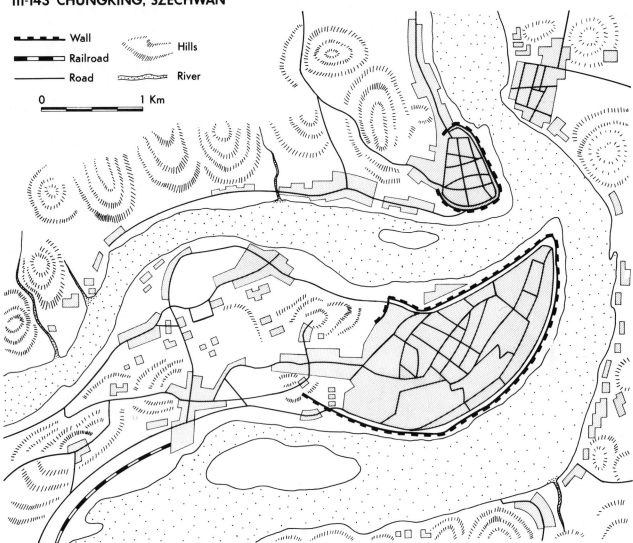

III-144 HANGCHOW, CHEKIANG

〰〰 Hills

〰〰 River

▬▬▬ Wall

▬▬▬ Railroad

─── Road

0 ▭▭▭▭ 1 2 Km

III-145   FOOCHOW, FUKIEN

Hills

Sandbar

River

Wall

Road

0   1 Km

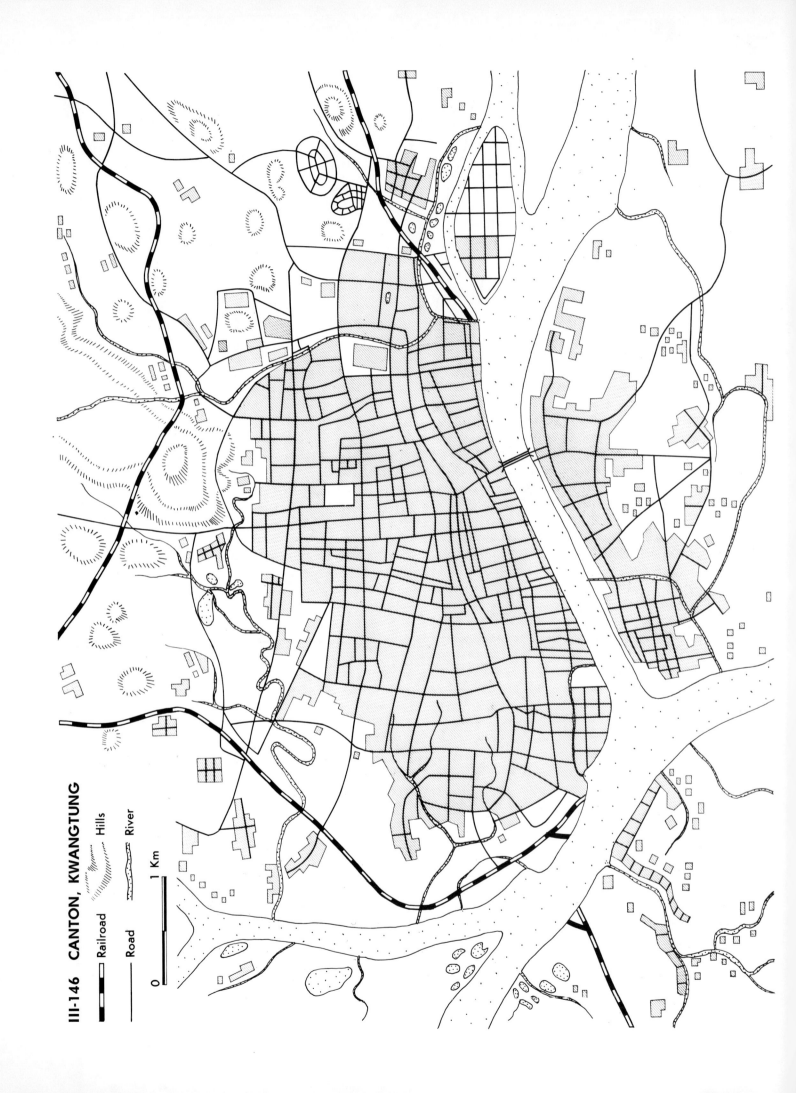

III-146 CANTON, KWANGTUNG

Railroad

Hills

Road

River

0   1 Km

III-147   NAN-NING, KWANGSI CHUANG AUTONOMOUS REGION

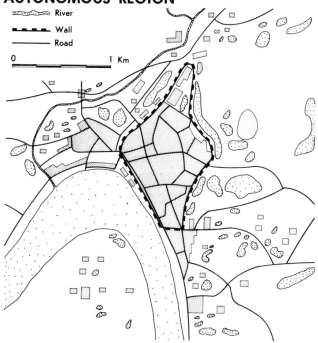

- River
- Wall
- Road

0   1 Km

III-148   KUEI-LIN, KWANGSI CHUANG AUTONOMOUS REGION

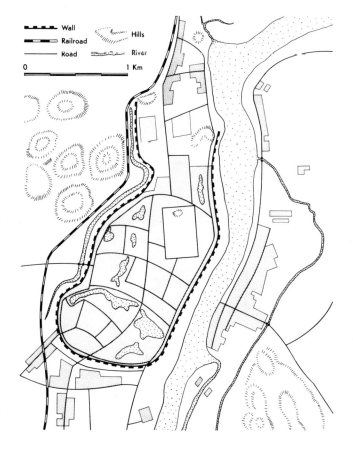

- Wall
- Railroad
- Road
- Hills
- River

0   1 Km

III-149   KUEI-YANG, KWEICHOW

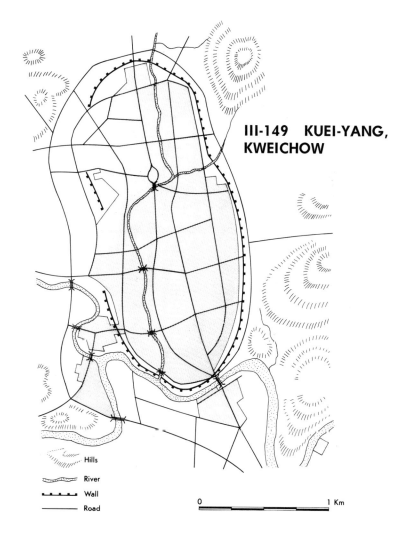

- Hills
- River
- Wall
- Road

0   1 Km

III-150   K'UN-MING, YUNNAN

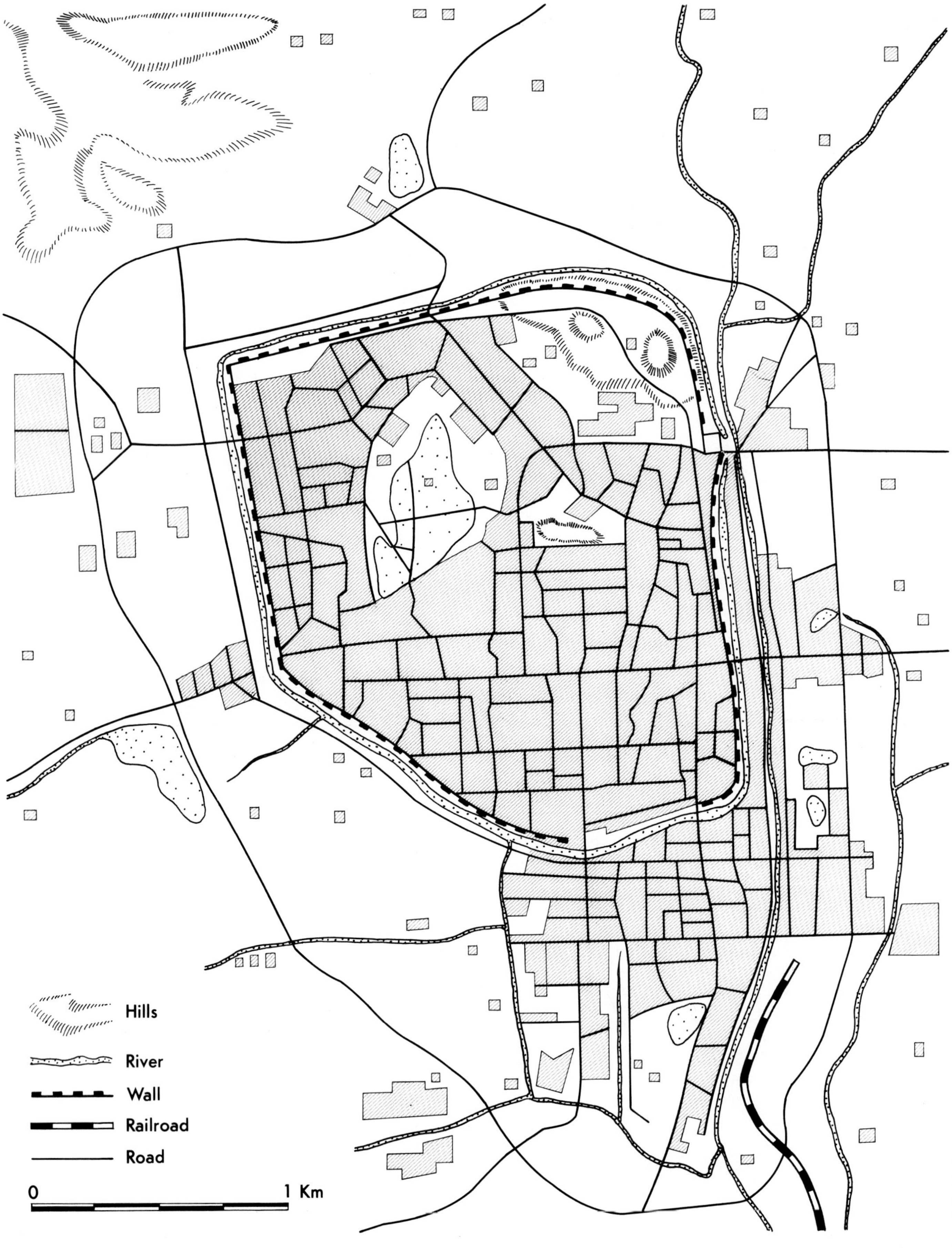

Hills

River

Wall

Railroad

Road

0   1 Km

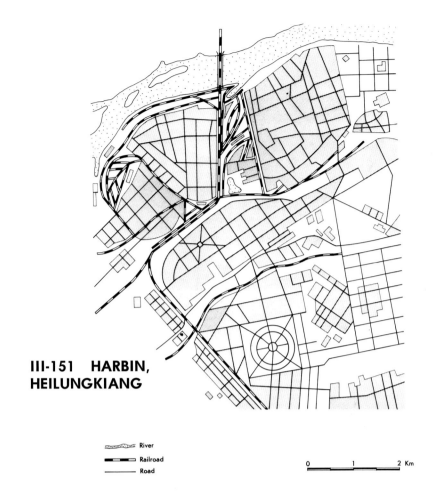

III-151 HARBIN, HEILUNGKIANG

~~~~~~~ River
▬▬▬▬ Railroad
──── Road

0   1   2 Km

III-152 SHEN-YANG, LIAONING

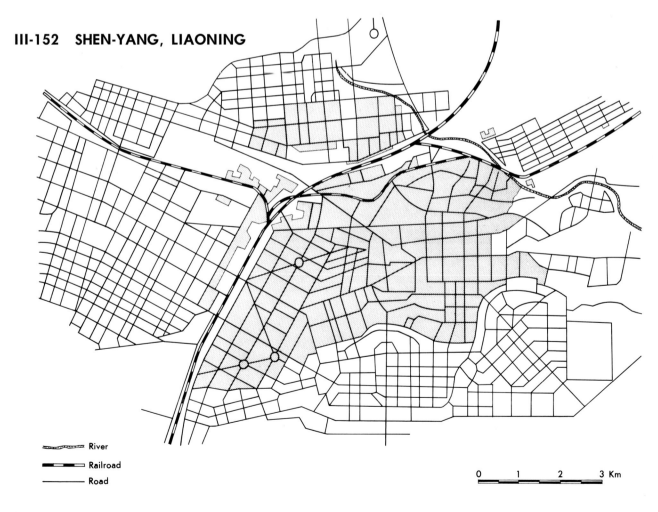

~~~~~~~ River
▬▬▬▬ Railroad
──── Road

0   1   2   3 Km

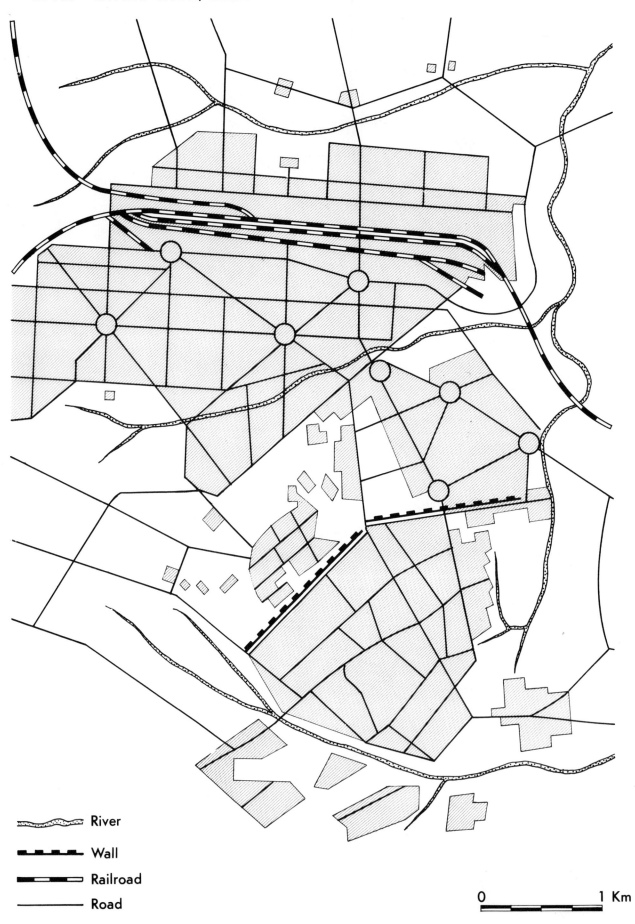

III-153 CH'ANG-CH'UN, KIRIN

~~~~~ River

▬ ▬ ▬ Wall

▬◻▬◻ Railroad

───── Road

0 ━━━━━━━ 1 Km

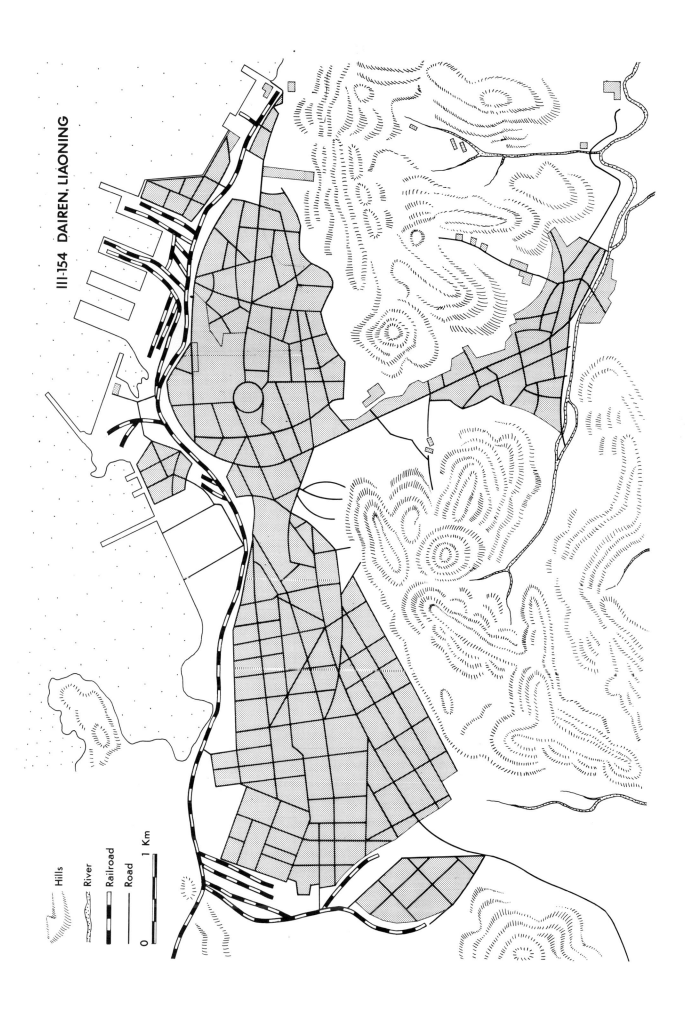

III-154 DAIREN. LIAONING

Hills

River

Railroad

Road

0   1 Km

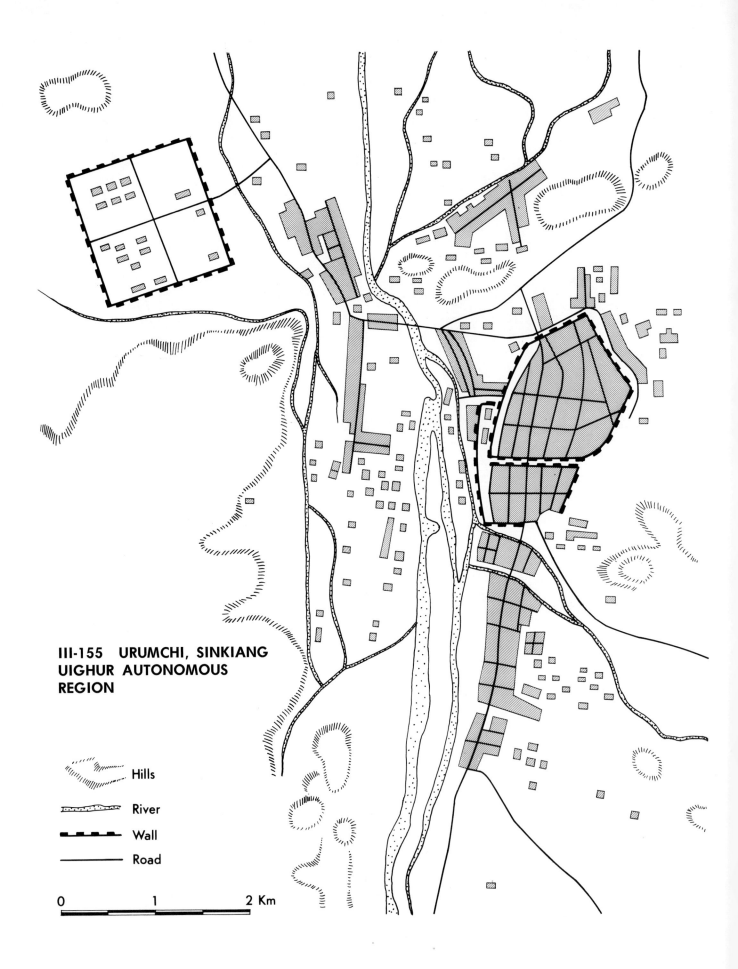

**III-155 URUMCHI, SINKIANG
UIGHUR AUTONOMOUS
REGION**

Hills

River

Wall

Road

0   1   2 Km

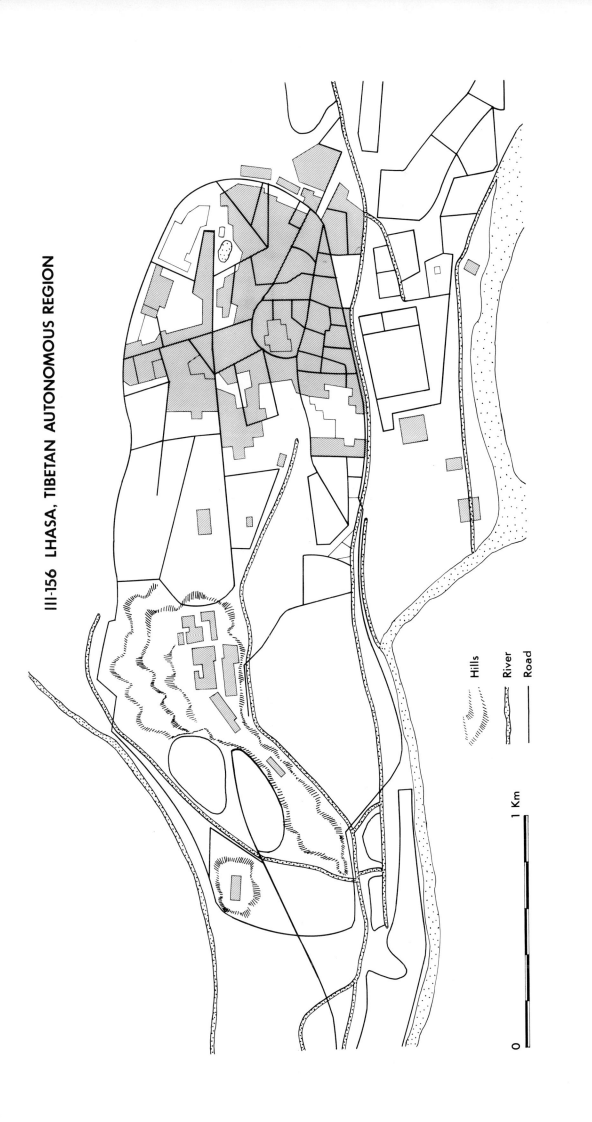

III-156 LHASA, TIBETAN AUTONOMOUS REGION

Hills

River

Road

1 Km

0

IV. HISTORICAL

China is often described as the world's oldest civilization. There is some justification for this claim, for China is the only civilization which has maintained a cultural continuity from the second millennium B.C. to the present. Other ancient centers of culture, such as Assyria, Egypt, and Greece, have not maintained their continuity with the same vitality as China. In these 3600 years, China's boundaries have of course changed many times (Map IV-1).

VERY EARLY HISTORY

There are many myths and legends about early Chinese history, but the Shang Dynasty (c. 1766-1122 B.C.) is the first dynasty for which there is significant archeological evidence. In 1928, in the North China Plain near present-day An-yang, the ruins of Ao, the major Shang capital, were initially excavated. This town had been built on a planned site, and houses were constructed of tamped earth. In addition, stone and bone tools were unearthed, along with ornate, highly decorated bronze vessels. Artifacts reveal that during the Shang Dynasty a highly organized agrarian society developed, founded on kingship and an elaborate class system. The people tilled the soil with hoes and used irrigation techniques; principal crops were millet, rice, and wheat. Workshops were found showing that bronze was used to make spears, arrows, needles, knives, and sacrificial vessels. Painting, music, and writing (in pictographic form) had developed.

In 1122 B.C. the Shang people were subjugated by the Chou people, who lived in the region now encompassed by Shensi and Kansu provinces, and whose capital was located at Hao, southwest of modern Sian (formerly also called Ch'ang-an). The Chou emperor divided his kingdom into semi-independent vassal states, which later became independent city-states. In 722 B.C. the Chou Dynasty was forced to move its capital eastward to the approximate location of Lo-yang. The Chou Dynasty is therefore divided into two periods with respect to the location of the imperial capital, the former period being the Western Chou, with the capital near present-day Sian, and the second (after 722 B.C.) being the Eastern Chou, when the capital was near Lo-yang.

The Chinese nation-state declined during this latter Chou period, while the smaller city-states became increasingly powerful. Since each of these states attempted to dominate the others, they were constantly at war. The Eastern Chou is subdivided into the Ch'un-ch'iu Period (722-481 B.C.) and the Period of the Contending States (480-221 B.C.).

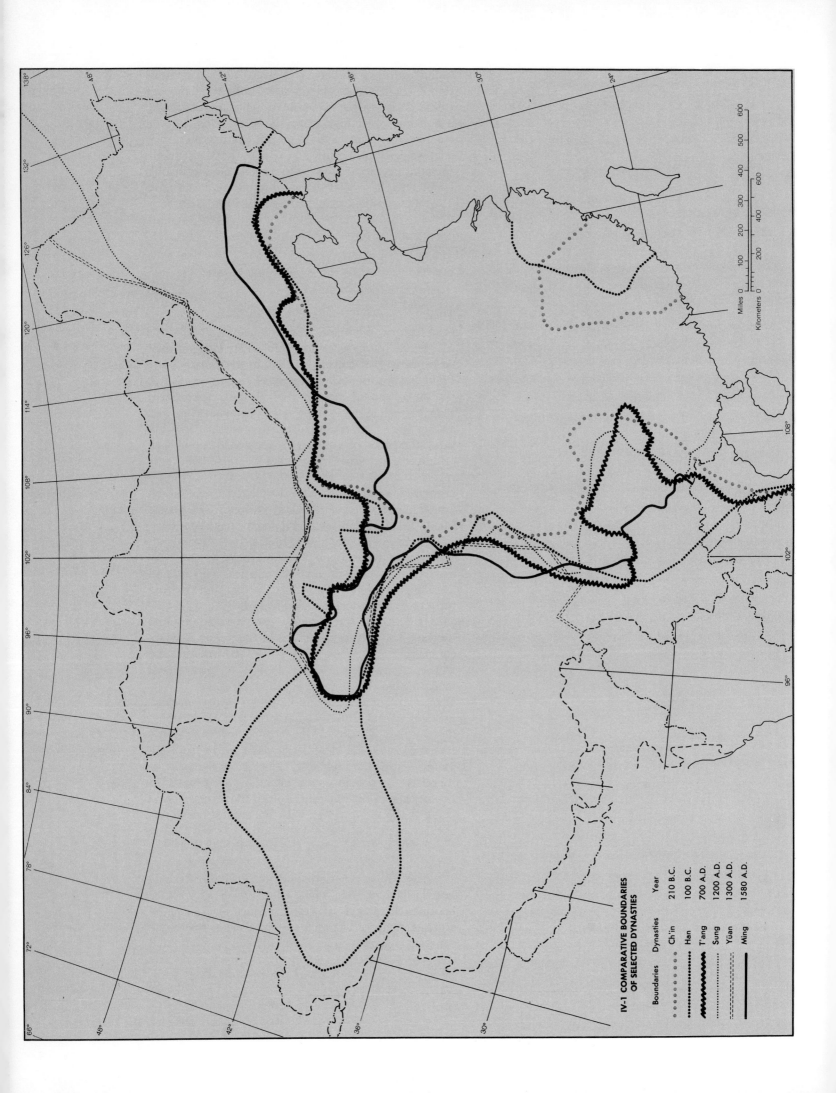

IV-1 COMPARATIVE BOUNDARIES
OF SELECTED DYNASTIES

Boundaries	Dynasties	Year
	Ch'in	210 B.C.
	Han	100 B.C.
	T'ang	700 A.D.
	Sung	1200 A.D.
	Yüan	1300 A.D.
	Ming	1580 A.D.

Miles 0   100   200   300   400   500   600

Kilometers 0   200   400   600

THE CH'UN-CH'IU PERIOD (722–481 B.C.)

The Ch'un-ch'iu Period derives its name from the book *Ch'un-ch'iu* (allegedly written in large part by Confucius), which recorded the history of the Chinese city-states between 722 and 481 B.C. (Map IV-2). The era was marked by constant warfare as these small states struggled among themselves for land and power. Despite the strife, however, population increased, art flourished, commerce expanded, and merchants rose to prominence. The most notable achievement of this period was the invention of iron smelting. Implements and weapons had formerly been made of bronze, the use of which had been a privilege of the elite; such tools and weapons as the peasantry possessed were mostly of wood. With iron tools newly available to commoners, agricultural production was stimulated and new land was brought under cultivation.

THE CONTENDING STATES (480–221 B.C.)

The division between the Ch'un-ch'iu and the succeeding period is arbitrarily set at 481 B.C., the last year recorded in the earlier Confucian history (Map IV-3). In actuality, however, the Period of the Contending States was largely a continuation and intensification of the contest that marked the Ch'un-ch'iu. After long and bitter internecine warfare, seven states—Ch'i, Ch'u, Yen, Han, Chao, Wei, and Ch'in—gradually gained in power.

The use of iron became widespread, and almost every state had an iron-smelting center, the most famous forges being at Han-tan in the state of Chao and at Wan in Ch'u. Blacksmiths made a wide variety of farm implements, tools, and weapons: Plowshares, hoes, sickles, spades, axes, chisels, saws, knives, swords, and halberds were all part of the metal tool inventory of China at this time.

Iron implements were essential to the construction of numerous public works. The state of Ch'in, for example, built the noted Tukiang Dam (in modern Szechwan). Other projects included the Canal of Cheng, also built by the state of Ch'in; canals dug by the states of Ch'i, Wei, and Ch'u, such as the Hankou and Hungkou canals; and portions of what later became the Great Wall. Construction of canals was also begun by the Kingdom of Wei in the Yellow River Basin.

Large surpluses of grain not only provided a commodity for trade but also enabled the growth of a larger urban population of merchants and craftsmen. The cities which arose during this period include Lin-tzu, in the state of Ch'i; Han-tan in

Chao; Lo-yang in the imperial state of Chou; Hsien-yang in Ch'in; and Ying in Ch'u. In addition, a money economy developed, and metal coins were widely used in commerce. Another familiar feature of Chinese life, chopsticks, had come into use by the end of this period.

The large number of states which existed during the early years of the Eastern Chou Period had been steadily reduced, and at the beginning of the Period of the Contending States only the seven principal ones remained. Although these states fought each other, the common enemy of six of them was the state of Ch'in (Ts'in), which had always been regarded as outside the inner core of the Chou city-states. Two strategists, Su Chin and Chang Yi, advocated unification, arguing that the existence of different states hampered trade, since each state had its own customs regulations and its own standard of weights and measures. Su Chin at first suggested a federation of the six powerful states of Ch'i, Ch'u, Yen, Chao, Han, and Wei to overthrow Ch'in, the strongest state, and thus unify all of China. But the six states failed to establish a stable alliance, and Ch'in retained its power.

Ch'in was bounded on four sides by significant physical barriers. The Ordos Desert was the border state on the north, and by way of this desert non-Chinese had continually attacked Ch'in. Through these invasions Ch'in acquired military experience and new tactics, especially the technique of conducting warfare on horseback. After Ch'in had extended its control over the fertile, cultivated Szechwan Basin, the state gradually expanded the economic bases of its power.

In view of Ch'in's waxing strength, Chang Yi then urged that each of the other six states ally itself with Ch'in and cooperate with it rather than fight against it. His efforts, too, met with only partial success. Instead of unifying with Ch'in voluntarily, the six were overcome between 230 and 221 B.C., and the empire was united for the first time by force.

THE CH'IN DYNASTY (221–206 B.C.), THE FIRST EMPIRE

The first Ch'in emperor of the unified empire assumed the title Shih-huang-ti, meaning "the First Emperor." During his conquest of the six states, Shih-huang-ti had never met strong resistance or suffered great losses. Thus when he ruled China he possessed sufficient resources and military power to allow for territorial expansion (Map IV-4).

The Ch'in Dynasty adopted a defensive policy toward the northern border region and an aggressive

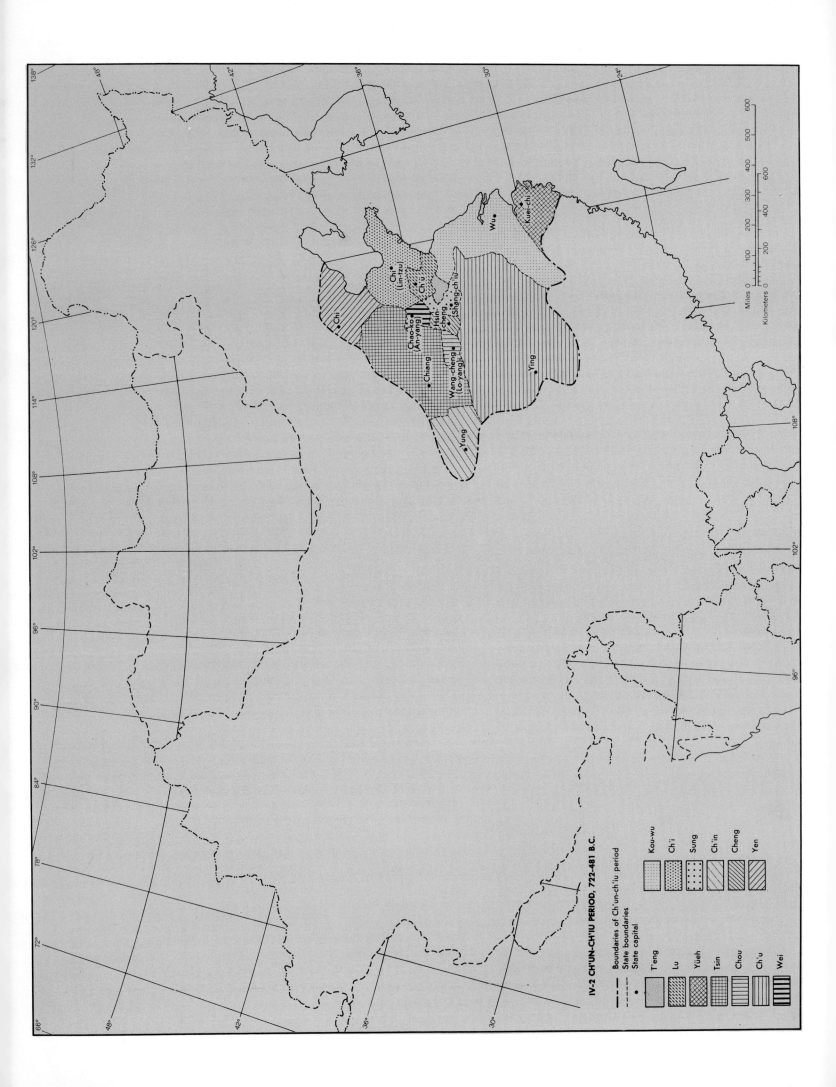

IV-2 CH'UN-CH'IU PERIOD, 722-481 B.C.

- - - - Boundaries of Ch'un-ch'iu period
········· State boundaries
• State capital

	Kou-wu
	Ch'i
	Sung
	Ch'in
	Cheng
	Yen

	T'eng
	Lu
	Yüeh
	Tsin
	Chou
	Ch'u
	Wei

Chi
Chi (Lin-tzu)
Ch'ü
Chao-ko (An-yang)
Hsin-cheng
Shang-ch'iu
Wu
Kuei-chi
Chiang
Wang-cheng (Lo-yang)
Ying
Yung

Miles 0   100   200   300   400   500   600
Kilometers 0   200   400   600

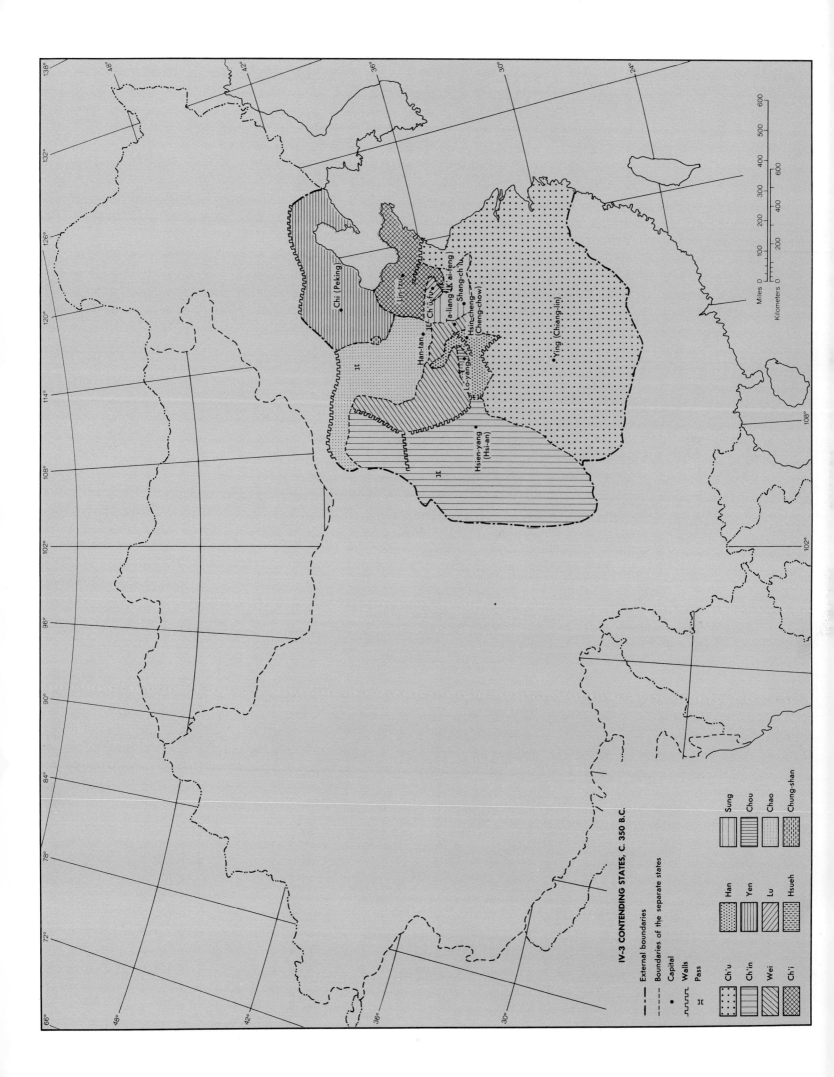

IV-3 CONTENDING STATES, C. 350 B.C.

External boundaries

Boundaries of the separate states

Capital

Walls

Pass

Ch'u

Ch'in

Wei

Ch'i

Han

Yen

Lu

Hsueh

Sung

Chou

Chao

Chung-shan

Chi (Peking)

Lin-tzu

Han-tan

Ta-liang (K'ai-feng)

Ch'ü-fu

Shang-ch'iu

Hsin-cheng (Cheng-chow)

Lo-yang

Ying (Chiang-lin)

Hsien-yang (Hsi-an)

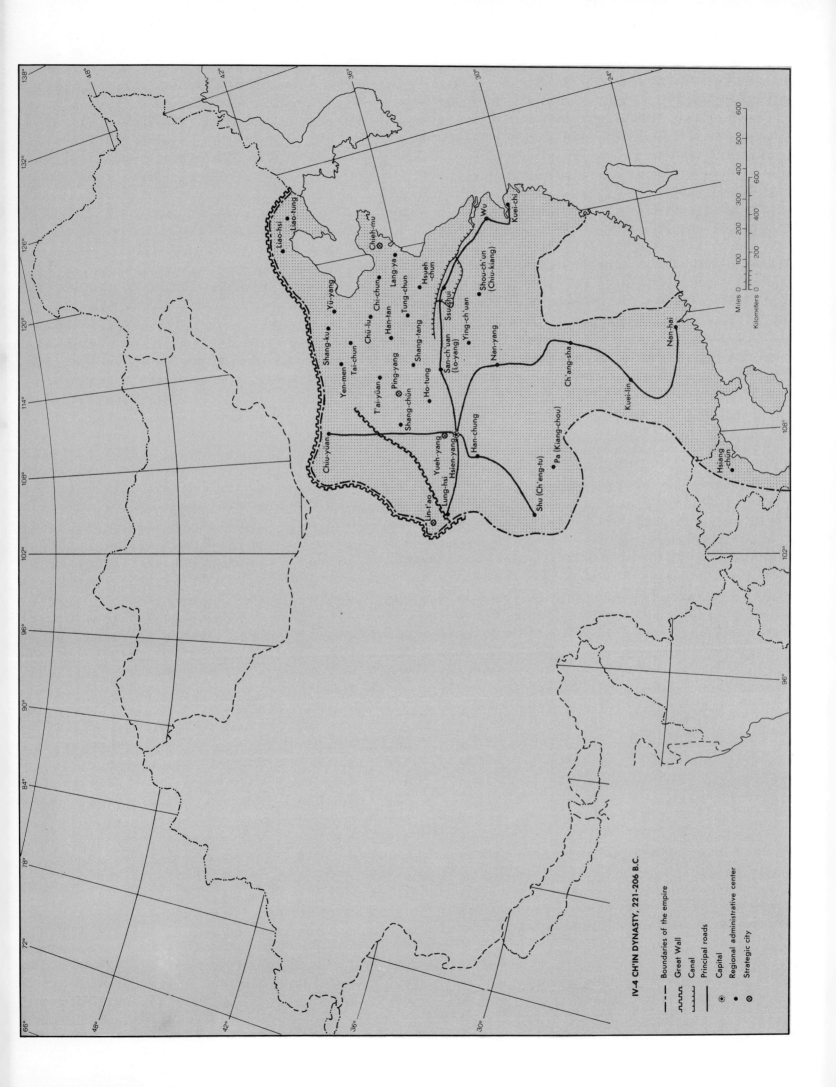

IV-4 CH'IN DYNASTY, 221-206 B.C.

Boundaries of the empire
Great Wall
Canal
Principal roads
Capital ⊕
Regional administrative center ●
Strategic city ⊗

Miles 0   100   200   300   400   500   600
Kilometers 0   200   400   600

Chiu-yüan

Liao-hsi
Liao-tung
Shang-ku
Yü-yang
Yen-men
Chieh-mu
Chü-lu
Chi-chün
Han-tan
Lang-ya
Tai-chün
Tung-chün
Hsüeh-chün
Wu
Kuei-chi
T'ai-yüan
Ping-yang
Shang-tang
Shou-ch'un
(Chiu-kiang)
Shang-chün
Ho-tung
San-ch'uan
(Lo-yang)
Ssu-shui
Ying-ch'uan
Nan-yang
Lung-hsi
Yüeh-yang
Hsien-yang
Han-chung
Lin-t'ao
Shu (Ch'eng-tu)
Pa (Kiang-chou)
Ch'ang-sha
Kuei-lin
Nan-hai
Hsiang-chün

policy toward the southern frontiers. The walls constructed by the former six states were joined to form a single long barrier known as the Great Wall. Thus, for the first time, the agricultural Chinese attempted to separate themselves from the nomadic horsemen of the north. The empire made no attempt to extend its territory into the northern steppe, since the Great Wall already enclosed all the land suitable for the intensive cultivation which had characterized traditional Chinese agriculture.

However, Ch'in was not content with a territory stretching south only to the southern boundaries of Ch'u, in modern Honan. In a series of campaigns between 221 and 214 B.C., the army of Shih-huang-ti pushed south beyond the Yangtze and reached the non-Han regions of Fukien, Kwangtung, and Kwangsi, and lands as far south as Annam.

The army met with little success in the south, where it was confronted not only by a tropical and malarial environment but also by hostile native tribes. Shih-huang-ti was never able to subdue this region completely; military agricultural settlements could only establish footholds in the more northerly regions of modern Hunan and Kwangsi.

The unification and centralization of the Ch'in Empire called for the standardization of units of weight and measure as well as language, currency, and the gauges of cartwheels. The emperor even imposed uniformity of thought and ideology. Since the end of the Chou Dynasty great social changes had given rise to different philosophic schools reflecting the outlooks of various social classes within Chinese society. Fearing that widespread debate and speculation would threaten his rule, Shih-huang-ti outlawed the philosophic schools. All books dealing with subjects other than technology, medicine, divination, and agriculture were ordered destroyed.

Along with these repressive measures, Shih-huang ti managed to accomplish some useful objectives. In addition to the needed standardization, he effected improvements in the transportation system. A network of roads was constructed throughout the empire. These roads, radiating outward from the capital of Hsien-yang in the Wei Ho Valley, were built for the purposes of supplying food for the populous capital and facilitating the emperor's inspections of his territories.

Ch'in divided the country into 36 administrative units, the civil and military governors of each being directly beholden to the emperor. After the partial success of the campaigns in the southern part of China extending as far south as the Hsi Chiang, four additional administrative units were created in that region.

The Ch'in Empire was based on the development of industry and commerce, an imperial policy which suited the merchants, but not the impoverished farmers. Large-scale peasant revolts erupted as a result of excessive taxation, conscription for frontier military service, and forced labor required to build the Great Wall and Ch'in Palace. As a result the dynasty fell in 206 B.C.

Nevertheless, the empire had a profound effect upon Chinese culture and history. The concept of centralization, for example, has persisted to the present day. In addition, some of Shih-huang-ti's specific policies and systems were preserved by the succeeding Han Dynasty, to such an extent that these two dynasties are often referred to collectively as the Ch'in-Han Period.

EARLIER AND LATER HAN DYNASTIES (206 B.C.–220 A.D.)

The Han Dynasty represents China's imperial period, a period contemporaneous with the Roman Empire (Map IV-5). One of the most important dynasties in Chinese history, the Han Dynasty lasted for more than 400 years.

During the Earlier Han (206 B.C.–9 A.D.), the now-united kingdoms were further organized and new territories were acquired, the whole being conjoined in a powerful empire. Also during this time certain measures were taken to improve the peasants' livelihood, and restrictions were imposed upon the merchants' power. This type of policy is known in Chinese history as "curbing commerce and stressing agriculture."

In the course of their expansion the Earlier Hans fought and defeated many of the nomadic peoples whose homelands bordered the Han heartland. These peoples included the Yüeh-chih in Liang, the Tung Hu in present Manchuria, and the Hsiung-nu in Mongolia. Of these, the Hsiung-nu, who inhabited the cold steppe and semidesert of the Mongolian Plateau, presented the greatest threat to the Hans.

The Earlier Han Empire, during the reign of Emperor Wu-ti (140–87 B.C.), extended its control over territories to the south, northeast, and northwest of the Han heartland. In 11 B.C. a Han emperor dispatched his army southward along five routes to conquer the Kingdom of Yüeh, the center of which was the Hsi Chiang delta, near Nan-hai (the present-day city of Canton). Yüeh was defeated and divided into nine districts, encompassing modern Kwangtung, Kwangsi, Hainan Island, and a part of Annam. Like Shih-huang-ti's earlier expedition in the south, this military conquest was not followed by colonization. Instead, the Han court ruled its southern territories through local tribes. As a result of the southern conquest, new foods, such as oranges, areca, and lichee, were introduced to the north.

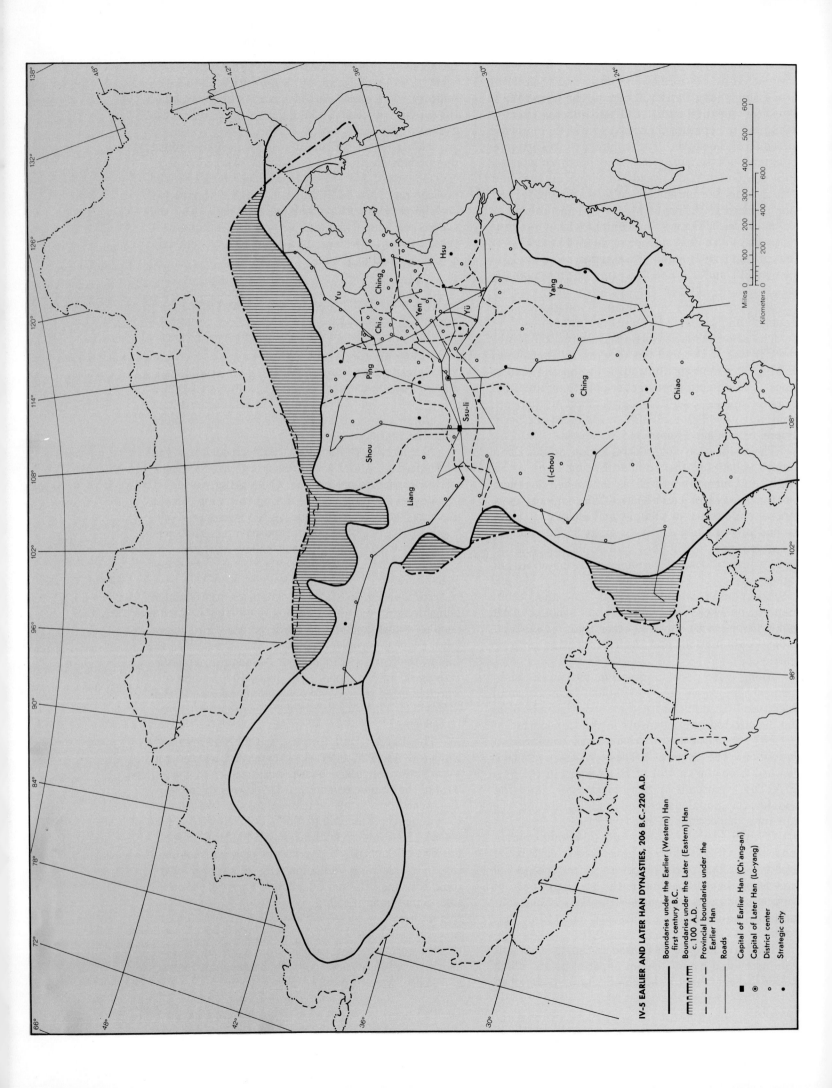

IV-5 EARLIER AND LATER HAN DYNASTIES, 206 B.C.–220 A.D.

	Boundaries under the Earlier (Western) Han first century B.C.
	Boundaries under the Later (Eastern) Han c. 100 A.D.
	Provincial boundaries under the Earlier Han
	Roads
■	Capital of Earlier Han (Ch'ang-an)
◉	Capital of Later Han (Lo-yang)
○	District center
•	Strategic city

The Hans developed southwestern China in the hope of establishing trade relations with India. The region, which included present-day Yunnan, Kwei-chow, and western Szechwan, was colonized by the Hans and divided into six administrative districts. Thus, except for parts of the southeast coast, all of southern China came under the control of the Han Dynasty.

Han territorial expansion on the northern frontier was more successful than Han southern colonization. For example, Emperor Wu-ti's forces established several garrisons in northern Korea in 108 B.C., and founded a colony with its capital at Lo-lang, near modern Pyongyang. The territory encompassed a region which extended as far south as present Seoul. This territory was more prosperous and populous than the Han colonies in Liaotung and Shantung and had a Chinese population of about 315,000.

The most important territorial expansion, however, was in the northwest, extending in a crescent from the Kansu Corridor, through the oases at the foot of the Ch'i-lien Shan-mo to the Tarim Basin. This colonization followed the Han army's victory over the Hsiung-nu in battles fought between 121 and 119 B.C., and the defeat of the kingdoms of the Tarim Basin and Inner Asia. To secure this territory, frontier agricultural colonies were established, and soldiers were sent to northwest garrisons to become permanent agrarian settlers. The Great Wall was extended westward to protect these settlers as well as the caravans of traders and government emissaries who traveled to the oases in the Kansu Corridor. Thus a new cultural feature appeared on the Chinese landscape: fortified, irrigated oases surrounded by barren desert. These agricultural colonies, however, further exacerbated the conflict between the sedentary Chinese and the nomadic pastoralists.

Trade and expansion in Han China were closely related. As a result of its western territorial expansion, the Earlier Han Dynasty established trading relations with the Roman Empire, and China's silk soon appeared in European markets. In addition, the products and some skills of Inner Asia were gradually introduced into China. Wu-ti's intrepid emissary, Chang Ch'ien, brought back from the lands west of the Pamirs viticulture, alfalfa, and a new breed of horse. The neighboring nomads traded hides, horses, and cattle for Han China's silk, food-stuffs, salt, woven goods, mirrors, iron, and bronze.

Chinese culture had first flourished in the upland basins, spreading to the eastern lowlands only after the Chinese had acquired greater confidence in controlling nature. During the reign of Wu-ti a canal was constructed along the south bank of the Wei Ho. The canal not only facilitated the transport of grain from the plain but also increased the irrigable farmland of the Wei Ho Basin. It is interesting to note that even during the Han Dynasty the Wei Ho Basin was easier to cultivate than the Yellow River Basin. Thus during the Earlier Han Period the Wei Ho Basin remained the economic center of China. The densest agglomeration of people was in the vicinity of the capital, Ching-chao (Ch'ang-an).

It is believed that periodic censuses began during the Earlier Han Dynasty, toward the end of which the first reliable census was taken and the total population was reported to be about 48 million. There was a short interregnum in the Han Dynasty from 9 to 23 A.D., when the throne was occupied by the usurper Wang Mang. After this there arose the Later Han, also called the Eastern Han because the capital was moved to Ho-nan (Lo-yang) on the North China Plain.

During the Later Han the economic and demographic center of China shifted from the eastern portion of the Wei Ho Basin to the great alluvial North China Plain. The majority of Chinese, approximately 43 million, lived in the Yellow River drainage area. The only other area of high population density was Szechwan (then called I or I-chou), which had settlements on the Shu (Ch'eng-tu) Plain and along several of the rivers of the basin.

Though some of the Later Han emperors proved to be strong rulers, the empire was gradually weakened by internal strife and rivalry and was finally over thrown in 200 A.D.

THE THREE KINGDOMS (220–265)

The period of turmoil had begun toward the turn of the third century; it lasted for three and a half centuries, during which much of the territory acquired during the Han Dynasty was lost.

For a while during the early part of this period China was divided into three kingdoms (Map IV-6). The Kingdom of Wei, with its capital at Ho-nan (Lo-yang), was the largest of these, and was divided into 13 districts. It was bounded on the north by the Great Wall, on the east by the Gulf of Chihli (modern Po Hai) and the Yellow Sea, on the south by the Tsin-ling Shan and the Huai Ho, and on the west by Tun-huang at the western end of the Kansu Corridor. Wu was the second largest kingdom; it controlled southeastern China north to the Yangtze and west to the Yangtze gorges and was divided into three districts: Ching, Yang, and Kuang. It encompassed the modern provinces of Chekiang, Fukien, Kiangsi, Hunan, Kwangtung, and Kwangsi, and portions of Kiangsu, Anhwei, and Hupeh, as well as northern Annam. The capital of the Kingdom of Wu was initially located at Chien-yeh (on the site of present Nanking) but was later moved to present Hankow. The King-

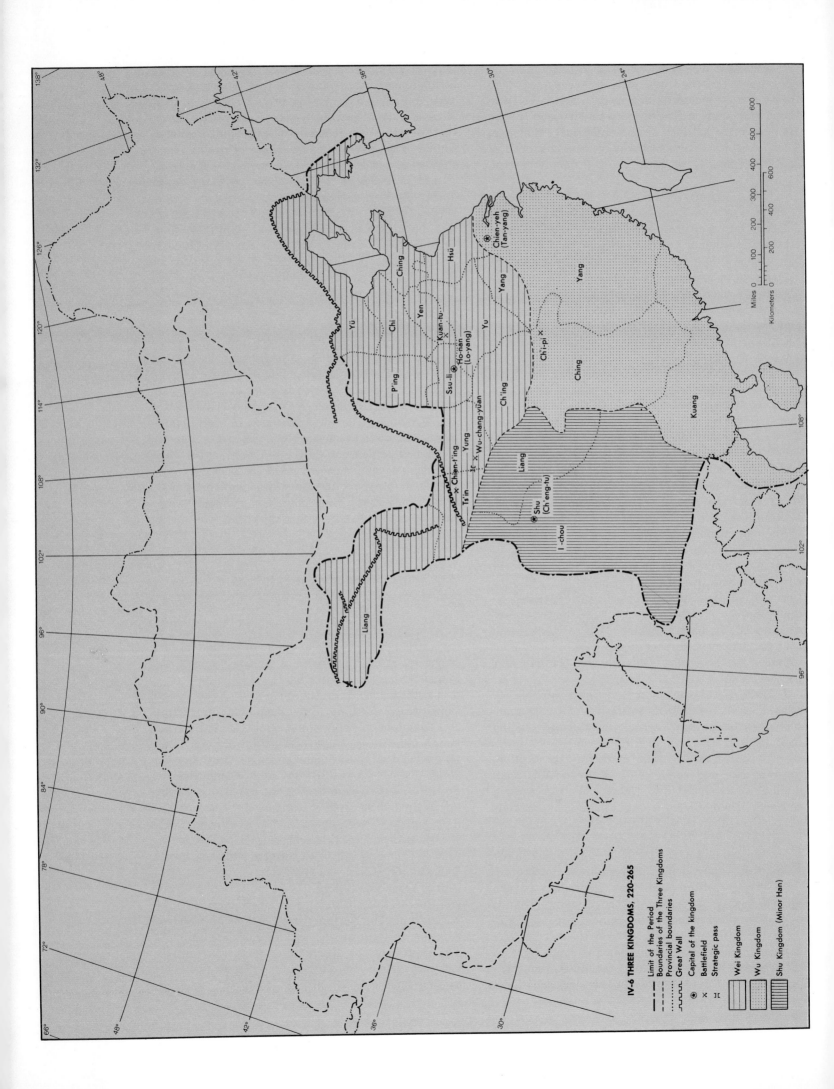

IV-6 THREE KINGDOMS, 220–265

Limit of the Period
Boundaries of the Three Kingdoms
Provincial boundaries
Great Wall
⊛   Capital of the kingdom
✕   Battlefield
Ⅱ   Strategic pass

Wei Kingdom

Wu Kingdom

Shu Kingdom (Minor Han)

Miles   0   100   200   300   400   500   600
Kilometers   0   200   400   600

Liang

Yü

Ch'i

P'ing

Yen

Kuan-tu
✕

Ssu-li
⊛ Ho-nan
(Lo-yang)

Ching

Hsü

Yang

Yu

Chien-yeh
(Tan-yang)
⊛

Yang

Ching

Ch'ing

Ch'ing

Chi-pi ✕

Kuang

Chien-p'ing
✕

Yung

✕ Wu-chang-yüan

Ts'in

Liang

Shu
(Ch'eng-tu)
⊛

I-chou

✕

dom of Shu, located in southwestern China, was divided into two districts, Liang and I, and had its capital at Ch'eng-tu.

The Period of the Three Kingdoms was characterized by a migration of people into southern China, by cultural and technological innovations, and by the increasing popularity of Buddhism. The population of the Yangtze Valley and southern China increased five-fold, primarily due to the influx of refugees from the floods and droughts in the Yellow River Basin. As a result of these migrations, hitherto uninhabited regions were settled. The mountainous southeastern coast and the Tung-t'ing Hu and P'o-yang Hu basins of Hupeh were all populated by emigrants from northern China.

As the population increased, the landscape underwent further modification. For example, the Yangtze was connected with the Huai Ho by two canals. Irrigation technology, employed in central China, was introduced to the relatively undeveloped south, and many dams and reservoirs were constructed. As the forests were cleared, indigenous tribes were driven into the mountainous areas, and the Han Chinese settled in increasing numbers in the fertile valleys.

Among the important consequences of the southern migrations was the experimentation with, and cultivation of, tea, which was first planted on the hillsides of present Chekiang and Kiangsi provinces. At the same time the porcelain industry began to develop in Kiangsi Province. Development of the wheelbarrow and the water mill were two other technological advances of the period. The wheelbarrow, supposedly invented by Chu-ko Liang, the premier of Shu, did not appear on the European landscape for another ten centuries. The water mill was used for grinding grain and for irrigation, not only lightening the farmer's work but also resulting in a more efficient use of arable land.

The continuous internecine warfare for nearly four decades, however, finally dissolved the Three Kingdoms, and a new empire, Tsin, arose in the second half of the third century.

THE WESTERN AND EASTERN TSIN DYNASTIES (265–420)

The Kingdom of Shu was conquered by the Kingdom of Wei in 263. Two years later, the Szu-ma family forced the Wei emperor to abdicate and inaugurated the Tsin Dynasty. The Earlier, or Western, Tsin Dynasty (265–316) chose Ho-nan (Lo-yang) as its capital, and the Later, or Eastern, Tsin Dynasty selected Chien-k'ang (present Nanking) (Maps IV-7 and IV-7a).

The Kingdom of Wu was conquered in the year 280 by the emperor of the Western Tsin Dynasty, and thus the former Three Kingdoms were unified. Under the Western Tsin, China was divided into 19 administrative provinces, 172 districts, and 1,232 counties (hsiens). The southeastern provinces, such as Yang, Ching, and Kuang, were generally larger than the other provinces. Communications were restored between northern and southern China, and trade gradually increased between these two regions.

The founder of the Western Tsin Dynasty was alleged to have fathered 25 sons, among whom he divided the principalities of his dominion. Gradually, these principalities became semi-autonomous kingdoms, each with its own administrative officials and army. When the founder died, civil war erupted between these kingdoms. At the same time, China was invaded by several nomadic tribes.

In 304 one of the Tsin princes made the mistake of seeking the assistance of one such tribe, the Huns of Inner Asia, while one of his rivals sought the aid of another, the Hsien-pis, also of Inner Asia. The Huns crossed the Yellow River, occupied Ho-nan, and brought the Western Tsin Dynasty to an end. Warfare ensued between the rulers of various tribes, and during this period of confusion many landlords fled south and established the Eastern Tsin Dynasty, locating its capital at Chien-k'ang (Nanking).

Northern China was politically unstable during the Eastern Tsin Dynasty, and 16 nations rose and fell in rapid succession. Most of these nations were established by nomadic tribesmen who vied with each other for land and power. This period in Chinese history is referred to as the era of "Five Alien Tribes and Sixteen Kingdoms." During the fourth century these northern tribes were gradually united and the Hsien-pis founded a new dynastic state of Wei. The people of the Eastern Tsin Dynasty longed to be reunited with their countrymen in northern China, while the northern alien tribes hoped to subjugate the south. War between the two regions was therefore inevitable. One of the most decisive battles in Chinese history took place in 383 when the Huns, Hsien-pis, and Ch'iangs, who had united to invade the south, were defeated by a numerically smaller force of the Eastern Tsin Dynasty along the Fei Ho in Anhwei Province. This victory thwarted the nomads' invasion of southern China and enabled the farmers of the Eastern Tsin Dynasty to cultivate land in what are now Honan and Shantung provinces, which the Eastern Tsin army had recaptured.

Also, many northern peasants migrated to southern China during the Eastern Tsin Dynasty introducing southern farmers to new agricultural techniques and some new tools. During this period in southern China wasteland was reclaimed, forests

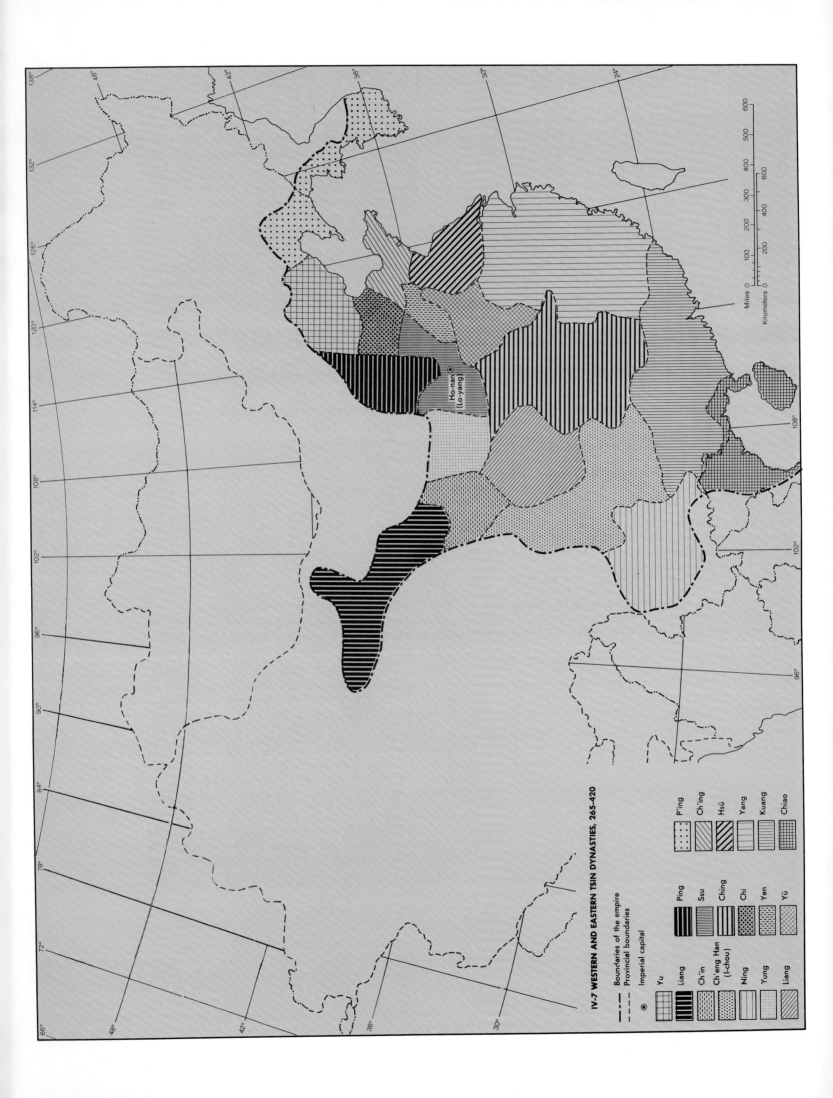

IV-7 WESTERN AND EASTERN TSIN DYNASTIES, 265–420

Boundaries of the empire
Provincial boundaries
⊛ Imperial capital

Yu	Ping	P'ing	Ch'ing	Hsü
Liang	Ssu	Yang	Kuang	Chiao
Ch'in	Ching			
Ch'eng Han (I-chou)	Chi			
Ning	Yen			
Yung	Yü			
Liang				

Ho-nan ⊛ (Lo-yang)

Miles 0 100 200 300 400 500 600
Kilometers 0 200 300 400 500 600

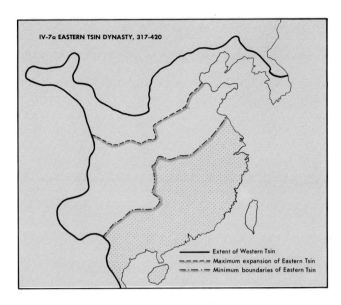

IV-7a EASTERN TSIN DYNASTY, 317-420

———— Extent of Western Tsin
— — — Maximum expansion of Eastern Tsin
—··—··— Minimum boundaries of Eastern Tsin

and scrub lands were cleared, dikes were built along the southeastern seacoast, and rivers and lakes were dredged. In addition, sericulture and the porcelain industry began to flourish in this region.

NORTHERN (439–581) AND SOUTHERN (420–589) DYNASTIES

The Eastern Tsin failed to recapture the northern territories but did retain control of southern China. The Tsin Dynasty was followed, in succession, by the four Southern Dynasties, Sung, Ch'i, Liang, and Chen (420-589), which established their capital in Chien-k'ang. Meanwhile, in the north, the Wei Dynasty, under which the Hsien-pis had unified other states founded by nomads, was likewise followed by a quick succession of ruling houses, known collectively as the Northern Dynasties (439-581) (Map IV-8). Four cities served as capitals during the period of the Northern Dynasties, Lo-yang being the most important.

This period was also one of extensive migration resulting from frequent warfare. The Northern Dynasties exerted control over a region which extended from the Yellow River Basin northward to the Great Wall, and the Southern Dynasties dominated an area which stretched from the Yangtze Basin southward to the Red River of Annam. The boundary between the two kingdoms, a matter of constant contest, ran through the present-day provinces of Kiangsu, Anhwei, and Hupeh and, for a time, shifted as far south as the Yangtze.

Some of the nomadic tribes of the northern and western borders of China gradually became assimilated with Han society in this period, as is evidenced by the changing of place names and surnames, the merging of languages, and intermarriage between the nomads and the Han Chinese. Meanwhile, in southern China, feudal Han culture continued to develop. Calligraphy, music, and painting flourished under imperial patronage, and the Buddhist, Confucian, and Taoist philosophies further evolved.

The economic development of southern China, as mentioned above, had lagged behind that of the Yellow River realm. The arable land of the south was initially cultivated during the Three Kingdoms, but farming methods were primitive, production was low, and large tracts of land remained uncultivated. The influx of migrants from northern China during the Eastern Tsin Dynasty had resulted in the more extensive development of the coastal regions and forest lands of the south.

Now, during the Northern and Southern Dynasties, the south began to rival the north in cultural, economic, and political importance. Irrigation and flood control projects were undertaken, wasteland was cultivated, and in some areas the land was double-cropped in rice. Agriculture was especially well developed in the provinces of Chiang and Yang (corresponding approximately to present Kiangsi, Chekiang, and Fukien provinces), the marshlands of Hsiang (present Ch'ang-sha in Hunan Province), the lower Yangtze area, and the T'ai Hu region. The principal trade center of northern China was Lo-yang, and that of southern China was Chien-k'ang. The extensive southward migrations during the Eastern Tsin Dynasty had led to the establishment of numerous hotels and inns, and even Buddhist temples were used as lodging. Despite such migration and economic development, however, the population of the south remained less than that of northern China, and the Northern Dynasties were politically stronger than the Southern.

By the beginning of the Northern and Southern Dynasties, Buddhism had attracted a wide following and exerted considerable political influence. The religious sculpture of this period, while recalling the traditional style of the Ch'in and Han Dynasties, also showed the influence of foreign culture, and particularly of Buddhism, on China's artistic development. In particular, numerous caves have been found which were dug into rock precipices, each cave containing many Buddhist statues which reflected the dignity and serenity characteristic of that tradition.

THE SUI DYNASTY (581–618)

Northern and southern China, which had existed as separate states for over 160 years, were unified by the Sui Dynasty in 581 when the Sui took control of Chien-k'ang, the southern capital (Map IV-9). The

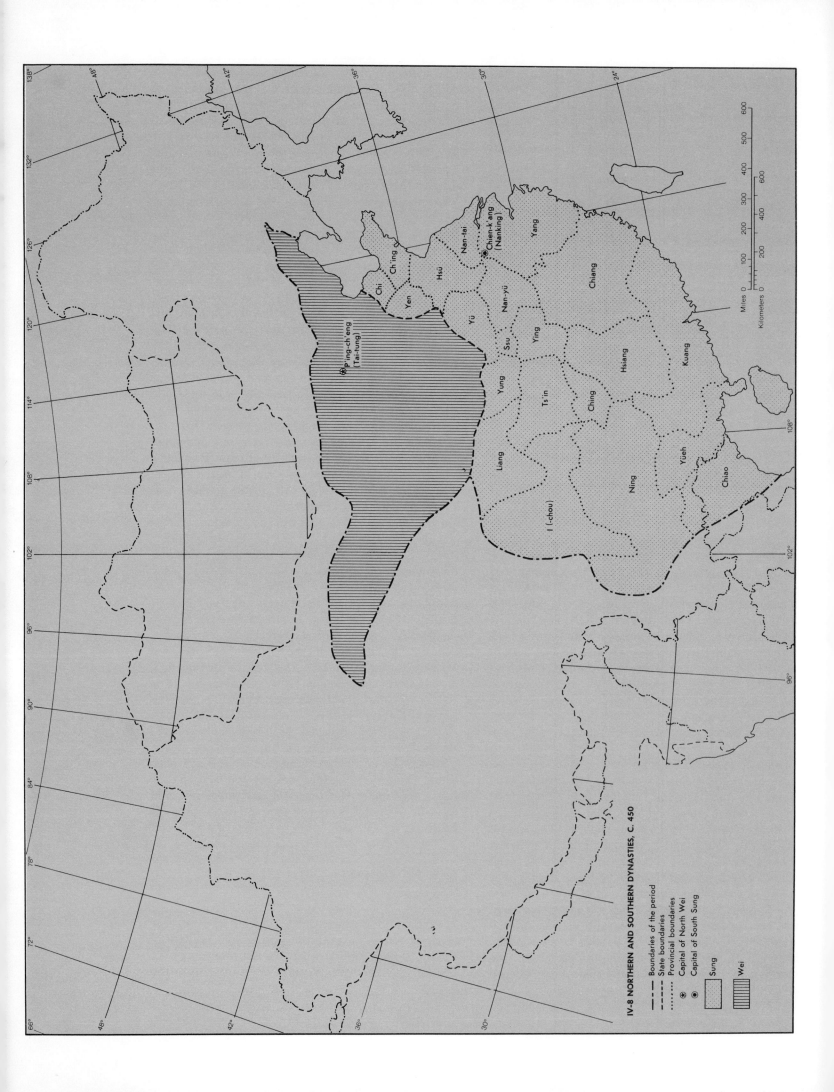

Chi

Ch'ing

Ch'ing

Yen

Hsü

Nan-tai

Chien-k'ang
(Nanking)

Yang

P'ing-ch'eng
(Tai-tung)

Yü

Nan-yü

Chiang

Ssu

Ying

Yung

Ts'in

Ching

Hsiang

Kuang

Liang

Ning

Yüeh

Chiao

I (-chou)

Miles 0   100   200   300   400   500   600

Kilometers 0   200   400   600

IV-8 NORTHERN AND SOUTHERN DYNASTIES, C. 450

— ·· — Boundaries of the period
— — — State boundaries
········· Provincial boundaries
⊛ Capital of North Wei
◉ Capital of South Sung

Sung

Wei

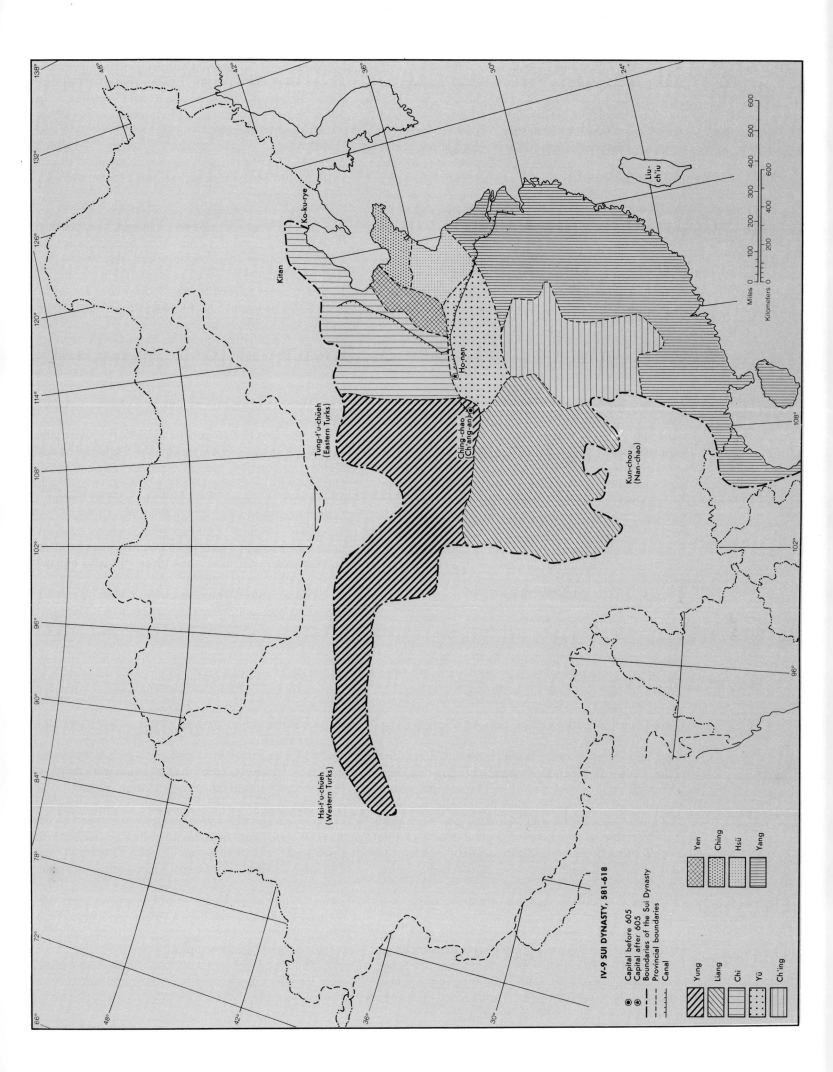

Kitan

Ko-ku-rye

Liu-
ch'iu

Ho-nan
⊛

Tung-t'u-chüeh
(Eastern Turks)

Ching-chao
(Ch'ang-an) ⊛

Kun-chou
(Nan-chao)

Hsi-t'u-chüeh
(Western Turks)

Miles 0   100   200   300   400   500   600

Kilometers 0   200   400   600

IV-9 SUI DYNASTY, 581–618

⊛ Capital before 605
⊛ Capital after 605
——— Boundaries of the Sui Dynasty
— · — Provincial boundaries
——— Canal

	Yung			Yen
	Liang			Ching
	Chi			Hsü
	Yü			Yang
	Ch'ing			

Sui and the following T'ang Dynasty are often considered as spanning a single historical period. In this respect they resemble, respectively, the Ch'in and the Han Dynasties. The Sui-T'ang era was a period of cultural rejuvenation. Traders, travelers, priests, and envoys introduced inventions and social innovations to the Chinese. There are several parallels between the Ch'in and the Sui. The Sui Dynasty laid the foundation for the cultural and political achievements of the T'ang Dynasty in much the same way as the Ch'in Dynasty set the stage for the Han. The leaders of the Ch'in and Sui Dynasties, Ch'in Shih-huang-ti and Sui Yang-ti respectively, were both capable but egotistic men who enjoyed luxury, lived extravagantly, and believed in military expansion. In addition, both rulers undertook the construction of massive public works projects, Ch'in Shih-huang-ti joining the sections of the Great Wall, and Sui Yang-ti building the Grand Canal.

The Sui Dynasty expanded its sphere of influence, established a new capital, and constructed an extensive network of canals. During the Sui reign over 800 miles of canals were constructed. These canals enabled grain to be transported throughout the country and increased the mobility of the army, which undertook expeditions to Central Asia and Korea. Obligatory military service and forced labor, however, aroused public discontent, and the peasants of the North China Plain initiated the rebellion which resulted in the collapse of the Sui Dynasty.

THE T'ANG DYNASTY (618–906)

The T'ang Dynasty, which spanned three centuries, is regarded by the Chinese as the most outstanding era in their country's history (Map IV-10). The impact of this dynasty upon Chinese culture is revealed by the fact that even today many overseas Chinese still call themselves "men of T'ang." Vigorously pursuing a policy of territorial expansion, the T'ang Dynasty created the largest Asian empire of its time. It reached its zenith during the first half of the eighth century, when Chinese suzerainty extended as far west as the Pamirs and included Mongolia, Manchuria, and Korea to the north and Annam to the south. The vast areal extent of this empire brought new legions of non-Han under the control of the T'ang Dynasty. In addition, Arabs, Jews, Greeks, Persians, Tartars, and Syrians came in contact with the Chinese through trade and travel.

An active commerce and awareness arose between China and several foreign countries during this period. Camel caravans traveled between Inner Asia and China, and many migrants, particularly Muslims from Lung-yu (Kansu), settled in China Proper (Map IV-11). In Kuang (present Canton) Arab merchants built China's first mosque. In addition, marine commerce developed between Yang (near present Nanking), Kuang, and the ports of the Persian Gulf. China exported silk, porcelain, and paper to the West, and the latter supplied China with perfumes, medicines, pearls, elephant tusks, and rhinoceros horns.

China maintained close relations with India during the T'ang Dynasty. Among the cultural importations resulting from this contact was the refining of sugar from sugar cane. Travel between the two countries was frequent. For example, Hsuan Tsang, a noted monk of the T'ang Dynasty, visited the birthplace of Sakyamuni (the founder of Buddhism) in Nepal as well as many of the monasteries in India; after spending more than ten years in India, he returned to China with many Buddhist scriptures. In addition, Buddhist monks traveled from India to China, and brought with them not only Buddhist scriptures but also medicines and medical knowledge.

China also had frequent contact with Korea and Japan. Korean students came to China to study history, astronomy, calendric science, and medicine, and during the T'ang Dynasty Korean music was introduced in China. During the eighth century, Japan sent envoys and students to China. The Japanese studied Chinese philosophy, history, political systems, literature, arts, and handicrafts. During this period a close relationship also existed between China and Tibet.

The southeastern coastal region was integrated into the Chinese Empire during the T'ang Dynasty. The growth of population and economic prosperity of this region was a result of new maritime industry and commerce. It was Arab traders, for example, who first established factories in the present Canton Delta and later in Fukien and Kiangsu; and Persian and Japanese merchants carried on trade with the southeastern coast. Yang, located north of the Yangtze delta, was the chief port of the region.

The T'ang Dynasty was also marked by urban growth. The major cities of this period were situated at the intersection of transportation routes. For example, Ching-chao (Ch'ang-an), the imperial capital, was the principal transportation node of the empire; and from here roads radiated outward to present Kansu, Szechwan, Hupeh, Shantung, and Hopeh. Ho-nan (Lo-yang), the eastern capital, located at the midpoint of the Grand Canal, functioned as an entrepôt for goods from northern and southern China. Ch'eng-tu was the commercial center of southwestern China, and Kuang was the largest seaport of the empire.

The T'ang government strengthened its control over its vast empire by stationing large numbers of

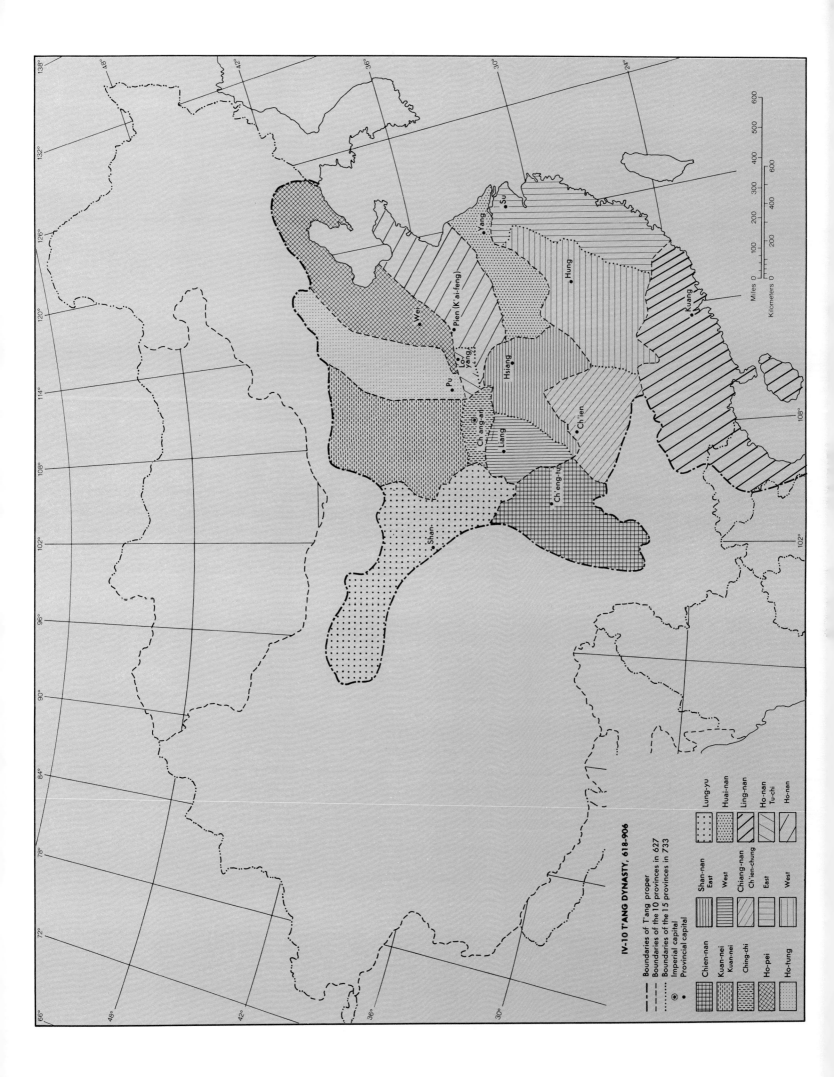

IV-10 T'ANG DYNASTY, 618-906

Boundaries of T'ang proper
Boundaries of the 10 provinces in 627
Boundaries of the 15 provinces in 733
⊛ Imperial capital
• Provincial capital

Chien-nan	Shan-nan East		Lung-yu
Kuan-nei Kuan-nei	West		Huai-nan
Ching-chi	Chiang-nan Ch'ien-chung		Ling-nan
Ho-pei	East		Ho-nan Tu-chi
Ho-tung	West		Ho-nan

Miles 0   100   200   300   400   500   600
Kilometers 0   200   400   600

Shan

Ch'eng-tu

Liang
Ch'ang-an ⊛
Hsiang
Ch'ien
Pu
Lo-yang
Pien (K'ai-feng)
Wei
Hung
Su
Yang
Kuang

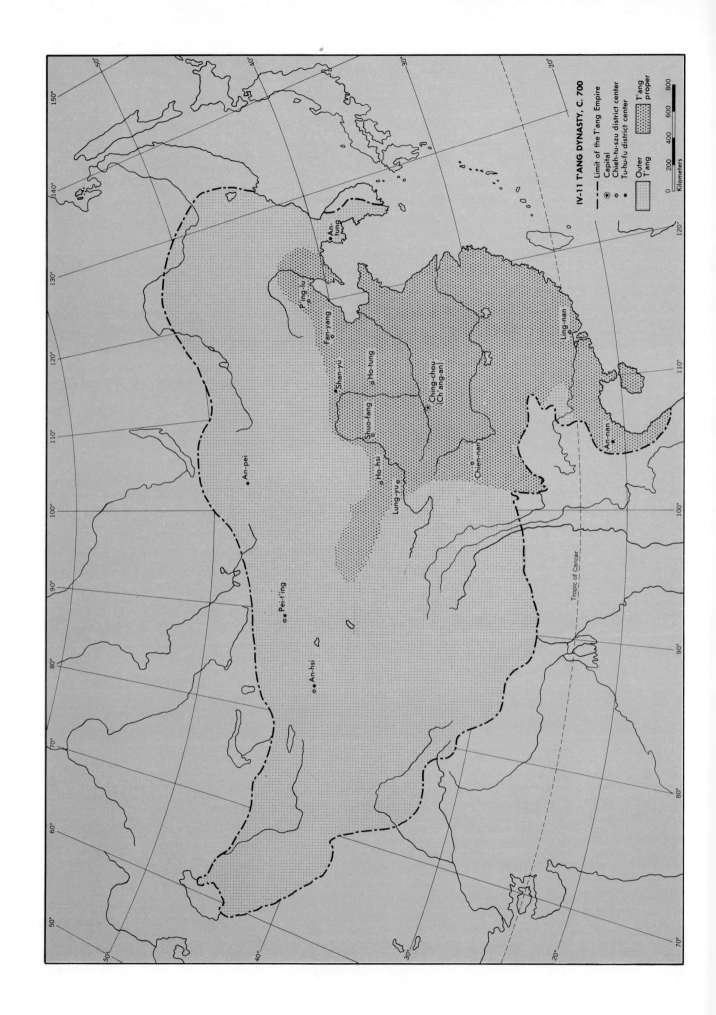

IV-11 T'ANG DYNASTY, C. 700

— · · — Limit of the T'ang Empire
⊛ Capital
☆ Chieh-tu-szu district center
● Tu-hu-fu district center

Outer T'ang

T'ang proper

Kilometers
0   200   400   600   800

An-tung

P'ing-lu

Fan-yang

Shan-yü

Ho-tung

Shuo-fang

Ho-hsi

Lung-yu

Ching-chou
(Ch'ang-an)

Chien-nan

Ling-nan

An-nan

An-pei

Pei-t'ing

An-hsi

Tropic of Cancer

troops in the frontier regions. These forces were commanded by viceroys, who exerted considerable control over the economic, political, and military affairs of their respective regions. There were sixteen viceroys, six of whom governed the nomads of their frontier regions and served a function comparable to that of the governor-general of a British colony. The name of each region controlled by a viceroy usually contained the word *an*, which means "pacified." For example, An-tung meant "pacified east," and An-nam meant "pacified south." The general name for such a region was *Tu-hu-fu*, or garrison district, and the *Chieh-tu-szu* were the officials who headed up these districts and had the responsibility for the organization and control of these outlying settlements.

The T'ang Dynasty divided China into 10 provinces on the basis of physical features and longitude and latitude. This was the first time that provincial boundaries were determined by natural features of the landscape.

In addition to Kuan-nei (the "land within the passes") and Lung-yu (the "right side of Lung"), there were three provinces whose names were closely linked to the Yellow River. Ho-tung ("east of the Yellow River") corresponded to modern Shansi. Ho-pei was located north of the Yellow River, and Ho-nan, including the modern province of the same name and Shantung Province, was situated south of the Yellow River. There were five provinces in southern China. Huai-nan ("south of the Huai River") encompassed all the land between the Yangtze and Huai Rivers, which is now divided into the provinces of Honan, Anhwei, and Kiangsu. Chien-nan ("south of the gorges") consisted of western Szechwan and portions of Yunnan and Kweichow and bordered Tibet on the west. Shan-nan ("south of the mountain") was located south of the Tsinling Shan and included eastern Szechwan, Hupeh, and northern Hunan. Chiang-nan ("south of the river") was situated south of the Yangtze and encompassed the area now divided into Chekiang, Kiangsi, and Fuchien Provinces and included portions of Hunan, Kiangsu, and Anhwei Provinces. Ling-nan ("south of the range") was located south of the Nan ling and included modern Kwangtung Province, Kwangsi Chuang Autonomous Region, and North Vietnam.

THE FIVE DYNASTIES (907–960)

Internal rebellions led by the Chieh-tu-szu and invasions by neighboring peoples resulted in the collapse of the T'ang Dynasty. A period of political chaos ensued, during which five dynasties rose and fell and the remainder of the former T'ang Empire was divided into several small independent states (Map IV-12). This era is considered by Chinese historians as one of the most turbulent in Chinese history. The map of this period reveals the extent of this disunity.

In contrast to the rest of China, few wars occurred in the south during this period; and agriculture and sericulture made significant progress in the Kingdom of Wu-yüeh, in the lower Yangtze flood plain. Cultivated fields and mulberry trees were ubiquitous features of this region. Large tracts of wasteland were reclaimed, an irrigation system was constructed near T'ai Hu, and a stone dike was built along the Ch'ien-t'ang Chiang. Hang (later Lin-an and now Hangchow), the capital of Wu-yüeh, became a large and prosperous metropolis. Silk textile manufacturing and tea processing were highly developed activities in Hunan, and marine commerce flourished in the large ports of the southeast coast.

The detailed history of the Five Dynasties Period is of little importance to the present discussion. However, one event is worthy of mention, since it profoundly influenced the future course of Chinese history. The first ruler of the Later Tsin Dynasty (936–946) was a Turkish adventurer who came to power with the assistance of the nomadic Ch'i-tans (Kitans). In return for Ch'i-tan support, he ceded to them the northeastern portion of the North China Plain, including the land between Peking and the Great Wall. Thus the nomads gained control of a strategic area through which they could invade China. This led to the control of northern China by the Ch'i-tans (Kitans) in the early part of the subsequent Sung Dynasty.

THE SUNG DYNASTIES (960–1279)

The Sung Dynasty, which spanned more than two centuries, differed in many respects from its predecessors the Ch'in, Han, Sui, and T'ang dynasties. The Sung Dynasty, for example, never ruled all of China Proper, nor did it exert effective political control over the border areas of the empire. The unification of the Sung Empire was accomplished through diplomacy rather than warfare: The royal family feared that dissent among government officials would weaken the dynasty, and therefore the rulers were chosen by consent of these officials and ruled with their approval. Consequently, the dynasty was seldom threatened with the internal rebellions which plagued the Han and T'ang dynasties. However, lacking a strong army, the Sung Dynasty was constantly in danger of invasion by the neighboring nomadic peoples who dominated the northern steppe.

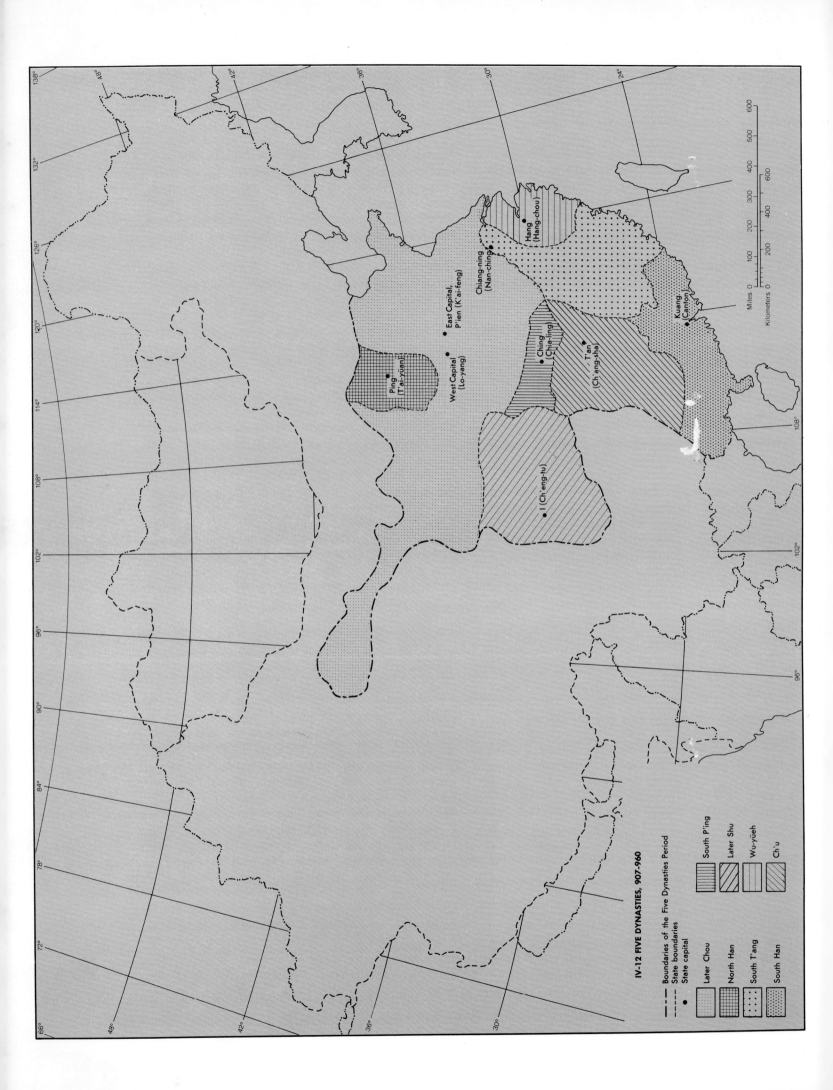

Ping
(T'ai-yüan)

West Capital
(Lo-yang)

East Capital,
P'ien (K'ai-feng)

Chiang-ning
(Nan-ching)

Hang
(Hang-chou)

Ching
(Chia-ling)

T'an
(Ch'ang-sha)

Kuang
(Canton)

I (Ch'eng-tu)

Miles 0   100   200   300   400   500   600

Kilometers 0   200   400   600

IV-12 FIVE DYNASTIES, 907-960

— · — ·   Boundaries of the Five Dynasties Period
— — —   State boundaries
●   State capital

	Later Chou		South P'ing
	North Han		Later Shu
	South T'ang		Wu-yüeh
	South Han		Ch'u

One of these nomadic groups, the Chiangs, who spoke a Tibeto-Burmese language, invaded northwestern China and established the kingdom of Hsi-hsia in northern Shensi and Kansu. During the twelfth century a nomadic people from Manchuria whom the Chinese called the Juchen founded the Chin Dynasty in the north after conquering the Ch'i-tans, who had founded the powerful Liao Kingdom of the North China Plain (Map IV-13). Because the Sung rulers had been forced to pay a high tribute to the Liao and Hsi-hsia kingdoms to maintain peace, the Sung emperor transferred his allegiance to the Juchen. However, the Juchen proved to be a greater menace than the Ch'i-tans. The Juchen invaded the Sung Empire, capturing the capital, K'aifeng, in 1126. As a result, the Sung Dynasty was forced to move its capital south to a city called Lin-an, or present Hangchow. Therefore Chinese historians distinguish between the Northern Sung Dynasty (960-1126), which had its capital at K'aifeng, and the later Southern Sung Dynasty (1127-1279), with its capital at Lin-an, which is the present Hung-chow.

This second partition of China between nomads and native Chinese lasted 152 years, after which the Chin and Sung empires were destroyed by the Mongols in the thirteenth century. Genghis Khan had strongly desired to conquer the Sung Empire. However, it was not until 1279 that his grandson, Kublai Khan, defeated the Sung and incorporated China into the vast Mongol Yüan Empire; and for the first time all of China Proper was controlled by a non-Han people. Thus the Sung fell victim to the nomads: Although the dynasty fostered the growth of literature and the development of economic and political theory, it was too civilized and pacific for the world of the eleventh century.

The Sung Dynasty was characterized by the development of industry and commerce, the growth of cities, and the continued expansion of agricultural land. During this period the dikes along the Yellow River were repaired and reservoirs were constructed in the Yangtze Valley. Mining and metallurgy were important activities, as was sericulture. The centers of the silk industry were K'aifeng, Ho-nan, and several places in Szechwan. The spinning and weaving mills of K'aifeng and Ho-nan also produced cotton textiles. In addition, ceramics had become a highly skilled craft, and porcelain was sold in domestic and foreign markets.

Other important activities included fishing, tea cultivation and processing, salt distillation, and various handicrafts. By the eleventh century, paper money and iron and copper coins were used extensively in commerce. Inventions which were developed during the T'ang regime were put to practical use during the Sung Dynasty. Gunpowder, for example, was used during the Sung Dynasty as a rocket propellant. Marine commerce also flourished; Kuang and Lin-an were two of the major ports.

As noted above, the Sung Dynasty was continually engaged in boundary disputes with the kingdoms of Hsi-hsia, Liao, and Chin. When a treaty was signed with one of these kingdoms, border trading posts were often established. To these southern China sent rice, silk, tea, spice, lacquerware, and ivory, in exchange for the sheep, horses, camels, cattle, jade, and wax of the northern nomads. The Sung Dynasty also carried on trade with the Arab merchants who visited the ports of southeastern China. This commerce not only increased the wealth of the southern Chinese provinces but also expanded Chinese knowledge of Western Asia. The nomadic invasions, however, disrupted the ancient caravan routes to Inner Asia and dealt a severe blow to the economy of northwestern China.

The focus of Chinese culture during the Sung Dynasty shifted to the south, particularly to the lower Yangtze. Although the first significant migration of people to southern China had occurred during the Three Kingdoms Period, the Sui and T'ang dynasties had kept their capitals in the north. Chinese culture, like that of many other countries, tended to follow the imperial capital. Thus when the nomadic invaders conquered northern China and forced the relocation of the Sung capital at Lin-an in the south, literature and the arts also moved south, and the Hsi Chiang Valley became an important cultural center. Moreover, not only did the principal economic areas of China shift southward, but so did the majority of the Chinese population. Regional self-sufficiency was replaced by regional interdependence. The northern and northwestern sections of China became increasingly dependent for rice upon the Yangtze Delta and the smaller, fertile areas of Szechwan, Hunan, and Kiangsi. In exchange, the less fertile north and northwest exported salt, tea, fish, and metals. Food production was increased not only by the more extensive use of fertilizer but also by the expansion of land under cultivation and the introduction of drought-resistant rice in Fu-chien and the Yangtze Delta.

China experienced, during the Sung Dynasty, a period of rapid urbanization, particularly in southern China. The cities of this region, in contrast to those of northern China, grew in size and economic importance as a result of their function as centers of commerce rather than as centers of government administration. A consequence of this rapid growth was the construction of irregular, rather than the traditional rectangular, city walls. By 1100 at least five cities had a population of over 1 million. Only one of these, K'aifeng, was located in northern China; three, Lin-an, P'ing-chiang (present Soochow), and Fu-chou (present Foochow), were located on the southeastern

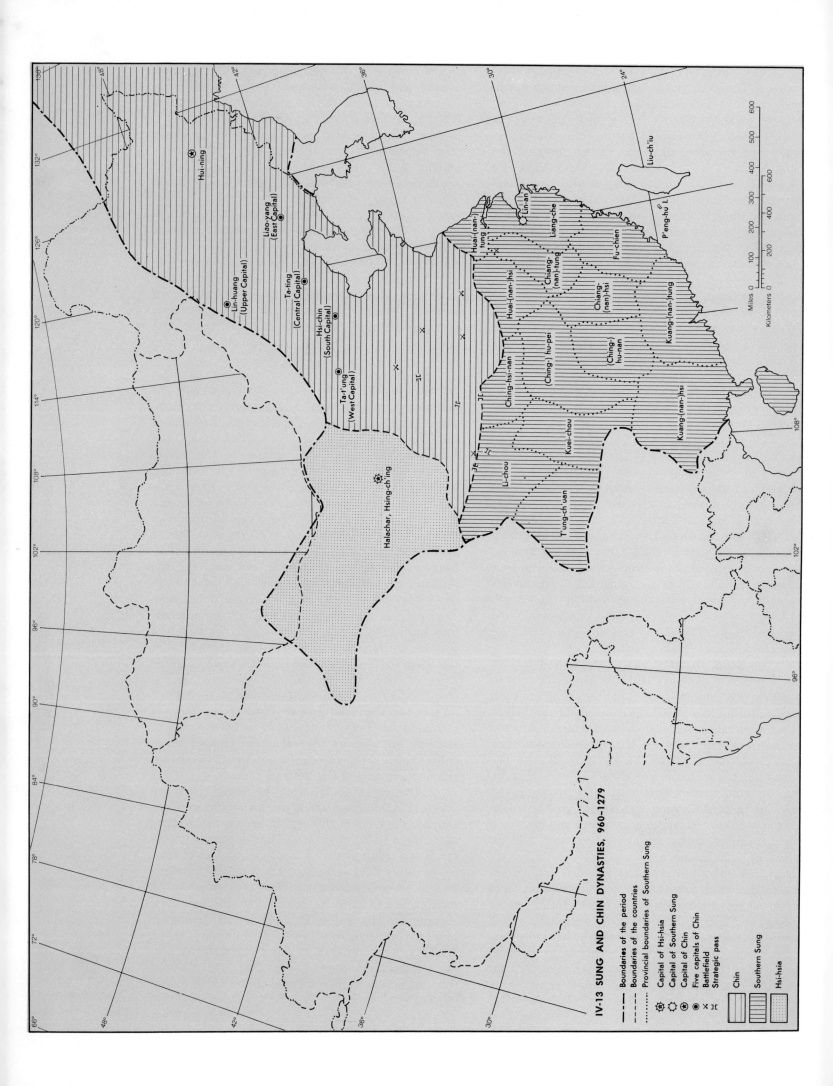

IV-13 SUNG AND CHIN DYNASTIES, 960–1279

Hui-ning

Liao-yang
(East Capital)

Lin-huang
(Upper Capital)

Ta-ting
(Central Capital)

Hsi-chin
(South Capital)

Ta-t'ung
(West Capital)

Halachar, Hsing-ch'ing

Huai-(nan-)
tung

Lin-an

Liang-che

Huai-(nan-)hsi

Chiang-
(nan-)tung

Fu-chien

Chiang-
(nan-)hsi

Ching-
hu-nan

Ching-hsi-nan

(Ching-) hu-pei

Kuang-(nan-)tung

Li-chou

Kuei-chou

Kuang-(nan-)hsi

T'ung-ch'uan

Liu-ch'iu

P'eng-hu I.

Miles 0   100   200   300   400   500   600

Kilometers 0   200   400   600

Boundaries of the period
Boundaries of the countries
Provincial boundaries of Southern Sung

Capital of Hsi-hsia
Capital of Southern Sung
Capital of Chin
Five capitals of Chin
Battlefield
Strategic pass

Chin

Southern Sung

Hsi-hsia

coast; and Jao (near present Nan-ch'ang) was situated near the trade route between the Yangtze and Kuang-chou. The marked increase in population during the Sung Dynasty, especially in the alluvial plains of southeastern China, was possible only because of increased agricultural productivity and expansion of cultivated land.

The Sung pursued a policy of appeasement with respect to the neighboring nomadic tribes and in domestic affairs stressed civilian, rather than military, needs. The dynasty's commercial development, technological achievements, monetary policies, and agricultural expansion were comparable to the accomplishments of the European Renaissance, which began over a century after the end of the Sung Dynasty.

THE YÜAN (MONGOL) DYNASTY (1280–1368)

In 1279 the Mongols conquered the kingdoms of Hsi-hsia, Chin, and the Southern Sung, as well as T'u-fan (Tibet), and annexed them all to their empire (Maps IV-14 and IV-15). This empire was one of the largest in world history. It extended from European Russia, Persia, and Mesopotamia in the west to the East China Sea in the east, and from Mongolia in the north to Annam in the south. The founder of the Yüan Dynasty, Kublai Khan, divided his empire into four kingdoms, each ruled by one of the four sons of his chief wife. The Ilkhan Empire was located in Persia, the Djagatai Empire in Central Asia, the Kip Chak Empire (Golden Horde) in southern Russia, and the Empire of the Great Khan in China. During the reign of Kublai Khan, the Yüan Dynasty ruled a larger area than did the Roman, Han, or T'ang Empire. Still, because of poor communications, Kublai Khan's control over much of this territory was nominal at best.

The Mongols ruled China for almost a century. However, although they were superior soldiers, they lacked the knowledge of bureaucratic organization which the agrarian Chinese had acquired, and consequently were forced to establish in China a government which was based upon the Chinese administrative system. Thus Chinese culture as a whole did not undergo drastic changes during this period of Mongol rule.

Chinese agriculture, commerce, and industry continued to flourish during the Yüan Dynasty. Sorghum was introduced and became an important crop, and for the first time cotton was extensively cultivated. Cotton textiles of high quality were manufactured in the lower Yangtze and Huai Ho valleys. Ceramics continued to be a highly skilled and creative craft, reflecting Persian influence. In addition, the abacus gradually came into wide use. Trade was carried on between Baghdad and Ta-tu (present Peking) by way of caravan routes, and between the Persian Gulf and the ports of southern China via marine routes. Ta-tu functioned as both the imperial capital of the Yüan Dynasty and the commercial center of northern and western China, while Hang-chou was the focus of foreign trade. The linkage between the central and northern regions was strengthened by improvements made to the Grand Canal under the Yüan (Map IV-16). Travel within the Mongol Empire was comparatively safe, and many people from Central Asia and Western Europe journeyed to China. Muslims, Dominican and Franciscan friars, Nestorian Christians, and Armenians brought with them new religions which had a profound influence upon Chinese society. The most noted of these travelers was Marco Polo, who was in the service of Kublai Khan for four years and who aroused European interest in China.

THE MING DYNASTY (1368–1644)

The gradual corruption and decline of the Yüan Dynasty resulted in the disintegration of its empire, the disruption of trade routes by bandits, and the subsequent exodus of European traders and missionaries from China. In 1368 it was overthrown by a popular leader from the south who established the last of the Chinese dynasties (Map IV-17).

During the Ming Dynasty, native rule and Chinese culture were restored after years of foreign domination. The dynasty revived Chinese customs; in particular, it encouraged a return to agricultural pursuits, the further development of sericulture, and the observance of the annual ceremonies and rituals of the seasons. The Ming Dynasty is noted for its works of fiction (much as the T'ang Dynasty is for its poetry and the Yüan for its drama) and for the compilation of the great encyclopedia, *Yung-lo Ta-tien,* the most significant scholarly achievement of the Ming Dynasty. It may be said, however, that in the fields of art, literature, and science, the Ming Dynasty perfected rather than created.

The names of previous dynasties had been derived from the classical names of the founders' native provinces or from the fiefs which they had ruled prior to becoming emperors. For example, Liu Pang, who was given the title Han Prince during the revolt against Ch'in, chose Han as the name of the dynasty which he founded after the fall of the Ch'in, and the first emperor of the T'ang Dynasty had been the Duke of T'ang, which was part of present Shansi Province during the Sui reign. The

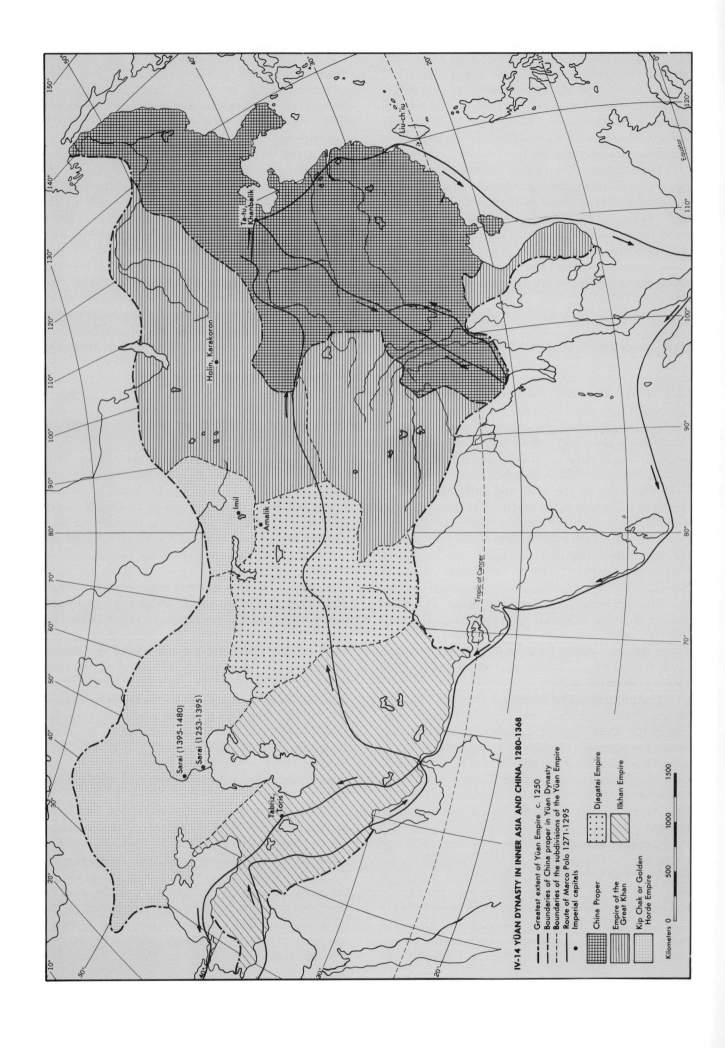

Te-tu
Khanbalik

Holin, Karakoron

Imil

Amalik

Sarai (1395-1480)

Sarai (1253-1395)

Tabriz, Toris

Liu-ch'iu

Tropic of Cancer

Equator

IV-14 YÜAN DYNASTY IN INNER ASIA AND CHINA, 1280-1368

— · — · — Greatest extent of Yüan Empire c. 1250
— — — — Boundaries of China proper in Yüan Dynasty
— — — — Boundaries of the subdivisions of the Yüan Empire
· · · · · · Route of Marco Polo 1271-1295
• Imperial capitals

China Proper

Empire of the
Great Khan

Kip Chak or Golden
Horde Empire

Djagatai Empire

Ilkhan Empire

Kilometers 0   500   1000   1500

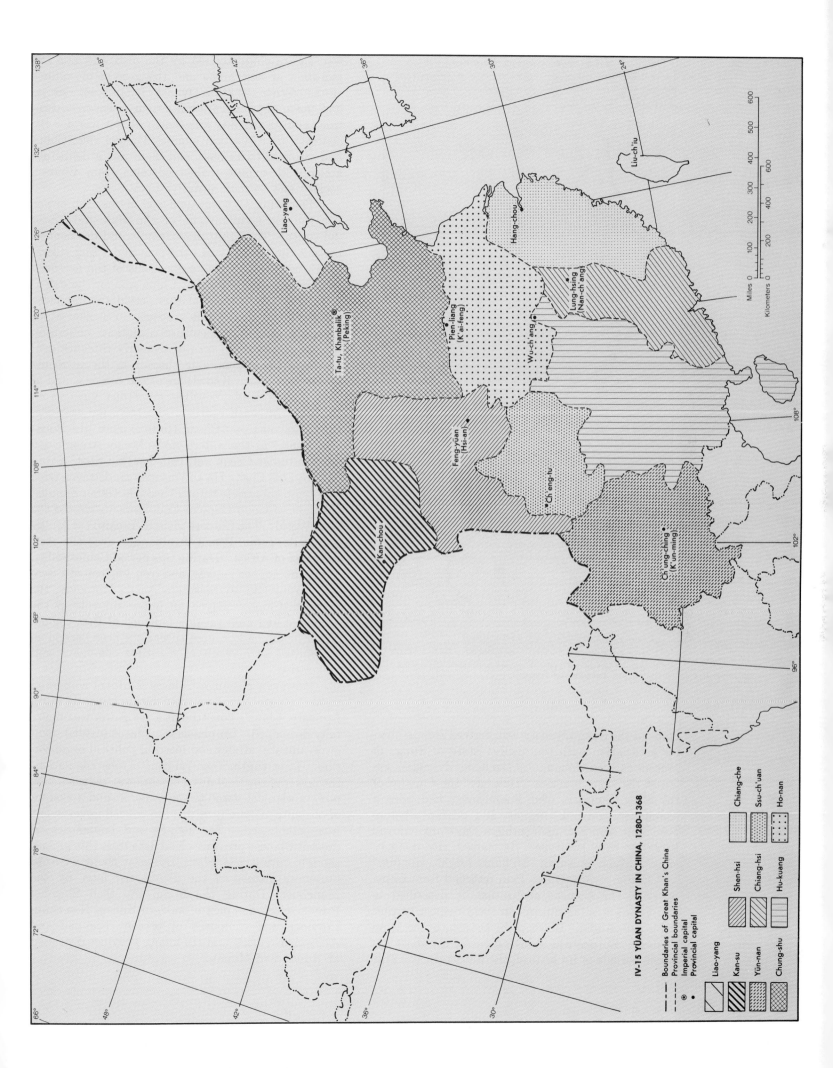

IV-15 YÜAN DYNASTY IN CHINA, 1280-1368

Liu-ch'iu

Liao-yang

Hang-chou

Ta-tu, Khanbalik
(Peking)

Pien-liang
(K'ai-feng)

Lung-hsing
(Nan-ch'ang)

Wu-ch'ang

Feng-yüan
(Hsi-an)

Ch'eng-tu

Kan-chou

Ch'ung-ch'ing
(K'un-ming)

Miles 0   100   200   300   400   500   600
Kilometers 0   200   400   600

--- — · — Boundaries of Great Khan's China
— · · — Provincial boundaries
⊛ Imperial capital
• Provincial capital

Liao-yang

Kan-su   Shen-hsi   Chiang-che

Yün-nan   Chiang-hsi   Ssu-ch'uan

Chung-shu   Hu-kuang   Ho-nan

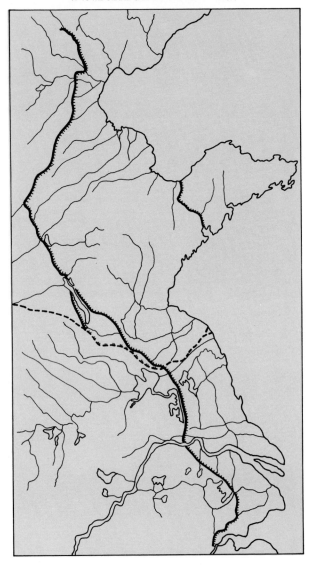

▬▬▬▬ The Grand Canal prior to the Yüan Dynasty

▲ ▲ ▲ ▲ The section of the Grand Canal added during the Yüan Dynasty

▬ ▬ ▬ Sections of the Yellow River used as part of the Grand Canal during the Yüan Dynasty

name of the Sung Dynasty was derived from a similar association with the ancient state of Sung, in present eastern Honan. All the minor dynasties followed the same practice. However, the founder of the Ming Dynasty, Chu Yuan-chang, had been a commoner—a monk, beggar, and peasant—before becoming emperor, and perhaps therefore enjoyed breaking with tradition: He named the dynasty simply Ming, meaning "brilliant, bright, shining."

Earlier, when Marco Polo returned from China in 1295, the Chinese civilization he described to Europeans was far superior in every respect to that of his native land. However, by the time of the Ming Dynasty, Europe was enjoying one of the most dynamic periods of its history, the Renaissance. This was an era characterized by the discovery and exploration of new lands and the growth of nation-states. When the Ming Dynasty fell in 1644, Europe had made significant advances in science, navigation, and geographic knowledge of the world. By contrast, as a reaction against Mongol rule, China had returned to its past, and there was a deliberate attempt to expunge alien customs from Chinese society and to restore native ones.

The Ming Dynasty achieved neither the power nor the territorial extent of the Han and T'ang dynasties. The Ming, for example, did not control present Sinkiang, as had the Han and T'ang rulers. Furthermore, the vast fortifications of the northern frontier were evidence that China was on the defensive; and during most of this period the Japanese repeatedly raided China's coast. Yet the Ming Dynasty, despite its cultural isolation, undertook numerous ocean voyages in the early fifteenth century and wrote a notable chapter in the maritime history of China. Knowledge of the compass and of shipbuilding made possible numerous voyages in the early fifteenth century. In 1405, for example, the Ming court sent Cheng Ho to explore "the Western Ocean," as the waters of the Malay Archipelago and the Indian Ocean were called at that time. From 1405 to 1433 Cheng Ho and his men made seven trips to foreign countries, before Vasco da Gama rounded the Cape of Good Hope or Columbus discovered the New World. The Chinese visited Annam, the Malay Peninsula, India, Persia, Arabia, and even the eastern coast of Africa. During this period Chinese silks, porcelain, copper vessels, and iron implements were sold throughout southeastern Asia. Moreover, the overseas Chinese played an important role in the economic and cultural development of that region. Never before had Chinese suzerainty been carried so far abroad as a result of maritime commerce and emigration.

However, although Chinese mariners embarked upon these ambitious voyages during the early Ming Dynasty, China's potential as a sea power was never fully developed. Emphasis was placed instead upon governmental affairs and internal political organization. To strengthen central control over the nation, the power of the local governments was reduced, new powers were delegated to the emperor, and a system of absolute monarchy with a centralized government was established. The names and boundaries of present Chinese provinces also date from this period, though during the Ming Dynasty there were 15 provinces instead of the 18 created later by the Manchus. During the Ming, the then Shen-hsi Province included part of modern Kansu, Nan-ching Province was composed of present Kiangsu and Anhwei provinces, and Hu-kuang Province consisted of Hunan and Hupeh.

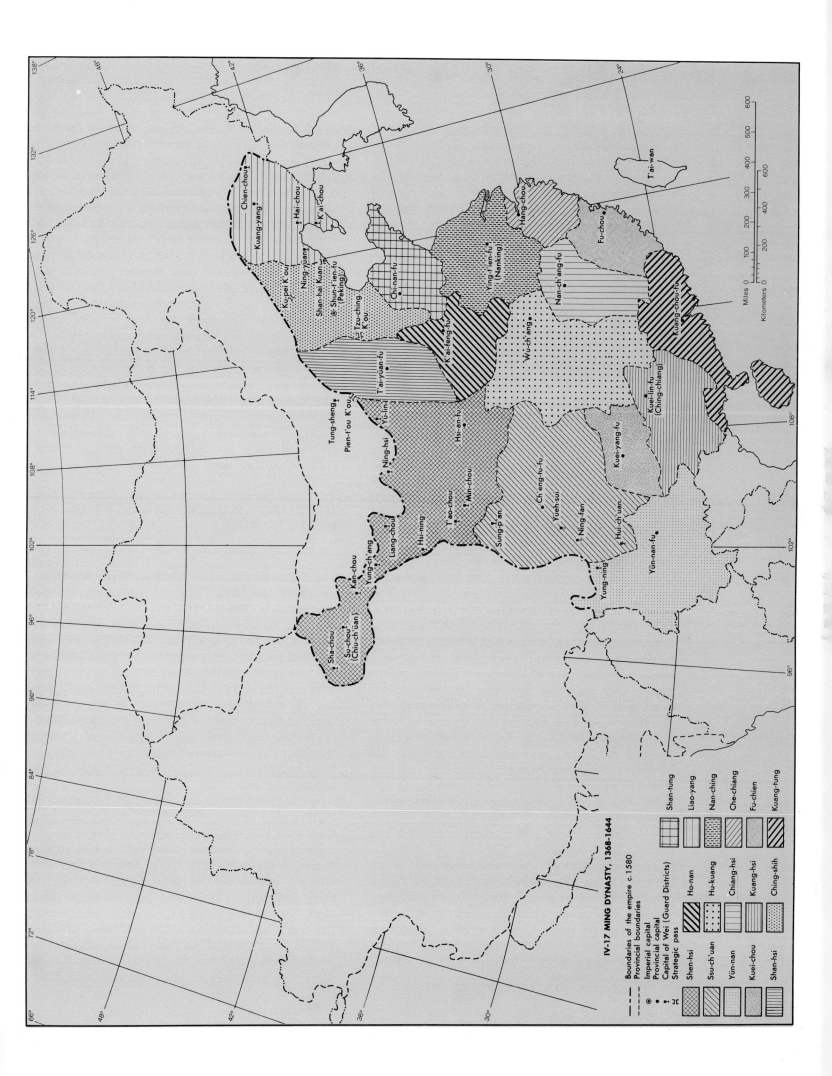

IV-17 MING DYNASTY, 1368-1644

		Shen-hsi			Shan-tung
	Boundaries of the empire c.1580		Ssu-ch'uan		Liao-yang
	Provincial boundaries		Yün-nan		Nan-ching
⊛	Imperial capital		Kuei-chou		Che-chiang
●	Provincial capital		Shan-hsi		Fu-chien
)(	Capital of Wei (Guard Districts)		Ho-nan		Kuang-tung
)(	Strategic pass		Hu-kuang		
			Chiang-hsi		
			Kuang-hsi		
			Ching-shih		

Chien-chou

Kuang-yang
Hai-chou
K'ai-chou

Ku-pei K'ou
Ning-yüan
Shan-hai Kuan
Shun-t'ien-fu (Peking)
Tzu-ching K'ou

Chi-nan-fu

Huang-chou
Ying-t'ien-fu (Nanking)

Nan-ch'ang-fu
Fu-chou

T'ai-yüan-fu

K'ai-feng-fu

Wu-ch'ang

Kuang-chou-fu

T'ai-wan

Tung-sheng
Pien-t'ou K'ou
Yü-lin
Ning-hsia

Hsi-an-fu

Kuei-lin-fu
(Ching-chiang)

T'ao-chou
T'ieh-chou
Min-chou
Ch'eng-tu-fu
Sung-p'an
Yüeh-sui
Ning-fan
Hui-ch'uan
Yung-ning

Kuei-yang-fu

Hsi-ning
Liang-chou
Yung-ch'ang
Kan-chou

Yün-nan-fu

Sha-chou
Su-chou (Chiu-ch'üan)

Miles
Kilometers
0 100 200 300 400 500 600
0 200 400 600

The Ming Dynasty, like the Sung, was an era of urban growth. Ying-t'ien-fu (present Nanking), the first capital of the Ming Dynasty, was situated in an area which had been a stronghold of resistance against the Mongols and which had been the center of Chinese population and wealth. To protect the city, a large and irregular wall was built around it. However, to better defend its northern frontier, the Ming Dynasty moved the capital to Shun-t'ien-fu (Peking) in 1421. Although Ying-t'ien-fu lost its political importance, it continued to prosper economically, as did most of southeastern China. Peking, in turn, became a majestic and beautiful city and a masterpiece of municipal planning with its broad avenues and walks, immense palaces, and artistically designed and handcrafted temples.

Numerous public works projects were undertaken during the Ming Dynasty. For example, the Grand Canal was repaired and deepened. This canal played an important role in the trade conducted between Shun-t'ien-fu and Ying-t'ien-fu. During the early part of the dynasty, the government also sponsored flood control projects. Levees and dams were built, canals and dikes were repaired, and river channels were dredged. In addition, the Ming government built military roads and bridges and established military-agricultural colonies in southwest China. However, it was not until 1420 that Yün-nan and Kuei-chou became Chinese provinces.

These flood control projects and military-agricultural colonies contributed to the increase in agricultural production during the Ming Dynasty. In addition, the government decreed that people who owned from 5 to 10 *mu* of land (approximately 1 to 1½ acres) must plant ½ *mu* in mulberry trees, cotton, and hemp. The consequent increase in the acreage of these crops ensured a large supply of raw materials for the textile industry. Cotton was grown on a large scale, and cotton cloth was sold throughout the empire. By the beginning of the fifteenth century China had become a major cotton-cultivating area. The areas of cotton growing spread beyond the North China Plain to the Yangtze Valley and even as far as Yün-nan and Kuei-chou, where cotton spinning and weaving became a common rural industry. Su-chou was the center of silk weaving. Cane sugar and indigo also brought prosperity to many regions of southern China.

Several new crops were introduced in China during the Ming period. These included maize, peanuts, and sweet potatoes, which were first planted in Fu-chien. These were brought from the Philippines, where they had become important following Spanish introduction from the New World. The introduction of these plants not only resulted in changes in land use and food habits but also stimulated the new use of slopelands for agricultural production. This, in turn, led to new population growth. Tobacco, which was first grown during the Ming Dynasty, was probably brought to southern China by traders from Manila. Many areas in China, such as the Ch'eng-tu Plain, Shan-hai Kuan on the North China Plain, and several areas in Fu-chien, prospered as a result of tobacco cultivation.

The growth of agriculture and handicrafts during the Ming Dynasty was an impetus to the development of an expanded commercial economy. More than 30 cities, the majority of which were in southern China, were trade centers, and a third were located in Nan-ching and Che-chiang provinces. The two capitals, Shun-t'ien-fu and Ying-t'ien-fu, were densely populated, and their streets were lined with shops. Situated at the junction of the Grand Canal and the Yangtze, Yang-chou was another important trade center. The Ming Dynasty was known in Central Europe and England for its porcelain, as the Han Dynasty had been noted in Rome for its silk. The demand for such Chinese goods resulted in the expansion of foreign trade during the Ming Dynasty, and Kuang-chou-fu (present Canton) and other Chinese ports achieved prominence. Portuguese traders established a permanent settlement at Macao in 1557; in addition, they gave the name Formosa to the island of T'ai-wan.

THE CH'ING (MANCHU) DYNASTY (1644–1911)

The Manchus, invaders from northeastern China, overthrew the Ming Dynasty in 1644 and founded the Ch'ing, or Manchu Dynasty, which amassed the most populous empire in Chinese history (Map IV-18). After about a century of Ch'ing rule, the Celestial Empire again extended from the Pamirs in the west to the Pacific Ocean in the east, and from Siberia in the north to the islands in the South China Sea. In the outlying provinces in the northwest and the Northeast, settlers brought new land under cultivation. Moreover, through political intrigue, the Manchus effectively controlled Mongolia and Tibet and forced Burma, Korea, and Annam to pay tribute to them.

The Han Chinese constituted 90 percent of the Chinese population during the Ch'ing Dynasty, but there were also other ethnic groups. Economic and cultural relations between these various nationalities improved under the aegis of the strong central government established by the Ch'ing. The foci of trade and cultural interaction between these ethnic groups were such cities as Shun-t'ien-fu (Peking), Lan-chou, and Hsi-ning. The products of China Proper—iron implements, cotton cloth, salt, and tea—were exchanged for the goods of the frontier regions—musk, saffron, and rhubarb from Tibet;

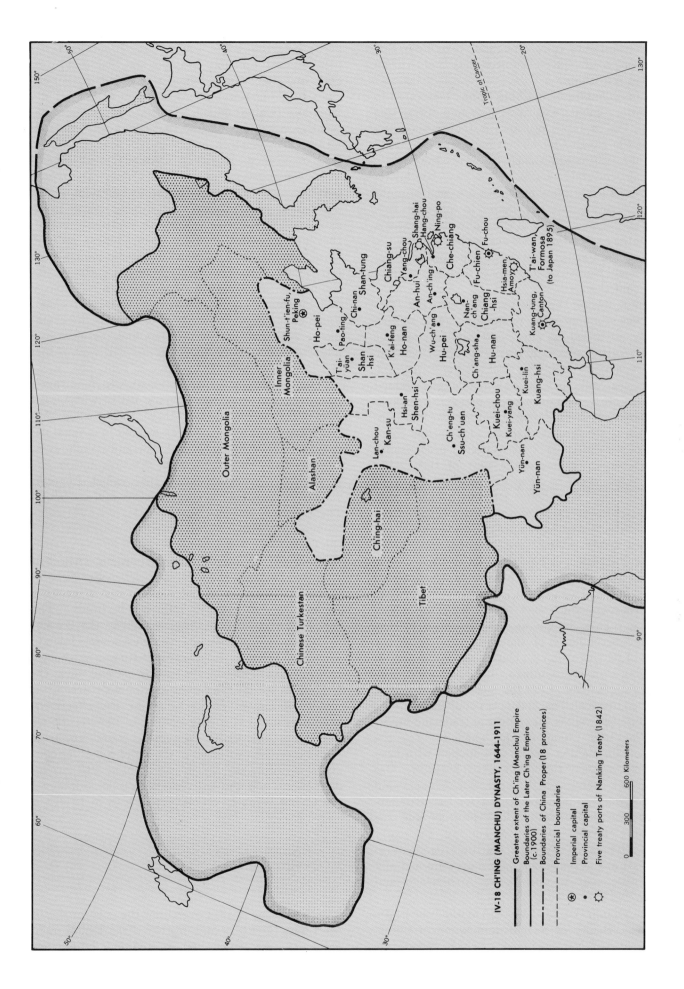

IV-18 CH'ING (MANCHU) DYNASTY, 1644-1911

Greatest extent of Ch'ing (Manchu) Empire
Boundaries of the Later Ch'ing Empire (c. 1900)
Boundaries of China Proper (18 provinces)
Provincial boundaries
⊛ Imperial capital
• Provincial capital
☼ Five treaty ports of Nanking Treaty (1842)

0   300   600 Kilometers

Outer Mongolia

Inner Mongolia

Alashan

Chinese Turkestan

Tibet

Ching-hai

Lan-chou
Kan-su

Hsi-an
Shen-hsi

Ch'eng-tu
Ssu-ch'uan

T'ai-yüan
Shan-hsi

Shun-t'ien-fu, Peking

Ho-pei
Pao-ting

Chi-nan
Shan-tung

K'ai-feng
Ho-nan

Wu-ch'ang
Hu-pei

Ch'ang-sha
Hu-nan

Kuei-yang
Kuei-chou

Yün-nan
Yün-nan

Kuei-lin
Kuang-hsi

Canton
Kuang-tung,

Nan-ch'ang
Chiang-hsi

An-ch'ing
An-hui

Yang-chou
Chiang-su

Shang-hai
Hang-chou
Che-chiang

Ning-po

Fu-chou
Fu-chien

Hsia-men, Amoy

T'ai-wan, Formosa (to Japan 1895)

Tropic of Cancer

livestock and furs from Mongolia; jade from Sinkiang; and medicinal substances and timber from southwestern China.

Many inhabitants of China Proper emigrated to the frontier regions to cultivate new land during this period. For example, peasants in the crowded sections of the North China Plain moved to the broad plains of northeastern Manchuria where they established agricultural colonies called *tun*. Gradually, the wasteland surrounding these *tun* was brought under cultivation and was planted in sorghum, soybeans, and maize. Early in the eighteenth century, much of the pasture land was also reclaimed, and the Ch'ing government encouraged the peasants of Shen-hsi and Kan-su to emigrate to Sinkiang to farm arable land there.

China, during the first part of the Ch'ing Dynasty, was economically prosperous and technologically advanced as any other contemporaneous empire. Agriculture, handicrafts, industry, and commerce expanded steadily for over one hundred years. Chinese tea, silk, cotton, and handicrafts gained popularity in Europe during this period. Paradoxically, however, Kuang-tung (Canton) was the only port open to foreign merchants. This narrow channeling of the European trade reflected a somewhat contradictory attitude on the part of the Ch'ing rulers: While eager to enjoy the benefits of foreign commerce, they nonetheless wished to keep China secluded from the rest of the world, and indeed adopted a self-satisfied stance vis-à-vis the West, believing firmly in their own cultural superiority.

The limitation of foreign trade to Canton also suggests that maritime commerce between China and Europe had completed a process of economic transformation which had begun with the T'ang Dynasty. This change was characterized by the economic ascendance of southern China and the decline of northern China. During the latter part of the Ch'ing Dynasty, southern China, and particularly the Yangtze Delta and the coastal tea districts, contained the wealthiest and most populous regions of the country as well as the centers of trade and industry. Southern Chiang-su, for example, was the center of silk making and, in conjunction with Che-chiang, the focus of the cotton textile industry. Ore mining was centered in Yün-nan, and Kuang-tung Province was the principal center for the manufacture of iron implements. Book printing and tea processing further progressed during the early Ch'ing Dynasty. Foreign maritime trade also flourished in the south, and porcelain ware and silk goods were sent to the Malay Archipelago and Europe.

The Opium War of 1839–1842 marked the beginning of a century of foreign domination of China. The Treaty of Nanking (1842), which ended this conflict between China and Britain, opened five ports to foreign trade: Kuang-tung (Canton), Hsia-men (Amoy), Fu-chou, Ning-po, and Shang-hai. In addition, Hong Kong Island was ceded to Britain. Thus the long self-imposed isolation of the Middle Kingdom (China) ended. By the end of the nineteenth century it appeared that China was the helpless prey of Eastern and Western powers—Japan, Russia, France, England, Germany, and others, which controlled various parts of China. The treaty ports themselves exemplified an incongruous juxtaposition of two cultures; and although these ports existed only briefly as symbols of political injustice, they had a profound effect upon Chinese society, since through them Western economic values were introduced. The power of the Manchus declined, and China was forcibly exposed to Western technology and customs. In the resulting cultural friction, much of the familiar structure of Chinese life crumbled. Although earlier invaders and travelers had adopted or admired China's culture and way of life, foreigners now held that culture in contempt.

Meanwhile, rapid population growth, food shortages, and a corrupt bureaucracy led to widespread riots. The most notable of these, the so-called T'ai-ping (Peaceful) Rebellion, was started by a fanatical religious leader, Hung Hsiu-ch'uan, and his followers, such as Shih Ta-k'ai, in 1850. (The revolutionaries established a government in 1851 called T'ai-ping Tien Kuo, meaning "the peaceful Celestial Empire.") The rebellion was not suppressed until 1864 after having devastated several provinces and threatened the Ch'ing imperial authority before it was quelled (Map IV-19). Meanwhile foreign power in China had increased considerably (Map IV-20). Russia controlled territory north of China, and after 1860 Japan began to exert its influence in Korea. The Sino-Japanese War of 1895 resulted in the cession to Japan of T'ai-wan and the Pescadores Islands as well as virtually full control of Korea. Although reforms were proposed, the reactionary and conservative forces within the Ch'ing government prevailed, making it impossible for China to deal effectively with the rapidly changing world. In 1900 the Boxer Rebellion, organized by a loosely bound group of secret societies dedicated to the expulsion of foreigners from China, also failed. Confronted with foreign domination and the outbreak of popular uprisings, the Ch'ing Dynasty officially collasped in 1911.

MODERN CHINA (1911-   )

The Revolution of 1911 overthrew the government of the Ch'ing Dynasty and destroyed the feudal monarchic system which had existed in China since before the Christian era. The Revolutionary League

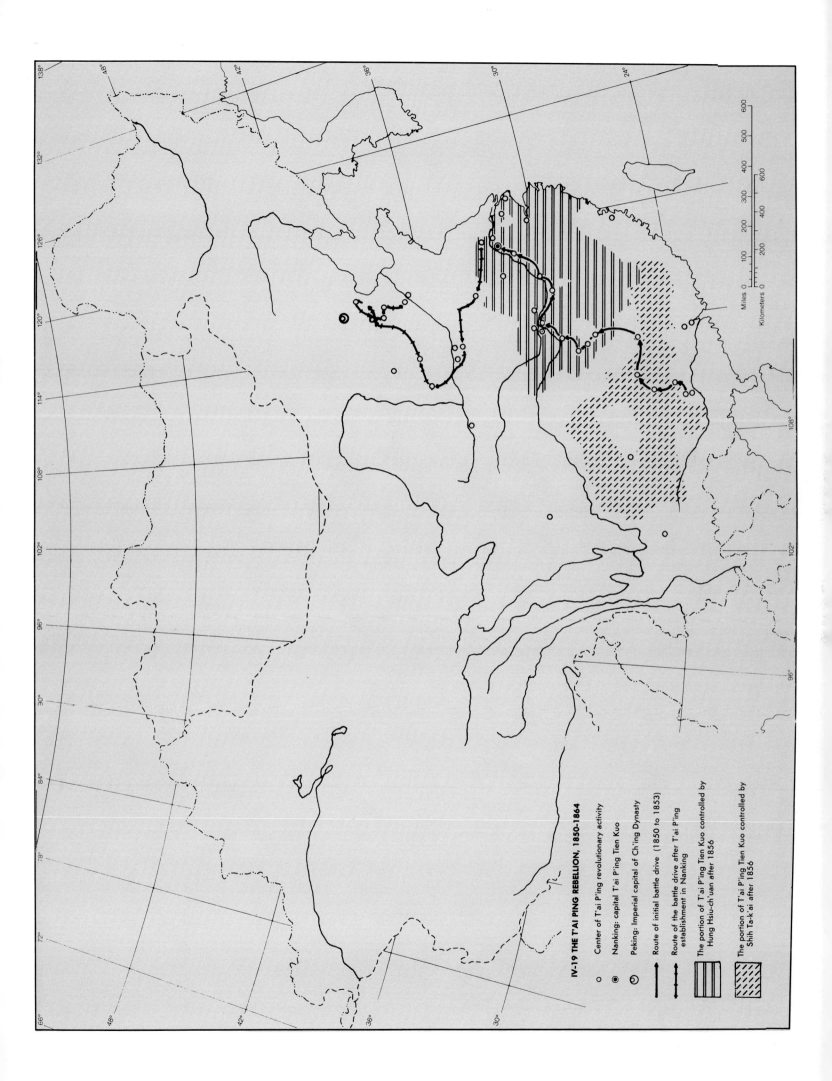

IV-19 THE T'AI PING REBELLION, 1850-1864

○   Center of T'ai P'ing revolutionary activity

◉   Nanking: capital T'ai P'ing Tien Kuo

◉   Peking: Imperial capital of Ch'ing Dynasty

→   Route of initial battle drive (1850 to 1853)

↕   Route of the battle drive after T'ai P'ing establishment in Nanking

▥   The portion of T'ai P'ing Tien Kuo controlled by Hung Hsiu-ch'uan after 1856

▨   The portion of T'ai P'ing Tien Kuo controlled by Shih Ta-k'ai after 1856

Miles 0   100   200   300   400   500   600

Kilometers 0   200   400   600

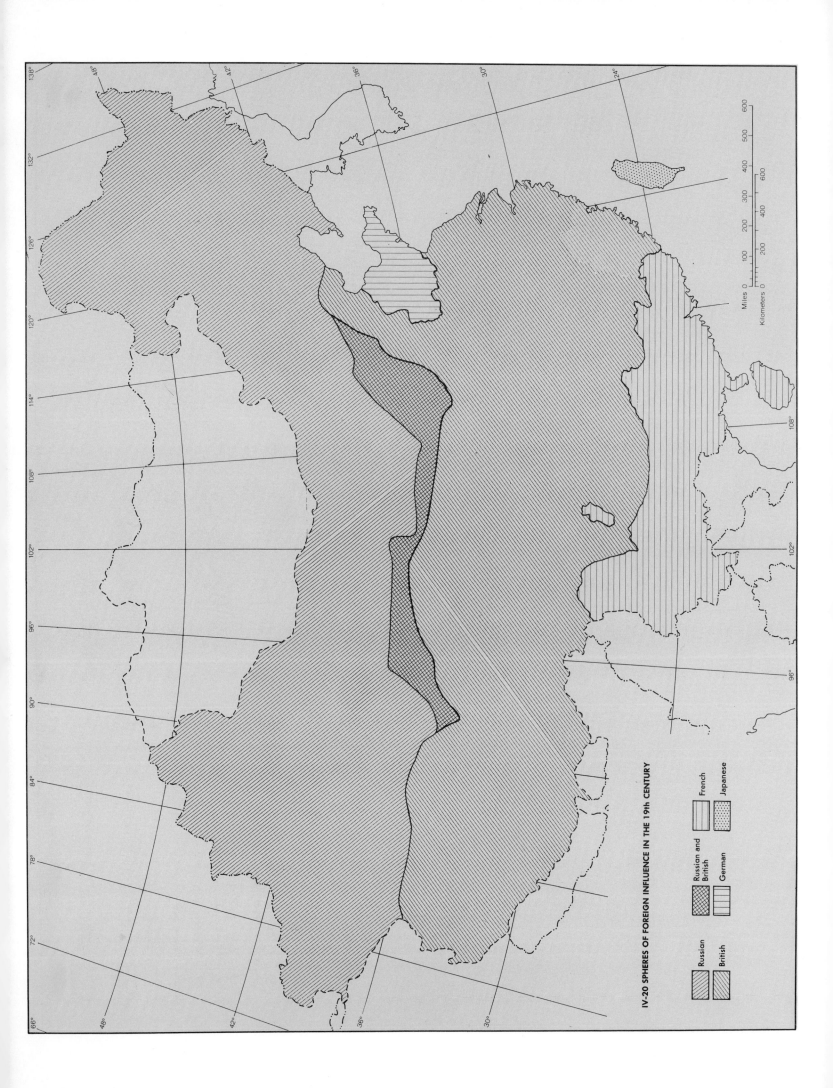

IV-20 SPHERES OF FOREIGN INFLUENCE IN THE 19th CENTURY

Russian   Russian and   French
            British

British   German   Japanese

declared the establishment of the Republic of China and organized a provisional government at Nanking, and Dr. Sun Yat-sen was elected president.

After the Chinese Republic was founded in 1911, the Revolutionary League was reorganized as the Kuomintang, the National People's Party (Nationalists), and Dr. Sun was retained as its leader. A new government was organized in Canton, and the Whampoa Military Academy was established, with Chiang Kai-shek as its dean. Dr. Sun planned to send the military force trained at this academy to northern China, which was controlled by the warlords. However, Dr. Sun died in 1925, and in 1926 Chiang Kai-shek led the Nationalist forces in a drive north from Canton. The following year Chiang moved the Nationalist government from Canton to Nanking and continued the northern military expedition. In 1928, the Nationalist army occupied Peking, and the warlords' government was dissolved. Thus China was again unified, this time under the Nationalist government in Nanking—a government that, for all its revolutionary beginnings, maintained a conservative position with regard to domestic policy, particularly in respect to land ownership.

In 1930, Mao Tse-tung and Chu Teh established a revolutionary political base in Kiangsi Province, and it was here that the first units of the Red Army (later called the People's Liberation Army, or PLA) were formed. In the areas under their control a policy of agrarian revolution was implemented, and guerrilla warfare was employed by the Red Army against the Nationalist forces, which were attempting to destroy the Communists. In 1934, the Nationalists drove the Communists out of their principal base in Kiangsi. Fighting as they went, the men of the Red Army began their famous Long March, traveling first west and then north to Shensi, which they reached in October 1935 (Map IV-21). They established their headquarters in Yen-an, and Mao Tse-tung soon emerged as the prime policy maker and leader.

The Japanese had seized Manchuria in 1931, while the Nationalists and the Communists were engaged in civil war in Shensi. The two native factions came to an agreement, however, to cooperate in their resistance against Japanese aggression. In 1937, Japan undertook a massive invasion of China, but was able only to control the coastal areas. The Chinese forces moved west, first to Hankow and then to Chungking. By 1941, the Nationalists controlled Szechwan and southwestern China, while the Communists occupied northern China. Japan occupied the coastal areas, the North China Plain, and the Northeast (Map IV-22).

The United States hoped that a renewal of the Chinese civil war could be avoided, and after the Japanese surrendered in 1945, discussions were held in Chungking, with the United States as mediator, between delegations representing the Communists and the Kuomintang. Although an agreement was reached, it was short-lived, for the division between the parties was too deep to be reconciled. Civil strife began anew, and in October 1949, in Peking, Mao Tse-tung proclaimed the formation of the People's Republic of China while the Nationalists, under Chiang Kai-shek, retreated to Taiwan and established their government at Taipei.

The First Five-Year Plan, implemented on the mainland in 1953, marked the beginning of a cooperative program which was to be the first stage in overall economic reform. In 1958, with the implementation of the Second Five-Year Plan, another stage in agrarian and industrial development began, and cooperative farms were combined into larger units, called communes, the purpose of which was to achieve the benefits of large-scale farming and cooperative organization. By 1959, the 500 million peasants of China were organized into approximately 26,000 communes (Map IV-23).

In addition to increasing agricultural productivity and instituting agrarian reforms, the Communist government also strove to further develop China's industries and railroad network. In October 1964, mainland China exploded its first atomic bomb, and thus became the fifth nuclear power in the world (Map IV-24).

The contemporary scene is further reflected in Maps IV-25 through IV-27, which shows the division of China into military administrative zones, the distribution of higher education centers in the mid-1960s, and the present political organization of the country under the Communist regime.

1966–1968 saw the chaos and consolidation of the Great Proletarian Cultural Revolution, and the decade of the sixties closed with the People's Republic of China still attempting to organize and use efficiently the forces of the revolution which lifted Mao Tse-tung and his followers to power in 1949.

In the winter of 1972 China opened its doors to the United States' President Richard Nixon and his retinue for an historic seven-day visit, and this journey gave rise to new hopes that Americans could travel in China to share the rich legacy of this mother nation of Asia.

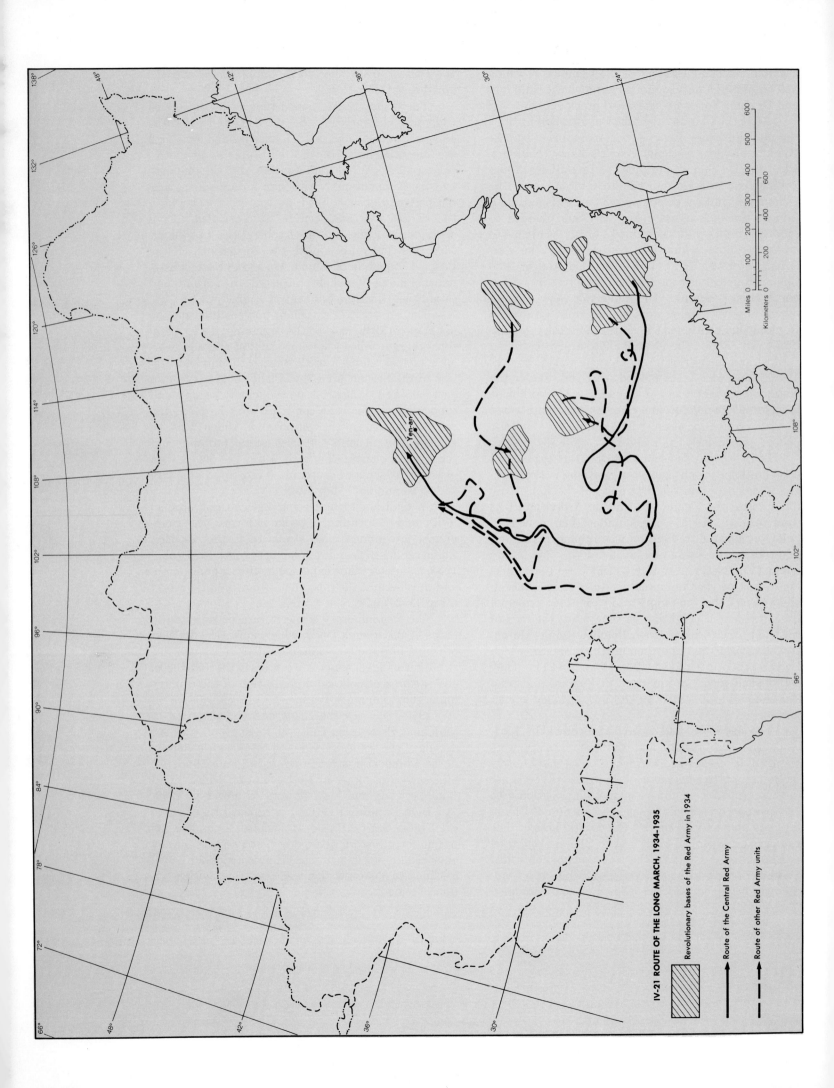

IV-21 ROUTE OF THE LONG MARCH, 1934-1935

Revolutionary bases of the Red Army in 1934

Route of the Central Red Army

Route of other Red Army units

Yen-an

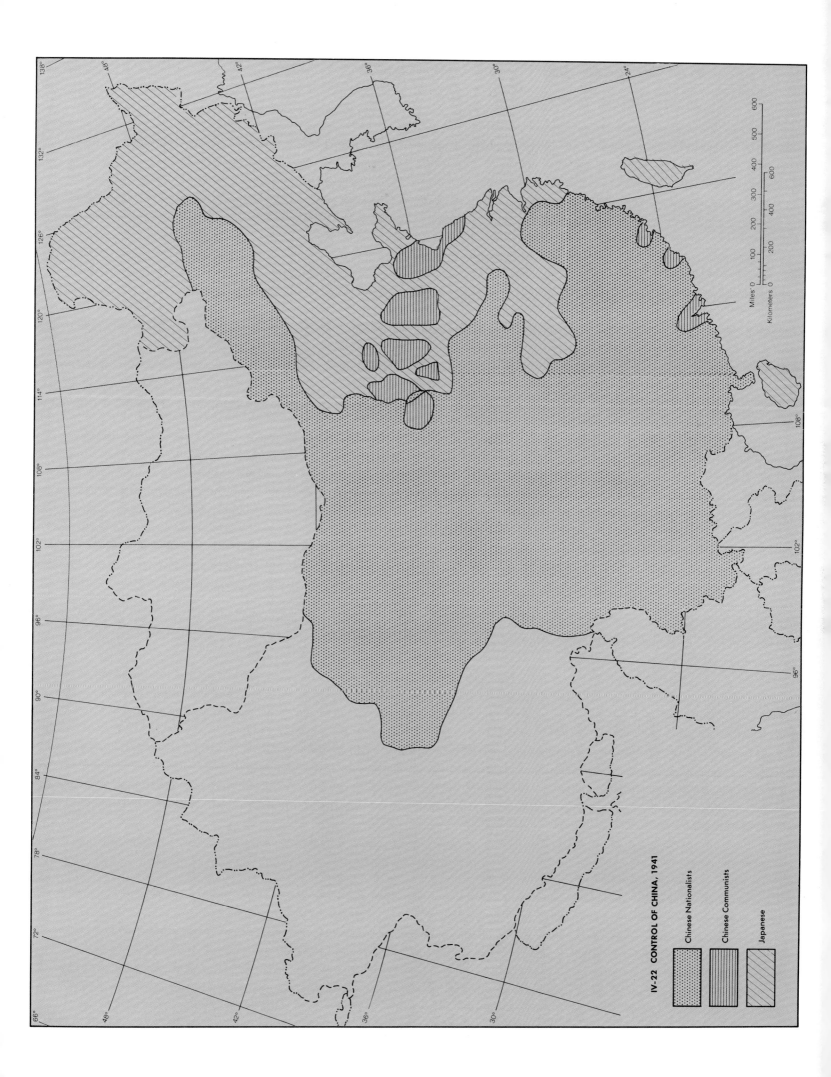

IV-22 CONTROL OF CHINA, 1941

Chinese Nationalists

Chinese Communists

Japanese

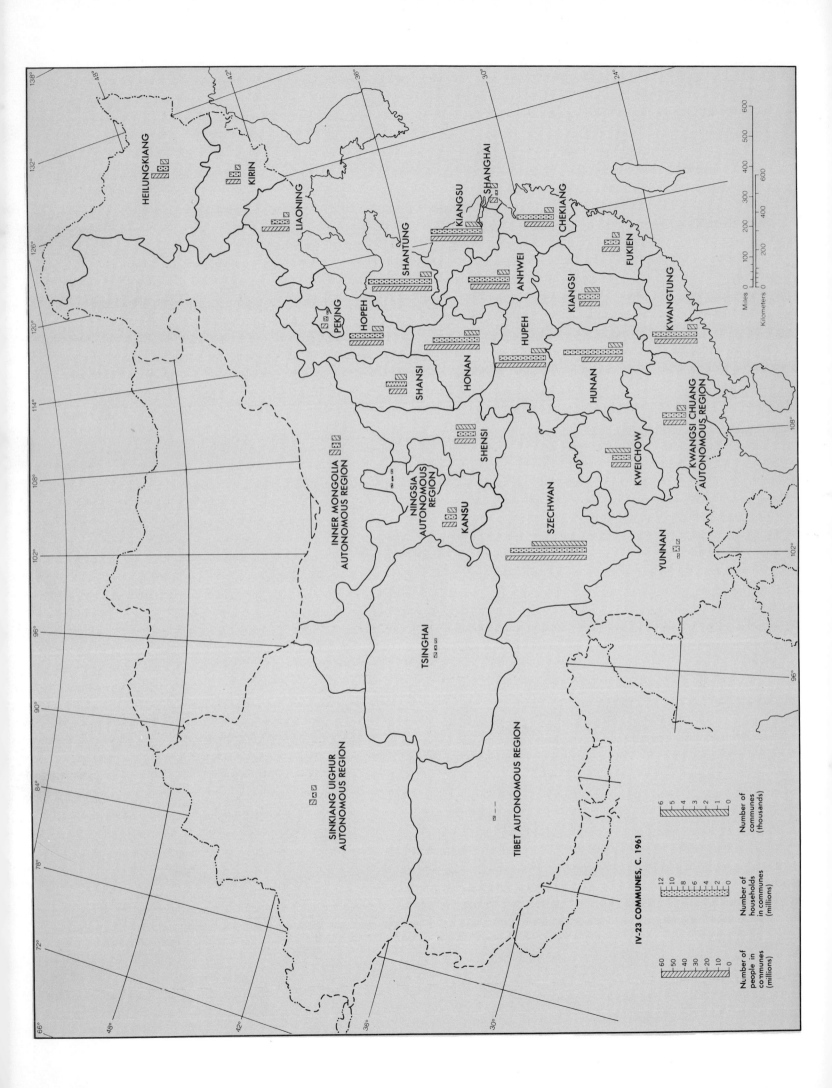

HEILUNGKIANG

KIRIN

LIAONING

SHANTUNG

SHANGHAI

KIANGSU

CHEKIANG

ANHWEI

PEKING

HOPEH

FUKIEN

SHANSI

HONAN

HUPEH

KIANGSI

KWANGTUNG

INNER MONGOLIA
AUTONOMOUS REGION

HUNAN

NINGSIA
AUTONOMOUS
REGION

KANSU

SZECHWAN

KWEICHOW

KWANGSI CHUANG
AUTONOMOUS REGION

YUNNAN

TSINGHAI

SINKIANG UIGHUR
AUTONOMOUS REGION

TIBET AUTONOMOUS REGION

IV-23 COMMUNES, C. 1961

Number of
people in
communes
(millions)

60
50
40
30
20
10
0

Number of
households
in communes
(millions)

12
10
8
6
4
2
0

Number of
communes
(thousands)

6
5
4
3
2
1
0

Miles 0   100   200   300   400   500   600
Kilometers 0   200   400   600

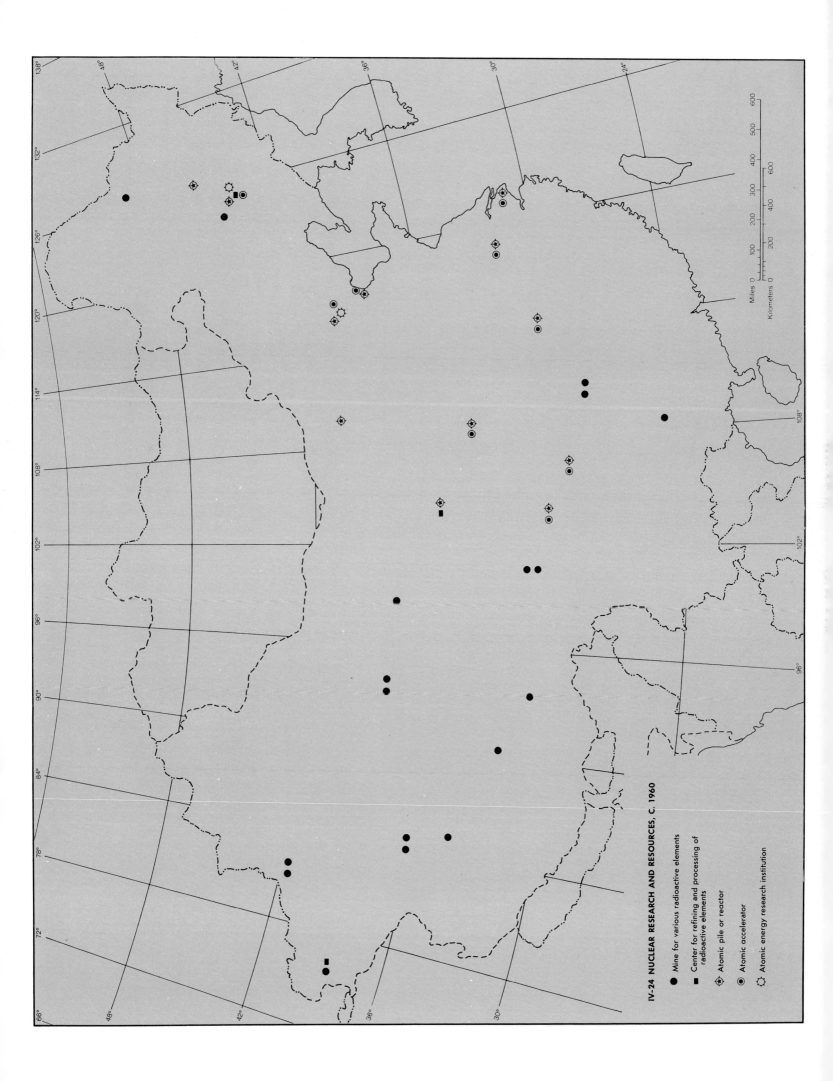

IV-24 NUCLEAR RESEARCH AND RESOURCES, C. 1960

● Mine for various radioactive elements

■ Center for refining and processing of radioactive elements

✦ Atomic pile or reactor

◉ Atomic accelerator

✺ Atomic energy research institution

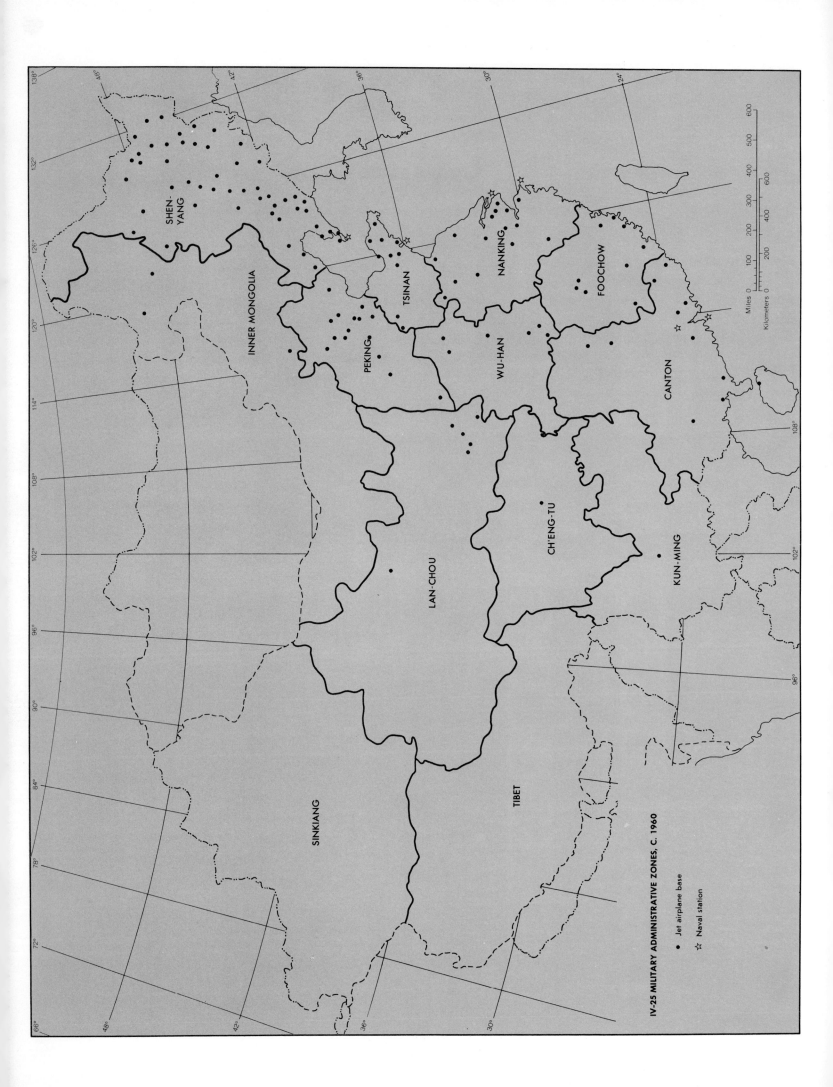

SHEN-
YANG

INNER MONGOLIA

TSINAN

NANKING

FOOCHOW

PEKING

WU-HAN

CANTON

LAN-CHOU

CH'ENG-TU

KUN-MING

SINKIANG

TIBET

Miles 0
Kilometers 0

• Jet airplane base

☆ Naval station

IV-25 MILITARY ADMINISTRATIVE ZONES, C. 1960

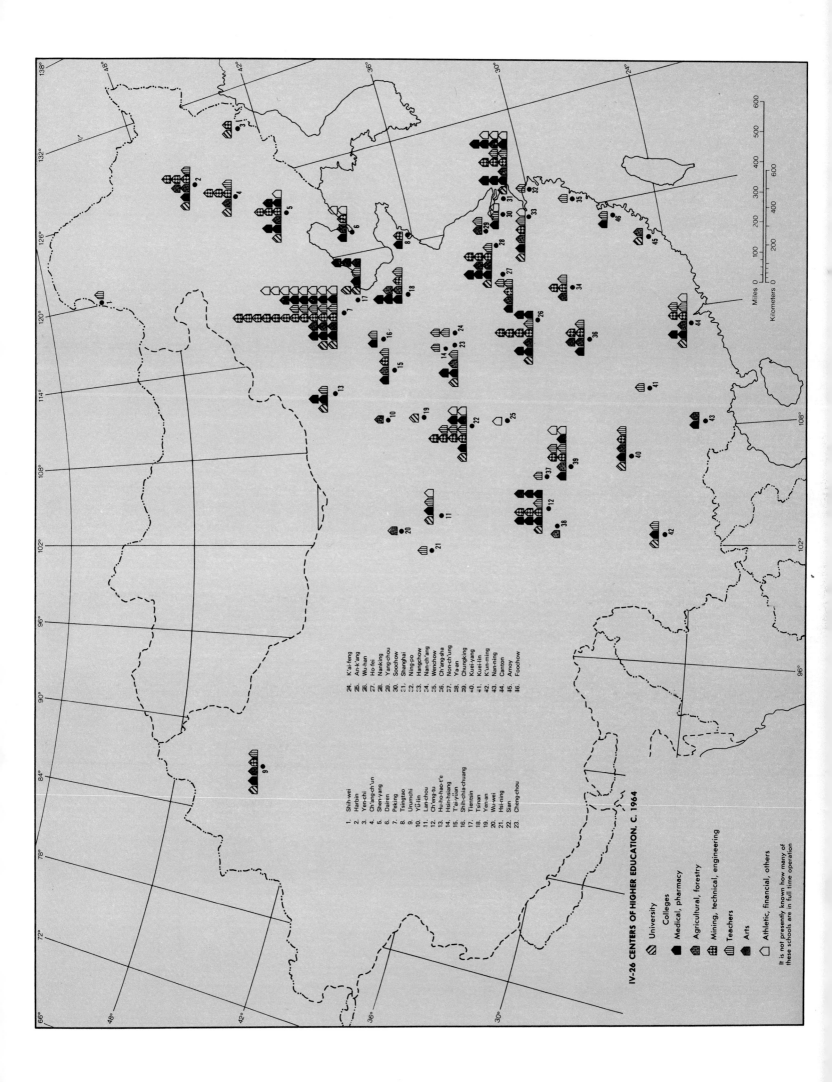

IV-26 CENTERS OF HIGHER EDUCATION. C. 1964

1. Shih-wei
2. Harbin
3. Yen-chi
4. Ch'ang-ch'un
5. Shen-yang
6. Dairen
7. Peking
8. Tsingtao
9. Urumchi
10. Yü-lin
11. Lan-chou
12. Ch'eng-tu
13. Hu-ho-hao-t'e
14. Hsin-hsiang
15. T'ai-yüan
16. Shih-chia-chuang
17. Tientsin
18. Tsinan
19. Yen-an
20. Wu-wei
21. Hsi-ning
22. Sian
23. Cheng-chou

24. K'ai-feng
25. An-k'ang
26. Wu-han
27. Ho-fei
28. Nanking
29. Yang-chou
30. Soochow
31. Shanghai
32. Ning-po
33. Hangchow
34. Nan-ch'ang
35. Wenchow
36. Ch'ang-sha
37. Non-ch'ung
38. Ya-an
39. Chungking
40. Kuei-yang
41. Kuei-lin
42. K'un-ming
43. Nan-ning
44. Canton
45. Amoy
46. Foochow

University
Colleges
Medical, pharmacy
Agricultural, forestry
Mining, technical, engineering
Teachers
Arts
Athletic, financial, others

It is not presently known how many of
these schools are in full time operation

Miles 0   100   200   300   400   500   600

Kilometers 0   200   400   600

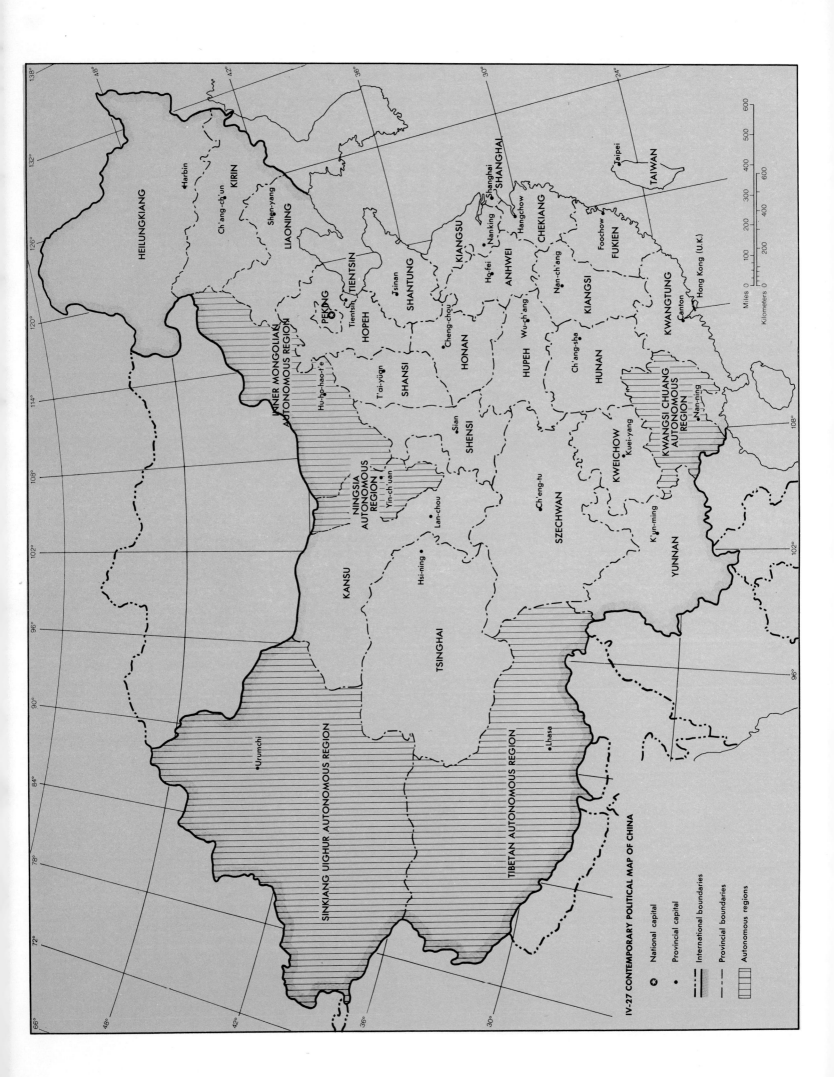

HEILUNGKIANG

•Harbin

KIRIN

Ch'ang-ch'un

Shen-yang

LIAONING

INNER MONGOLIAN AUTONOMOUS REGION

Hu-ho-hao-t'e•

PEKING ✪

Tientsin• TIENTSIN

HOPEH

SHANSI

T'ai-yüan•

Sian•

SHENSI

NINGSIA AUTONOMOUS REGION

Yin-ch'uan•

Lan-chou•

KANSU

Hsi-ning•

TSINGHAI

SINKIANG UIGHUR AUTONOMOUS REGION

Urumchi•

TIBETAN AUTONOMOUS REGION

Lhasa•

Jsinan•

SHANTUNG

Cheng-chou•

HONAN

HUPEH

Wu-ch'ang•

Ch'eng-tu•

SZECHWAN

KWEICHOW

Kuei-yang•

YUNNAN

K'un-ming•

KIANGSU

Nanking•

Shanghai• SHANGHAI

Hangchow•

CHEKIANG

Ho-fei•

ANHWEI

Nan-ch'ang•

KIANGSI

Ch'ang-sha•

HUNAN

KWANGSI CHUANG AUTONOMOUS REGION

Nan-ning•

FUKIEN

Foochow•

Canton•

KWANGTUNG

Hong Kong (U.K.)

Taipei•

TAIWAN

Miles 0   100   200   300   400   500   600

Kilometers 0   200   400   600

IV-27 CONTEMPORARY POLITICAL MAP OF CHINA

✪ National capital
•   Provincial capital

⎯··⎯··⎯ International boundaries

⎯·⎯·⎯   Provincial boundaries

▨ Autonomous regions

EPILOGUE

After completion of the maps for this atlas, post-1970 boundary changes came to light. For example, the Inner Mongolian Autonomous Region is greatly reduced in size, and the Ningsia Autonomous Region now extends to the border of Outer Mongolia. Map IV-27, *Contemporary Political Map of China*, shows the new boundaries, and the following table shows the associated area and population changes.

Political units (30)	Area (sq. km.)	Population
Peking*	17,800	7,570,000
Tientsin*	4,000	4,280,000
Hopeh†	190,000	41,410,000
Shansi†	150,000	12,350,000
Inner Mongolia‡	450,000	6,240,000
Liaoning†	230,000	29,500,000
Kirin†	290,000	17,890,000
Heilungkiang†	710,000	21,390,000
Shanghai*	5,800	10,820,000
Shantung†	150,000	55,520,000
Kiangsu†	100,000	44,500,000
Chekiang	100,000	28,320,000
Anhwei†	130,000	31,240,000
Kiangsi†	160,000	21,070,000
Fukien†	120,000	16,760,000
Taiwan†	36,000	12,040,000
Shensi†	190,000	20,770,000
Ningsia‡	170,000	2,160,000
Kansu†	530,000	12,650,000
Tsinghai†	720,000	2,140,000
Sinkiang‡	1,600,000	7,270,000
Honan†	160,000	50,320,000
Hupeh†	180,000	33,710,000
Hunan†	210,000	37,180,000
Kwangtung†	220,000	42,800,000
Kwangsi‡	230,000	20,840,000
Szechwan†	560,000	67,960,000
Kweichow†	170,000	17,140,000
Yunnan†	380,000	20,510,000
Tibet‡	1,200,000	1,250,000
Total	9,363,600	697,600,000

* Cities (3).
† Provinces (22).
‡ Autonomous Regions (5).
SOURCE: Data from *World Atlas* published by China Cartographic Institute, Peking. December 1971.

Bibliography and Map Sources

The major portion of the information contained in this atlas has been garnered from library research both in the United States and abroad. Even though many materials on China's natural environment and economic development have been published in mainland China since the Peking government was established in 1949, these materials have not been permitted to flow freely to America; but they are obtainable in other Western world cities. Attendance at international conferences in Tokyo, Stockholm, Canberra, and Budapest; service as an external examiner in geography in Hong Kong; and a lectureship at the University of Leeds in England have afforded me an opportunity to tap library resources in major Oriental study centers while also allowing me to purchase materials not readily available in the United States. Secondly, much information was obtainable from library facilities in the United States. Washington, D.C., provided excellent sources, such as the Library of Congress and many government agencies. Libraries located in other cities were also helpful. The Harvard-Yenching Library at Harvard University and the Hoover Library of Stanford University are examples.

Chinese materials have been the most significant source for the atlas, though information has also come from Russian, Japanese, German, French, and English sources.

The Chinese materials include new data on the physical resources and environment of China from the reports of survey parties sent out by government agencies. These reports have appeared in Chinese scientific journals of the different disciplines.

Information on economic development from a much wider range of sources, including books, newspaper and magazine articles, and reports in professional and technical journals have also been utilized. Not only have their texts been examined, but accompanying maps, charts, and photographs have been scrutinized, a process that provided a most valuable key to other information or to the evaluation of the work itself.

It is recognized that much of the information from the popular press and to some extent even the technical journals is spotty and incomplete. However, I have engaged in a systematic program of reading these materials over a long time span, and my hundreds of notes gathered over the years from different sources, when pieced together, have often given a complete and reliable picture that would not have been otherwise available.

The bibliography which follows cites some of the sources most useful in the creation of the *Atlas of China*. The map numbers attached to the articles, such as **(II-15)**, indicate that the article is the major source for the construction of the map.

Afanasyesky, Ye A., *Szechuan* (in Russian) (Moscow: Publishing House in Oriental Literature, 1962).

An Atlas of Chinese Climatology (Chung-kuo Ch'i-hou T'u) (Peking: Central Meteorological Bureau, 1960). **I-17, I-32**

Atlas of the People's Republic of China (Chung-hua Jen-min Kung-ho-kuo Ti-t'u Chi) (Shanghai: Map Publishing Company, 1957). **(I-3, II-2)**

Barbour, G. B. *The Geology of the Kalgan Area, Memoirs of the Geological Survey of China,* Series A, No. 6, 1929. **(III-6)**

Barbour, George B., *Physiographic History of the Yangtze* Mem. Geol. Survey of China, Series A. No. 14, 1930. **(III-25)**

Buchanan, Keith. *The Chinese People and the Chinese Earth* (London: G. Bell & Sons, Ltd., 1966). **(II-37)**

Buchanan, Keith. *The Transformation of the Chinese Earth* (New York: Praeger Publishers, Inc., 1970). **(II-37, II-38)**

Carin, Robert. *River Control in Communist China* (Hong Kong: Union Research Institute, 1962).

Chang, C. L., "The Distribution of Fresh Fisheries in China," *Acta Geographica Sinica,* XX, No. 3, 1954.

Chang, Chi-yun, (ed.) *The Physical Environment of China* (Chung Kuo tse Tzu Shan Yuan Ching) (Taipei, Taiwan: China Cultural Publication Foundation, 1956).

Chang, Chi-yun (ed.), *A New Geography of Tsun-Yi,* National Cheking University, Hangchow, 1948.

Chang, Kuei-sheng, "The Changing Railroad Pattern in Mainland China," *Geographical Review,* L1, No. 4, October 1961. **(II-7)**

Chang, Jen-hu. "Air Mass Maps of China Proper & Manchuria" *Papers on the Climate of China and Ground Temperatures* (Taipei: Chinese Geographical Research Institute, 1958). **(I-18, I-19)**

Chang, P. S., "A Discussion of the development of Yellow River and its deposit of Loess" Quaternaria Sinica, I, No. 1, Science Press, 1958. **(III-15)**

Chang, Sen-dou, "The Distribution and Occupation of Overseas Chinese," *The Geographical Review,* Vol. 58, No. 1, January 1968. **(II-3)**

Chang, W. Y. *Principles of Geotectonics of China, Geological Monograph,* No. 1 (Peking: Institute of Geology, Academia Sinica, Science Press, 1959). **(I-4, I-5)**

Chang, Yung-tsu. "The Distribution of Mammals in China," *Ti-li Chih-shih,* Peking, January 1955. **(I-47, I-48, I-49)**

Chang, Yung-tsu and Tso-hsin Cheng. "A Tentative Scheme for Dividing Zoogeographical Regions of China," *Acta Geographica Sinica,* XXII, No. 1, Peking, 1956. **(I-46)**

Chao, S. G., *The Territory of China* (Chung-kuo ti Pan T'u) (Taipei, Taiwan: Chung Hwa Publishing Company, 1955). **(IV)**

Chen, C. S., *Hosi Corridor,* Geographical Monograph, No. 4, National Central University, Chungking, 1943). **(III-18)**

Chen, C. S., Sun T. H., and Huang, T. H., *Climatic Classification and Climatic Regions in China,* Fu-Min Geographical Institute of Economic Development, Research Report No. 68, Taipei, Taiwan: 1956. **(I-27)**

Chen, C. T. and C. Y. Mao. "Erosional Remnants in the Loess Landscape of Ningsia Basin," *Ti-li chih-shih* Peking, 1957.

Chen, En-feng, *Soil Geography of China,* (Shanghai: Commercial Press, 1954). **(I-43)**

Chen, Hsin-wen, "Reconstruction of the Electric Power Industry During the Past Four Years," *Reconstruc-tion Monthly,* (Chien-She Yueh-Kan), No. 7, 1957. **(II-38)**

Chen, Meng-hsiung. "Studies of the Classification of Ground Water of the Provinces of China," *Ti-chih Lun-ping,* XVII, No. 4, Peking, 1957. **(I-39)**

Chen, S. P. and L. P. Yang, "Settlement Geography of Tsun-yi, Kweichow" *Journal of the Geographical Society of China,* Chungking, 1943. **(III-94)**

Chen, S. S., "The Development of Tropical Resources in South China," *Tili Chih Shih,* July 1956.

Cheng, H. N., "The Highway Transportation in China's Ethnic Minority Regions," *Tili Chih Shih,* November 1956. **(II-12)**

Cheng, Kwang-yu and Sheng-mu Hsu. *An Historical Atlas of China (Chung-kuo Li-shih Ti-t'u Chi)* (Taipei: (1956). **(IV)**

Cheng, li-chien, *The New Geography of Szechuan (Sze-chuan Hsin ti chih)* (Shanghai: 1947).

Cheng, Tso-hsin. "The Animal Regions of China," *Ti-li Chih-shih,* Peking, April 1956. **(I-46)**

Cheng Lu, S. P. Chen, M. K. Sung, and P. C. Huang, "The Land Utilization of Tien-Chih, Yunnan" *Acta Geographica Sinica,* XIV, No. 2, 1945. **(III-96-III-99)**

Chiang, N. C., "Soybeans in China," *Tili Chih Shih,* No. 11, 1957. **(II-18)**

Chiang, Y. C., "The Production of China's Cotton" *Tili Chih Shih,* October 1957. **(II-26)**

Chiang, Y. C., "The Distribution of Chemical Industry in China," *Tili Chih Shih,* No. 5, 1958. **(II-36)**

Chien, S. S., C. Y. Wu and C. T. Chen. "The Vegetation Types of China," *Acta Geographica Sinica,* XXII, No. 1, Peking, March 1956. **(I-45)**

Chinese Water Resources (Chung-kuo Ch'u-yu Shui-wen Ti-chih Kai-lun) (Peking: Ministry of Geology, 1958).

Cho, C. *Geography of Agriculture in China* (Peking: Scientific Expansion Publication Society, 1957). **(II-15)**

Chou, Li-san, H. T. Hou, and S. E. Chen, *Economic Atlas of Szechuan (San chuen Ching-chi li-tu chih)* (Chungking: Institute of Geography, 1946). **(III-41, III-46, III-50)**

Chow, H. C. "The Characteristics of China's Karst," *Ti-li,* No. 2, Peking, March 1965. **(I-13)**

Chow, T. J. and Pei-tung Liu, *The Landforms and Soil Types of China* (Peking: San Lien Book Company, 1956). **(I-42)**

Chu Chi, *The Selected Historical Material of China's Grand Canal* (Chung Kuo Yun-Ho Tzu-Liao Hsüan Chi) (Peking: Chung Hwa Publishing Company, 1962). **(IV-16)**

Chu, Chien-keng, "Fog in Peking," *Weather Monthly,* No. 10, Peking, 1957. **(I-32)**

Chu, H. Y., "Silk in Chekiang Province: *Tili Chih Shih,* January 1960. **(II-27)**

Chu, K. K. "A Preliminary Analysis of the Water Balances of China's Rivers," *Acta Meteorologica Sinica,* II, No. 1, 1957. **(I-36)**

Chu, Kang-kun and Jen-chang Yang, "A Study of the Evaporation Distribution in China," *Acta Meteorologica Sinica* XXVI, No. 1-2, Peking, 1955. **(I-31)**

Chung, P. E., "The Vegetation and Their Distribution in Tibet," *Acta Botanic Sinica,* No. 10, 1954.

Chung, Tsao, "The Past, Present, and Future of China's Railway," *Current Affairs (Shih-Shih Shou-tse),* No. 2, January 1957. **(III-6, II-11)**

"Coal Research and Techniques in Communist China," *Coal Age,* October 1959.

Communist China Administrative Atlas (Washington, D.C.: Central Intelligence Agency, 1969).

Communist China Map Folio (Washington, D.C.: Central Intelligence Agency, 1967).

"The Distribution of Glacier Remnants," *Quaternaria Sinica*, VII, No. 1, Peking (Institute of Geology, Academia Sinica, Science Press), 1964. **(I-15)**

"Distribution of Snow Cover Depth in the People's Republic of China," *Tien-ch'i Yueh-k'an*, No. 11, 1959, pp. 24–25.

Economic Geography of China (for High School), *(Chung-Kuo Kao-chung Tili)* 2 vols., (Canton: Hsin Chung Publishing Society, 1956.

Economic Geography of Inner Mongolia (Nei Mon-ku Tzu chih ch'u ching-chi Tili) Monography of China's Regional Geography, No. 1, Acadamia Sinica, Science Press, Peking, 1956. **(III-113)**

Fong, Jen, "The Number of Ethnic Minority Groups and Their Distribution in China," *Tili Chih Shih*, June 1958. **(II-4)**

Fong, T. F., *Cotton In China* (Peking: Treasury and Economic Publishing Society, 1956). **(II-26)**

Growth of Civil Aviation in Communist China, (Hong Kong: Union Research Service, May 1965). **(II-13)**

Hao, Sheng-jung. "Using the Waters of the Yellow River for Irrigation," *Huang-ho Chien-she*, No. 10, 1959.

He, Chi-li. "Achievements in the Construction of Irrigation Works in China in Ten Years," *Shui-li Shui-tien Chien-she*, No. 18, 1959, pp. 13–17.

Herrmann, Albert. *An Historical Atlas of China* (Chicago: Aldine Publishing Company, 1966). **(IV)**

Highlights of Chinese History, (Peking: China Reconstructs, 1962). **(IV)**

Ho, Yu-Chung, "A New Page in the History of China's Machine-building Industry," *Ching-chi Tao-pao*, June 1957. **(II-39)**

Hsieh, Chiao-min, *Taiwan: Ilha Formosa*, (Washington: Butterworth Company, 1964). **(III-57, III-70)**

Hsieh, Chiao-min, "Physical and Human Geography of Eastern Szechuan," *Tili*, China Institute of Geography, Peipei, III, No. 3-4, Chungking, 1943.

Hsieh, Chiao-min and Jean Kan Hsieh, *The Coast of Southeastern China—Submergent or Emergent?—*, Chinese Geographical Institute, Taipei, Taiwan, 1958.

Hsiao, C. E., "The Physical Environment, Agriculture and Pasture of Tibet," *Scientia*, No. 10, 1954. **(III-128)**

Hsu, C. M., "Special Physical Features of the Pearl River" *Tili Chih Shih*, May 1959. **(III-52)**

Hsu, P. S., "The Geography of Petroleum Industry in China," *Tili Chih Shih*, Octobor 1957. **(II-32)**

Hu, Huan-Yung, *The Geography of Szechuan (Szechuan Ti-li)* (Chungking: Chung-Chang Book Company, 1938).

Hu, S. W., "The Achievement of the Railway's Construction in the First Five Year Plan in our Country," *Tili Chih Shih*, January 1958. **(II-10, II-11)**

"The Huai Ho Drainage," *Ti-li Chih-shih*, II, No. 10, Peking, 1951.

Huang, Chi-ch'ing. "Basic Features of the Tectonic Structure of China," *International Geology Review*, V, No. 4. **(I-6)**

Huang, F. P., "A Preliminary Study of the Karst Sinkhole in Kwangsi," *The Selected Essays on China's Karst*, Academia Sinica, Science Press, 1962. **(I-14)**

Huang, Ping-wei, "The Experience Obtained from making the Soil Erosion Map of the Middle of Huang Ho," *Scientia*, 1955. **(III-16, III-17)**

Huang, S. H. "Soil Temperature in Eastern China and its Relation to Soil Distribution," *Ti-li*, No. 6, Peking (Science Press), 1963. **(I-43)**

Huang, T. K. "The Main Characteristics of the Geologic Structure of China: Preliminary Conclusions," *Ti-chih Lun-ping*, XL, No. 1, February 1960. **(I-5)**

Hursch, Erhard, "Industrialization in China," *Nene Zuricher Zeitung (New Zurich Journal)* March 1964.

Hwa Chao Chic (Overseas Chinese), (Taipei, Taiwan: Overseas Chinese Affairs Commission, 1957). **(II-3)**

Inner Mongolia Today (Peking: Nationalities Publishing House, 1957).

Jen, M. N., "The Geology and Landform of the Northeast," *Tili Chih Shih*, XI, 1953.

Jen, Yu-ti, *A Concise Geography of China* (Peking: Foreign Language Press, 1964).

Ku, Chieh-kang and Chang S., *An Historical Atlas of China*, *(Chung-Kuo Li-shih Ti-t'u Chi)* (Peking: Map Publishing Company, University of Peking, 1956). **(IV)**

Ku, Chieh-kang and Shih, Y. H., *A Changing History of China's Territory (Chung-Kuo Chiang-yueh Yen-k'e Shih)* (Shanghai: Commercial Press, 1938). **(IV)**

Kuo, Ching-hui. "Hydrography of the Rivers in China," *Ti-li Chih-shih*, IX, No. 2, Peking, February 1958. **(I-37)**

Kuo, Ching-hui. "Making a Map of Isolines of the Runoff Modulus of China," *K'e-hsueh T'ung-pao*, No. 6, 1958, pp. 190–191. **(I-38)**

Kuo, Ching-hui. "On the Calculation of China's Run-off Resources," *K'e-hsueh T'ung-pao*, September 1957.

Kuo, Ching-hui. "The Physical Factors of China's Surface Runoff," *Acta Geographica Sinica*, XXIV, No. 2, May 1958. **(I-36)**

Kuo, Ching-hui. "The Surface Run-off in China," *Acta Geographica Sinica*, XXI, No. 4, 1955. **(I-38)**

Kuo, W. K. "The Basic Characteristics of the Formation Conditions of the Major Minerals in China," *Ti-chih Lun-ping*, XIX, No. 3, 1959, pp. 103–109.

Lee, C. S. "Glacial Remnants in Szechwan," *The Research Volume of Glacial Remnants in Quaternry in China* (The Scientific Publishing Society, Peking: 1964).

Lee, J. "Sea Surface Temperature and Floods and Droughts in China," *Journal of the Chinese Geophysical Society*, II, Nanking, 1950.

Lee, S. P. "Maps of Seismology in China," *Science Records*, I, No. 5, Peking (Institute of Geophysics, Academia Sinica), 1957. **(I-78)**

Li, L. C., "The Physical Regions of Tibet," *Acta Geographica Sinica* XX, No. 3, 1954. **(III-126)**

Li, M. S. "Antimony in China," *Ti-li Chih-shih*, January 1960. **(II-33)**

Li, T., "The Hydrography of Sinkiang's River and Some Problems of Their Utilization," *Tili Chih Shih*, June, 1958. **(III-119)**

Liang, J. T., *Economic Geography of Kwangtung (Kwangtung Ching-Chi Tili)* Science Press, 1956. **(III-84)**

Ling, Hung-hsun, *A Comprehensive Survey of Railway Development in China. (Chung Kuo Tieh-lu chih)* (Taipei, Taiwan: 1954).

Liu, C. S. and H. C. Chang, "A Great Change in China's Industrial Location for the Ten Years (1949–59)" *Tili Chih Shih*, November 1959. **(II-36)**

Liu, S. N., "Tobacco in China," *Tili Chih Shih*, July 1955. **(II-21)**

Liu, S. O., C. Y. Foong, and T. C. Chao. "Some Principal Problems in Classifying the Vegetation Regions in China," *Acta Botanica Sinica*, VII, No. 2, June 1959. **(I-45)**

Liu, T. H., *The Transportation Geography of China (Wo Kuo Chiao-tung ti-li)*, Chinese Geography Knowledge Series, Science Promoting Publishing Society, 1957. **(II-12, II-14)**

Liu, T. S., "The Physical Features of Inner Mongolia," *Tili Chih-Shih,* October 1955. **(III-111)**

Liu, Chung-gen and Mou-tsang Tang. "The Climatic Characteristics of Hail in China," *Acta Geographica Sinica,* XXXII, No. 1, 1966. **(I-29)**

Liu, Tsai-min, "China's Machine-building Industry on the Road to Self-Sufficiency," *Ching-chi Tao-pao,* May 1964.

Liu, Tung-sen and Tsung-hu Chang. "The Loess of China," *Acta Geologica Sinica,* XLI, No. 1, Peking, 1962. **(I-11)**

Liu, Tung-sen. *The Deposition of Loess in China* (Peking: Institute of Geology, Academia Sinica, Science Press, 1965). **(I-12)**

Liu Ting, Vice Minister of the First Ministry of M-B Industry, "Great Achievements of the Machine-building Industry in the Past Decade," *Chi-hsieh Kung Cheng Hsueh pao,* No. 1, 1959.

Lo, C. C. and T. C. Wang. "The Chemical Characteristics of China's Rivers," *Acta Geographica Sinica,* XXIX, No. 1, March 1963. **(I-40, I-41)**

Lo, K. F. and T. Li. "Hydrography," *Materials for Physical Geography of North China,* Peking (Scientific Publishing Company), III, December 1957.

Lo, K'ai-fu, et al. "Runoff Regimes in China," *K'e-hsueh T'ung-pao,* No. 16, 1957. **(I-37)**

Lu, A. "Climatic Regions of China," *Acta Geographica Sinica,* XII–XIII, 1949. **(I-27)**

Lu, A., "A Preliminary Study of Coastal Fog in China," *The Meteorological Magazine,* XIII, No. 9, Nanking, 1937. **(I-32)**

Ma, H. Y., "The Comprehensive Utilization of Tilh-Chih," *Ti-li Chih Shih,* VI, 1958. **(III-98, III-99)**

Ma, Tse-Ching, "Railway Construction in People's China," *People's China,* No. 1, November 1954. **(II-6-II-9)**

Ma, Yung-chih. "General Principles of Geographical Distribution of Chinese Soils," *Report for the Sixth International Congress of Soil Science,* Soil Science Society of China, Peking, (Nanking: Institute of Soil Science, Academia Sinica), 1956. **(I-44)**

Murzaev, E. M., *The Mongolian People's Republic* (in Russian) Moscow, State Publishing House for Geographic Literature, 1952.

Okazaki, Ayakoto, *The Technical Level of Iron and Steel Industry and Machine-building Industry in China (Chugoku no Tekkogyo te Kikai Kogyo no gijutue suijuh)* (Tokyo: Ajia Keizai Kenkyujo, 1962). **(II-39)**

Ou-yang, Ying. *An Historical Atlas of Chinese Territorial Wars (Chung-kuo Li-tai Chiang-yu Chang-cheng Ho-t'u)* (Shanghai: 1931).

Ovdienko, Ivan Kharitonovich, *Inner Mongolia* (in Russia) (Moscow: State Publishing House for Geographic Literature, 1954).

"Paochi-Chengtu Railway," *People's China,* No. 14, July, 1956. **(II-8)**

Peng, Y. Y., "The New Railways Constructed During the First Five Year Plan," *Tili Chih Shih,* March 1956. **(II-6)**

People's Republic of China Atlas (Washington, D.C.: Central Intelligence Agency, 1971).

Porch, Harriet, E., *Civil Aviation in Communist China Since 1949* (Santa Monica, California: The Rand Corporation, 1966). **(II-13)**

Raper Arthur, Chuan Han-sheng, and Chen Shao-Hsing, *Urban and Industrial Taiwan—Crowded and Resourceful* Foreign Operation Administration & National Taiwan University, Taipei, Taiwan, 1954. **(III-71, III-77)**

"Rapid Development of China's Civil Aviation Enterprise," *Ta Kung pao,* Peking, Oct. 4, 1964.

Richardson, H. L., *Soils and Agriculture of Szechuan,* National Agricultural Research Bureau, Ministry of Agricultural and Forestry, Special Publication, No. 27, Chungking, 1942. **(III-43, III-44)**

Shen, H. N., *Paddy Rice,* Science Press, Peking, 1955. **(II-17)**

Shen, Y. C., "The Distribution of Wheat Regions and Their Future Development in China," *Tili Chih Shih,* No. 8, 1957. **(II-18)**

Shen, Y. C. "A Discussion of the Classification of China's Landforms," *Quaternaria Sinica,* I, No. 1, Peking, 1958. **(I-16)**

Shin Chugoku no Kikai Kogyo (The Machine-building Industry in New China), Tokyo: Tao Keizai Kenkyuhai, 1960. **(II-39)**

The Selected Geographical Sources of Major Cities in China (Chung Kuo Cheng-Shih Ti-li Tze-liao) Compiled by Kaifen Teacher's College, Dept. of Geography Honan Branch of Institute of Geography, Academia Sinica, Commercial Press (Peking: 1959). **(III-129, III-156)**

Song, C. T., "The Husbandry of New China" *Tili Chih Shih,* No. 4, 1953. **(II-22-II-25)**

Sources of Physical Geography of North China (Hua-pei Chu Tzu Jan tili Tze-Liao) Monography of China's Regional Geography, No. III, Science Press, Peking, 1957. **(III-5)**

Sources of Physical Geography of the Northeast (Tung-pei Chu Tzu shan Tili Tze-liao) Monography of Regional Geography of China, No. II. Science Press, Peking, December 1957. **(III-102)**

Sun, C. T., "Teaching Geography of Inner Mongolia" *Tili Chih-Shih,* No. 6, 1951. **(III-114)**

Sun, K. T., "The Husbandry of Inner Mongolia," *Tili Chih-Shih,* November 1957. **(III-112)**

Sun, N., "The Underground Resources and Industrial Reconstruction," *Tichih Chih Shih* (Geological Knowledge) I, 1955.

Sun, Ching-chih, et al. (eds.), *Economic Geography of Central China* (Hupei, Hunan, and Kiangsi) *(Hua-chung Ta-chu Ching-chi Tili)* Monography of China's Regional Geography, No. III, Science Press, Peking, 1958. **(III-35-III-39)**

Sun, Ching-chih, et al (eds.), *Economic Geography of North China* (Hopei, Shansi, Shentung, and Honan) *(Hua-pei Ch'u Ching-chi Tili)* Monography of China's Regional Geography, No. II, Science Press, Peking, 1957. **(II-7-II-11)**

Sun, Ching-chih, et al. (eds.), *Economic Geography of South China* (Kwang tung, Kwangsi, and Fukien) *(Hua-nan Ti Ch'u Ching-chi Tili)* Monography of China's Regional Geography, Science Press, Peking, 1959. **(III-55, III-56, III-80, III-82-III-85)**

Sun, Ching-chih, et al. (eds.), *Economic Geography of Southwest China* (Yunnan, Kwei chow, and Szechuan) *(Si-Nan Ti-Ch'u Ching-chi Tili)* Monography of China's Regional Geography Science Press, Peking, 1960. **(III-45, III-47-III-49, III-88-III-93)**

Sung, C. T., *The Tsaidam Basin,* Geographical Monography, No. 6, National Central University, Chungking, 1944. **(III-20)**

Tai Chu Nihon Kosaki Kikaikogyo Shisatzudan Hokokusho (Report of Japanese Machine-tool Industry Delegation to China) (Tokyo: Nihou Kokusai Boeki Sokushikai and Nihon Kosaku Kikai Kogyokai, 1965). **(II-39)**

Tan, Chi-Hsiang, "The Changes of Huang Ho and the Grand Canal" *Tili Chih Shih*, August 1955. **(III-4)**

Teng, C. C. "A Preliminary Study on the Demarcation of the Agricultural Regions of China," *Acta Geographica Sinica*, XXIX, No. 5, Peking, December 1963. **(II-30)**

Teng Ching-Chung, Kao Yung-Yuan, Hou Hsueh-tao, and Chang P'ei, *A Study of the Methodology of the Division of Agriculture Regions of China*, Edited by Institute of Geography, Academia Sinica, published by Scientific Press, Peking, January 1960. **(II-30)**

Thiel, Erich, *The Mongols, Land, People, and Economy* (in German) (Munich: Isar Publishing House, 1958).

Ts'ui, Tse-chiu. "Observations of Present Glaciers on Kung Ka Shan," *Acta Geographica Sinica*, XXIV, No. 3, 1958, pp. 318–338.

Tu, Chi Pao. *A Dictionary on Geology and Mineralogy (Ti-chih K'uong-wu-hsueh Ta Tzu-tien)* (Hong Kong: New Asia Publishing Company, 1956).

Tung, C. K., *Turfan Basin of Sinkiang (Sinkiang Turfan peng-ti)* National Central University, Geographical Monograph, No. 3, Chungking, 1943. **(III-121)**

Tung, Tso-ping. *Illustrations and Maps in Chinese History, (Chung-kuo Li-shih Chen Yu Tu Pu)* (Taipei, 1953). **(IV)**

Tung, Tung-ho, *Languages of China*, (Taipei, Taiwan: China Cultural Publishing Foundation, 1953). **(II-5)**

Tung Chi-ming, *Outline of History of China*, (Peking: Foreign Language Press, 1958).

Wang, M. H., "The Development and Distribution of Coal Mining in China," *Tili Chih Shih*, No. 4, 1957.

Wang, K. P. *Rich Mineral Resources Spur Communist China's Bid for Industrial Power* (Washington, D.C.: Bureau of Mines, Department of Interior, 1960). **(I-32)**

Wang, S. S., "Inland Waterways in New China," *Tili Chih Shih*, January 1954. **(II-14)**

Wang, S. S., et al. *Historical Atlas of China, (Chung-Kuo Li-shih Ti-T'u)*, (Shanghai: Hsin-ya Book Company, 1956). **(IV)**

Wang, T. C., et al. (eds.), *A Geographical Survey of Han-Chung Basin*, Geographical Monograph, No. 3, China Institute of Geography, Chungking, 1946. **(III-14)**

Wang, W. P. "A Preliminary Study of Karst Sinkholes in Kwangsi," *The Selected Essays of the Research Committee on Karst*, Academia Sinica, Science Press, (Peking 1962).

Wang, Ching. "A Sketch of Chinese Agricultural Geography," *People's China*, Peking, 1957. **(II-15, II-16)**

Wang, Chi-wu. "The Forests of China, with a Survey of Grassland and Desert Vegetation," *Maria Moors Cabot Foundation Publication No. 5*, Harvard University, 1961. **(I-45)**

Wang, Chun-heng, *A Simple Geography of China*, (Peking: Foreign Language Press, 1957).

Wang, Chung-Chi, *The Geography of China (Chung Kuo Tili)* (Taipei, Taiwan: Chung Cheng Book Company, 1956).

Wang, Wei-ping, *Kiangsu—The Water Country (Shui-hsiang Kiangsu)* (Shangai: Hsin-chih-shih [New Knowledge] Publishing House, 1956). **(III-27–III-29)**

Wang, Wei-ping, "The Great Achievement of Agriculture in Our Country" *Tili Chih Shih*, January 1958. **(II-19)**

Wataru, Yanal *An Historical Atlas of East Asia (Tôyô Tokushi Chizu)* (Tokyo, 1926). **(IV)**

Wei, Anton W. T., "Minerals in China in 1961" *The Mining Journal*, London, 1961. **(II-32-II-35)**

Wu, C. C., C. L. Sun, et al. (eds.), *Economic Geography of the Western Part of the Middle Yellow River (Huang Ho Chung Yu Si Pu-ti Ch'u Ching-chih Tili)* Science Press, Peking, 1956.

Wu Chao-su, "The Ecological Classifications and Demarcations of Wheat in China," *Chung-Kuo Nung-yeh Ko-Hsueh* (China Agricultural Science) No. 2, Peking, 1962. **(II-18)**

Wu, Julian C. C. *The Rice Economy of China* (Liverpool: University of Liverpool, M. A. Thesis, 1948). **(II-17)**

Yang, J. C., "The Climate of the Northeast" *Acta Geographica Sinica*, XXVI, 1950. **(III-103-III-105)**

Yang, N. Y., "The Regional Classification & Evaluation of the Physical Condition for the Highway's Transportation in China," *Acta Geographica Sinica*, XXX, No. 4, December 1964. **(II-12)**

Yao, Kai-yuan, "The Distribution of Forest in China," *Tili Chih Shih*, September 1955.

Yeh, L. C., "The Geology of the Northeast," *Tili Chih Shih*, VI. 1951.

Yeh, Y. C., "A Note on Population Density Wall Map of China," *Tili Chih Shih*, November 1956. **(II-2)**

Yeh, Tu-cheng, "The Development of Research on Atmospheric Circulation in New China," *Scientia*, Peking, 1957. **(I-20, 21)**

Yeh, Tu-Cheng, Lo, Szu-wei, and Chu, Pao-chen, "The Wind Structure and Heat Balance in the Lower Troposphere over Tibetan Plateau and Its Surroundings," *Acta Meteorologica Sinica*, XXVIII, No. 2, Peking, 1957. **(I-24-I-26)**

Yeh, Yung-i. "Floods of the Yellow River," *Acta Geographica Sinica*, XXII, No. 4, November, 1956, pp. 325–337.

Yen, K. I., *The Sinking Uigur Autonomous Region (Hsin Chiang Wei-Nu-er Tzu-chih Chu)*, (Peking: Science promoting publishing society, 1957). **(III-122, III-123)**

Yu, H. S., *Tobacco of China*, (Peking: Science Press, 1955). **(II-21)**

Yuan, Kuan, "The Distribution of Spring Wheat in China," *Jen-min Jih-pao (People's Daily)*, Peking, March 10, 1963.

Yung, Chung, "Silk in China" *Tili Chih Shih*, April 1955. **(II-27)**

Glossary

The following list of terms is taken from the 1971 *People's Republic of China Atlas* (Central Intelligence Agency) and is included because the system of orthography utilized in this atlas is the same as that of the CIA atlas. The following terms occur as generic parts of index names.

chen	second-order administrative division (administrative town)
ch'eng	wall
ch'i	second-order administrative division (banner)
chiang	stream, section of stream, estuary, lagoon, stream channel
ch'iao	bridge
ch'ih	lake, pool
ch'ü	canal
ch'uan	stream
hai	bay, lake(s), salt lake(s), sound
ho	stream, section of stream, canal, section of canal, lake, tidal creek, marine channel
ho-k'ou	stream mouth
hsia	strait, gorge
hsien	second-order administrative division (hsien)
hsü	island(s), rocks in water
hu	lake, section of lake, lagoon, marsh, reservoir, wetland
kang	bay, harbor, inlet, tidal creek, sound, marine channel, lagoon, estuary, cove, stream mouth
k'eng	stream
k'ou	bay, stream mouth, inlet, cove, pass
kuan	pass
la (Tibetan)	pass
lieh-tao	islands
ling	mountain(s), mountain range, hill, pass
miao	temple, shrine
pan-tao	peninsula
po	lake
shan	mountain(s), hill(s), peak, range, island(s), rocks in water, point, headland
shan-k'ou	pass
shan-mo	mountain range, mountains
shih	administrative division (municipality)
shui	stream, section of stream, distributary
ssu	monastery
tao	island(s), peninsula, section of island
ts'o (Tibetan)	lake
wan	bay, cove, inlet, lagoon
yen-ch'ih	lake

Appendix

DETAILED AGRICULTURAL REGIONS OF CHINA

1 Northern Dry Agricultural and Pastoral Regions

  A Northeast one-crop-yearly dry agricultural and forestry regions

    1 Khingan Mountains forestry and agricultural regions

    2 Ch'ang-pai Shan agricultural and forestry regions

      (1) Mu-tan Chiang soybeans, maize, rice, spring wheat, and forestry region

      (2) Ch'ang-pai Shan (mid-southern sector) soybeans, rice, maize, and forestry region

    3 Sungari-Nen Plain soybeans, maize, spring wheat, sugar beet regions

      (1) Plain of the Three Rivers soybeans, spring wheat, maize, sugar beet region

      (2) Nen Chiang Plain soybeans, millet, maize, spring wheat, sugar beet region

      (3) Sungari Plain soybeans, maize, sugar beet, flax region

      (4) Ch'ang-pai (west) soybeans, rice, maize region

    4 Liaoning kaoliang, maize, fruit, and aquatic products regions

      (1) Liaoning hill country maize, rice, groundnuts, fruit, silk, and aquatic products region

      (2) Middle and lower Liao Ho kaoliang and maize region

      (3) Liao highland (west) kaoliang, millet, cotton, fruit region

  B Inner Mongolia one-crop-yearly dry agricultural and pastoral regions

    1 Pastoral regions of Inner Mongolian Plateau

    2 Agricultural and pastoral regions of southeast Inner Mongolia

      (1) Khingan (east) maize, millet, grazing region

      (2) Hsi-liao Ho kaoliang, maize, millet, grazing region

      (3) Chi-je Mountain millet, oats, kaoliang, maize, grazing region

      (4) Ta-ching Plateau spring wheat, oats, potatoes, sesame, grazing region

      (5) North Shensi millet and grazing region

      (6) Ningsia (southeast) millet, spring wheat, sheep region

    3 Agricultural regions of mountains along the Great Wall

      (1) Chi-pei Shan millet, maize, soybeans, kaoliang region

      (2) North Shansi oats, millet, hemp region

      (3) Ta-ching Shan oats, hemp region

    4 Kansu-Tsinghai Plateau semidry agricultural regions

      (1) Liu-p'an Shan sesame, oats, sheep region

      (2) Lung-chung spring wheat, millet, potatoes, hemp region

(3) T'ao Ho spring wheat, barley, potatoes, region

C North China three-crops-biennially dry agricultural regions
  1 Hopeh wheat, millet, maize, rice, fruit region
    (1) Central Hopeh wheat, kaoliang, rice region
    (2) Yen Shan millet, maize, wheat, fruit region
  2 Loess Plateau wheat, maize, millet regions
    (1) Southeast Shansi millet, wheat, maize, subsidiary forestry region
    (2) Central Shansi wheat, millet, kaoliang region
    (3) West Shansi–north Shensi millet, wheat region
    (4) Wei Ho–northern plateau wheat, soybeans, maize, millet region
    (5) Ching Ho wheat, millet, oats, sesame region
    (6) Upper Wei Ho wheat, maize, hemp region
  3 North China Plain cotton and wheat regions
    (1) Hopeh-Shantung-Honan cotton, wheat regions
    (2) West Honan wheat, cotton region
    (3) South Shansi-Kuan-chung cotton, wheat region
  4 Shantung Peninsula wheat, soybeans, groundnuts, tobacco, fruit, fisheries regions
    (1) [sic]
    (2) T'ai-Yi Mountains wheat, sweet potatoes, groundnuts region
    (3) Central lowland wheat, soybeans, tobacco region
  5 Yellow-Huai River lowlands wheat, soybeans, tobacco, sesame regions
    (1) North Anhwei wheat, soybeans, tobacco regions
    (2) East Honan–west Shantung wheat, soybeans region
    (3) East Honan wheat, tobacco, sesame region
    (4) Fu-niu Shan wheat, maize, sweet potatoes, subsidiary forestry region

2 Southern Wet-Field Agriculture and Commercial Forestry Regions
  A East and central China double-cropping wet rice and subtropical forestry regions
    1 Yangtze-Huai interlocking wet-field and dry agriculture region
      (1) North Kiangsu Plain rice, wheat, cotton region
      (2) Huai-nan (south of Huai River) rice, wheat, tobacco region
    2 Ta-pieh Shan wheat, rice, and forestry regions
      (1) Foothills wet rice, wheat, tea, and forestry region
      (2) Nan-yang Basin wheat, wet rice, cotton, sesame region

    3 Middle and lower Yangtze Plain rice, cotton, silk, hemp, and fish regions
      (1) Lower plain rice, cotton, silk, jute, and fish region
      (2) Central Anhwei and P'o-yang Hu Plain double-cropping rice, wheat, and fish region
      (3) Tung-t'ing Plain double-cropping rice, cotton, ramie, and fish region
    4 Chiang-nan rice, tea, and commercial forest regions
      (1) Anhwei-Chekiang-Kiangsi border rice, tea, and forestry region
      (2) Central south Kiangsi rice, tea-oil, and forestry region
      (3) Hunan-Kiangsi-Hupeh border double-cropping rice, tea, and ramie region
      (4) Hunan (south central) rice, sweet potatoes, tea, and tea-oil region
    5 Chekiang-Fukien hills rice, tea, fruit, and timber regions
      (1) Chekiang-Fukien coastlands region of double-cropping rice, tea, oranges, fish, and forestry
      (2) Fukien (western hills) rice and forestry region
    6 Nan Ling hills rice, tea oil, and forestry regions
      (1) Northern Nan Ling rice, tea-oil, and forestry regions
      (2) Southern Nan Ling double-cropping rice and subtropical fruit region

  B Southwestern highlands and basins double-cropping wet-field agriculture and forestry regions
    1 Upper Han Shui maize, wheat, forestry regions
      (1) Southern Tsinling maize, winter wheat, and forestry region
      (2) Ta-pa Shan maize, winter wheat, and forestry region
      (3) Pai-lung Chiang maize, winter wheat, and livestock region
    2 Szechwan-Hupeh-Hunan-Kweichow border rice, maize, and forestry regions
      (1) Yangtze and southwestern Hupeh maize and forestry region
      (2) Southeastern Szechwan and eastern Kweichow rice, maize, tung oil, and forestry region
      (3) Western Hunan rice, tung oil, and forestry region
    3 Szechwan Basin rice, sugar cane, tung oil, and pig-rearing regions
      (1) Ch'eng-tu Plain rice, rapeseed, and tobacco region
      (2) Southern Szechwan double-cropping rice, sugar cane, pig-rearing, and citrus region
      (3) Northern Szechwan rice, sweet potatoes, and silk region
      (4) Eastern Szechwan rice, maize, and tung oil region
    4 Kweichow Plateau rice, maize, and forestry regions

(1) Central Kweichow rice, tobacco, and forestry region

(2) Western Kweichow-northeast Yunnan maize and livestock region

(3) Kweichow-Kwangsi-Yunnan border rice, maize, and forestry region

5 Yunnan Plateau rice, maize, and forestry regions

(1) Eastern Yunnan rice and tobacco region

(2) Chin-sha Chiang (upper Yangtze) rice and forestry region

(3) Western Yunnan rice, wheat, and forestry region

6 Ta-liang Shan maize, forestry, and livestock region

C South China treble-cropping wet-field and tropical tree-crop regions

1 Taiwan (see Map III-65)

2 Fukien-Kwangtung coast rice, sugar cane, tropical and subtropical fruits and fisheries regions

(1) Southern Fukien rice, sugar cane, tea, fruit, and fisheries region

(2) Eastern Kwangtung rice, sugar cane, fruit, and fisheries region

(3) Central Kwangtung rice, sugar cane, silk, fruit, and fisheries region

3 Kwangtung-Kwangsi lowlands rice, maize, and tropical tree-crops regions

(1) Kwangtung-Kwangsi rice, sugar cane, and tropical tree-crops region

(2) South central Kwangsi rice, maize, and tropical tree-crops region

(3) Yunnan-Kwangsi border maize, rice, cattle, and tree-crops, and fisheries region

4 Western Kwangtung-Hainan rice, sugar cane, tropical crops, and fisheries regions

(1) Western Kwangtung rice, sweet potatoes, sugar cane, tropical crops, and fisheries region

(2) Northern Hainan rice, sweet potatoes, tropical tree-crops, and fisheries region

(3) Southern Hainan rice, sweet potatoes, tropical tree-crops, and fisheries region

5 Southern Yunnan rice, maize, and tropical crops regions

(1) Southern Yunnan rice, maize, tea, and tropical crops regions

(2) Hsi-shuang-Pan-na T'ai Autonomous District rice and tropical crops region

3 Northwestern Arid and Irrigated Agricultural and Pastoral Regions

A Inner Mongolia–Ningsia–Ho-hsi one-crop-yearly irrigated agriculture and pastoral regions

1 Central and western Inner Mongolia spring wheat, millet, and arid pastoral regions

(1) Siwu Desert nomadic region

(2) Pao-t'ou spring wheat, millet, and sugar beet region

(3) Western Ordos settled pastoral region

2 Ningsia-Ho-hsi spring wheat, rice, irrigated agricultural regions

(1) Ningsia Plain wheat, rye, and sheep region

(2) Ho-hsi corridor spring wheat and rye region

3 Ala Shan Desert camel-rearing nomadic region

B Northern Sinkiang-Tien Shan one-crop-yearly irrigated agriculture and upland grazing region

1 Altai spring wheat agricultural and pastoral regions

2 Northern Tien Shan spring and winter wheat, cotton, and pastoral regions

3 Tien Shan spring wheat and upland grazing regions

C Southern Sinkiang multiple-cropping irrigated agricultural regions

1 Tun-huang-Yü-men wheat and cotton region

2 Turfan-Ha-mi spring wheat, cotton, melons, and other fruit region

3 Southern Tien Shan spring and winter wheat, maize, and cotton regions

4 Northern Karakoram wheat, maize, and cotton regions

4 Tsinghai-Tibet High Cold Agricultural and Pastoral Regions

A Northern Tibet high cold pastoral regions

1 Ch'iang-t'ang cold desert nomadic pastoral region

2 Northern Tibet pastoral region

3 Ari River Valley barley and goats region

B Tsinghai-Tibetan Plateau mixed agricultural and pastoral regions

1 Valleys of southern Tibet barley and rapeseed regions

2 Northeastern uplands of Tibet barley, potatoes, and goats region

3 Upper valley of Yellow River yaks and barley region

4 Ch'i-lien Shan-mo and Koko Nor lake district barley and sheep region

5 Tsaidam Basin spring wheat and sheep region

C Southeastern Tibetan Plateau warmer and humid agricultural and forestry regions

1 Southeastern semitropical agricultural and forestry region

2 Chamdo-Szechwan border maize, wheat, barley, forestry, and pastoral region

Indexes

INDEX FOR PHYSICAL (I), CULTURAL (II), AND REGIONAL (III) SECTIONS

(Many of these places appear on more than one map; the location given is the most apparent for easiest reference.)

Place Name	Location: Lat. (° 'N.)	Long. (° 'E.)	Map Number
A-erh-shan	47 13	119 59	III-110
A-ho-ch'i	40 50	78 01	III-116
Ai-hui	50 16	127 28	III-101
A-k'o-su	41 09	80 15	II-13
Ala Shan	39 00	105 00	I-2
A-le-t'ai	47 52	88 07	I-17
A-li Shan	23 15	120 40	III-60
Altai Mountains	48 00	89 00	I-2
Amoy	24 27	118 05	III-53
Amur River	50 00	127 00	I-2
An-ch'ing	30 31	117 02	III-26
An-hsi	40 30	96 00	III-12
Anhwei	32 00	117 00	III-26
An-k'ang	32 42	109 12	III-12
An-lung	25 06	105 31	III-86
An-shan	41 07	122 57	II-37
An-shun	26 15	105 56	III-86
An-ta	46 24	125 19	III-101
An-yang	36 05	114 21	I-17
A-pa	32 55	101 42	III-40
A-pa-ha-na-erh-ch'i	43 58	116 02	II-13
Brahmaputra River	30 00	89 00	I-2
Canton	23 07	113 15	I-17
Cha-hsi-kang	32 32	79 41	III-125
Chan-chiang	21 12	110 23	III-78
Chang-chia-k'ou	40 50	114 56	II-13
Ch'ang-chiang	19 19	108 43	III-78
Ch'ang-chih	36 11	113 06	III-3
Chang-chou	24 31	117 40	III-53
Ch'ang-ch'un	43 52	125 21	I-17
Chang-hua	24 05	120 32	III-68
Ch'ang-pai Shan	42 00	128 00	I-2
Ch'ang-sha	28 12	112 58	I-17
Ch'ang-te	29 02	111 41	III-33
Ch'ang-tu	31 10	97 14	III-125
Chang-yeh	38 56	100 37	III-12
Chan-i	25 36	103 49	III-86
Ch'ao-an	23 41	116 38	III-78
Chao-hsien	31 36	117 52	III-26
Ch'ao Hu	32 00	117 00	I-2
Chao-su	43 10	81 07	III-116
Ch'ao-yang	41 33	120 25	II-13
Charkhlik (*see* Jo-ch'iang)			
Cha-ta	31 32	79 50	III-125
Chefoo	37 32	121 24	III-3
Chekiang	28 30	120 00	III-53
Chen-chiang	32 13	119 26	III-26
Cheng-chou	34 45	113 40	III-3
Ch'eng-te	40 58	117 53	III-3
Ch'eng-tu	30 40	104 04	I-17
Ch'eng-tu Plain	31 00	104 00	I-2

Place Name	Lat. (°'N.)	Long. (°'E.)	Map Number
Ch'eng-tzu-t'uan	39 30	122 30	III-101
Ch'en-hsien	25 48	113 02	III-33
Chia-hsing	30 46	120 45	III-26
Chia-i	23 29	120 27	III-69
Chia-li	19 42	109 39	III-78
Chia-ling Chiang	32 00	106 00	I-2
Chia-mu-ssu	46 50	130 21	II-13
Chi-an	27 08	115 00	III-33
Chi-an	41 06	126 10	III-101
Chiang-ling	30 21	112 11	II-13
Chiang-men	22 35	113 05	III-78
Chiang-tzu	28 57	89 38	III-125
Chiang-yu	31 47	104 45	III-40
Chiao-tso	35 15	111 13	III-3
Ch'i-chiao-ching	43 28	91 36	III-116
Ch'i-ch'i-ha-erh	47 22	123 57	III-101
Ch'ieh-mo	38 08	85 32	I-17
Ch'ien-chiang	29 31	108 46	III-40
Chien-ou	27 03	118 19	III-53
Ch'ien-t'ang Chiang	30 00	118 00	I-2
Ch'ih-feng	42 17	118 53	I-17
Chihli, Gulf of	39 00	120 00	I-2
Chi-hsi	45 18	130 58	III-101
Chi-lai Shan	24 00	121 25	III-60
Ch'i-lien Shan-mo	39 00	98 00	I-2
Chi-lung	25 08	121 45	III-68
Chi-mu-nai	47 32	85 38	III-116
Chi-nan	36 40	117 00	II-13
Chin-chou	41 07	121 06	II-10
Ch'ing-chiang	28 05	115 31	III-33
Ch'ing-chiang	33 35	119 02	II-13
Ching-chou (see Chiang-ling)			
Ch'ing Hai (see Koko Nor)			
Ching Ho	36 00	108 00	I-2
Ching-ho	44 39	82 50	I-17
Ching-hsi	23 08	106 25	III-78
Ching-hsien	30 42	118 23	II-13
Ching-po Hu	43 30	128 30	III-102
Ching-te-chen	29 16	117 11	III-33
Ch'ing-yang	36 05	107 40	III-12
Chin-hsi	40 45	120 50	III-101
Chin-hua	29 07	119 39	III-53
Ch'in-huang-tao	39 56	119 37	III-3
Chi-ning	35 24	116 33	III-3
Chi-ning	40 57	113 02	III-110
Chin-kua-shih	25 10	121 50	III-68
Chin-sha Chiang	30 00	99 00	I-2
Chin-t'a	40 05	99 00	III-18
Chin-t'ang	30 51	104 57	III-40
Ch'i-t'ai	44 01	89 28	III-116
Chiu-chiang	29 44	115 59	III-33
Chiu-ch'üan	39 46	98 34	III-12
Chiung-lai Shan	32 00	102 00	I-44
Chomolungma, Mount (see Everest, Mount)			
Ch'üan-chou	24 54	118 35	III-53
Chu-chou	27 50	113 09	III-33
Chu-ma-tien	32 58	114 03	III-3
Chungking	29 34	106 35	I-17
Ch'ung-ming Island	31 36	121 33	III-26
Chung-wei	37 30	105 09	III-12
Chung-yang Shan-mo	23 30	121 15	III-60
Chu-yun-kuan	40 18	116 08	III-3
Dairen	38 55	121 39	III-101
Dzungarian Basin	45 00	87 00	I-2
East China Sea	29 00	124 00	I-2
En-shih	30 18	109 29	III-33
Erh-lien	43 45	112 02	III-110
Erh-shui	23 50	120 35	III-70
Everest, Mount	28 00	87 00	I-2
Feng-feng	36 28	114 12	III-3
Feng-hsien	33 55	106 32	II-8
Fen Ho	35 00	111 00	I-2
Foochow	26 05	119 18	I-17
Formosa Strait	24 00	119 00	I-2
Fo-shan	23 02	113 07	III-78
Fou-yang	32 57	115 51	III-26
Fu-an	27 04	119 37	III-53
Fu-chin	47 16	132 01	III-101
Fu-hsien	39 38	122 00	III-101
Fu-hsin	42 06	121 46	III-101
Fukien	26 00	117 00	III-53
Fukien Massif	26 00	118 00	I-2
Fu-la-erh-chi	47 15	123 40	III-101
Fu-shun	41 52	123 53	II-37
Fu-yang	32 57	115 51	II-13
Fu-yüan	47 40	132 30	III-101
Gobi Desert	42 00	108 00	I-2
Great Himalaya Range	28 00	86 00	I-2
Greater Khingan Range	48 00	121 00	I-2
Hai-an	20 16	110 13	III-78
Hai Ho	39 00	115 00	I-2
Hai-k'ou	20 03	110 19	III-78
Hailar	49 12	119 42	I-17
Hai-lun	47 27	126 56	III-101
Hai-men	28 41	121 27	III-53
Hainan	19 00	110 00	I-2
Hai-yen	36 58	100 50	III-12
Ha-mi	42 48	93 27	I-17
Han Chiang	26 00	117 00	I-2
Han-chung	33 08	107 02	III-12
Han-chung Basin	33 00	108 00	I-2
Hangchow	30 15	120 10	II-13
Hangchow Bay	30 00	122 00	I-2
Hankow	30 35	114 16	III-33
Hanoi	21 04	105 50	II-13
Han Shui	33 00	111 00	I-2
Han-tan	36 35	114 29	III-3
Han-yang	30 35	114 02	III-33
Harbin	45 45	126 39	I-17
Hei-lung Chiang (see Amur)			
Heilungkiang	50 00	130 00	III-101
Heng-tuan Mountains	27 00	99 00	I-2
Heng-yang	26 58	112 21	III-33
Ho Chiang	23 30	111 30	III-52
Ho-ch'ih	24 42	108 02	III-52
Ho-fei	31 51	117 17	II-13
Ho-kang	47 05	130 20	III-101
Ho-k'ou	22 36	103 58	III-86
Honan	34 00	112 00	III-3
Hopeh	40 00	118 00	III-3
Ho-p'u	21 41	109 09	III-78
Ho-t'ien	37 07	79 55	I-17
Ho-yüan	23 44	114 41	III-78

Place Name	Lat. (°N.)	Long. (°E.)	Map Number	Place Name	Lat. (°N.)	Long. (°E.)	Map Number
Hsia-kuan	25 34	100 14	III-86	K'an-chu-erh-miao	48 22	118 07	III-110
Hsiang Chiang	27 00	112 00	I-2	K'ang-ting	30 03	112 02	I-17
Hsiang-fan	32 03	112 05	II-13	Kansu	37 00	103 00	III-12
Hsiang-t'an	27 51	112 54	III-33	Kansu Corridor	40 00	101 00	I-2
Hsia-tung	40 50	95 57	III-12	Kan-tzu	31 38	100 01	III-40
Hsi-ch'ang	27 53	102 18	III-40	Kao-hsiung	22 37	120 17	III-69
Hsi Chiang	23 00	112 00	I-2	Kao-pao Hu	33 00	120 00	I-2
Hsien-yang	34 22	108 42	III-12	Kao-t'ai	39 20	99 58	III-18
Hsi-kuei-t'u-ch'i	49 17	120 44	I-44	Kara Irtish (see			
Hsi-liao Ho	44 00	119 00	I-2	O-erh-ch'i-ssu Ho)			
Hsi-lin-hoa-t'e (see				Karamai	45 30	84 55	II-13
A-pa-ha-na-erh-ch'i)				K'a-shih	39 29	75 58	II-13
Hsin-chu	24 48	120 58	III-68	Khotan (see Ho-t'ien)			
Hsing-an	25 37	110 40	III-78	Kiangsi	27 30	116 00	III-33
Hsing-hai	35 50	99 59	I-4	Kiangsu	33 00	120 00	III-26
Hsin-hsiang	35 19	113 52	III-3	Kirin	43 51	126 33	II-10
Hsi-ning	36 37	101 46	I-17	Kirin	45 00	121 00	III-101
Hsin-kao Shan	23 35	120 55	III-60	Ko-chiu	23 23	103 09	II-86
Hsin-t'ai	35 54	117 44	III-3	K'o-erh-ch'in-yu-i-ch'ien-	46 05	122 05	III-110
Hsin-yang	32 03	114 05	III-3	ch'i			
Hsin-ying	23 20	120 20	III-68	Ko-erh-mu	36 22	94 55	I-4
Hsüan-hua	40 38	115 06	III-3	Koko Nor	38 00	101 00	I-2
Hsüan-wei	26 16	104 01	III-86	K'o-shan	48 04	125 54	III-101
Hsü-ch'ang	34 01	113 49	III-3	Kowloon	22 28	114 20	III-78
Huai-an	33 31	119 08	III-26	Kuang-chou (see Canton)			
Huai Ho	33 00	117 00	I-2	Kuang-hua	32 22	111 40	III-33
Huai-nan	32 40	117 00	III-26	Kuang-yüan	32 26	105 52	III-40
Hua-lien	23 59	121 36	III-68	Kuan-hsien	31 00	103 37	III-40
Huang Ho (see Yellow River)				Kuan Shan	23 10	121 05	III-60
Huang-liu	18 30	108 46	III-78	K'u-ch'e	41 43	82 54	I-17
Huang Shan	30 00	117 00	I-2	Kuei Chiang	23 28	111 18	III-52
Huang-shih	30 13	115 06	III-33	Kuei-lin	25 17	110 17	I-17
Hu-ho-hao-t'e	40 47	111 37	I-17	Kuei-te	36 03	101 28	III-19
Hui-li	26 41	102 15	III-40	Kuei-yang	26 53	106 43	I-17
Hu-lin	45 48	132 59	III-101	K'u-lu-k'o Shan-mo	42 00	88 00	III-121
Hu-lu-tao	40 43	121 00	III-101	Kunlun Mountains	36 00	86 00	I-2
Hunan	27 30	111 00	III-33	K'un-ming	25 04	102 41	I-17
Hung-shui Ho	25 00	107 00	I-2	K'u-shui	42 03	94 35	III-116
Hung-tse Hu	34 00	119 00	I-2	Kwangsi Chuang	22 30	109 00	III-78
Hupeh	31 00	113 00	III-33	Autonomous Region			
I-ch'ang	30 42	111 17	I-17	Kwangtung	24 00	114 00	III-78
I-ch'un	47 42	128 54	III-101	Kweichow	26 00	107 00	III-86
I-erh-hsieh	47 18	119 45	I-17	Lan-chou	36 03	103 41	I-17
I-hsien	41 32	121 15	III-101	Lan-ts'ang Chiang			
I-lan	24 46	121 45	III-70	(see Mekong)			
I-liang	27 35	104 01	III-86	Lat-zu	29 10	87 45	III-125
I-li Basin	44 00	82 00	I-2	Lei-yang	26 25	112 51	III-33
I-ning	44 00	81 40	I-17	Leng-hu	38 57	93 25	III-12
Inner Mongolian	45 00	119 00	III-110	Lesser Khingan Range	49 00	127 00	I-2
Autonomous Region				Lhasa	29 39	91 06	I-17
I-pin	28 46	104 34	I-17	Liao Ho	42 00	123 00	I-2
I-ping-lang	25 06	101 53	III-86	Liaoning	42 00	118 00	III-101
I-t'u-li-ho	50 44	121 56	III-110	Liaotung Peninsula	40 00	122 00	I-2
I-yang	28 36	112 20	III-33	Liao-yang	41 17	123 11	III-101
Jih-k'a-tse	29 15	88 53	III-125	Liao-yüan	42 55	125 09	III-101
Jih-t'u	33 27	79 42	III-125	Li-chiang	26 48	100 16	III-86
Jo-ch'iang	39 02	88 00	III-116	Lien-yün-chiang	34 43	119 27	III-26
Ka-erh	31 45	80 22	III-125	Lien-yün-chiang-shih	34 36	119 13	III-26
K'ai-feng	34 51	114 21	I-17	Lin-chiang	41 44	126 55	III-101
K'ai-yuan	42 32	124 01	III-101	Lin-ch'uan	28 01	116 20	III-33
Kan Chiang	27 00	115 00	I-2	Lin-fen	36 05	111 32	II-13
Kan-chou	25 51	114 56	I-17	Lin-hsi	43 31	118 02	III-110

Place Name	Lat. (°N.)	Long. (°E.)	Map Number	Place Name	Lat. (°N.)	Long. (°E.)	Map Number
Lin-hsia	35 28	102 55	III-12	Ning-ming	22 12	107 05	III-78
Li-t'ang	23 12	109 08	III-78	Ning-po	29 53	121 33	III-26
Liu-chia	35 30	102 55	III-19	Ningsia Oasis	38 00	106 00	I-2
Liu Chiang	23 48	109 31	III-52	North China Plain	35 00	116 00	I-2
Liu-chou	24 19	109 24	III-78	Nu Chiang (see Salween)			
Liu-p'an Shan	36 00	106 00	I-2	O-erh-ch'i-ssu Ho	47 00	87 00	I-2
Loess Plateau	37 00	110 00	I-2	O-mei Shan	29 00	102 00	I-2
Lo Ho	36 00	110 00	I-2	Ordos Desert	39 00	109 00	I-2
Lo-ho	33 14	114 02	III-3	Ou Chiang	28 00	120 00	I-2
Lop Nor	40 00	90 00	I-2	Ou-p'u	52 47	126 01	III-101
Lo-shan	29 34	103 44	III-40	Pa-ch'u	39 46	78 15	I-17
Lo-tung	24 40	121 45	III-69	Pai-ch'eng	45 37	122 49	III-101
Lo-yang	34 41	112 48	III-3	Pai-se	23 54	106 37	III-78
Luan Ho	41 00	118 00	I-2	Pai-t'ou Shan	42 00	128 03	III-102
Lu-chou	28 53	105 23	III-40	Pai-yün-o-po	41 46	109 58	III-110
Lu-feng	22 57	115 38	III-78	Pa-li-k'un	43 52	92 51	I-17
Luichow Peninsula	21 00	110 00	I-2	Pamir Mountains	38 00	74 00	I-2
Lung Chiang	21 18	105 25	III-52	Pang-pu	32 57	117 21	III-26
Lung-k'ou	37 38	120 18	III-3	P'an-hsien	25 46	104 39	III-52
Lü-shun	38 48	121 16	III-101	Pao-an	22 32	114 08	III-78
Lü-ta (see Dairen)				Pao-chi	34 21	101 23	II-8
Ma-an-shan	31 44	118 28	III-26	Pao-shan	25 07	99 09	III-86
Ma-lung	25 18	103 20	III-86	Pao-ting	38 52	115 20	III-3
Ma-na-ssu	44 18	86 13	III-116	Pao-t'ou	40 36	110 03	I-17
Man-chou-li	49 36	117 26	I-17	Pa-t'ang	30 00	99 00	III-40
Manchurian Plain	46 00	125 00	I-2	Pa-tung	31 02	110 20	III-33
Mandalay	22 00	96 08	II-13	Pa-yen-k'a-la Shan	35 00	98 00	I-2
Mang-yai	37 50	91 38	III-12	Pearl (Delta)	22 00	114 00	I-2
Mao-ming	21 39	110 54	III-78	Pei-an	48 16	126 36	III-101
Mei-hsien	24 18	116 07	III-78	Pei Chiang	24 00	113 00	I-2
Mekong	30 00	98 00	I-2	Pei-hai	21 29	109 06	III-78
Meng-tzu	23 22	103 24	III-86	Pei-li	19 09	108 40	III-78
Miao-li	24 33	120 49	III-68	Pei-p'an Chiang	25 07	106 01	III-52
Mien-yang	31 28	104 46	III-40	Pei-p'iao	41 48	120 44	III-101
Min Chiang	29 00	104 00	I 2	Peking	39 56	116 24	I-17
Min Chiang	27 00	118 00	I-2	Pen-ch'i	41 17	124 07	III-101
Min-ch'in	38 42	103 11	III-12	P'eng-hu	23 30	119 40	III-58
Min-lo	38 26	100 54	III-18	P'eng-shan	30 14	103 53	III-40
Mukden (see Shen-yang)				Pi-chieh	27 18	105 16	III-86
Mu-tan Chiang	45 00	130 00	I-2	P'ing-hsiang	22 06	106 44	III-78
Mu-tan-chiang	44 35	129 36	II-10	P'ing-hsiang	27 37	113 51	III-33
Na-ch'ü	31 30	92 00	III-125	P'ing-liang	35 32	106 41	III-12
Na-mu Hu	31 00	90 00	I-2	P'ing-lo	38 56	106 34	III-12
Nan-ch'a	47 08	129 16	III-101	P'ing-ting-shan	33 44	113 18	III-3
Nan-ch'ang	28 33	115 56	I-17	P'ing-tung	22 41	120 29	III-69
Nan-ch'ung	30 48	106 04	II-13	Po Hai (see Chihli, Gulf of)			
Nan-hu-ta Shan	24 20	121 35	III-60	Po-ko-to Shan	43 15	89 00	I-44
Nanking	32 03	118 47	I-17	Port Arthur (see Lü-shun)			
Nankow Pass (see Chu-yun-kuan)				Po-shan	36 29	117 50	III-3
Nan Ling	26 00	111 00	I-2	P'o-yang Hu	29 00	117 00	I-2
Nan-ning	22 49	108 19	I-17	P'u-erh	23 05	101 03	III-86
Nan-p'ing	26 38	118 10	I-17	P'u-lan	30 15	81 10	III-125
Nan Shan	39 00	96 00	I-2	P'yŏngyang	39 03	125 48	II-13
Nan-tan	24 59	107 32	III-78	Red River	24 00	102 00	I-2
Nan-t'ou	23 50	120 50	III-58	Salween River			
Nan-t'ung	32 06	121 05	III-26	San-men-hsia	34 50	111 05	III-3
Nan-yang	33 00	112 32	I-17	San-sui	26 58	108 41	III-86
Nei-chiang	29 35	105 03	III-40	Shang-ch'iu	34 23	115 37	III-3
Nen Chiang	50 00	125 00	I-2	Shanghai	31 07	121 22	I-17
Nien-ch'ing-t'ang-ku-la Shan	30 00	89 00	I-2	Shang-shui	33 38	114 38	III-3
				Shan-hai-kuan	40 01	119 44	III-3

Place Name	Location: Lat. (°N.)	Long. (°E.)	Map Number	Place Name	Location: Lat. (°N.)	Long. (°E.)	Map Number
Shansi	37 00	112 00	III-3	T'ang-ku-la Shan-mo	33 00	92 00	I-2
Shansi Plateau	38 00	112 00	I-2	T'ang-shan	39 38	118 11	III-3
Shan-tan	38 45	101 15	III-18	T'ao-an	45 20	122 47	III-101
Shantung	36 00	119 00	III-3	Tao-liu	23 42	120 32	III-68
Shantung Peninsula	37 00	121 00	I-2	T'ao-yüan	25 00	121 10	III-58
Shao-hsing	30 00	121 35	III-26	Ta-pa Shan	32 00	109 00	I-2
Shao-kuan	24 48	113 35	III-78	Ta-pieh Shan	32 00	115 00	I-2
Shao-wu	27 18	117 30	III-53	Tarim River	41 00	81 00	I-2
Shao-yang	27 00	111 12	I-17	Tarim Basin	39 00	83 00	I-2
Sha-shih	30 19	112 14	III-33	T'a-shih-k'u-erh-kan	37 47	75 14	III-116
Sha-shih Reservoir	39 19	112 14	I-2	Tash Kurgan (see T'a-shih-k'u-erh-kan)			
She-hsien	29 52	118 26	III-26	Ta-t'ung	36 56	101 40	III-12
Shensi	33 00	108 00	III-12	Ta-t'ung	40 05	113 18	I-17
Shen-yang	41 48	123 27	I-17	Ta-yao Shan	24 00	110 00	III-52
Shih-chia-chuang	38 03	114 29	III-3	Ta-yeh	30 05	114 57	III-33
Shih-ch'üan-ho	32 30	79 46	III-125	Te-chou	37 27	116 18	III-3
Shih-p'ing	24 43	102 30	III-86	T'e-la-to-mu	29 39	84 10	III-125
Shuang-ch'eng-tzu	40 26	99 58	III-110	T'eng-ch'ung	25 02	98 28	III-86
Shuang-ya-shan	46 40	131 21	III-101	Teng-k'ou	40 18	106 59	III-110
Shu-yang	34 07	118 45	III-26	Tengri Nor (see Na-mu Hu)			
Sian	34 16	108 54	I-17	Tibetan Autonomous Region	33 00	86 00	III-125
Sinkiang Uighur Autonomous Region	30 00	84 00	III-116	Tien Ch'ih	25 00	103 00	I-2
So-ch'e	38 24	77 15	I-17	Tien Shan	43 00	83 00	I-2
Soochow	31 18	120 37	III-26	T'ien-shui	34 38	105 45	III-12
South China Sea	21 00	114 00	I-2	Tien-tsang Shan	25 00	102 00	I-44
Ssu-p'ing	43 10	124 20	III-101	Tientsin	39 08	117 12	II-13
Su-ao	20 35	121 50	III-68	T'ien-tung	23 36	107 08	III-78
Süchow	34 16	117 11	III-26	Ting-hsin	40 21	99 42	III-18
Sui-fen-ho	44 24	131 10	III-101	Ting-jih	28 34	86 38	III-125
Sui-hua	46 39	126 59	III-101	T'o-k'o-hsün	42 47	88 38	III-116
Sui-ning	30 32	105 32	III-40	T'o-li	45 47	83 37	III-116
Sui-te	37 32	110 12	III-12	To-lun	42 10	116 25	III-110
Sungari River	46 00	128 00	I-2	Tonkin, Gulf of	21 00	108 00	I-2
Sung-p'an	32 36	103 36	I-17	Tsaidam Basin	37 00	94 00	I-2
Sun-moon Lake	23 45	120 55	III-60	Ts'ang-chou	38 19	116 52	III-3
Swatow	23 22	116 40	III-78	Tse-tang	29 16	91 46	III-125
Szechwan	31 00	102 00	III-40	Tsinan	36 40	117 00	I-17
Szechwan Basin	30 00	105 00	I-2	Tsinghai	35 00	95 00	III-12
Ta-chai	37 40	113 39	III-3	Tsingtao	36 04	120 19	I-17
Ta-ch'ai-tan	37 50	95 18	III-12	Tsinling Shan	34 00	109 00	I-2
T'a-ch'eng	46 45	82 57	III-116	Tsun-i	27 33	106 50	III-86
Ta-ch'ing	46 10	126 18	III-101	Tu-lan	36 10	98 16	I-17
Ta-hsien	31 16	107 31	I-17	T'u-lu-fan	42 56	89 10	I-17
Ta-hsüeh Shan	30 00	102 00	I-2	Tumen River	43 00	130 00	I-2
T'ai-chung	24 10	120 40	III-69	T'u-men	42 58	129 49	III-101
T'ai-chung Basin	24 00	121 40	III-60	Tung Chiang	24 00	115 00	I-2
T'ai-hang Shan	36 00	114 00	I-2	T'ung-chiang	47 40	132 30	III-101
T'ai Hu	32 00	120 00	I-2	T'ung-ch'uan	35 05	109 05	III-12
T'ai-nan	22 59	120 12	III-68	Tung-fang	19 06	108 37	III-78
Taipei	25 02	121 30	III-68	T'ung-hua	41 41	125 55	III-101
Tai-pei Basin	25 05	121 25	III-60	T'ung-kuan	34 36	110 15	III-12
T'ai Shan	37 00	118 00	I-2	T'ung-liao	43 37	122 16	I-17
T'ai-shan	22 15	112 47	III-78	Tung-sheng	39 49	109 59	II-13
T'ai-tung	22 45	121 09	III-68	Tung-t'ing Hu	30 00	112 00	I-2
T'ai-tung Rift Valley	23 20	121 20	III-60	Tun-huang	30 10	94 50	III-12
Taiwan	23 00	122 00	I-2	Turfan (see T'u-lu-fan)			
T'ai-yüan	37 46	112 30	I-17	Turfan Depression	42 00	90 00	I-2
Takla Makan Desert	38 00	83 00	I-2	Tu-shan-tzu	44 20	84 51	III-116
Ta-li	28 30	98 20	I-17	Tu-yün	26 16	107 31	III-86
Ta-lo	21 42	100 03	III-86	Tzu-kao Shan	24 20	121 10	III-60
T'ang-ku	39 01	117 40	III-3				

Place Name	Lat. (°N.)	Long. (°E.)	Map Number
Tzu-kung	20 24	104 47	III-40
Tzu-po	36 48	118 93	III-3
Urumchi	43 48	87 35	I-17
Ussuri River	46 00	133 00	I-2
Wan-hsien	30 49	108 24	III-40
Wan-t'ing	24 05	98 04	III-86
Wei-fang	36 43	119 06	III-3
Wei-hai	37 30	122 06	III-3
Wei Ho	34 00	108 00	I-2
Wenchow	28 01	120 39	I-17
Wen-shan	23 22	104 14	III-86
Whampoa	23 06	113 26	III-78
Wu-ch'ang	30 21	114 10	III-33
Wuchow	23 29	111 19	III-78
Wu-chung	38 00	106 10	III-12
Wu-han	30 35	114 16	I-17
Wu-ho	33 08	117 54	I-34
Wu-hsi	31 35	120 18	III-26
Wu-hu	31 21	118 22	III-26
Wu-i Shan	27 00	116 00	I-2
Wu-lan-hao-t'e	46 05	122 05	III-110
Wu-liang Shan	24 00	101 00	I-2
Wu-lung Shan	40 47	117 30	I-44
Wu-lun-ku Ho	47 00	89 00	I-2
Wu Shan	32 00	110 00	I-2
Wu-shan	31 02	109 56	III-25
Wu-su	44 27	84 37	III-116
Wu-wei	37 58	102 48	I-17
Wu-yüan	41 06	108 16	III-110
Wu-yün	49 17	129 40	III-101
Ya-an	29 59	103 05	III-40
Ya-k'o-shih (see Hsi-kuei-t'u-ch'i)			
Yalu River	41 00	126 00	I-2

Place Name	Lat. (°N.)	Long. (°E.)	Map Number
Ya-lung Chiang	30 00	101 00	I-2
Yang-chiang	21 51	111 58	III-78
Yang-chou	32 24	119 26	III-26
Yang-ch'üan	37 54	113 36	III-3
Yangtze River	31 00	112 00	I-2
Ya-tung	27 29	88 54	I-17
Yeh-ch'eng	37 54	77 26	III-116
Yellow River	35 00	112 00	I-2
Yellow Sea	35 00	123 00	I-2
Yen-an	36 38	109 27	II-13
Yen-ch'ang	36 31	110 08	III-12
Yen-ch'eng	33 23	120 08	II-13
Yen-chi	42 53	129 31	III-101
Yen-ch'i	42 04	86 34	III-116
Yen-chou	35 33	116 50	III-3
Yen-t'ai (see Chefoo)			
Yin-ch'uan	38 28	106 19	II-13
Ying-k'ou	40 38	122 30	III-101
Ying-t'an	28 14	110 00	III-33
Yin-shan Shan-mo	41 00	110 00	I-2
Yüan Chiang	29 00	111 00	I-2
Yüan-ling	28 27	110 23	III-33
Yu Chiang	24 00	107 00	I-2
Yüeh-yang	29 23	113 06	III-33
Yü-lin	18 14	109 30	III-78
Yü-lin	38 18	109 45	III-12
Yü-men	39 50	97 44	II-13
Yung-an	25 58	117 22	III-53
Yün-lin	23 40	120 20	III-58
Yunnan	24 00	102 00	III-86
Yunnan-Kweichow Plateau			
Yü-tu	25 57	115 16	III-33
Yü-tz'u	37 42	112 44	III-3

INDEX FOR HISTORICAL (IV) SECTION

In the indexing of the Historical Section of *The Atlas of China* hypens, apostrophes, and commas do not influence the order in alphabetizing, e.g., Hai Ho is after Hai-an. However, it two words are spelled exactly alike except for such a punctuation mark, then the one without the mark will precede the one with it, e.g., Ching Ho precedes Ching-ho. Place names with identical spelling are listed in the index in chronological order, e.g., Ch'ang-sha of the Ch'in dynasty precedes Ch'ang-sha of the contemporary period. In some cases the locations may be exactly the same, while in other cases, there may be some distance between the sites. All place names noted on maps of the post Ch'ing period (after 1911) have a blank entry under the column "Dynasty/Period" in the index which means that they are contemporary sites and may be found in the index to the other sections of *The Atlas of China* as well. A word in parentheses is ignored in alphabetizing unless it is an integral part of the name being alphabetized, e.g., (Ching-)hu-nan is listed under the C's.

Place Name	Lat. (°N.)	Long. (°E.)	Map Number	Dynasty/ Period
Alashan	40 00	102 00	IV-18	n
Amalik	45 00	81 00	IV-14	i
Amoy	24 47	118 05	IV-26	
An-ch'ing	31 00	117 00	IV-18	n
An-hsi	41 00	83 00	IV-11	i
An-hui	32 00	118 00	IV-18	n
Anhwei	31 00	117 00	IV-27	
An-k'ang	32 42	109 12	IV-26	
An-nan	21 00	105 00	IV-11	i
An-pei	47 00	103 00	IV-11	i

Key for Dynasty/Period

Ch'un-ch'iu	a	Sui	h
Contending States	b	T'ang	i
Ch'in	c	Five Dynasties	j
Han	d	Sung and Chin	k
Three Kingdoms	e	Yuan	l
Tsin	f	Ming	m
North and South Dynasty	g	Ch'ing	n

Place Name	Lat. (°N.)	Long. (°E.)	Map Number	Dynasty/ Period
Canton	23 07	113 15	IV-27	
Ch'ang-an	34 00	109 00	IV-10	i
Ch'ang-ch'un	43 52	125 21	IV-27	
Ch'ang-sha	28 00	113 00	IV-4	e
Ch'ang-sha	28 00	113 00	IV-18	n
Ch'ang-sha	28 12	112 58	IV-27	
Chao	39 00	113 00	IV-3	b
Chao-ko (An-yang)	36 00	116 00	IV-2	a
Che-chiang	29 00	120 00	IV-17	m
Che-chiang	29 00	120 00	IV-18	n
Chekiang	29 00	120 00	IV-27	
Cheng	34 00	115 00	IV-2	a
Cheng-chou	34 45	113 40	IV-27	
Ch'eng Han (I-chou)	29 00	106 00	IV-7	f
Ch'eng-tu	31 00	104 00	IV-10	i
Ch'eng-tu	31 00	104 00	IV-15	i
Ch'eng-tu	31 00	104 00	IV-17	m
Ch'eng-tu	31 00	104 00	IV-18	n
Ch'eng-tu	30 40	104 04	IV-27	
Chi	40 00	116 00	IV-2	a
Chi (Lin-tzu)	37 00	119 00	IV-2	a
Chi (Peking)	40 00	117 00	IV-3	b
Chi	38 00	116 00	IV-5	d
Chi	38 00	115 00	IV-6	e
Chi	38 00	116 00	IV-7	f
Chi	38 00	118 00	IV-8	g
Chi	38 00	114 00	IV-9	h
Ch'i	37 00	119 00	IV-2	a
Ch'i	37 00	119 00	IV-3	b
Chiang	35 00	112 00	IV-2	a
Chiang	27 00	117 00	IV-8	g
Chiang-che	27 00	118 00	IV-15	l
Chiang-hsi	26 00	115 00	IV-15	l
Chiang-hsi	27 00	116 00	IV-17	m
Chiang-hsi	27 00	116 00	IV-18	n
Chiang-nan: Ch'ien-chung	28 00	109 00	IV-10	i
Chiang-nan: East	27 00	119 00	IV-10	i
Chiang-(nan)-hsi	27 00	116 00	IV-13	k
Chiang-(nan)-tung	29 00	117 00	IV-13	k
Chiang-nan: West	27 00	115 00	IV-10	i
Chiang-ning (Nan-ching)	32 00	119 00	IV-12	j
Chiang-su	34 00	120 00	IV-18	n
Chiao	24 00	110 00	IV-5	d
Chiao	22 00	108 00	IV-7	f
Chiao	22 00	106 00	IV-8	g
Chi-chun	37 00	118 00	IV-4	c
Chieh-mu	37 00	120 00	IV-4	c
Ch'ien	29 00	108 00	IV-10	i
Chien-chou	43 00	127 00	IV-17	m
Chien-k'ang (Nanking)	32 00	119 00	IV-8	g
Chien-nan	29 00	104 00	IV-10	i
Chien-t'ing	35 00	106 00	IV-6	e
Chien-yeh (Tan-yang)	32 00	119 00	IV-6	e
Chin	42 00	120 00	IV-13	k
Ch'in	34 00	108 00	IV-2	a
Ch'in	34 00	107 00	IV-3	b
Ch'in	35 00	105 00	IV-7	f
Chi-nan	36 00	117 00	IV-18	n
Chi-nan-fu	37 00	117 00	IV-17	m
Chinese Turkestan	41 00	88 00	IV-18	n
Ching	29 00	110 00	IV-5	d
Ching	37 00	118 00	IV-5	d
Ching	28 00	112 00	IV-6	e
Ching	37 00	119 00	IV-6	e
Ching	29 00	112 00	IV-7	f
Ching	28 00	111 00	IV-8	g
Ching	37 00	120 00	IV-9	h
Ching (Chia-ling)	30 00	112 00	IV-12	j
Ch'ing	33 00	111 00	IV-6	e
Ch'ing	37 00	121 00	IV-7	f
Ch'ing	36 00	119 00	IV-8	g
Ch'ing	28 00	113 00	IV-9	h
Ching-chao (Ch'ang-an)	34 00	109 00	IV-9	h
Ching-chao (Ch'ang-an)	34 00	109 00	IV-11	i
Ch'ing-hai	37 00	97 00	IV-18	n
Ching-hsi-nan	32 00	112 00	IV-13	k
(Ching-)hu-nan	27 00	112 00	IV-13	k
(Ching-)hu-pei	30 00	113 00	IV-13	k
Ching-shih	39 00	117 00	IV-17	m
Ch'i-pi	30 00	114 00	IV-6	e
Ch'iu-yüan	41 00	110 00	IV-4	c
Chou	34 00	114 00	IV-2	a
Chou	34 00	113 00	IV-3	b
Ch'u	31 00	114 00	IV-2	a
Ch'u	30 00	115 00	IV-3	b
Ch'u	27 00	112 00	IV-12	j
Ch'ü	35 30	116 00	IV-2	a
Ch'ü-fu	36 00	117 00	IV-3	b
Chü-lu	38 00	116 00	IV-4	c
Ch'ung-ching (K'un-ming)	25 00	103 00	IV-15	l
Chungking	29 34	106 35	IV-26	
Chung-shan	39 00	115 00	IV-3	b
Chung-shu	39 00	115 00	IV-15	l
Dairen	38 55	121 39	IV-26	
Djagatai Empire	40 00	75 00	IV-14	l
East Capital, Pien (K'ai-feng)	34 00	115 00	IV-12	j
Fan-yang	40 00	117 00	IV-11	i
Feng-yüan (Hsi-an)	34 00	109 00	IV-15	l

Key for Dynasty/Period

Ch'un-ch'iu	a	Sui	h
Contending States	b	T'ang	i
Ch'in	c	Five Dynasties	j
Han	d	Sung and Chin	k
Three Kingdoms	e	Yuan	l
Tsin	f	Ming	m
North and South Dynasty	g	Ch'ing	n

Place Name	Lat. (°N.)	Long. (°E.)	Map Number	Dynasty/ Period
Foochow	26 05	119 18	IV-27	
Fu-chien	26 00	118 00	IV-13	k
Fu-chien	26 00	118 00	IV-17	m
Fu-chien	27 00	119 00	IV-18	n
Fu-chou	26 00	119 00	IV-17	m
Fu-chou	26 00	119 00	IV-18	n
Fukien	26 00	118 00	IV-27	
Great Khan, Empire of the	40 00	90 00	IV-14	l
Hai-chou	41 00	123 00	IV-17	m
Halachar, Hsing-ch'ing	39 00	106 00	IV-13	k
Han	34 00	113 00	IV-3	b
Han-chung	33 00	108 00	IV-4	c
Hang (Hang-chou)	30 00	120 00	IV-12	j
Hang-chou	30 00	120 00	IV-15	l
Hang-chou	30 00	120 00	IV-17	m
Hang-chou	30 00	120 00	IV-18	n
Hangchow	30 15	120 10	IV-27	
Han-tan	37 00	115 00	IV-3	b
Han-tan	37 00	115 00	IV-4	c
Harbin	45 45	126 39	IV-27	
Heilungkiang	46 00	129 00	IV-27	
Ho-fei	31 51	117 17	IV-27	
Ho-hsi	38 00	102 00	IV-11	i
Holin, Karakoron	48 00	103 00	IV-14	l
Honan	33 00	113 00	IV-27	
Ho-nan (Lo-yang)	35 00	113 00	IV-6	e
Ho-nan (Lo-yang)	35 00	113 00	IV-7	f
Ho-nan	35 00	113 00	IV-9	h
Ho-nan	32 00	115 00	IV-15	l
Ho-nan	35 00	113 00	IV-17	m
Ho-nan	34 00	114 00	IV-18	n
Ho-nan: Ho-nan	35 00	117 00	IV-10	i
Ho-nan: Tu-chi	34 00	112 00	IV-10	i
Hong Kong	22 15	114 40	IV-27	
Hopeh	38 00	115 00	IV-27	
Ho-pei	39 00	116 00	IV-10	i
Ho-pei	39 00	117 00	IV-18	n
Ho-tung	35 00	111 00	IV-4	c
Ho-tung	39 00	113 00	IV-10	i
Ho-tung	38 00	112 00	IV-11	i
Hsia-men, Amoy	24 00	118 00	IV-18	n
Hsi-an	35 00	110 00	IV-18	n
Hsi-an-fu	34 00	109 00	IV-17	m
Hsiang	26 00	112 00	IV-8	g
Hsiang	32 00	112 00	IV-10	i
Hsiang-chün	21 00	106 00	IV-4	c
Hsi-chin (South Capital)	40 00	117 00	IV-13	k
Hsien-yang (Hsi-an)	35 00	109 00	IV-3	b
Hsien-yang	34 00	109 00	IV-4	c
Hsi-hsia	39 00	102 00	IV-13	k
Hsin-cheng	34 00	115 00	IV-2	a
Hsin-cheng (Cheng-chow)	34 00	116 00	IV-3	b
Hsin-hsiang	35 19	113 52	IV-26	
Hsi-ning	37 00	102 00	IV-17	m
Hsi-ning	36 37	101 46	IV-27	
Hsi-t'u-chüeh (Western Turks)	40 00	87 00	IV-9	h
Hsu	34 00	119 00	IV-5	d
Hsü	34 00	119 00	IV-6	e
Hsü	34 00	119 00	IV-7	f
Hsü	34 00	118 00	IV-8	g
Hsü	35 00	118 00	IV-9	h
Hsueh	35 00	117 00	IV-3	b
Hsueh-chun	35 00	118 00	IV-4	c
Huai-nan	32 00	117 00	IV-10	i
Huai-(nan-)hsi	32 00	117 00	IV-13	k
Huai-(nan-)tung	33 00	120 00	IV-13	k
Hu-ho-hao-t'e	40 47	111 37	IV-27	
Hüi-ch'uan	26 00	102 00	IV-17	m
Hui-ning	45 00	129 00	IV-13	k
Hu-kuang	26 00	110 00	IV-15	l
Hu-kuang	29 00	112 00	IV-17	m
Hunan	27 00	111 00	IV-27	
Hu-nan	27 00	111 00	IV-18	n
Hung	28 00	116 00	IV-10	i
Hupeh	31 00	112 00	IV-27	
Hu-pei	30 00	112 00	IV-18	n
I (Ch'eng-tu)	31 00	104 00	IV-12	j
I-chou	30 00	103 00	IV-6	e
I(-chou)	30 00	106 00	IV-5	d
I(-chou)	30 00	104 00	IV-8	g
Ilkhan Empire	35 00	55 00	IV-14	l
Imil	47 00	82 00	IV-14	l
Inner Mongolia	42 00	112 00	IV-18	n
Inner Mongolian Autonomous Region	40 00	107 00	IV-27	
K'ai-chou	40 00	122 00	IV-17	m
K'ai-feng	35 00	115 00	IV-18	n
K'ai-feng	34 51	114 21	IV-26	
K'ai-feng-fu	35 00	115 00	IV-17	m
Kan-chou	39 00	101 00	IV-15	l
Kan-chou	40 00	99 00	IV-17	m
Kansu	35 00	104 00	IV-27	
Kan-su	40 00	101 00	IV-15	l
Kan-su	35 00	105 00	IV-18	n
Kiangsi	27 00	116 00	IV-27	

Key for Dynasty/Period

Ch'un-ch'iu	a	Sui	h
Contending States	b	T'ang	i
Ch'in	c	Five Dynasties	j
Han	d	Sung and Chin	k
Three Kingdoms	e	Yuan	l
Tsin	f	Ming	m
North and South Dynasty	g	Ch'ing	n

Place Name	Lat. (°N.)	Long. (°E.)	Map Number	Dynasty/Period
Kiangsu	33 00	119 00	IV-27	
Kip Chak or Golden Horde Empire	50 00	55 00	IV-14	l
Kirin	43 00	127 00	IV-27	
Kitan	42 00	120 00	IV-9	h
Ko-ku-rye	41 00	123 00	IV-9	h
Kou-wu	32 00	120 00	IV-2	a
Kuang	24 00	109 00	IV-6	e
Kuang	24 00	111 00	IV-7	f
Kuang	23 00	112 00	IV-8	g
Kuang	24 00	113 00	IV-10	i
Kuang (Canton)	23 00	113 00	IV-12	j
Kuang-chou-fu	23 00	113 00	IV-17	m
Kuang-hsi	24 00	109 00	IV-17	m
Kuang-hsi	24 00	109 00	IV-18	n
Kuang-(nan-)hsi	24 00	110 00	IV-13	k
Kuang-(nan-)tung	24 00	114 00	IV-13	k
Kuang-tung	23 00	113 00	IV-17	m
Kuang-tung, Canton	23 00	113 00	IV-18	n
Kuang-yang	43 00	124 00	IV-17	m
Kuan-nei: Ching-chi	34 00	109 00	IV-10	i
Kuan-nei: Kuan-nei	37 00	108 00	IV-10	i
Kuan-tu	35 00	114 00	IV-6	e
Kuei-chi	30 00	121 00	IV-2	a
Kuei-chi	30 00	121 00	IV-4	c
Kuei-chou	29 00	109 00	IV-13	k
Kuei-chou	26 00	107 00	IV-17	m
Kuei-chou	27 00	107 00	IV-18	n
Kuei-lin	26 00	111 00	IV-4	c
Kuei-lin	25 00	110 00	IV-18	n
Kuei-lin	25 17	110 17	IV-26	
Kuei-lin-fu (Ching-chiang)	26 00	110 00	IV-17	m
Kuei-yang	27 00	107 00	IV-18	n
Kuei-yang	26 53	105 43	IV-27	
Kuei-yang-fu	27 00	107 00	IV-17	m
Kun-chou (Nan-chao)	27 00	106 00	IV-9	h
K'un-ming	25 04	102 41	IV-27	
Ku-pei-k'ou	42 00	118 00	IV-17	m
Kwangsi Chuang Autonomous Region	24 00	109 00	IV-27	
Kwangtung	24 00	114 00	IV-27	
Kweichow	27 00	107 00	IV-27	
Lan-chou	36 00	104 00	IV-18	n
Lan-chou	36 03	103 41	IV-27	
Lang-ya	36 00	120 00	IV-4	c
Later Chou	34 00	112 00	IV-12	j
Later Shu	31 00	106 00	IV-12	j
Lhasa	29 39	91 06	IV-27	
Liang	37 00	105 00	IV-5	d
Liang	32 00	107 00	IV-6	e

Place Name	Lat. (°N.)	Long. (°E.)	Map Number	Dynasty/Period
Liang	31 00	108 00	IV-7	f
Liang	39 00	101 00	IV-7	f
Liang	33 00	107 00	IV-8	g
Liang	32 00	107 00	IV-9	h
Liang	33 00	107 00	IV-10	i
Liang-che	28 00	120 00	IV-13	k
Liang-chou	38 00	103 00	IV-17	m
Liao-hsi	42 00	121 00	IV-4	c
Liaoning	41 00	123 00	IV-27	
Liao-tung	41 00	123 00	IV-4	c
Liao-yang (East Capital)	41 00	123 00	IV-13	k
Liao-yang	41 00	123 00	IV-15	l
Liao-yang	45 00	126 00	IV-15	l
Liao-yang	42 00	123 00	IV-17	m
Li-chou	33 00	107 00	IV-13	k
Lin-an	30 00	121 00	IV-13	k
Ling-nan	22 00	110 00	IV-10	i
Ling-nan	23 00	114 00	IV-11	i
Lin-huang (Upper Capital)	45 00	119 00	IV-13	k
Lin-t'ao	35 00	104 00	IV-4	c
Lin-tzu	37 00	118 00	IV-3	b
Liu-ch'iu	24 00	121 00	IV-9	h
Liu-ch'iu	23 00	122 00	IV-13	k
Liu-ch'iu	25 00	121 00	IV-14	l
Lo-yang	35 00	113 00	IV-3	b
Lo-yang	35 00	113 00	IV-10	i
Lu	35 00	118 00	IV-2	a
Lu	36 00	117 00	IV-3	b
Lung-hai	35 00	104 00	IV-4	c
Lung-hsing (Nan-ch'ang)	28 00	116 00	IV-15	l
Lung-yu	38 00	102 00	IV-10	i
Min-chou	34 00	105 00	IV-17	m
Nan-ch'ang	29 00	117 00	IV-18	n
Nan-ch'ang	28 33	115 56	IV-27	
Nan-ch'ang-fu	28 00	116 00	IV-17	m
Nan-ching	32 00	118 00	IV-17	m
Nan-ch'ung	30 48	106 04	IV-26	
Nan-hai	23 00	113 00	IV-4	c
Nanking	32 00	119 00	IV-19	n
Nanking	32 03	118 47	IV-27	
Nanning	22 49	108 19	IV-27	
Nan-tai	33 00	120 00	IV-8	g
Nan-yang	32 00	114 00	IV-4	c
Nan-yü	31 00	117 00	IV-8	g
Ning	25 00	102 00	IV-7	f
Ning	26 00	106 00	IV-8	g
Ning-fan	28 00	102 00	IV-17	m
Ning-hsi	38 00	107 00	IV-17	m
Ning-po	30 00	122 00	IV-18	n

Key for Dynasty/Period

Ch'un-ch'iu	a		Sui	h
Contending States	b		T'ang	i
Ch'in	c		Five Dynasties	j
Han	d		Sung and Chin	k
Three Kingdoms	e		Yuan	l
Tsin	f		Ming	m
North and South Dynasty	g		Ch'ing	n

Place Name	Lat. (°N.)	Long. (°E.)	Map Number	Dynasty/Period
Ning-po	29 53	121 33	IV-26	
Ningsia Hui Autonomous Region	37 00	106 00	IV-27	
Ning-yüan	41 00	121 00	IV-17	m
North Han	37 00	113 00	IV-12	j
Outer Mongolia	47 00	105 00	IV-18	n
Pa (Kiang-chou)	29 00	107 00	IV-4	c
Pao-ting	38 00	116 00	IV-18	n
Pei-t'ing	45 00	90 00	IV-11	i
Peking	39 56	116 24	IV-27	
P'eng-hu Islands	23 00	119 00	IV-13	k
Pien (K'ai-feng)	34 00	115 00	IV-10	i
Pien-liang (K'ai-feng)	35 00	115 00	IV-15	l
Pien-t'ou K'ou	40 00	111 00	IV-17	m
Ping	39 00	113 00	IV-5	d
Ping	38 00	112 00	IV-7	f
Ping (T'ai-yüan)	38 00	113 00	IV-12	j
P'ing	38 00	112 00	IV-6	e
P'ing	39 00	126 00	IV-7	f
P'ing-ch'eng (Tai-tung)	40 00	113 00	IV-8	g
P'ing-lu	41 00	120 00	IV-11	i
Ping-yang	37 00	111 00	IV-4	c
Pu	35 00	110 00	IV-10	i
San-ch'uan (Lo-yang)	34 00	113 00	IV-4	c
Sarai (1253–1395)	46 00	48 00	IV-14	l
Sarai (1395–1480)	48 00	46 00	IV-14	l
Sha-chou	41 00	94 00	IV-17	m
Shan	36 00	102 00	IV-10	i
Shan-nan: East	31 00	111 00	IV-10	i
Shan-nan: West	32 00	112 00	IV-10	i
Shang-ch'iu	34 00	116 00	IV-2	a
Shang-ch'iu	34 00	116 00	IV-3	b
Shang-chün	37 00	110 00	IV-4	c
Shanghai	31 07	121 22	IV-27	
Shang-hai	31 00	121 00	IV-18	n
Shang-ku	40 00	116 00	IV-4	c
Shang-tang	36 00	113 00	IV-4	c
Shan-hai Kuan	40 00	120 00	IV-17	m
Shan-hsi	38 00	112 00	IV-17	m
Shan-hsi	37 00	113 00	IV-18	n
Shansi	37 00	112 00	IV-27	
Shantung	36 00	117 00	IV-27	
Shan-tung	36 00	118 00	IV-17	m
Shan-tung	36 00	119 00	IV-18	n
Shan-yü	40 00	111 00	IV-11	i
Shen-hsi	35 00	106 00	IV-15	l
Shen-hsi	35 00	106 00	IV-17	m
Shen-hsi	34 00	109 00	IV-18	n
Shensi	34 00	108 00	IV-27	
Shen-yang	41 48	123 27	IV-27	
Shih-chia-chuang	38 03	114 29	IV-26	
Shih-wei	51 20	119 54	IV-26	
Shou	39 00	108 00	IV-5	d
Shou-ch'un (Chiu-kiang)	32 00	117 00	IV-4	c
Shu (Ch'eng-tu)	30 00	104 00	IV-4	c
Shu (Ch'eng-tu)	32 00	104 00	IV-6	e
Shu Kingdom	30 00	105 00	IV-6	e
Shun-t'ien-fu (Peking)	40 00	117 00	IV-17	m
Shun-t'ien-fu, Peking	40 00	117 00	IV-18	n
Shuo-yang	38 00	107 00	IV-11	i
Sian	34 16	108 54	IV-27	
Sinkiang Uighur Autonomous Region	40 00	84 00	IV-27	
Soochow	31 18	120 37	IV-26	
South Han	23 00	112 00	IV-12	j
South P'ing	30 00	112 00	IV-12	j
South T'ang	27 00	117 00	IV-12	j
Southern Sung	27 00	113 00	IV-13	k
Ssu	34 00	113 00	IV-7	f
Ssu	31 00	114 00	IV-8	g
Ssu-ch'uan	31 00	107 00	IV-15	l
Ssu-ch'uan	30 00	105 00	IV-17	m
Ssu-ch'uan	30 00	105 00	IV-18	n
Ssu-li	34 00	110 00	IV-5	d
Ssu-li	35 00	112 00	IV-6	e
Ssu-shui	34 00	117 00	IV-4	c
Su	31 00	121 00	IV-10	i
Su-chou (Chiu-ch'üan)	41 00	97 00	IV-17	m
Sung	34 00	116 00	IV-2	a
Sung	35 00	116 00	IV-3	b
Sung	27 00	112 00	IV-8	g
Sung-p'an	32 00	104 00	IV-17	m
Szechwan	30 00	104 00	IV-27	
Tabriz, Toris	38 00	47 00	IV-14	l
Tai-chun	39 00	115 00	IV-4	c
Taipei	25 02	121 38	IV-27	
Taiwan	23 00	121 00	IV-27	
T'ai-wan	24 00	121 00	IV-17	m
T'ai-wan, Formosa	23 00	119 00	IV-18	n
T'ai-yüan	38 00	112 00	IV-4	c
T'ai-yüan	38 00	113 00	IV-18	n
T'ai-yüan	37 46	112 30	IV-27	
T'ai-yüan-fu	38 00	113 00	IV-17	m

Key for Dynasty/Period

Ch'un-ch'iu	a	Sui	h
Contending States	b	T'ang	i
Ch'in	c	Five Dynasties	j
Han	d	Sung and Chin	k
Three Kingdoms	e	Yuan	l
Tsin	f	Ming	m
North and South Dynasty	g	Ch'ing	n

Place Name	Lat. (°N.)	Long. (°E.)	Map Number	Dynasty/Period
Ta-liang (K'ai-feng)	35 00	115 00	IV-3	b
T'an (Ch'ang-sha)	27 00	113 00	IV-12	j
T'ao-chou	35 00	104 00	IV-17	m
Ta-ting (Central Capital)	41 00	119 00	IV-13	k
Ta-tu, Khan-balik (Peking)	40 00	116 00	IV-15	l
Ta-t'ung (West Capital)	40 00	113 00	IV-13	k
T'eng	34 00	117 00	IV-2	a
Tibet	33 00	91 00	IV-18	n
Tibetan Autonomous Region	31 00	88 00	IV-27	
Tientsin	39 08	117 12	IV-27	
Tsin	36 00	113 00	IV-2	a
Ts'in	35 00	105 00	IV-6	e
Ts'in	30 00	101 00	IV-8	g
Tsinan	36 40	117 00	IV-27	
Tsinghai	35 00	96 00	IV-27	
Tsingtao	36 04	120 19	IV-26	
T'ung-ch'uan	30 00	104 00	IV-13	k
Tung-chun	36 00	116 00	IV-4	c
Tung-sheng	41 00	111 00	IV-17	m
Tung-t'u-chüen (Eastern Turks)	42 00	110 00	IV-9	h
Tzu-ching K'ou	39 00	115 00	IV-17	m
Urumchi	43 48	87 35	IV-27	
Wang-cheng (Lo-yang)	34 00	114 00	IV-2	a
Wei	36 00	116 00	IV-2	a
Wei	36 00	112 00	IV-3	b
Wei	36 00	110 00	IV-8	g
Wei	36 00	115 00	IV-10	i
Wei Kingdom	36 00	114 00	IV-6	e
Wenchow	28 01	120 39	IV-26	
West Capital (Lo-yang)	34 00	114 00	IV-12	j
Wu	31 00	121 00	IV-2	a
Wu	31 00	121 00	IV-4	c
Wu-ch'ang	31 00	114 00	IV-15	l
Wu-ch'ang	30 00	115 00	IV-17	m
Wu-ch'ang	31 00	115 00	IV-18	n
Wu-ch'ang	30 21	114 19	IV-27	
Wu-chang-yüan	34 00	109 00	IV-6	e
Wu-han	30 35	114 16	IV-26	
Wu Kingdom	26 00	114 00	IV-6	e
Wu-wei	37 58	102 48	IV-26	
Wu-yüeh	30 00	120 00	IV-12	j
Ya-an	29 59	103 05	IV-26	
Yang	28 00	116 00	IV-5	d
Yang	28 00	117 00	IV-6	e
Yang	32 00	117 00	IV-6	e
Yang	28 00	118 00	IV-7	f
Yang	29 00	120 00	IV-8	g
Yang	26 00	115 00	IV-9	h
Yang	33 00	119 00	IV-10	i
Yang-chou	33 00	119 00	IV-18	n
Yang-chou	32 24	119 26	IV-26	
Yen	39 00	117 00	IV-2	a
Yen	40 00	120 00	IV-3	b
Yen	36 00	116 00	IV-5	d
Yen	36 00	116 00	IV-6	e
Yen	35 00	116 00	IV-7	f
Yen	36 00	117 00	IV-8	g
Yen	36 00	117 00	IV-9	h
Yen-an	36 38	109 27	IV-26	
Yen-chi	42 53	129 31	IV-26	
Yen-men	40 00	114 00	IV-4	c
Yin-ch'uan	38 28	106 19	IV-27	
Ying	30 00	112 00	IV-2	a
Ying (Chiang-lin)	31 00	112 00	IV-3	b
Ying	30 00	114 00	IV-8	g
Ying-ch'uan	33 00	114 00	IV-4	c
Ying-t'ien-fu (Nanking)	32 00	119 00	IV-17	m
Yu	39 00	108 00	IV-5	d
Yu	40 00	116 00	IV-6	e
Yu	40 00	117 00	IV-7	f
Yü	33 00	115 00	IV-5	d
Yü	35 00	115 00	IV-6	e
Yü	33 00	115 00	IV-7	f
Yü	33 00	115 00	IV-8	g
Yü	34 00	114 00	IV-9	h
Yüeh	29 00	121 00	IV-2	a
Yüeh	24 00	107 00	IV-8	g
Yüeh-sui	29 00	103 00	IV-17	m
Yueh-yang	35 00	109 00	IV-4	c
Yü-lin	39 00	110 00	IV-17	m
Yü-lin	38 18	109 45	IV-26	
Yung	34 00	108 00	IV-2	a
Yung	35 00	108 00	IV-6	e
Yung	35 00	109 00	IV-7	f
Yung	32 00	112 00	IV-8	g
Yung	36 00	125 00	IV-9	h
Yung-ch'ang	39 00	101 00	IV-17	m
Yung-ning	27 00	101 00	IV-17	m
Yunnan	24 00	102 00	IV-27	
Yün-nan	26 00	102 00	IV-15	l
Yün-nan	25 00	101 00	IV-17	m
Yün-nan	24 00	100 00	IV-18	n
Yün-nan	25 00	102 00	IV-18	n
Yün-nan-fu	25 00	103 00	IV-17	m
Yü-yang	40 00	116 00	IV-4	c

Key for Dynasty/Period

Ch'un-ch'iu	a		Sui	h
Contending States	b		T'ang	i
Ch'in	c		Five Dynasties	j
Han	d		Sung and Chin	k
Three Kingdoms	e		Yuan	l
Tsin	f		Ming	m
North and South Dynasty	g		Ch'ing	n